THE CHRISTA

A SOCIOLOGY OF CHRIST

PhD Thesis
Sociology of Religion
King's College London
Awarded on 30 November 2000

Supervisor:
Peter B Clarke
Professor of Sociology of Religion,
King's College London

Examiners:
Keith Ward
Regus Professor of Divinity,
Oxford University
David Martin
Emeritus Professor of Sociology,
London School of Economics

AMDG
© **Daren Kemp 2003**
Kempress Ltd
www.Christaquarian.net

ACKNOWLEDGEMENTS

No thesis would be complete without an acknowledgement to the supervisor. My thanks goes to my supervisor, Professor Peter Clarke, at the Centre for New Religions, King's College, University of London, and to Professor Peter Byrne and Dr Madawi Al-Rasheed, also in the Department of Theology and Religious Studies at King's College, for reading drafts of the thesis.

I am also grateful for the input of scholars outside of King's College, including Stuart Rose, Steven Sutcliffe and Matthew Wood. Useful reactions were obtained to papers presented at a number of conferences and seminars. Significant subjects of the research, including Revd Donald Reeves, Dr William Bloom, Eileen Conn, Petra Griffiths, Canon Peter Spink, Revd Jim Hill, Fr Adrian Smith, Janice Dolley and Gillian Paschkes-Bell have also commented on drafts of relevant chapters. Of course, any errors that may remain are my own. An acknowledgement must also be made to the anonymous subjects of the study, who freely gave up their own time to be interviewed and to fill in the questionnaire.

Financial assistance, approximating 70% of course fees, was received from King's College London Theological Trust and St Olave's & St Saviour's Grammar School Foundation, plus a number of smaller conference grants. Both major sources of funding required written reports at the end of each year of study but otherwise imposed no restrictions on the research, and did not attempt to influence the writing up. I am grateful for the generous support of these bodies, and also for the indulgence of my various employers in the City of London who cast a blind eye when I read texts, typed chapters, analysed results and printed drafts whilst in their employ. My parents also subsidised my living expenses and fees through the first two years of study. I would not have embarked on the financially challenging project of an unfunded PhD without a legacy from my great uncle, George Kent.

The thesis is dedicated to my wife, Ewa, in gratitude for the solitary evenings she endured during our first year of marriage when I devoted attention to my books. Without Ewa's support through a year of illness taken out in the middle of the doctorate, it is doubtful whether I would have had the will to continue. We married in the third year of research, in one of the churches used as a case study.

Sidcup, Kent
Easter 2000
(On original submission of thesis)

Lynch, Frederick R, 1977, "Toward a Theory of Conversion and Commitment to the Occult", *American Behavioral Scientist* 20.6 p895 diagram reprinted by permission of Sage Publications, Inc.

Acknowledgements of other copyrighted material will gladly be made in future editions on request.

ABSTRACT

The thesis begins with a hypothesis: that there is a movement of New Age Christians. The neologism, "Christaquarians", named after the new astrological Age of Aquarius, is coined to refer to these New Age Christians. New Age is defined along family resemblance lines, and the methodology involves participant observation, semi-structured interviews and a postal questionnaire survey of over 700 people. An extended survey of the literature rediscovers some neglected studies.

Three case studies are examined to test the hypothesis. St James's church, Piccadilly, is an Anglican church renowned for its New Age project, Alternatives. Christians Awakening to a New Awareness, "CANA", is a nationwide network and mailing list of over 100 people which has produced a paper outlining its vision for Christianity in the new millennium. The Omega Order is a small community of New Age Christians living and worshipping in a large manor house near Bristol.

Fourthly, for a control group, an evangelical Anglican church is subjected to the same tests. The results of the surveys are presented in the appendix, together with data from previous surveys of New Age groups and magazine readers. Analysis of the data affords much confirmation of the hypothesis that there is a movement of Christaquarians.

However, consideration of the notion of a "movement" with regard to the arguments of other scholars, leads to the conclusion that a movement must be conscious of itself as a movement. This has not yet happened with Christaquarians, and so the hypothesis is rejected for the time being.

PREFACE TO 2003 EDITION

The purpose of this 2003 edition of my doctoral thesis is to make it available in a readily accessible format. The full, original text has been available for some time at www.Christaquarian.net, generating some interest from both scholars and Christaquarians, and I am grateful for the contacts made in this way. I hope this 2003 edition will generate further interest.

A number of further debts have been incurred to bring this edition to fruition, not least a financial obligation to Christians Awakening to a New Awareness, who kindly loaned me the small amount necessary to finance this edition. I am grateful also for the fellowship and stimulation CANA has continued to offer me since I completed my research with them. Especial mention must go to Rev Adrian B Smith, who acted as editor for my CANA publication on contemporary New Age Christians (see www.canaweb.info), and was instrumental in organising the Meta-Net Round Tables in 2001 and 2002, which brought together a number of the groups I researched (see www.Meta-Net.info).

The Christaquarian website, through its ScholarsOfNewAge (SONA) discussion list, has also led, with the collaboration of James R. Lewis and Marion Bowman, to a conference on Alternative Spiritualities and New Age Studies (ASANAS) at The Open University, Milton Keynes, England, 30 May – 1 June 2003 (see www.asanas.org.uk). This promises to be an important step of consolidation in New Age studies, just as Meta-Net promises to be an important step in consolidation of Christaquarians.

The text has also been used by a researcher for the Bible Society, in attempting to map contemporary spirituality for evangelistic purposes. I always realised when conducting my research that, if successful, the final product would prove useful for a number of audiences. This has already proven true for three audiences: Christaquarians, scholars and evangelicals. But the text was also purposely written in a popular, accessible style with a fourth audience in mind: the general spiritual public. I hope that, as well as maintaining interest among the first three audiences, this edition will reach that fourth audience.

Portions of the text have previously been published by Maney Publishing in *Implicit Religion* (Kemp 2001a) and a précis of the thesis has been published by Edinburgh University Press in *Studies in World Christianity* (Kemp 2001b) and Prometheus Books in *The Encyclopedic Sourcebook of New Age Religions* (Lewis ed 2003).

Needless to say, my wife has continued to suffer my interest in New Age, put up with ridiculous amounts of the household budget spent on book purchases now that I have no access to an academic library, and further hours in the study.

Daren Kemp, January 2003

CONTENTS

TABLES AND FIGURES

I. INTRODUCTION

A spectre is haunting Europe – the spectre of Communism. All the Powers of old Europe have entered into a holy alliance to exorcise this spectre: Pope and Tsar, Metternich and Guizot, French Radicals and German police-spies.
(Marx & Engels 1990/1848:221)

Marilyn Ferguson opens her seminal New Age manual, *The Aquarian Conspiracy: Personal and Social Transformation in the 1980s* (1989/1980) with an allusion to Marx and Engels' *Communist Manifesto* (1848):

> A leaderless but powerful network is working to bring about radical change in the United States. Its members have broken with certain key elements of Western thought, and they may even have broken continuity with history.
>
> This network is the Aquarian Conspiracy. It is a conspiracy without a political doctrine. Without a manifesto.
> (Ferguson 1989/1980:23)

If it was not already the case, with Ferguson's work New Agers finally became conscious of themselves as a movement. Ferguson suggested that a New Ager's aim is social transformation through personal transformation.

This thesis poses the hypothesis that there exists an identifiable group of New Age Christians who occupy the crossover between Christianity and the New Age movement. These people are given the name, 'The Christaquarians'. Who are the Christaquarians? What do they believe? How do they differ from Christians and how similar are they to Aquarians – to New Agers? These are some of the questions this thesis seeks to answer.

But nobody calls themselves a Christaquarian. This is a neologism coined for the present study, a shorthand way of saying "Christians in the New Age, the Age of Aquarius". Terms used by other scholars (eg Jorgensen 1982:387; D'Andrea 1997) to refer to the same sort of people are inadequate: "New Age Christians" implies people who are fundamentally Christian, but with some New Age attributes; "Christian New Agers" implies people who are fundamentally New Age, but with some Christian attributes[1]. Christaquarians may identify themselves as Christian, or as New Age – or, as is often the case – as neither Christian nor New Age. Yet, from a scholarly perspective, in view of the similarities of their beliefs, practices and social characteristics, it is useful to consider them as belonging to an identifiable sociological grouping – to what we may call Christaquarianism. Since it is one of my major aims to investigate whether the term 'Christaquarian' has any substance, I nevertheless retain usage of the phrases 'New Age Christian' or 'Christian New Ager'. All three designations are used interchangeably.

The neologism 'Christaquarian' was introduced at a late stage in writing up to provide a unifying label to order my material and for the purposes of analysis. The question, "Is there a Christaquarian movement?" provided a useful overarching rationale for grouping together the diverse materials contained in the thesis. As will be seen, the hypothesis that there is a substantive Christaquarian movement is rejected for a number of reasons. It has been argued (by both Professor Keith Ward and Dr Matthew Wood), that the term "Christaquarian" should therefore be deleted from the thesis since it has no referent. I have chosen to retain the term for reasons of style and presentation, but it must be emphasised that this is not an attempt to bring the hypothesis back into play through a semantic back door.

Methodology

Research methodology is important in the sociology of religion, and it will be seen in the survey of the literature (Chapter II) that many existing studies of New Age are weak on this count. Most recommendations made in the literature on methodology follow the dictates of common sense in the quest to present an unbiased picture of the phenomena under observation.

My research began with a period of familiarization with the emic literature. I had a personal interest in New Age for several years prior to the commencement of the research[2], and was already familiar with a number of evangelical tracts on the subject. During the first year of study, I read on average one book per day – not as remarkable a feat as it sounds, since New Age texts are often repetitive and easy to skim.

Following this familiarization period, I began making tentative explorations into the field[3]. These were initially with people already known to me through my attendance at the local parish church and through other informal networks. Gradually, my circle of study widened, and I began to write letters to various organizations, and conduct telephone interviews with contacts who were too far away to visit in person. My first foray into face-to-face interviewing was at the local branch of the National Federation of Spiritual Healers, where I conducted several structured interviews. These do not form a part of the present study, as I did not find Spiritual Healers to be overtly Christian, although many claimed some allegiance to Christianity.

After several months of study I had located the three Christian New Age groups which I found most interesting. These were: St James's church, Piccadilly, a large Anglican city church with a New Age project called Alternatives; The Omega Order, a residential New Age Christian community near Bristol; and a small network based around a nationwide mailing list, Christians Awakening to a New Awareness. In addition, my own local Anglican evangelical church[4] was studied as a control group. In the absence of a wider survey requiring much more intensive resources than were available for this study, it cannot be seen whether these three groups are representative of positive Christian responses to the New

Age. Thus in no way do I claim that this survey of Christaquarianism is comprehensive, as there will be many groups and countless more individuals with whom I had no contact, that could have been relevantly considered. This is the most serious methodological weakness in the present study. However, my impression is that the groups studied give useful insights into the sociological issues raised by positive Christian responses to the New Age movement.

In early 1996 I wrote to the Rector of St James's church, Piccadilly asking for permission to conduct fieldwork in his church. A positive response was obtained, and formal participant observation began in May 1996. I attended on average once every three weeks until December 1996. I was introduced by the Rector to the congregation on my first official visit, but found that I frequently needed to remind people, who perhaps had not been present on that occasion, that I was interested in what they were saying to me for research purposes. At all times I attempted to make my role as an observer clear, and in addition, when asked, I affirmed my Christian faith and fascination with the New Age. I did not find it necessary to make notes during the fieldwork, and this would have been inappropriate. Instead I typed up a one- or two- page report as soon as possible after each session of fieldwork.

Similar procedures were adopted for fieldwork at The Omega Order, except that because of the nature of the community and its distance from my home in Kent, my visits here were residential. Fieldwork with the mailing list, Christians Awakening to a New Awareness, was limited to a number of conferences and workshops held throughout the period of study. Pilot telephone interviews were conducted with CANA in November 1997, to test the questions for a postal survey, which were largely taken from previous studies so as to provide comparable results. From this pilot survey, a number of questions asked by previous researchers were found to be unintelligible to respondents and thus rejected.

Telephone interviewing was an ideal method to reduce input of time and expenses. I had just two rejections of my request for a telephone interview. Permission had been obtained from the mailing list's compilers prior to commencement of the telephone survey. By keeping to a written text of introduction and questions, interview bias was reduced to a minimum. Due to the conversational nature of the medium, however, it was possible to detect and develop nuances of opinion that were not available from the later postal survey. I do not believe that responses on the telephone to an unkown researcher are any more or less trustworthy than anonymous replies to a postal questionnaire, although I did avoid asking personal questions such as, for example, the matter of income.

Face-to-face interviews were held at a location convenient to the interviewee, usually their home or the religious centre under observation. All formal interviews were prepared in advance with a structured list of questions, which is included in the Appendix. For many of the less formal interviews, some of the questions were phrased identically so as to obtain comparable responses.

11

Permission was usually obtained verbally to record the interview on a portable cassette recorder and the interviews typically lasted between 45 and 90 minutes. Notes were taken during the interview in case of tape failure and as an aid to directing the interview through showing interest in a particular answer or lack thereof. All recorded interviews were transcribed by me onto a wordprocessing package with the aid of these notes to decipher inaudible words. This part of the research was the most time-consuming prior to writing-up.

Various leaders of Christaquarian groups are named in this study, as far as possible with their permission. Significant actors in the text have viewed drafts of the thesis, which have then been amended in disagreements of a factual nautre – and in one or two cases my interpretation has been amended. The churchWarden of St James's asked me at one point to withdraw the chapter concerning her church. Instead, I negotiated some alterations to the chapter and offered space to present St James's views.

Where I have used a surname in this thesis, these are the actual names of those involved. However, where I have used only a first name, these are pseudonyms designed to protect the identity of the individuals concerned. Such pseudonymous subjects are usually followers rather than leaders. Occasionally I have altered some of these people's personal details so as to preserve their anonymity, but no arguments in the thesis rest on such altered details. One consequence of identifying the groups I have studied is that the danger of anonymous interviewees (other than named leaders) also being identified, is very real. It is because of this danger that at times the descriptions of interviewees may seem rather bare. However, I hope that the anonymous surveys give an adequate understanding of the life patterns of those involved.

The participant observation role is not ideal. On the one hand, the sociologist must participate fully in the activities at hand, and become integrated with the group under observation. However, at the same time, the sociologist may not believe in or agree with, on a personal level, all that is being done or said, and may at times feel unable to participate fully. But even were he or she to become fully immersed in the field, the sociologist must at the same time maintain mental distance between the participants and him/herself as observer, in order for useful analysis to be achieved. An account by a sociologist should be fundamentally different in style and content from an account by an insider.

The extent to which I integrated with the groups in this thesis varies. The evangelical church was well-known to me but paradoxically this may have caused some respondents to be reticent, even in the anonymous postal surveys. I got on extremely well with the elderly residents at The Omega Order and received their well-wishes when I was forced to abandon one research trip through ill-health. CANA was less easy to become acquainted with since the major effort of the group is a newsletter, with only infrequent meetings; accordingly, I conducted a telephone survey to get to know members better. I found integration into the large city church of St James's difficult despite the relatively large number of research visits, and perhaps this lack of rapport explains the difficulties I experienced after the completion of fieldwork.

Permission was obtained for the postal surveys of three of the groups studied, and a covering letter introducing the research was provided by their leaders. Excellent response rates of up to nearly 60% were received, perhaps attributable to the advanced age of many of the respondents, and also because I had gone to the expense of supplying a stamped addressed envelope with each questionnaire. In view of the large response rate received for The Omega Order, I doubled the size of the questionnaire for St James's and CANA. For a copy of the questionnaire survey and more detailed notes on its preparation, see the Appendix.

St James's withdrew permission for the survey at the last moment and thus no covering letter was provided. As I had invested months of participant observation in this group with the agreement for a postal survey in place, I decided to go ahead with the survey without the permission of the leaders, who had already supplied me with the address list. Perhaps because of the lack of covering letter, a reduced but still respectable response rate of nearly 30% was achieved at St James's. CANA was surveyed one year later than the other groups, because by that time it had doubled in size to over 100 members and could then provide a large enough sample.

Each returned questionnaire was anonymous and, after return, provided with a unique identification number. A code book of answers was compiled and the results entered into a computer spreadsheet package as they arrived through the post. Percentage results were calculated manually by sorting these spreadsheets. I decided that the level of interpretation required for this study was not sufficient to warrant the time required to analyse the results on a more sophisticated statistical package such as SPSS. In each case, a small number of responses was received after the cut-off date on which analysis began, and these returns were not included in the calculations. Also, because the questionnaires had been printed on coloured paper, I was able to reject questionnaires which anonymous individuals had kindly photocopied and passed to co-religionists!

Towards a Definition

It is a paradox within the sociology of religion that a starting definition of the subject under consideration is often given before the investigation has ascertained the proper limits of the enquiry. In the course of the study, it may become apparent that the criteria initially used to define the boundaries of the fieldwork were in some way not wholly pertinent to the sociologist's aim. The criteria are hence constantly modified throughout the study until the report is produced when it may be assumed that, within stated limits, definite criteria for membership of the group have been outlined (cf Weber 1956/1922:1).

The New Age movement is such a wide-ranging phenomenon, that it is often referred to as an "umbrella" term (eg Chandler 1989:18; Terrin 1992:7), covering a far broader spectrum than any one example of New Age merits in itself, and is thus difficult to classify (cf Maciejko 1994:1). One method of overcoming this difficulty in definition is family resemblance categorisation theory, also known as polythetic classification, which is outlined below. This allows both exposition of the similarities between New Age phenomena and acknowledgement of their differences. So, what is the starting definition of New Age?

A list of beliefs is the conventional evangelical method of defining New Age (eg Groothuis 1991/1986), and has also been used by scholars such as Hanegraaff (1996). Indeed, Hanegraaff has provided such a comprehensive exposition of New Age belief that this need not be repeated here. Typical New Age beliefs would include reincarnation, holism, monism, a spiritual hierarchy and pelagianism. Again, the exact content of these beliefs varies from individual to individual, and what is a matter of faith to one New Ager is often anathema to another. Typical New Age practices include body therapies, psychotechnologies, environmental concerns and various spiritual disciplines. One New Ager may concentrate entirely on bodywork, while another is interested only in the more spiritual aspects of the Interfaith movement, for example.

Historically, New Age may be seen as a continuation of what Aldous Huxley called *The Perennial Philosophy* (1946). This is an esoteric collection of occult philosophies, which have usually resided outside the mainstream of the Western tradition. Thus it includes Gnosticism and other Christian heresies, Hermeticism, Neoplatonism, alchemy, Sufism and the Eastern religions in the West. More recently, New Age is a continuation of the counterculture of the 1960s, so-called 'baby boomer' spirituality (Roof 1994/1993). Hanegraaff (1996) sees New Age as the occult milieu becoming aware of itself as a movement, which is said to have happened in the mid- to late- 1970s.

To give examples of New Age is problematic, because often any particular example will not exhibit all criteria proposed in the definition of New Age.

> Formally, a definition to be valid must apply to every instance of the phenomena to be defined; hence even one exception is sufficient to refute the definition.
> (Southwold 1978:367)

This problem is eased if we use family resemblance categorization theory, which allows emphasis of difference as well as similarity. Family resemblance theory was outlined, but not fully developed, by Ludwig Wittgenstein in *Philosophical Investigations* (1994/1953). Its basic functions may be simply summarized with a tabulated example. Below are three distinct items under consideration in rows numbered 1 to 3, and characteristics observed in columns lettered A-G.

Table I.1 Family resemblance theory

	A	B	C	D	E	F	G
1	✓	✓	✓				
2			✓	✓	✓		
3					✓	✓	✓

Items 1 and 3 have no characteristics A to G in common. They initially appear dissimilar. However, a middle term, item 2, has characteristic C in common with item 1 and characteristic E in common with item 3. Items 1 and 3 may therefore be seen to have a family resemblance through the middle item 2, despite *prima facie* dissimilarity.

A development of family resemblance theory is to have a shortlist of items considered typical to the family. This 'common core' holds the benchmark criteria for family resemblance, and would be represented in the above table by item 2. Items for possible inclusion in the family are first compared and contrasted with the core members, and admitted according to the significance of the relationships.

Family resemblance categorization theory is similar to Needham's (1975) description of polythetic classes.

> A monothetic class is a set of phenomena such that there is some set (or 'bundle') of attributes which is common to all of them – which is possessed by each and every member of the class. With a polythetic class there is again an associated bundle of attributes; but in this case it is not necessary that all the attributes in the bundle be possessed by a member of the class. A phenomenon may be treated as a member of the class if it possesses only some of the attributes. Since different members of the class may possess different selections from the bundle of attributes, there is no guarantee that any one of these attributes is common to all the members. Indeed a class must be regarded as polythetic when there is no attribute which is both common to all the members and important for understanding them.
> (Southwold 1978:369)

I started my research with a simplistic picture of two divergent Christian assessments of New Age: hostile evangelicals and sympathetic Christaquarians. While these opposing camps are the main features of the terrain, there are also many similarities and exchanges between the two 'ideal type' Christian reactions which are not captured by such a map[5].

Definitions of the New Age movement by Christians, New Agers and non-partisan observers reveal wide divergences both in abstract theorizing as to what sort of thing New Age is, and in specifically cited concrete examples. The examples of New Age given by sympathizers (see survey results in the Appendix) differ not only from those rather more inclusive indices given by conspiracy theorists like Roy Livesey (1987, 1989, 1990), but also from those of other so-called 'insiders'. This is evident in comparing examples cited in two works widely regarded as seminal, Marilyn Ferguson's *The Aquarian Conspiracy* (1980) and William Bloom's *The New Age* (Bloom ed 1991).

Fieldwork and the questionnaire surveys also suggest divergent definitions of New Age. For example, Fr Adrian B Smith does not think of New Age as a movement or religion but as a wider 'natural' cultural process of consciousness evolution[6]. Conversely, a Catholic retreat leader at The Omega Order speaks of a sinister leaderless "network"[7]. I have yet to encounter first-hand a fundamentalist Christian who thinks New Age an orchestrated conspiracy[8], but respondents at the Anglican evangelical church studied do tend towards such a view of New Age. These definitions of New Age are not easy to reconcile in a singular definition, and nowhere in this thesis do I attempt to provide such a concise definition.

The distribution of examples of New Age in the literature and given by respondents appears to be a centrally-weighted normal bell curve. Focused interviews suggested a common core of examples of New Age – which include David Spangler, crystals, astrology, Findhorn, reflexology – and the survey questionnaire gave statistical backing to such a common core of consensual examples of New Age[9].

There is some academic authority for the usage of family resemblance theory in the definition of New Age. Implicit or unevaluated use of family resemblance theory seems to occur when scholars wish to study *prima facie* diverging religious phenomena under one pre-existing label that might otherwise seem inappropriate to critics. This may unnecessarily weaken their argument, as my contention is that family resemblance theory is a justifiable philosophical basis for analysis.

Tony Walter uses an implicit family resemblance theory in a paper on "Death in the New Age" (1993) in order to justify consideration of various seemingly disparate groups under the New Age label.

> My delineation below of New Age 'core beliefs' about death is not a delineation of a creed or dogma, and there are vast differences within the New Age orbit between ... [various groups]
> (Walter 1993:134)

Walter concentrates on one core belief, that of an "inner essence", the bases of this belief being located in "various religious sources" and "near (or 'after') death experience" and having "core practices: care of the dying" (Walter 1993:136-89).

Wouter Hanegraaff has confirmed to me[10] that his use (Hanegraaff 1996:14) of Snoek's cluster association of contiguity is based on Wittgensteinian family resemblance. His concern is to analyze New Age literature with a philosophical basis that does not predetermine whether it will be possible to speak of one New Age movement on the basis of association by similarity of beliefs.

Ruth Prince (1992) outlines a family resemblance model of New Age which explicitly refers to Needham's polythetic classification theory, although it does not form a significant part of her analysis. Eileen Barker's usage of family resemblance theory for New Age is consigned to an appendix (Barker 1992:189).

While not related to New Age, Clarke & Byrne's (1993) use of the theory stems from their perception of the inadequacy of essentialist (whether functionalist or substantive) definitions of religion (cf Byrne 1980). Mattausch[11] likewise rejects previous accounts of Campaign for Nuclear Disarmament ("CND") for relying on a "covert" "essentialist theory of categorisation" (Mattausch 1986:32):

> In this paradigm, there lurks the presumption that there will be a common explanation for the activists' behaviour ... terms such as 'CND' and 'Movement' ... appear as the name for something ... [whereas] CND is a social praxis and not an entity ..."
> (Mattausch 1986:35)

Common Core Examples of New Age

It clear, therefore, that academic authority exists for the application of family resemblance theory to religious and social movements. I will now describe various members that I consider form a common core of examples of New Age phenomena. These are David Spangler, David Icke, aromatherapy and the Mind-Body-Spirit festival.

David Spangler (b 1945) began his New Age lecturing career at an early age in 1964. He soon teamed up with Myrtle Glines, a friend of the family and a relations counsellor, and stayed at the spiritual community at Findhorn in Scotland with her for three years from 1970. The Findhorn Foundation was established in 1962 by Eileen and Peter Caddy and Dorothy MacLean, building on a group led by Sheena Govan which had disbanded in 1957 (Sutcliffe 1998a:50). Spangler's arrival and leadership turned the community from a small membership of a dozen or so that expected imminent apocalypse in the New Age, into a burgeoning centre with visitors and members in the hundreds that taught that the New Age had already arrived. While at Findhorn, Spangler received communications from an entity that called itself "Limitless Love and Truth" (Spangler 1978/1971). These transmissions told that the New Age had already been born.

Emergence: The Rebirth of the Sacred (Spangler 1984) gave a definition and critique of New Age that has had wide currency. Spangler distinguished different facets of the New Age: a commercial level; "new age as glamour" with people living out occult millenarian fantasies; New Age as paradigm shift; and New Age as an incarnation of the sacred (Spangler 1984:78). Spangler located his work for a new consciousness within the last facet of New Age. His criteria for recognizing the New Age spirit included a positive image of the future; a guiding worldview; positive action; and the presence of a spirit rather than just a vision (Spangler 1984:82-83). He wrote that the New Age "is a process, not a sudden event" (Spangler 1984:160). (See also Spangler 1978/1971, 1996; Spangler & Thompson 1991).

David Icke is an example of somebody whom we would wish to style a New Ager, but who himself explicitly rejects the movement[12]. He acknowledges many typical New Age beliefs including reincarnation, UFOs and a conspiracy of freemasons, illuminati and world governments – beliefs which he claims

Christianity and Science have hindered. One way we can help the Higher Beings is to channel positive energy at significant places on the Earth's surface. A triangle of land with points at the Glastonbury Tor, Warwickshire and Hampshire is the heart chakra of the planet; and the Earth is the heart chakra of the universe. According to Icke, Lucifer took over a small planet, now called the Moon, which was originally in the Horse Head Nebula, and directed it at the Earth, hoping to deincarnate the Earth Spirit. However, the two did not collide, but the Earth's axis was changed and Lucifer resorted to humanity to further his plans. Merlin and Arthur, father and son, led a group who went around the world, closing down energy sites at this time to prevent them being used as open valves for Lucifer's negative energies. Lucifer is intent on disrupting the ley lines that crisscross the Earth's surface with negative energy. (See Icke 1992, 1993a, 1993b, 1994, 1995).

One typical, and very popular, practice in New Age is aromatherapy, the use of natural oils for therapeutic ends. At one workshop I attended in the course of my research, use of essential oils was combined with a basic form of reflexology and meditation. Sitting cross-legged on the floor of a darkened flat, we removed our shoes and socks. Earlier we had prepared our own special mixture of essential oils from the leader's large collection – mine was lavender with jasmine and lemon. A guided visualisation put us into a relaxed state of mind. We then proceeded to massage our own feet with our individual mixtures of essential oils. Certain parts of the feet were said to connect, via meridian lines, to various parts of the body. It was a very relaxing experience.

A representative example of a New Age event is the regular Mind-Body-Spirit exhibition held in the Alexandra Palace, London. This is a huge festival, attracting all from the hardcore New Age to the merely curious, and presents a staggering variety of stands – from New Age bookshops and Native American goods to demonstrations of Rudolf Steiner's eurhythmic dancing and the benefits of overtone chanting; from the National Federation of Spiritual Healers and Reiki practitioners to hi-tech sensory deprivation hoods and traditional Chinese acupuncture; from individual astrologers and tarot card readers to such established new religious movements as the Aetherius Society and Christian Science.

Many other examples could be given to form the common core of typical examples to build our family resemblance model of New Age. In a sense, every example of New Age given in this thesis forms a gestalt from which an understanding of New Age can be derived. But even so, it is not a comprehensive definition.

Such is the starting definition of New Age which will inform the rest of the study. Previous academic definitions of New Age are of course also crucially important and are considered in the literature review (Chapter II). The starting definition is far from conclusive or concise, but it gives a good working indication of the sort of phenomena I am concerned with. But how do I intend to use this definition? This thesis will explore recent claims (eg Introvigne 1994[13]; Sutcliffe 1998a; Wood 1999b) that the New Age does not qualify as a 'movement'. It will do this by examining one section of the New Age movement, that which overlaps with Christianity, and exploring whether it is valid to name it as a distinct movement, which I have called Christaquarianism.

The New Age is often referred to as a 'spirituality' rather than a 'religion', although Hanegraaff (1996) makes much of the term "New Age religion". In general, it may be noted that religion implies a more strict definition of boundaries of membership, whereas spirituality is a more open concept. The New Age does not have a central list of beliefs or members, but is a shifting phenomenon, changing according to what criteria we apply to it. Under some criteria, X may be considered a New Ager, but under a different definition she may be definitely Christian. New Agers are by nature eclectic, having what is often called a 'pick-n-mix' approach to philosophies.

Similarly, the application of the suffix 'movement' to New Age indicates a less cohesive organization than is apparent in a religion. (This is not to say that all religions are cohesive organizations, as is clear with 'Christianity', which covers such a vast range of denominations, but even more so with 'Hinduism'.) Scholars have not located a central organization of the New Age movement despite fundamentalist accusations of a conspiracy for a New World Order (eg Livesey). There are, however, some acknowledged leaders and oft-cited authors. As Rose's survey (1996:375) of readers of the New Age magazine *Kindred Spirit* showed, these include Denise Linn, Sir George Trevelyan, Matthew Manning, Eileen Caddy and David Icke. But none has ascendancy and each may be rejected by any individual New Ager.

Massimo Introvigne (1994:18-21) argues that movements are social edifices with a minimum of structure, a recognizable hierarchy and a precise programme. He defines New Age as a 'metanetwork', that is, a network of networks. A metanetwork is not a movement in his definition for it does not appear in a rigid form with a head or stable hierarchical organization. My understanding of 'movement' differs from that of Introvigne; so far as I can see, phenomena that are usually regarded historically as movements have not always had discernable structures and are often akin to loosely-structured networks.

Stephen Sutcliffe makes a useful distinction between a network and a matrix:

> the network is a metaphor for processes of intercommunication amongst seekers. The material by-products, spin-offs, and (sometimes) outcomes

of this activity – the establishment of communities and societies, the purchase or erection of buildings, publishing of written media, production of material artifacts – constitute a sustaining, if hitherto weak, empirical matrix.

(Sutcliffe 1998a:223-224)

In place of the term 'movement', the New Age is defined by Sutcliffe as a 'collectivity' in the following way:

In terms of the sociology of collective behaviour, we can think of the alternative network as a 'diffuse crowd' ... a scattered collectivity articulated and mobilised through two complementary mechanisms: the 'interaction net' – 'communication from individual to individual and small group to small group' – and the mass media ...

(Sutcliffe 1998a:221)

We may retain Sutcliffe's useful gradation of terms from the diffuse crowd or scattered collectivity, through the network to the fully-fledged movement. At the final stage, or partially along the way, a movement may institutionalize to form a matrix. In this sense it is now similar to a sect or church, but it has reached this stage through a different process of institutionalization than that envisaged by the traditional cult-sect-church hypothesis.

Sutcliffe's charge that New Age is not a movement fails partly because he does not clearly define what it means to be a movement. This thesis will explore that very question, using the example of Christaquarianism. Scholars of new religious movements make surprisingly little use of the literature on the so-called 'new social movements'[14], in spite of the similarity of the nomenclature. In fact, the 'NRM' style is often used merely as a politically correct alternative for 'cult', with the hierarchical and organizational input of that latter concept, rather than indicating the more flexible structure of a social movement. Examples of new social movements are the American civil rights movement, the women's movement, the student movement of 1968 and the environmental movement. In my understanding, New Age shares a family resemblance with these new social movements, in the fact that its primary concern is social: a concern for life-style rather than political power (Scott 1995/1990:17). Furthermore, the New Age movement shares with the new social movements their typically loose organizational structure.

Alan Scott defines a social movement as follows:

A social movement is a collective actor constituted by individuals who understand themselves to have common interests and, for at least some significant part of their social existence, a common identity. Social movements are distinguished from other collective actors, such as political parties and pressure groups, in that they have mass mobilization, or the threat of mobilization, as their prime source of social sanction, and hence power. They are further distinguished from other collectivities, such as voluntary associations or clubs, in being chiefly concerned to defend or change society, or the relative position of the group in society.

(Scott 1995/1990:6)

Scott suggests that the term 'social network' may in some cases be more appropriate than 'movement' (Scott 1995/1990:30). To be particularly noted in Scott's definition of a social movement is the requirement for self-perception of common identity. Without an emic understanding of themselves as a movement, a collective of actors cannot be regarded as such.

Another important commentator on social movements, Sidney Tarrow, defines social movements as follows:

> those sequences of contentious politics that are based on underlying social networks and resonant collective action frames, and which develop the capacity to maintain sustained challenges against powerful opponents.
> (Tarrow 1998/1994:2)

Of note in this definition of social movements is that they are based on existent social networks, such as the kinship ties located by Wood (1999a; 1999b) in the New Age movement. Secondly, "resonant collective action frames" is Tarrow's way of describing what Scott calls "understanding of collective identity". Tarrow argues that recent theorists have shifted the focus in studies of social movements from structural factors to the cultural framing of collective action (Tarrow 1998/1994:17). Frames may be described, after Erving Goffman (1974), as the matrices of interpretation that allow actors to situate events within their life-world.

Johnston et al (1994) outline eight characteristics of New Social Movements (NSMs). NSMs are not related to socio-structural bases such as class or gender. They do not have a unifying ideology but exhibit pluralism of ideas and values. There is an expansion of civil versus political dimensions of society. New or formerly weak dimensions of identity often emerge. NSMs are 'acted out' in individual actions rather than through mobilized groups. They often involve personal and intimate aspects of life. Radical mobilization tactics are employed. NSMs are related to a crisis in the credibility of conventional channels for participation in Western democracies. They are segmented, diffuse and decentralized. Many of these characteristics may be seen to apply to New Age and Christaquarianism.

Touraine defines a social movement as a "particular form of struggle."

> *I use the term struggle for all forms of organized conflictual action carried out by a collective actor against an adversary for control of a social field.*
> (Touraine 1981:85, *original emphasis*)

He sets four criteria for the recognition of a struggle. Firstly, it must be waged by a committed population. Secondly, the struggle must be organized and not exist purely at the level of opinion. Thirdly, it must fight against an adversary. Fourthly, the conflict with the adversary should not be specific but should concern the whole of society. Clearly, neither New Age nor Christaquarianism satisfy all these criteria, most obviously in the level of organization. However, there are some developments in one of the groups studied here (CANA) that may organize the Christaquarian movement to a greater degree (see Chapter IV).

Touraine is also valuable for his methodological suggestions. He describes his method as "permanent sociology" involving "intervention" (Touraine 1981:passim). To summarise this method as outlined in the second half of *The Voice and The Eye* (1981) and as utilised in his studies of Solidarity (Touraine 1990/1982) and the anti-nuclear movement (Touraine 1983/1980), we may note that the researcher acts as co-ordinator of a number of field researchers. These field researchers are integrated in the movements studied, to quite a great extent, for a period of up to several years prior to the research. The research itself involves setting up focus groups with members from various organizations within the movement. Through interaction with the researchers over the course of several months, these groups are led through a "conversion" which makes them more aware of their situation.

> It must be stated quite openly that the purpose of this research work is to *contribute to the development of social movements*.
> (Touraine 1981:148)

Touraine's methodology could easily be applied to Christaquarianism. It is perhaps fortunate that I do not have the resources to attempt this, though. Instead, I have taken a cue from Touraine's search for new social movements. At the outset of my research, nobody had developed the idea of a movement along the lines of Christaquarianism. To this extent, then, the hypothesis I test could lead members of the field through a 'conversion'. However, at no point during my fieldwork did I attempt to provide any analysis to people in the field. Indeed, to have done so would have been fundamentally opposed to my research style. Instead, the 'intervention' I supply comes with the production of this thesis. This thesis may be seen as the 'conversion'[15].

David Snow et al (1986) delineated four forms of 'frame alignment', whereby mobilization in social movements is encouraged by the harmonization of cultural frames between movement activists and the public at large (a distinction of populations which may in any case be blurred). These processes can be seen at work in Christaquarianism. 'Frame bridging' is occurring where sectors of popular opinion which might otherwise remain separate are brought together. For example, at St James's church, the ecological activists of Creation Spirituality are brought into the sphere of influence of metaphysical communities such as *A Course in Miracles*, through the bridging frame of an Earth spirit. 'Frame amplification' articulates interpretations of the world which would otherwise remain unarticulated – this very thesis could be interpreted as the amplification of the Christaquarian frame, building on primary material from CANA and The Omega Order in particular. 'Frame extension' brings the specific issues of the movement to more general public concerns, such as for the improved quality of life through holistic or alternative medicine. 'Frame transformation' brings the values of the movement more in line with dominant public cultural frames. In Christaquarianism, this occurs when, for example, believers in reincarnation express this in terms that are compatible with the resurrection of the dead as in orthodox Christianity.

Scott (1995/1990:52), Tarrow (1998/1994:3) and Touraine (1981:58) all warn against constructing a general theory of the development of social movements, arguing from history that they are too diverse to conceptualize usefully in this way. In any case, such a grand narrative could not be deduced from the empirical data used in this study, which is limited to one particular movement, the New Age movement, and a section of this movement which I have named Christaquarianism. Furthermore, this study has not been diachronic to any great extent. Nevertheless, some analysis may be made of the development of new religious movements. I save these comments for Chapter VIII, after consideration of the fieldwork and statistical data in my four case studies.

Scott writes,
> 'Success' takes the form of integrating previously excluded issues and groups into the 'normal' political process. If there is a telos of social movement activity then it is the normalization of previously exotic issues and groups. Success is thus quite compatible with, and indeed overlaps, the disappearance of the movement as a movement.
> (Scott 1995/1990:10)

Will New Age disappear within Christianity? How far will its 'exotic' cultural frames – such as reincarnation and altered states of consciousness – be incorporated into Christianity? How successful will New Age be? These are speculative questions which we cannot hope to answer, but by understanding the success of the New Age movement to date, we may come closer to understanding its future.

In their introduction to *Comparative Perspectives on Social Movements* (1996), Doug McAdam and his co-editors synthesize scholarship of social movements as concentrating on three factors:
> (1) the structure of political opportunities and constraints confronting the movement; (2) the forms of organization (informal as well as formal), available to insurgents; and (3) the collective processes of interpretation, attribution, and social construction that mediate between opportunity and action.
> (McAdam et al 1996:2)

McAdam focused in an earlier work (McAdam 1994)[16] on the links between culture and social movements. He presented three ways in which culture facilitates movement emergence: the cultural resonance with mainstream society of the frames advanced by the organizers; the role of long-standing activist subcultures; and the expansion of cultural opportunities and interpretations of structural, political opportunities. For Christaquarians, more orthodox aspects of their thought resonate with mainstream Christianity. Secondly, there is a longaeval subculture of esoteric or alternative Christianity, outlined in Chapter V, which is available to movement activists.

Thirdly, McAdam details the cultural opportunities that facilitate movement emergence: the demonstration of contradictions between cultural values and conventional social practices; "suddenly imposed grievances" (Walsh 1981) such as human-made disasters, major court decisions or official violence; dramatization of system vulnerability such as the collapse of Communist party rule in Poland which led to 'copy-cat' revolutions across Eastern Europe in the early 1990s; and the availability of "master protest frames" (Snow & Benford 1988) legitimating collective actions. New Age may itself be considered a "master frame" of cultural protest, to which Christaquarianism, the holistic health movement, the human potential movement and the Neopagan movement (among others) are related. Mainstream Christianity shows its vulnerability, for example, in sex scandals involving senior clergy or in Latin America with the delegitimation of the state-backed church. Awareness of environmental crises is also a cultural opportunity that facilitates organisation of New Age movements, such as Bridge Trust, which is specifically focused around environmental issues (see Chapter IV).

In discussion of St James's church, I suggest that the postmodern or late modern condition is an opportunity structure which is particularly germane to the formation of New Age and similar movements on the fringe of Christianity. The most explicit formulation of the cultural frame of Christaquarianism is made by Christians Awakening to a New Awareness, which is examined in Chapter IV. In discussion of The Omega Order, I shall outline a historical tradition of thought which is used to frame the spirituality of Christaquarians. These variously-formed cultural frames are argued by many commentators to form an alternative tradition, whose mobilizing structures I examine in the final chapter.

Synopsis

This Introduction has outlined my main hypothesis and the research methods employed to illuminate it, before attempting an initial definition of New Age along family resemblance lines. I then discussed the insights of new social movement theorists, which have been neglected among scholars of new religions. The integrating core of the thesis is an examination of whether Christaquarianism can properly be identified as a New Age movement within Christianity.

The second chapter is an extended survey of the literature on New Age and Christianity, rediscovering a number of neglected works.

The next four chapters are case studies that deal with various UK groups in more detail. There are three New Age Christian groups, and one Anglican evangelical congregation which is meant to act as a contrasting control group. In each case, participant observation, focused interviews with leaders and followers, and a questionnaire survey were conducted. Additionally, the literature produced by each group is summarised and reviewed.

Chapter III explores St James's Church, Piccadilly, an Anglican church in the centre of London that hosts a New Age project called Alternatives. It is suggested that the diverse array of projects at St James's, including Alternatives and the post-evangelicals, are indicative of a postmodern spirituality.

Chapter IV considers the group Christians Awakening to a New Awareness, which is a nation-wide mailing list and network of Christians associated with the small New Age organisation Bridge Trust. It provides a clear articulation of

Christaquarian beliefs, and these are explored in connection with the notion of cognitive dissonance and with theories of conversion.

Chapter V discusses The Omega Order, a residential community near Bristol, England of New Age Christians that is run by an Anglican canon-turned Roman Catholic. The second half of the chapter focuses upon historical religious movements that were either in some way precursors of contemporary Christian New Age groups, or that have had some influence on today's New Age Christians. These are the Essenes, the Gnostics, Neoplatonists, Christian Qabbalah, the Rhineland Mystics, the Celtic tradition, Jacob Boehme, Emanuel Swedenborg, William Blake, Theosophy, Anthroposophy, the Arcane School, Christian Science, New Thought, Carl Jung, Edgar Cayce, Dion Fortune and Pierre Teilhard de Chardin.

Chapter VI contrasts evangelical responses to New Age. In the absence of a readily identifiable 'normative' Christian control group, this chapter attempts to provide benchmarks against which to compare New Age Christians. The church chosen is in fact the church in which I grew up, and was married during the course of the research, an Anglican evangelical church which is typically hostile to the New Age and thus provides interesting points of comparison. Additionally, evangelical literature that is hostile to New Age is reviewed. The analysis picks up on some suggestions that evangelical Christianity is similar to New Age, and examines in particular The Omega Order's roots in Burrswood Home of Healing (which is now evangelical), and the evangelical roots of the Nine O'Clock Service.

Chapter VII gives an overview of Christian responses to the New Age movement. The official responses of the main Christian denominations are considered, followed by examination of a number of independent Christian outreach groups to the New Age. Examples of positive Christian responses to the New Age movement covered are *A Course in Miracles*, neognostic groups, Paulo Coelho, Creation Spirituality, the Quaker Universalists, retreat centres, New Age Catholics and New Age Psychology.

The final chapter suggests an answer to the question, Is there a Christaquarian movement? An Appendix lists the results of the postal questionnaire surveys in tabular form. Also included are results of previous surveys for comparison, including Stuart Rose's 1996 survey of *Kindred Spirit* magazine and Michael York's 1990 survey of Alternatives. Some national statistics are also included where relevant. A copy of the survey is included, together with the interview structure generally used and a log of fieldwork dates.

Notes to Chapter I

[1] Canon Professor Edward Bailey has suggested there is a similar problem with the term Christaquarian, preferring the emphasis in "Aquario-Christian" on the fact that these people consider themselves primarily as Christian. Comment from the chair, 49th Winterbourne Study Day, 21 October 1999.

[2] I outline the unusual origin of my interest in Kemp (2000), but it is not of relevance here.

[3] Fieldwork in this thesis is mainly limited to England. New Age is also present in, for example, Poland (see eg Dobroczynski 1991, 1995), Japan (see eg Manabu & Kisala 1995) and Africa (see eg Hackett 1992; Steyn 1994). For a fuller bibliography of New Age worldwide, see Heelas 1996a:131 note 13.

[4] For the avoidance of confusion, I must declare my own religious preferences. During the course of the research I was on the electoral roll of this Anglican church, in which I grew up and was married. However, I have never considered myself evangelical at heart, and profess a developing liberal and non-realist faith. I now attend from time to time a Roman Catholic church with my family.

[5] In parallel fashion, Paul Greer (1994; cf 1995) provides a typology within New Age of two opposite 'poles' or 'tendencies' of patriarchal and ecological spirituality.

[6] Interview: 21 November 1996.

[7] Interview: 2 October 1996.

[8] Except perhaps Margaret Brearley, currently advisor on the Holocaust to the Archbishops' Council of Church of England..

[9] A previous attempt at a characterization of New Age along similar lines has been published in *Cultic Studies Journal* by Dole et al (1990, 1993):

> ... two panels of experts, one consisting of scientific skeptics and the other consisting of cult researchers, were asked to rate 340 items deemed at least remotely related to the concept "New Age". Subsequent ratings and statistical analyses permitted the identification of six statements that appear to characterize the "New Age". ...
> * "An eclectic collection of psychological and spiritual techniques."
> * "Inadequate scientific data regarding effectiveness."
> * "Create zealous promoters."
> * "Rooted in eastern mysticism."
> * "Idealization of a leader who claims founding transformative vision."
> * "Contradict my beliefs."
> (Dole et al 1990:69,74)

Despite claiming to have culled their 340 statements from the literature and to have approximated a scientific approach, the common core statements identified (particularly the sixth) and the rejected characterizations appear overly biased to a hostile approach to New Age.

[10] Conversation, April 1996.

[11] Mattausch's detailed presentation and analysis of a sample of 62 life-history interviews at two CND groups bear out the usefulness of this approach. Three groupings of supporters are suggested (welfare state employees, non-welfare state employees, and elected office holders) and within and between these groups both

similarities and differences are highlighted for consideration. In conclusion, Mattausch points out that the family resemblance approach is more suited to providing description than causal explanation (Mattausch 1986:236, 287), but claims to have illustrated "the feasibility of social inquiry based upon the spirit of Wittgenstein's philosophical position" (Mattausch 1986:288).

[12] At an open lecture in Cardiff University in March 1994, I asked Icke how he relates to the New Age movement. He said he was pleased to answer the question as it enabled him to express his deep-seated reservations about the movement, which he views as just another "ism" or another religion. He prefers the term "Spiritual Renaissance" to "New Age". He pictured a group of people on a walk. Some, in the environmental movement, pitch their tent early; the New Age pitches its tent slightly later. He, however, keeps walking, he said. See Kemp (1994a).

[13] Cf Introvigne (nd), where he argues that New Age has suffered a crisis due to over-commercialisation. "The Next Age could be described as the passage of the New Age from the third to the first person singular" (ibid). He writes that it is difficult to predict the evolution of Next Age into a New Religious Movement.

[14] New social movement theory is one analysis of social movements among many extant theories. Marxist analysis recognizes only one type of movement: the class movement. Collective behaviour analysis concentrates on the disorientation of society and the mobilization of movements as compensators for individual deprivation (eg Kornhauser 1959). Rational choice theory asks how to involve in collective action as high a proportion of a group as possible without incurring the problem of 'free riders' (eg Olson 1965). Resource mobilization theory posits the solution in professional movement organizations (eg McCarthy & Zald 1987). However, new social movement theory appears to be most appropriate to extend to analysis of new religious movements.

[15] I am now working on a book for John Hunt Publishing, provisionally titled, *A New Age Christian Theology*, which is more confessional than this current work of sociology. The methodology of this thesis is that of the sociology of religion, and as such it seeks to exclude partisan approaches. Despite my significant personal interest in the subject matter, I attempted to remain as impartial and objective as possible throughout the work, both in fieldwork and in writing up. The writing of a Christaquarian Theology is a separate project from my sociological thesis. Any "evangelical" aspirations for a putative Christaquarian movement that I may entertain should not be apparent in this study. I consciously took the decision during my doctoral research not to follow Touraine's methodology in which the sociologist provides an interpretation of the movement to the subjects and suggests ways of developing the movement. Nevertheless, having completed the thesis, I became editor of the CANA newsletter in addition to beginning a Christaquarian Theology.

[16] The editors of this volume explicitly include New Age as a new social movement (Johnston, Laraña & Gusfield 1994:3,9).

II. LITERATURE SURVEY

Why this thesis on Christians in the New Age? Is there a need in the academic literature for a further study of a particular section of the New Age movement? Although I selected the subject of my thesis for reasons of personal interest prior to undertaking a thorough literature search, by good fortune I can show that there is a significant gap in academic knowledge on the Christian subsection of the New Age movement. Moreover, much of the literature that is available is not widely discussed. Therefore, I have made this Chapter an extended literature review, which seeks to expose to a wider audience some of the less well-known works on the New Age.

Just a few years ago, scholars could claim with some justification that there had been little academic discussion of the New Age movement (York 1995:3 [submitted in 1991]; cf Lewis & Melton eds 1992:11). Even at this time, though, there were significant early studies relevant to New Age which were overlooked by scholars of the movement. Neither York nor Lewis & Melton, for example, make mention of June Anne English' excellent thesis (1985), which presented an ethnography of holistic health practitioners in Southern California. Furthermore, it is unfortunate that few English speaking students of the New Age have the facility to access the large amount of German literature on the movement available since the late 1980s[1].

Similar, more recent claims that "to date there has been little theoretical enquiry into the contemporary New Age" (Rose 1996:5-6) are more difficult to uphold. Rose's brief literature review (Rose 1996:5-10) dismisses York (1995) and Heelas (1996a) in one sentence for failing to provide "a comprehensive portrayal of the New Age and its British participants in the 1990s" (Rose 1996:8). Sutcliffe's similarly brief literature survey (Sutcliffe 1998:13-21) does not adequately discuss the major theses on New Age either. His discussion is mainly limited to consideration of Melton, York, Heelas, Steyn and Hanegraaff. This is not sufficient for a doctoral thesis that aims to refute earlier understandings of a phenomenon. Similarly, Wood (1999b) concentrates his review on Heelas, York, Melton and Hanegraaff. Again, this is a limited perspective for a thesis which is described as "a challenge to New Age Movement studies" (Wood 1999b:2). As my literature survey will show, academic discussion of New Age is now a wide-ranging enterprise. Nevertheless, there remain serious limitations in much of the extant literature on the New Age movement, and this is particularly the case in discussion of Christians in the New Age.

Although no scholar has yet considered Christians in the New Age as a distinct religious movement which may be named Christaquarianism, a number of texts do discuss the crossover between Christianity and the New Age. But not only is this more restricted field of Christaquarians less widely discussed than the New Age in general, but most of the available texts are of a confessional nature. The main exception to this rule is John Saliba's excellent study (1999) of Christian literary responses to the New Age movement, which I consider first below.

Saliba is both a Christian and an internationally-renowned scholar of new religious movements; who better to assess Christian responses to the New Age movement? The book is clearly structured, with an opening attempt at definition of the New Age followed by three chapter-length discussions of various Christian responses: evangelical/fundamentalist, Protestant and Orthodox, and Catholic. A final chapter gives Saliba's own "Christian evaluation" of the New Age.

The initial definition of New Age that is outlined follows emic attempts at definition, including David Spangler, Marilyn Ferguson and that given by the editors of the American *Body, Mind and Spirit* magazine. However, the consideration of scholarly definitions of the New Age is too brief to do justice to the wide range of literature now available[2]. While there are bound to be omissions in any review of such a burgeoning literature, in the main Saliba's search tools on the various hostile Christian responses seem to have been rather more successful than my own searches. One unfortunate effect of covering such a large number of works, however, is that the text sometimes becomes repetitive in its summary of yet another critique of New Age. Indeed, Saliba comments several times (eg Saliba 1999:77) that the hostile responses to New Age are often very similar.

The analysis that Saliba provides of these texts is as follows. Evangelical and fundamentalist responses to New Age, which are considered together, are said to converge under three headings:
  (1) confrontational, in which the New Age is resisted;
  (2) apologetical, where Christian doctrine is clearly expressed and New Age teachings evaluated from a biblical standpoint; and
  (3) pastoral, where advice is given to Christians to prepare themselves to counteract the movement's influence or to New Agers to draw them back into the Christian fold.
  (Saliba 1999:63)
As might be expected, Saliba is not complimentary of the scholarship in evangelical/fundamentalist accounts of New Age (Saliba 1999:73-76). Furthermore, he concludes that such responses are likely to be ineffective in engaging New Agers in dialogue (Saliba 1999:78).

A tripartite analysis of Protestant and Orthodox reactions to the New Age is also presented, according to the theologies of religion operative in the understanding of the New Age movement:
  (1) an exclusive theology that maintains that only Christianity is the true religion ...;
  (2) an inclusive theology which, while taking Christianity as the normative faith, allows for some truth and goodness in other religions ...; and
  (3) a pluralistic theology that argues that all religions are equally valid paths to revelation and salvation.
  (Saliba 1999:124)
However, it is unclear why Protestant and Orthodox reactions should be

considered together. For example, why cannot some the Protestant reactions be considered in the previous chapter on evangelicals and fundamentalists? Indeed, Tony Higton is considered in both chapters. Neither is it clear why other authors – such as Ernest Lucas – are considered to be Protestant rather than evangelical/fundamentalist. One omission is Barton English' thesis (1994) on the challenge New Age poses to Christian theology. Finally, it might have been insightful to group Protestant authors under their denominations rather than thematically.

The analysis of Catholic responses to the New Age is fourfold. The first response is described as traditional and concentrates on dogmatic issues. A second approach is also traditional, but is willing to look at the positive side of the New Age. The third response is the official Catholic reaction which incorporates materials from the first two methods. Finally, an innovative fourth response is said to attempt to harmonise New Age and Catholic world views. Again Saliba omits discussion of important documents, for instance the Irish Theological Commission's *Response* (1994) to the movement, the Congregation for the Doctrine of the Faith's condemnation of Anthony de Mello (1998), and a doctoral dissertation by a Catholic priest on bridging the New Age and Christianity (Legere 1993) (see below). Discussion of Catholics with a New Age bias – such as Anthony de Mello, Teilhard de Chardin, Bede Griffiths, John Main, Laurence Freeman, Basil Pennington, Thomas Merton, Enomiya-Lassalle and JM Déchanet – could usefully be extended.

The final chapter presents Saliba's own evaluation of the the New Age movement, for which he rather imperiously adopts the adjective "Christian". His consideration concentrates on several major topics of debate between Christians and New Agers: namely, Christology, reincarnation, crystals and channelling. A very brief and rather disappointing conclusion describes the New Age as a "mixed blessing for Christians" which may present an opportunity to the Christian Church to adapt to the 'signs of the times'.

In this work, Saliba performs the redactive role of documenting the vast literature on Christian responses to the New Age movement. Although there are serious omissions, as we have seen, by and large a representative cross-section of the various responses are covered. Indeed, at times Saliba may be over-inclusive and repetitive. However, the major drawback of this literary approach is that it is not grounded in empirical, sociological observation. It is not made clear to what extent Christians actually read these texts, and to what extent church-goers have similar beliefs to these authors. For example, in a structured interview programme at an Anglican evangelical church (below), I found that few people had read texts such as Cumbey (1983) or Cole et al (1990), although they certainly had a clear idea of the approach to the New Age that these texts represent. How far is New Age of common concern among Protestants and Orthodox? It might also have been profitable to do some participant observation at some of the groups that Saliba mentions as accommodating New Age within Christianity. My thesis will provide the fieldwork that Saliba's study lacks; but first in this chapter I will continue with analysis of some doctoral theses that

Saliba neglects.

Of restricted academic influence, Barton Dean English's thesis, *The Challenge of the New Age to Christian Theology and Life* (1994) is conservatively Christian in its bias. Although New Age is defined as non-Biblical, English does allow for some overlap between Christianity and New Age in his analysis of Christian responses to the New Age. He describes this overlap as Christians who have "gone native" (English 1994:i), covering as examples Peter Spink, Donald Reeves and Matthew Fox (English 1994:327-364). Indeed, this is the most lengthy consideration of Christaquarians available prior to my thesis.

English concludes

> a biblical approach would suggest gleaning from the New Age and the various responses to the New Age, those themes and challenges which can awaken a Christian apologetic response without the subjectivism that has manifested itself on the one hand in conjuring conspiracies or narrow millennial views or on the other hand "going native".
> (English 1994:366)

He identifies

> five areas where the New Age specifically challenges Christian theology and the body-life of churches.
> 1. **The Challenge and Need for Spirituality ...**
> 2. **The Challenge to Establish Balance Between Utility and Innate Value. [consumerism vs ecology] ...**
> 3. **The Quest for Hope and Divine Presence ...**
> 4. **The Sense of community, healing, unity and love – Liberation ...**
> 5. **The Challenge to Faith and Doctrine.**
> (English 1994:368-384, **original emphasis**)

Alan Roxburgh's *On Being the Church in a New Age* (1991) is also biased to a conservative Christian point of view in its approach. Indeed, Roxburgh writes that it was "written for pastors and church leaders" (Roxburgh 1991:iii) and the ultimate aim is to provide an understanding of New Age as a basis for evangelization (Roxburgh 1991:64). This is described as "contextualization". It details the response of Roxburgh's church (in Canada) to the arrival in 1983 of the Big Carrot, a health food store which grew into a small mall called the Carrot Common. 50 people were interviewed; 60% of these were women aged 20-40 (Roxburgh 1991:13)[3].

New Age is presented as a rejection of post-Enlightenment culture and a drive for transcendence. The primary response of the church to New Age is thought to be liturgy, and comparisons are made to John Wimber's Vineyard movement. There is also said to be a need for a renewed understanding of the earth (Roxburgh 1991:146). Overall the New Age is seen as a positive challenge to the church: "The New Age is not to be feared." (Roxburgh 1991:147).

Unless our churches switch their focus to strategies aimed at engagement with the emerging culture, then they will lose the new generation and experience shock because the world which they are trying to maintain in their structures, orders and understanding no longer exists.
(Roxburgh 1991:157)

An Examination and Evaluation of the New Age Christology of David Spangler (1986) by Ron Rhodes is an early Christian academic critique of New Age theology. Rhodes' starting point is declared to be "orthodox" (Rhodes 1986:8) and "scholarly evangelical" (Rhodes 1986:3), and his influence has been limited to such Christians. What is done in order to reject Spangler's theology is that he is demonised[4]. The central point of Rhodes' demonization of Spangler is expressed as follows:

The goal of the whole process is <u>Luciferic Initiation</u>. This refers to a crisis point that one must come to where he [sic] fully accepts all of his [sic] experiences on earth without any negative feelings. ... Such a person is a New Age person.
(Rhodes 1986:243, <u>original emphasis</u>)

Rhodes demonstrates a deep acquaintance with the intricacies of this Mephistophelean metaphysics, which may be reduced to a simple oppositional dualist position: Christ versus Lucifer. Rhodes goes on to suggest that,

In the present writer's view, Spangler's theory is inspired by the very Satanic being he denies.
(Rhodes 1986:244)

Subsequently, Rhodes became associate editor of the *Christian Research Journal*, a publication of the Christian Research Institute which has produced a number of critiques of the New Age movement. *The Counterfeit Christ of the New Age Movement* (1991/1990), a CRI book, is not a straight adaptation of Rhodes' 1986 thesis for the popular Christian market, although it does include a section on Spangler's christology (Rhodes 1991/1990:135-141). Rather, it is a detailed examination of the presentation of New Age christology across the board, from Spangler to Blavatsky.

Thomas Legere is a Catholic priest who wrote *A Popular Book: Christianity for a New Age* (1993) for his PhD in the philosophy of spiritual psychology, dealing

with the central question of how orthodoxy and the best of so-called New Age thinking can be bridged by the insights of spiritual psychology.
(Legere 1993:1)

Legere sees the New Age movement as a result of Western Christianity's "failing in its purpose of leading people to an experience of the sacred" (Legere 1993:24). A keystone to Legere's bridge between Christianity and New Age is Needleman's "intermediate Christianity" as outlined in *Lost Christianity* (1985/1980). This is a form of spirituality which somehow bridges conventional life and the unattainable mysticism of the saints, and takes much from Eastern religions.

In one of the few statistical considerations of New Age, Donahue (1993) considers the "Prevalence and Correlates of New Age Beliefs in Six Protestant

Denominations".

Table II.1 New Age Beliefs in Six Protestant Denominations

Question (n=3349)	Percentage
Human nature is basically good.	72
I believe in reincarnation – that I have lived before and will experience other lives in the future.	8
I believe in astrology.	9
Through meditation and self-discipline I come to know that spiritual truth and wisdom is within me.	32
I am in charge of my own life – I can be anything I want to be.	54
It is possible to communicate with people who have died.	7
An individual should arrive at his or her own religious beliefs independent of any church	32

(from Donahue 1993:178,181)

Donahue found that members of the conservative Southern Baptist Convention ranked lowest on each of the seven statements, and members of the liberal United Church of Christ ranked highest on four statements. The most frequently endorsed God image was that of panentheism, endorsed by between 39% and 49% of the six congregations; theism was endorsed by between 24% and 34% and pantheism by between 6% and 13%. However, neither pantheism nor panentheism correlated with the seven New Age beliefs. Donahue concluded that while specific supernatural beliefs, such as reincarnation, astrology and communication with the dead, are rather infrequent, the attitudes that might support this type of spirituality were more common: "Human nature is basically good" and "I am in charge of my own life – I can be anything I want to be."

This handful of works represents the sum of current academic knowledge on Christians in the New Age. As I have shown, much of it is of a confessional nature, leaving space for an objective sociological enquiry. But Christaquarians are also considered, albeit briefly, in literature on the New Age movement in general. There is now a sizeable body of literature on the New Age movement. Moreover, a number of postgraduate students[5] are currently researching further theses, and this trend is likely to continue as undergraduate courses take up the New Age theme. I will now consider theses on the New Age in general.

Matthew Wood (1999b) describes his thesis as "a study of a religious network ... that would normally be described as part of the New Age Movement" (Wood 1999b:1). In some ways, his main argument is semantic: Nottinghamshire Networkers do not like being described as New Age, and some alternative term, such as "nonformative spirituality" (Wood 1999b:110f) should be substituted.

Although it is obvious that some New Agers are ambiguous about their descriptor, this is not evident from the fieldwork Wood presents. Indeed, a number of his informants use the term "New Age", without any qualification, to describe their spirituality (eg the Lovells at Wood 1999b:191f; "Michael" at Wood 1999b:220f; "Noel" at Wood 1999b:264). Eileen Barker has questioned[6] whether Wood's research covered New Age *spirituality* or rather a continuation of lower-social class based *Spiritualism*. Thus, if Wood's informants were ambiguous about the term New Age, perhaps this was because he was not studying the New Age movement.

Wood's conclusions would be refuted by the claim that what he calls *the* Nottinghamshire Network is simply *a part of* a wider 'New Age' network (or whatever substitute term we choose). Given the wide spread of New Age groups uncovered by my research in several locations over Britain, I find it difficult to believe that the handful of groups studied by Wood represents the totality of New Age involvement in Nottinghamshire; due to the nature of the movement, many groups will remain invisible to outsiders.

There is a tension in Wood's thesis between discussing New Age and denying it. Thus, if the Nottinghamshire Network is not New Age, why are the "New Age Movement studies" discussed in his literature review, such as those by Heelas, York, Melton and Hanegraaff, relevant? Similarly, how do the "four main practices" of channelling, meditation, holistic health therapies and divination (Wood 1999b:2) differ from New Age practices?

Wood admits that there is a problem with the "relatively small time-scale [of fieldwork] and numbers of persons encountered" (Wood 1999b:4), but his thesis contains more fieldwork than many other studies of New Age. The Nottinghamshire Network, as he calls it, consists mainly of an Essene Meditation group which met fortnightly with up to 20 meditators; and a Spiritual Fair which attracted about 150 people each Sunday it was held (Wood 1999b:220f). In addition to these two core groups, Wood briefly considers Spiritualism, the Anthroposophical Society, an Occult Study Group and paganism (Wood 1999b:5). The individual life histories he presents are not derived from formal (or even semi-formal) interviews, but seem to be an overall impression derived from interaction with the group concerned. There is no discussion of methodology.

The Essene Meditation group could perhaps be considered Christaquarian, in that Christ is often said in New Age circles to have been instructed at Qumran. Indeed, Wood mentions the Anglican church, Christian Science and other Christian churches as important influences on his informants. However, he does not explore the belief structure of his groups in great detail and is more concerned with relations of power.

The first chapter of Wood's thesis is a dense theoretical discussion of social power, the sociology of knowledge and the relationships between self and society. This broadens in the second chapter to the context of the Nottinghamshire Network, and Wood's concept of 'nonformative spirituality'.

> As a sociological concept, nonformative refers to three elements: the attitude of the participants, including leaders, both in behaviour and beliefs; the social organisation of particular groups and events; and the social organisation of the Network as a whole.
> (Wood 1999b:111)

In fact, Wood concentrates his discussion of 'nonformativeness' on structures of power in his groups, and for this reason, perhaps 'nonformational' would be a more suitable term.

While it is obvious that New Age groups are less hierarchical in their power structures than other groups, it is difficult to describe them as *non*-hierarchical, *non*-formational or *non*-formative. Indeed, on the evidence Wood presents, it is clear that the Essene Meditation was organised by the Lovells and Spencers, and the Spiritual Fair was organised by Michael. New Age may not be described as anarchic.

Wood's final chapter tantalisingly refers to theoretical issues in the study of NRMs, strangely absent from the rest of the thesis. He interestingly suggests that the Network

> was an enduring social phenomenon, for it drew upon formative traditions in order to maintain its own lack of organisation. Thus, the Network did not appear to fit into sociological patterns of religious transformation, from cultic milieu to cult to sect. Rather, it appeared to arise from cults and sects.
> (Wood 1999b:333)

Wood calls for further research into this suggestion, but concludes that

> cults and sects do not appear to arise from nonformative spiritualities.
> (Wood 1999b:344)

If the Essene Meditation is typical of nonformative spirituality, and similar to some Christaquarian groups I have studied, then my thesis will seek to show that some of these groups may in fact lead to the formation of a distinct movement.

Steven Sutcliffe's thesis (1998a)[7] on the New Age is to date the most balanced in terms of scholarship and breadth of analysis. His main idea is that New Age is not a movement but a "collectivity" of seekers. The argument is presented as both an ethnography and a historical enquiry, concentrating mainly on Findhorn[8]. The second half of the thesis contains ethnographical sketches[9]: full-moon meditations of a Lucis Trust Unit of Service, the experience week at the Findhorn Community, a weekend Scottish Alternative Health Exhibition in Glasgow and a firewalking evening.

Sutcliffe concludes his thesis with a chapter of analysis, "Beyond 'New Age': Seekers and Alternative Spirituality" (Sutcliffe 1998a:211-251). He presents the case that the so-called New Age movement is no more than a "collectivity" of individual seekers that happen to use the New Age emblem. The argument is that, because it has "no essential purpose or goal", the collectivity cannot be classed as a movement. However, *pace* Sutcliffe, this is not necessarily a *sine qua non* of a movement, for Joseph Gusfield (1994) has distinguished between the "linear" old social movements with an explicit goal such as the labour movement, and the "fluid" new social movements, such as New Age, which seek change in values and the conception of reality without having explicit goals. Two further reasons are enumerated by Sutcliffe, firstly that emic affiliation with New Age is optional, episodic and in decline, and secondly that the phenomena

> lack most of the requisite sociostructural features for viable differentiation from slacker types of collective behaviour, such as the 'crowd', 'fads', 'crazes' and 'public' ... for example, they lack coordinating bodies, historical awareness, a plausible degree of stability and continuity, evidence of boundary and belonging, a realistic level of critical debate and mobilization (presupposing in turn the existence of an explicit level of ideological norm and practice) .
> (Sutcliffe 1998a:220)

New Age is, according to Sutcliffe, merely an emblem that is invoked *within* the networks, rather than defining them. In an earlier work, Sutcliffe's thesis is perhaps more succinctly explained:

> Thus New Age is not a 'movement' but a populist collectivity: a cluster of seekers affiliated by choice – if at all – to a particular term in a wider synchronous and diachronous network of religious alternativism.
> (Sutcliffe 1997:98)

Sutcliffe then goes on to define three modes of seekership: singular, serial and multiple, as outlined in Sutcliffe (1997). But in my opinion, singular seekers are perhaps not best defined as seekers at all, for by definition they do no seeking[10]. Again, it is questionable whether the distinction between serial and multiple seekership in New Age is a useful one. While the majority of respondents to my surveys were multiple seekers, they were also generally able to identify themselves within a specific tradition (which was New Age in only a minority of cases). They were able in a later answer to acknowledge adoption of New Age practices and beliefs.

> The purpose of this excursion into the definition of seekership is to claim that a movement of seekers ... must be an operative contradiction. One's subjective freedom – indeed *imperative* – to 'seek' inevitably undermines the minimum requirements of a viable movement. Instead, a fluxional aggregate of individual seekers stands revealed, the wider context of which is not a movement, but shifting networks of human cultural experimentation.
> (Sutcliffe 1998a:234)

Ignoring the fact that Sutcliffe has earlier denied New Age is a network, we must still question whether his reasoning here is valid. Unfortunately, because Sutcliffe nowhere sufficiently defines his understanding of a movement, it is impossible to see why there may not be a movement of seekers. In my understanding, a movement is precisely a loose collectivity of individuals who do not have a central organisation, standard text or other trappings of more institutionalised groups. Where is the Bible of the civil liberties movement? Where is the Christ of the feminist movement? Where is the headquarters of the environmental movement? If Sutcliffe is saying that none of these movements are in fact movements, but are merely collectivities of individuals with similar aims, then surely his point is, like Wood's, mainly semantic.

It is surprising that Sutcliffe does not discuss more widely the earlier thesis of Stuart Rose (1996). Here also there is some uncertainty as to the status of the New Age: Rose thinks York's use of Gerlach and Hine's definition of movement is misleading because the New Age lacks an element of structure or authority (Rose 1996:16). It is suggested by Rose that the New Age comprises several Movements – with the given examples of ecology, spirituality and psychotherapy.

New Age in the 1990s is "categorized [by Rose] into core domains or fields of interest ... matters of a change or empowerment of an individual's spirituality, their healing practices, and their community activity (which includes environmental concerns)" (Rose 1996:45). Rose's characterization of New Age draws from William Bloom's definition of "four major fields: New Paradigm/ New Science, Ecology, New Psychology, Spiritual Dynamics" (Bloom ed 1991:xvi). Rose does not explain the decision to exclude New Science from his own categorization, and the exclusion of ecology is attributed to considerations of space (Rose 1996:58) – strange exclusions, if these indeed are fundamental categories of New Age. The thesis concentrates on just two of the four domains: spiritual empowerment and healing.

The bulk of the thesis (Rose 1996:120-275) relates the results of a 908-strong response to a survey of *Kindred Spirit* magazine subscribers, and an ethnographic account of a five-day New Age workshop. 70% of respondents were female, and there was some female bias to body therapies over spiritual or social activities. 57% of respondents were aged 35-54. However, only 26% of respondents had been associated with New Age for over 10 years, suggesting that it may not be as directly derivative from the counter-culture as Rose claims. 31% of respondents were social group B, 48% social group C1. These results are tabulated in more detail in my Appendix where they are compared with results from my own postal surveys. One flaw with Rose's unprecedented survey of New Age is that, until my own surveys, it had no bank of control data against which to be compared.

The survey Rose used explicitly defined New Age as follows:
> For our purposes, "New Age" covers any activity or idea in our culture – for example, including healing, self-development, ecology, etc – whose value can be considered new or alternative to the traditional Western mainstream.
> (Rose 1996:362)

Three sentences later, question 3 asks
> In a few words please describe what you think the New Age is.
> (ibid)

It could therefore be argued that the survey prompted its own results. Further methodological weaknesses are the almost total absence of interviews and contextualising fieldwork. The sole ethnographic study of a workshop is a diary of Rose's own thoughts which might have been interesting if his perceptions were calibrated against those of other participants.

"The Christian Response to the New Age" (Rose 1996: 279-301) should be the most relevant chapter to my study of Christians in the New Age. Rose first outlines Cumbey as representative of the extreme response to New Age, before a limited purview of Peters, Drane and Perry on a scale of less hostile approaches. In total, Rose mentions 13 Christian writers on New Age: Cumbey, Matrisciana, Hunt, Groothuis, Peters, Miller, Streiker, Drane, Perry, Peck, Griffiths, Spink and Fox; just three sentences are devoted to St James's church, Piccadilly. This list is far from comprehensive: what of Livesey, Chandler, Carr, Vitz, Cole et al, Mangalwadi, Smith, Johnston, Marrs, Hunt & McMahon, etc (see Chapter VI)? In other ways, though, the shades of opinion considered are rather over-inclusive: neither the Inter Faith Network nor the Quakers (except perhaps the Quaker Universalists) are particularly concerned with New Age. The conclusion is that "the Church appears to consider that New Age spirituality represents a competitive threat" (Rose 1996:288). Rose uses Drane to summarize Christian arguments against the New Age:

1. We are not all God.
2. Going within will not solve all our problems.
3. It is wrong to deny evil.
4. It is wrong to deny absolute values.

(from Rose 1996:289)

The Spiritual Dynamics of the New Age Movement (Greer 1994) is a PhD thesis completed under John Drane. The examples Greer uses of his patriarchal and ecological poles of New Age are respectively Lectorium Rosicrucianum, Trevelyan, Ramtha; Creation Spirituality and Wicca. His aim was to provide "a framework which highlights and explains many of the fundamental contradictions of the movement" (1994:ii), and his early observation that New Age is difficult to characterize is reflected in his final qualification that the typology is to be used as a sliding continuum. The main problem with Greer's approach is that it is not philosophically neutral but favours one end of the continuum – the approach is explicitly ecofeminist (Greer 1994:ii), so other possible continua within New Age are neglected or distorted: for example, his consideration of Fox does not adequately explore the interesting continuum between Creation Spirituality, Wicca and the Churches. A wider problem is whether it is helpful to frame the thesis in terms of "contradictions" in the New Age movement: not only does this supply an implicit value-judgement (self-contradictory therefore false), but at a fundamental level is inappropriate for consideration of a movement which explicitly rejects such Aristotelian logic. Greer has had little influence in discussion of the New Age other than one article in the *Journal of Contemporary Religion* (Greer 1995).

It is likely that Sutcliffe (1998a) and Rose (1996) will be central to academic discussion of New Age in Britain in years to come. At the moment the debate is dominated by York (1995) and Hanegraaff (1996).

In 1991, when York completed his doctoral thesis[11], *The Emerging Network: A*

Sociology of the New Age and Neo-Pagan Movements (published as York 1995), it represented a huge leap in scholarly work on the New Age, containing nearly as much detailed information on various groups as Melton et al's *Encyclopaedic Handbook* (1992/1986) and *Almanac* (1991), but with the added bonus of an academic analysis and interpretation. Much of York's information seems to have been derived from a thorough submersion in the newsletters of the movements, from *Circle Network News* and *The Cauldron* to the New Age magazine, *Body, Mind and Spirit*. He seems to have become acquainted with a large range of people in the field – possibly assisted by his own membership of a coven in San Francisco in the late 1960s (York 1995:224). Exemplary presentations of both the New Age movement and the Neopagan movement are given, drawing on a large bank of data that at the time of his writing was not readily available.

York's fieldwork concentrated on the Alternatives lecture series at St James's church, Piccadilly, for the New Age; and Shan's House of the Goddess for Neopaganism. Although it can be seen from footnotes throughout the thesis that York spent much time in the field, the actual presentation of the participant observation is minimal, just nine pages (York 1995:223-232). The statistical surveys are similarly disappointing (although all achieved respectable response rates) – consisting of just 17 responses from the House of the Goddess; 25 from the Pagan Moon festival held at the University of London Union buildings; and 48 from an Alternatives lecture. It is not going too far to say that York's 'control groups' are irrelevant: why should he pick a centre for people suffering from AIDS, an American high school reunion and a group of ten lawyers "vacationing in the south of France" (York 1995:209 n1)?

The academic discussion in the thesis concentrates on a résumé of church-sect typologies developed by sociologists (York 1995:237-314). It is interesting to see how many different typologies have been proposed, but these are generally not related by York to the New Age or Neopagan movements except at the end of the chapter when their relevance is questioned. In their place, York suggests (York 1995:324f) application of Luther Gerlach and Virginia Hine's concept of SPIN – segmented, polycentric, integrated networks – which was developed by them to describe such movements without leaders as the Black Panthers and Palestinian guerrillas (Gerlach 1971; Gerlach & Hine 1968).

The remit of Wouter Hanegraaff's thesis (1996) is limited due to the fact that he considers only literary sources, and furthermore limits this to literary sources that were available in continental bookshops (Hanegraaff 1996:13). However, within this remit, Hanegraaff's study is unparalleled in the detail of its exposition and should be the starting point for any understanding of the intellectual history of New Age. He outlines four major trends in New Age religion: channelling, healing and personal growth, New Age Science and Neopaganism. The philosophy of New Age is then explored, considering attitudes to reality through the ideas of holism and evolution; meta-empirical and human beings; the philosophy of mind; death and survival; good and evil; visions of the past; and the idea of a New Age. The final definition he gives of New Age is as follows:

The New Age movement is the cultic milieu having become conscious of itself, in the later 1970s, as constituting a more or less unified "movement". All manifestations of this movement are characterized by a popular western culture criticism expressed in terms of a secularized esotericism.
(Hanegraaff 1996:522, *original emphasis*)

He describes the relationship between "New Age Religion and Western Culture" as one of both reaction and reflection, the underlying model being that of "dialectic tension".

... New Age religion emerged from traditions of western esotericism, as reflected "in the mirror of secular thought".
(Hanegraaff 1996:441)

These mirrors are detailed as: causality; evolution; study of religions and theosophy; psychologization of occultism. New Age is thus understood as "Culture Criticism" which nevertheless expresses itself in the terms of the dominant culture:

As a religious reaction to rationalism and scientism, it [New Age holism] has to demarcate itself from its principal religious rival, Christianity; but in its reaction to traditional Christianity it frequently allies itself with reason and science, and therefore has to demarcate itself from rationalist and scientific ideologies. The solution to this dilemma is, of course, the affirmation of a "higher perspective" in which religion and science are one.
(Hanegraaff 1996:515)

According to Hanegraaff, New Agers react to Christianity by finding an esoteric Christianity which accords with New Age. Hanegraaff allows Neopagans to affirm an "esoteric core of Christianity" (Hanegraaff 1996:77 n2), even though he defines Neopaganism as

firstly, based on the conviction that what Christianity has traditionally denounced as idolatry and superstition actually represents/represented a profound and meaningful religious worldview ...
(Hanegraaff 1996:77)

Despite these qualifications, Hanegraaff's application of his definition of New Age remains squarely within an 'oppositional' tradition of definition which defines 'alternative' religious movements in relation to a 'mainstream'. This is particularly disappointing given Hanegraaff's (1995) perceptive critique of approaches that define "the occult"

indirectly, i.e., as derivations from a given norm defined in terms of scientific rationalism.
(Hanegraaff 1995:119)

He lists three limitations of these approaches: failing to see occultism as a modern continuation of traditions that predate modernism itself; assuming an artificial duality between science and the irrational; and precluding any possibility of understanding occultism in its own terms. In place of an oppositional definition of esotericism, Hanegraaff here (1995) favours Antoine Faivre's substantive definition of esotericism. Faivre's characteristics for esotericism are summarized as: a theory of correspondences; nature as a living *milieu*; imagination mediating between higher and lower worlds; the experience of transmutation; the practice of concordance (ie syncretism); transmission of a tradition (Hanegraaff 1995:111-112). However, it must be noted that Faivre (1994:42) has explicitly rejected New Age as an example of esotericism.

Hanegraaff has written a number of articles which have not been widely discussed in academic debate of the New Age. The article discussed above repeats some of the detailed discussion in Dutch of Hanegraaff (1992b), which clarifies the terms esotericism, occultism and (neo)gnosticism. Another article concerned with the technical debate in establishing esotericism as a field of study in the history of religions is Hanegraaff (1992a), which delineates an analysis that applies to the whole of gnostic studies, including what he calls its modern, "post-gnostic" developments (ie New Age). An earlier article (Hanegraaff 1991) considered "Channeling-literatuur", explicitly in a New Age setting. A useful summary of Hanegraaff's work, uniting his treatment of New Age and approaches to the study of esotericism, is to be found in van den Broek and Hanegraaff eds (1998).

Hanegraaff (1994) resumes for a Dutch audience the academic debate over characterizing NRMs. A section of this article deals with the New Age movement, which is described as a "chameleonic meta-religiosity" (Hanegraaff 1994:29). Here is outlined for the first time what became in his thesis New Age *sensu stricto* ("New Age in engere zin") and New Age *sensu lato* ("New Age in algemene zin") (Hanegraaff 1994:29).

> ... *New Age sensu stricto* (i.e., New Age in a restriced sense). This movement had its roots primarily in England, a country where Theosophy and Anthroposophy have traditionally been strongly represented. ... Typical for this New Age *sensu stricto* is the absolute centrality of the expectation of a New Age of Aquarius. ...
> ... *New Age sensu lato* (i.e., in a wide sense) ... emerged when increasing numbers of people, by the later 1970s, began to perceive a broad similarity between a wide variety of "alternative" ideas and pursuits, and started to think of these as parts of one "movement". ... the expectation of an Aquarian Age is not necessary in order for a movement or trend to be part of the New Age *sensu lato* ... the influence of typically American movements in the "metaphysical" and "New Thought" tradition is strong.
> (Hanegraaff 1996:97)

This is a useful distinction which separates the later fully-fledged New Age movement from the early British 'New Age'-style movement centred around Universal Link, Findhorn and Trevelyan which expected the catastrophic arrival of an Aquarian Age (usually through nuclear disaster) in 1967. Christians were also involved in this movement, and I possess a copy of David Vaughan's *A Faith for the New Age* (1967) annotated with handwritten notes by Vaughan to explain the nonappearance of this eschaton. Universal Link from the early 1960s under Anthony Brooke produced a worldwide 'round robin' newsletter, and in 1968 Universal Foundation was based in Findhorn, to which it introduced David Spangler (Sutcliffe 1998a:82). 1967 is therefore a useful cut-off date between

New Age *sensu stricto* and New Age *sensu lato*, although the process was gradual, and still today strands of the former remain extant in the latter. To take examples other than Spangler and Findhorn: Bridge Trust leader Janice Dolley (see below) remains involved in Trevelyan's Wrekin Trust; and Shaune Crockett-Burrows, editor of *Positive News with Planetary Connections* (a New Age[12] newspaper founded in 1993 and with a print run of 75,000) received Universal Link newsletters when she ran Global Link-Up from the early 1980s.

To judge from the photographs of Paul Heelas in his study of *The New Age Movement* (1996a), it is this transitional period of New Age into which he was socialised. In the 1980s, Heelas carried out academic fieldwork research on New Age training seminars, and this is evident in the material used to explain his theories. *The New Age Movement* is largely based upon Heelas' earlier understanding of "Self-religions" now renamed "Self-spirituality".

Self-religions were described (Heelas 1982) as "secondary institutions" that socialize the subjective in the face of "the demise of traditional, externalized forms of Christianity and other institutions" (Heelas 1982:75), and in the context of "cultural obsessions ... with psychology and with meaning" (Heelas 1982:69). Later papers claimed Self-religions were "basically Eastern in nature" (Heelas 1988:925), and Heelas suggests India "has always been the most important home of the New Age" (Heelas 1993:113). These claims are not fully discussed (cf Heelas 1996a:121-123), and in practice Heelas concentrates far more on New Age as a development of (western) modernity, in particular the centrality of the Self.

The precise nature of the relationship between New Age in 1996 and Self-religions, the Human Potential Movement of the 1970s, and the counter-cultural scene of the 1960s is not adequately explored, calling into question the relevance of frequent citations of *est* (37 are indexed) and other senior New Age groups (eg Rajneesh indexed 17 times) to illustrate points concerning contemporary New Age. Below are the most detailed explanations of the relationship:

> given the fact that many New Age teachers combine, say, Human Potential teachings with Eastern, or Jungian themes with paganism, a great deal supports the contention that teachings and practices – at heart – are all about Self-spirituality.
> (Heelas 1996a:29)
> Paths addressing Self-actualization are often discussed under the headings 'Human Potential Movement' or 'transpersonal psychologies'. However, the growth of this Movement, since the 1960s, has been associated with a shift of emphasis away from the neo-Freudian therapeutic legacy to eastern spiritualities. (See Charles Tart (ed.) 1975.) To some extent, the HPM has lost its 'psychological' distinctiveness, the New Age today drawing on many resources to actualize human potential.

(Heelas 1996a:57)
Heelas here locates the essential difference between HPM and New Age – New Age is HPM de-psychologized and applied globally.

'Degrees' of involvement are outlined from the "fully-fledged" (Heelas 1996a:117) to the "culturally diluted" New Age of the "casual part-timer" (Heelas 1996a:119), with the suggestion that a similar gradational model could be applied to other New Age topics (Heelas 1996a:115f). This fits in well with the family resemblance model of New Age discussed above, where individuals or groups are considered more or less New Age according to their relationship with core family members. Heelas' allusion to his understanding of New Age as a "cultural resource" (Heelas 1996a:128) could be profitably developed to elucidate his view of the nature of New Age, which he claims is not a NRM (Heelas 1996a:9).

A number of passing references is made to the relation between Christianity and New Age, but these are not given a full consideration. There are several unsourced claims that New Age is present in Christianity. In particular, Heelas considers "rave services" (Heelas 1996a:129; repeated on 1996:149) to be New Age; but the 'rave worship' held during my period of fieldwork by members of St James's Piccadilly in a nearby nightclub was conducted by post-evangelicals rather than New Agers. 'New Agey' vicars referred to in the book apparently refer to such liberal non-realists as Revd Don Cupitt and others in his Sea of Faith network[13]. Heelas' claim that "many have become more-or-less New Age – within Christianity" (Heelas 1996a:163) refers solely to the demise of authoritarian epistemology (ie reliance on Scripture) and of exclusivistic traditionality (ie lack of dialogue with other faiths).

Amy Simes has criticised (Simes 1995:491) Heelas for defining self-religions as 'groups'[14], since much of his observation derives from encounter group therapy which meets only sporadically or temporarily in workshops and seminars. Anthony D'Andrea (1997/1996) criticizes the work of Heelas and Amaral (1994) on New Age in Rio de Janeiro for being imprecise and over-inclusive in their definition of New Age (D'Andrea 1997/1996:98). The heart of New Age resides for D'Andrea in reflexive mysticism. Using Anthony Giddens' (1995/1990) concept of an emergent post-traditional order within Late Modern societies, D'Andrea situates New Age within the decline of tradition which forces the individual to experiment in questions of social and subjective identity, particularly the questions of perfectibility of the self and the self-cultivation ideal. This "cosmovision" is, according to D'Andrea, the religion of a new global culture.

There have been a large number of other studies of the New Age which have at least some bearing on the present subject in their clarification of the nature of the movement. These include Prince (1992), Scott (1980), Roberts (1989), Melton et al (1991), Albanese (1988, 1990, 1992, 1993), Bednarowski (1989, 1991), and Roof (1994/1993)[15].

Ruth Prince's (1992) original input to academic study of New Age (although her methodology is weak[16]) is an analysis of individualism and holism through her fieldwork at Glastonbury. She makes the simple logical observation that individuals cannot exist without the support of society and vice versa, but in fact this does not mean that self-transformationist ideas cannot exist without holistic ideas, nor that methodological atomism cannot exist without collectivism. Thus her conclusion, that holism and individualism are complementary, is achieved only through theoretical confusion.

Gini Graham Scott's *Cult and Countercult: A study of a spiritual growth group and a witchcraft order* (1980) is based on PhD fieldwork conducted between 1974 and 1976. The groups studied were a workshop-based group called the Inner Peace Movement, with c20,000 members, and the Aquarian Age Order (a pseudonym for a neopagan group in the San Francisco Bay area) with c150 members. Unfortunately, the two groups are considered rather in isolation and their part in a wider cultic milieu is not fully explored. Scott's main thesis is to contrast the two groups as mainstream and alternative:

> While mainstream groups accept mainstream values and help members function better in this world, countercultural groups reject these principles and seek alternative structures and values.
> (Scott 1980:8)

Susan Roberts' *Consciousness shifts to psychic perception: the strange world of New Age services and their providers* (1989), was based on participant observation and 36 taped interviews[17] in the California area. In fact, the majority of the thesis is taken up by simple transcripts of extracts from the interviews, although they are grouped into three classes: those with psychic abilities, those who had experienced trauma leading to a reevaluation of worldview, and those who are on a purposeful search. Roberts is generally not referred to by the academic community.

J Gordon Melton, one of the international authorities on New Age and also a Unitarian Minister, predicted in 1992 that

> As a revivalist movement, the New Age (like the healing revivals, the Ecumenical movement, and the Jesus People movement) will come and go. Its major impetus will be absorbed by the older bodies from which the movement derived its basic ideas.
> (Melton 1992:16)

By 1994 he was confidently pronouncing its obituary (Melton 1998:133-149). Melton takes a brief look at Christianity and the New Age in the *New Age Almanac* (Melton et al 1991:310f) but concentrates on negative responses. There are individual entries dealing with sympathetic Christian relations with New Age, such as on Matthew Fox (Melton et al 1991:324-326) and Spiritual Frontiers Fellowship (Melton et al 1991:354-355), but these are not united into a coherent analysis – a problem stemming from the encyclopaedic nature of the *Alamanac*.

Catherine L Albanese's contribution to Lewis and Melton's *Perspectives on the New Age* (Albanese 1992:68-84) depicts New Age as a "new healing religion" (Albanese 1992:75) with a "planetary dimension" that is expounded "under the metaphorical sign of the quantum" (ibid). Albanese's suggestion is that quantum metaphors are central to New Age; however, in my estimation New Age is not bound to quantum mechanics, but to ultra-modern science in whatsoever form it happens to take. A different but similarly limited conception of New Age was presented by Albanese in 1988. Here healing is listed as just one of a number of similarities between New Age and fundamentalism (Albanese 1988:349) which are presented to illustrate the thesis that New Age is an ethnic American response to secularism.

Mary Farrell Bednarowski's limited consideration of New Age (1989) also concentrates on American theological preoccupations, and is structured around imaginary discussion of basic questions such as, "Who or What Is God Like?" (Bednarowski 1989:19f). While eminently readable, the very structure of this work as a conversation precludes proper analysis of the theological issues; and does not even claim to consider their sociology. New Age, although defined by Bednarowski according to Spangler (Bednarowski 1989:15), is at times equated with Theosophy (eg Bednarowski 1989:39) apparently forgetting an early caveat that New Age is more planetary in its concerns (Bednarowski 1989:17). A later article by Bednarowski (1991) compensates for her abstract approach in the earlier book with consideration of primary and secondary sources. As always with such reviews of the literature, criticisms may be made about her selection of these 14 books, which includes New Age, academic and Christian works without properly distinguishing the various merits of each.

Roof's *Generation of Seekers* (1994/1993) are defined as the 76 million Americans (one third of America's total population) born between 1946 and 1962 – dates chosen "arbitrarily" (Roof 1994:266) but significantly located after World War II and before the assassination of President Kennedy. Given such a formidable task, Roof's wide-ranging comments on the religious attitudes of a population larger than that of the UK sound quite convincing[18]. His central thesis is that the 1960s divided the country between two worldviews – traditional and counterculture – and that this has repercussions in attitudes to religion and spirituality today just as it did in Wuthnow's study in the 1970s. The book is an accessible read, using seven individuals as 'ideal type' presentations of various trends and claiming wider validity with a wealth of statistics and charts from Roof's surveys.

"Mollie Stone" is presented as an ideal type of a New Ager – Roof prefers the term "highly active [spiritual] seeker" (Roof 1994/1993:79f) – for what he claims is "about 9% of the boomer population" (Roof 1994/1993:80).

> Compared with others of their generation, they are older [sic], more of them are white collar and professionals, and they are better educated. However, they earn less in their jobs and careers. More are female. Fewer are married. They are more liberal in political views. As we would expect, these seekers have low levels of institutional religious involvement.
> (Roof 1994/1993:80)

Roof then uses Troeltsch's concept of "mystical religion" to describe the New Age worldview, and noting the difficulties of researching the category, depicts five differentiating "beliefs and practices". The statement which does indeed seem to separate New Agers from much of the rest of the population is "People have God within them, so churches aren't really necessary", to which 60% of the "highly-active seekers" agreed, but only 27% of all others. Roof also finds significant the larger proportion of New Agers believing in reincarnation, psychic powers, ghosts and practising meditation.

Having provided an introduction to scholarship on the New Age movement, I will now widen my consideration to include more general works on NRMs. Virtually without exception, scholars have identified the tradition of thought current in Christaquarian circles, as 'marginal' or 'deviant'. Revd Donald Reeves, formerly rector of St James's church, Piccadilly, has mentioned to me on a number of occasions that Theodore Roszak's *The Making of a Counter Culture* (1969) was an important influence on his life. J Milton Yinger took up this terminology with his study of *Countercultures* (1982). Other scholars to use concepts of marginality include Campbell (1972), Tiryakian (1974), Marty (1970), Webb (1976), Ellwood (1979), Stark & Bainbridge (1987), Wuthnow (1976), Harper (1982), McGuire (1988, 1993) and Beckford (1985).

NRMs have been given various typologies, many of which contain insights for the study of New Age. However, the analysis presented here suggests that existing typologies are cut across by the New Age movement, and therefore inadequate. Considered are Berger (1981/1973), Wilson (1975/1973), Glock & Stark (1965) and Wallis (1984). Jorgensen (1982, 1983) (cf Jorgensen & Jorgensen 1982) has depicted a tripartite typology of the psychic fair movement, and suggests that marginality is the unifying factor in the esoteric community. Later, I develop Jorgensen's suggestion of a continuum from cultic marginality to mainstream cultural movements, which are no longer marginal, using the insights of scholars of the so-called new social movements.

Campbell introduced the notion of the "cultic milieu" in 1972, ostensibly as a conceptual tool to enable sociologists to study "cults" (which he described as ephemeral) within a more stable context.

> Such a milieu is defined as the sum of unorthodox and deviant belief-systems together with their practices, institutions and personnel and constitutes a unity by virtue of a common consciousness of deviant status, a receptive and syncretistic orientation and an interpenetrative communication. In addition, the cultic milieu is united and identified by the existence of an ideology of seekership and by seekership institutions. (Campbell 1972:134-135)

The origin of the concept as a means to the end of studying cults has been largely forgotten in the literature, with the cultic milieu becoming hypostasized for study in itself rather than just as a means to the end of studying institutionalised cults. Indeed, Hanegraaff defines New Age as *"the cultic milieu **having become conscious of itself**"* (Hanegraaff 1996:17, ***original emphasis***).

The cultic milieu was defined as dichotomous with "non-Christian religious ideas and the weakened position of the churches as agencies of cultural control" (Campbell 1972:119). Campbell has since reconsidered (Campbell 1987) the basis of the "common dichotomy" between normal-anomalous, exoteric-esoteric and accepted-rejected, for three reasons. Firstly, normality is a value-judgement. Secondly, in the seventeenth and eighteenth centuries, occultism was mainstream and so there may be difficulties in defining it as esoteric. Thirdly, present-day occultism is not the only past knowledge that has been rejected, so there must be something other than its rejection that defines it as occult. Campbell speaks in this later paper in terms similar to Hanegraaff (1996) of an ambiguous relationship between occultism and established religion:

> It is also possible that established religion and the occult possess a somewhat symbiotic relationship, from which each benefits in its struggle against its "revival". It is hard to judge how true this is although Christian fundamentalism clearly does help to encourage belief in magic, witchcraft and demons ...
> (Campbell 1987:51)

Campbell, then, shows awareness of some of the problems of defining occultism in contradistinction to mainstream religion, but does not go so far as to reject such a polarized mode of definition.

Peter Berger suggests that "youth culture" (Berger 1981/1973:181) is in rebellion against modern society's main characteristic: rationality. Later, he explored what he called *The Heretical Imperative* (1980/1979), which is the apparent near-necessity today of choosing a non-traditional faith. The final chapter explicitly gives the example of the influence of the "Age of Aquarius" (Berger 1980/1979:165) on Christianity, and suggests that the dominant tradition must modify in the face of the influence of the East.

Berger is one among a number of sociologists who have described influential typologies of NRMs, but I will now show that the New Age movement often cuts across these typologies. The table below explores the general validity of Berger's typology with reference to the New Age.

Table II.2   *Berger's typology of NRMs*

Berger's type		My New Age example of Berger's type
Enthusiastic:	Revivalist/Pentecostalist	Channelling
	Pietist/Holiness	Divine spark within
Prophetic:	Chiliastic	Harmonic convergence
	Legalistic	Arcane School
Gnostic:	Oriental	Tao of Physics
	New Thought	Louise Hay
	Spiritist	Guardian angels

Bryan Wilson similarly suggests that "the new cults" (Wilson 1979/1976:passim) are a response to secularization. Despite his obvious bias for *Rationality* – the title of a volume he edited in 1970 – Wilson's detailed study of *Magic and the Millennium* (1975/1973) is valuable not only for its collection of diverse materials, but also for the widely-used schematization. But Wilson's suggestions on typifying sects according to their response to the world are difficult to apply to the New Age. Below I suggest one New Age group or central New Age idea that could belong to each *typos*:

Table II.3   Wilson's typology of NRMs

Wilson's type	My New Age example of Wilson's type
Conversionist	*The "You create your own reality" belief*
Revolutionist	*Aquarian Conspiracy*
Introversionist	*Gnostic Studies (aka Esoteric Psychology)*
Manipulationist	*Affirmations*
Thaumaturgical	*Crystal work*
Reformist	*Gaia hypothesis*
Utopian	*Natural Law Party (TM)*
Acceptance	*New Age businesses and management training courses*

Because the New Age is so diverse and contains groups with contradictory aims and *rationales*, parts of the New Age can be seen to manifest aspects of all Wilson's proposed divisions. There is no immediately apparent "typical" typification of the New Age *in toto* according to Wilson's typology.

Roy Wallis, in *The Elementary Forms of the New Religious Life* (1984), presented a popular typology constructed, like Wilson's, according to orientation to the world:

Table II.4   Wallis' typology of NRMs

Wallis' type	My New Age example of Wallis' type
Rejection	*Rejection of science and technology*
Affirmation	*Prosperity workshops*
Accommodation	*Adapting traditional rituals to New Age settings*

Yet again, while the New Age can generally be said to be world-affirming, there are necessary qualifications:

> Although the New Age Movement and the New Age religions in general will be seen to conform to Wallis's world-affirming type, in many cases there are important world-rejecting features as well (eg millenarianism, inner elite corps, charismatic leader, etc) and even, in some cases, elements of the world-accommodating movement.
> (York 1995:294)

Glock and Stark in *Religion and Society in Tension* (1965) outline five kinds of deprivation, suggesting that each leads to a different form of sectarianism:

Table II.5   *Glock and Stark's typology of NRMs*

Glock and Stark's types of deprivation		*My New Age example of their types*
Economic	Sect	*Prosperity workshops*
Social	Church	*Rave masses*
Organismic	Healing movement	*National Federation of Spiritual Healers*
Ethical	Reform movements	*Environmental concern groups*
Psychic	Cult	*Psychic fairs*

As the examples in italics show, each of these forms can be applied to some aspect of New Age which therefore is not usefully analyzable by the schema.

We have seen that there is now a well developed collection of literature on the New Age movement in general which must be considered before we can attain a sufficient understanding of Christians within the New Age. Many works on New Age do not adequately discuss this literature. Those that discuss the crossover between Christianity and the New Age are often of a confessional nature. A number of the works are limited to literary sources. To remedy these limitations, the next four chapters of this thesis present fieldwork case studies of Christaquarian groups and, for comparison, an evangelical church.

III. ST JAMES'S CHURCH, PICCADILLY

St James's, Piccadilly, is a large Anglican church in the centre of London where Revd Donald Reeves was Rector from 1980 to 1998. It is well-known, especially among Christaquarians and evangelicals, for its welcoming of New Age speakers. The observations in this chapter are garnered from visits to about a dozen Sunday services at St James's between May and December 1996, a series of semi-structured interviews with the clergy and other leaders as well as members of the congregation, and a postal questionnaire sent to the 179 members of the electoral roll for which a respectable response rate of 28% was achieved. Many lecture evenings and a number of religious services other than the main Sunday worship were also attended[19]. Additionally, primary literature has been reviewed, including transcriptions of sermons where available, a "Parish Profile" prepared for applicants during the inter regnum in 1998-1999, an internal theological audit conducted in 1996, a ten-year "Vision" statement printed in 1990, the parish magazine, Piccadilly Press, and the many publications of the leaders of the church.

St James's might almost be said to be the Canterbury of Christaquarianism, in that it is a place for spiritual pilgrimage and viewed as a centre of New Age Christianity in Britain. Over two-thirds of CANA respondents and half of the *Omega News* respondents (members of both groups are scattered across the country) have been to St James's, Piccadilly, and this is probably true of most other Christian New Agers. A memorial service held (like those of many other illustrious people) for Sir George Trevelyan, the New Age leader, conducted by Revd Donald Reeves at St James's during the course of my research, was an occasion for the reunion of many Christian New Agers and also New Agers who were not Christian but wanted to mark Trevelyan's death (*Positive News* Issue 10:32, June 1996). According to internal figures ('Parish Profile' 1998), the average congregation at the main service on a Sunday is 177, while special services and festivals attract over 500 people.

It must be emphasised at the outset of this report, that New Age is only one influence among many at St James's. There are a multitude of other ministries and events held at the church, given its central location. These include classical concerts, consultations at the Centre for Health and Healing[20], and the various meetings of the Centre for Creation Spirituality (now GreenSpirit), Church Action on Poverty, the asylum seekers' projects, the small choir, the Blake Society, Bible study groups, Julian meditation groups, the catechumenate, the Taizé group, the lesbian and gay group, Christian Aid, the Vagabonds group and the liturgical dancing group. They are not considered here, as in my experience the concerns of these various groups are not frequently expressed at the New Age events (mostly organised by the Alternatives group) held in the church. The weekly programme of St James's is centred on the two-hour Sunday Eucharist. This is the main celebration of the church, although Eucharist is also held throughout the week (except Mondays and Saturdays), with various other services aswell.

The New Age project of St James's is Alternatives, a weekly lecture series held at the church on a Monday night, that invites New Age and pagan speakers. Entrance is by a mid-priced ticket (in 2000 this cost £10, £5 for concessions), and the church is usually quite full with around 300 people; a press release dated October 1998 claims the Alternatives programme attracts over 15,000 people every year. Alternatives developed out of a group known as Turning Points (formed in the late 1970s by Sabine Kurjo and Malcolm Stern) and was run from 1988 by Dr William Bloom, his partner Sabrina Dearborn, and Malcolm Stern. Dr Bloom is heavily involved with the Findhorn Foundation, and although he still occasionally attends Alternatives and gives lectures and his name and biography sometimes appears on the fliers, he has little day-to-day involvement with their organisation, which passed to Nick Williams in 1994[21]. Some members of the church congregation are highly critical of Dr Bloom and the "parallel church" they claim he developed at St James's in Alternatives, while Dr Bloom denies that Alternatives was ever a "satellite" under his leadership. The churchWarden emphasises that the audience at these New Age events is different from the audience on a Sunday morning, just as these are both different from the audiences at the concerts and the Blake Society events, for example.

All Alternatives literature distributed in St James's includes what is described as a "friendly disclaimer" (written by Dr Bloom during a period of controversy with evangelicals in the early 1990s) that

> Although St James's Church, in its openness of heart and mind, includes Alternatives, the ideas in the programme are not representative of the church itself.
> (Alternatives Brochure)

The PCC of St James's, in considering earlier drafts of this chapter, also provided the following statement:

> The PCC, while welcoming the presence of Alternatives, does not expect to be in agreement with everything it does and has at times been questioning of some of Alternatives' activities. It remains, however, of the view that Alternatives is a valuable project and is committed to offering it hospitality at St James's.

A second statement, written by Revd Reeves and Revd Robins, was also provided:

> The Sunday Eucharist is central to the worshipping life of St James's, which also includes prayer, bible study and discussion groups. St James's, while being true to its Anglican tradition, has seen its ministry as open and inclusive, and extending beyond its core community to include offering hospitality to all those who ask for it, including many who feel themselves marginalised or on the edge, who have perhaps been hurt by institutional religion and need a space for exploration and healing. In this spirit, St James's welcomes New Age enquirers and provided a base for the Alternatives project. St James's recognises that some New Age ideas strive for a reconciliation of body, mind and spirit that the Church, to its loss, has sometimes failed to acknowledge.

According to my survey, less than one in three members of the electoral roll have not been to Alternatives. Until 1999, there was no institutional distinction between the church and the lecture series. Indeed, during Dr Bloom's leadership the three leaders and administrative staff at Alternatives were provided with a PAYE salary by the church and also supported with free office accommodation at the central Piccadilly rectory, free telephone usage and a float which paid for printing and advertisements. The PCC have indicated to me that this financial assistance was not part of a policy to support Alternatives, but rather an administrative oversight[22]. They also point out that from circa 1993 an annual charge of up to £5,000 was levied, while in 1999 this changed to a charge of £100 per evening[23] held in the church.

It is now emphasized by the PCC that Alternatives is not a 'ministry' of St James's, as this would mean it was Christian, but a 'project' of the church; during the period of Dr Bloom's leadership, no such distinction was made. In 1996, a small steering group was set up to discuss the interface between St James's church and Alternatives, on which Revd Reeves, Revd Robins and Nick Williams (then director of Alternatives) sat with a couple of others, but this was not entirely successful and disbanded by 1998. Williams is

> aware that Alternatives is a gateway for people back into the church. That's not our stated purpose, but I'm thrilled if people find a way back to something meaningful through us, whether you call it Christian or New Age, that's great.
> (Interview, 29 July 1998).

Statistical Surveys

Michael York distributed 121 surveys to an Alternatives lecture audience in 1990, receiving a respectable 45% return[24] (York 1995:179f). In common with my survey responses of Christian New Age groups, as well as that of the evangelical Anglican church, York found that 71% of respondents were female. The social composition of the audience was mixed: 17% were involved in "teaching, crafts, etc", 12% in therapy, 11% in computer programming and 11% were unemployed. The average income was fairly low: 35% earned £10-15,000, 23% £5-10,000 and 21% below £5,000, with only 4% above £20,000. 61% came from a Protestant background, and York remarks on the high presence of former Jews at 12.5%. There was great diversity in the expression of current religious preference: 23% claimed none and only 8% claimed New Age identity, the same percentage that identified themselves as Christian. Accordingly, 6% believed God to be a real personality, 33% an impersonal force. 75% of respondents were familiar with the term "New Age", 42% with "Neo-paganism".

The only statistical survey of the whole congregation at St James's church was conducted in 1992 by Professor Eileen Barker of the London School of Economics, at the request of the then Bishop of London in his efforts to diffuse criticism about the ministry at St James's. However, perhaps because of the immensity of this survey – which continued for 37 pages with around 500 questions – these results remain unanalysed.

My survey at St James's used the electoral roll as its population[25], receiving a 28% response rate. For full details of this survey and the comparative statistics used below, please see the Appendix. Compiled during the course of my research in 1996, the electoral roll contains 179 names of which 55 or 31% are male. Most reside within London postal districts, but there are a couple from surrounding counties and one from York; one questionnaire was even returned to me, having been forwarded to an English teacher in France.

From the survey, there appears little sociologically remarkable about the congregation: largely post-middle aged, middle-class with conventional religious and educational backgrounds, approximately 3:7 male:female. Nearly half of the electoral roll respondents were over the age of 55 – this is nearly double the national size of this age group, but similar to that of the evangelical church which was used as a control group[26]. Interestingly, Rose's *Kindred Spirit* readers (1996) for this age group approximate the national statistics. Around one third of those who responded at St James's are single, and slightly more are married. Incomes were much higher at St James's than the national average, other New Age groups and the control congregation. Nearly one quarter reported incomes in excess of £35,000, and another quarter in excess of £20,000 (see Appendix). Not surprisingly, nearly two thirds of respondents were in employment and nearly 80% had completed a university degree or professional qualification.

From my participant observation, I have concluded that St James's main Sunday congregation may be considered under three distinct headings: the core[27] of 'regulars' who are generally heavily involved with the various ministries hosted by the church; a floating section of less regular 'associates'; and a large number of 'occasional visitors', many from abroad. These three segments of the congregation may also be discernable from the survey results, where approximately one third attended once a week (regulars), one third attended every few weeks (associates) and a final third attended less frequently (occasional visitors).

Table III.1   Question 21. How often do you attend a Christian service at St James's church?

Regularity	%
Never	4
Occasionally	31
Every few weeks	27
Once a week	33
More than once a week	2
No answer	2

Over 20% of respondents have moved from the church of their upbringing to Anglicanism, but the overall level of reported Christian religious affiliation has remained constant at around 90% in both religion of upbringing and current religious affiliation. 14% regarded God as a real personality, in contrast with 58% of the control church; 27% regarded God as an impersonal force, a similar figure to that obtained in York's survey of Alternatives. Asked whether there are varying types of spirituality – eg New Age spirituality, Buddhist spirituality, Christian spirituality – or whether spirituality is universally the same, St James's responded respectively 57:29, that is to say, in proportions closer to that of the control church than that of Rose's (1996) *Kindred Spirit* readers, where 70% thought spirituality universally the same. Similarly, frequency of the practice of meditation was closer to that of the control church than that of other New Age groups. St James's respondents pray the least among those surveyed, with over 60% praying only every few days or less. It may therefore be that electoral roll respondents are atypical in their use of traditional Christian practices of worship, but further studies of similar city-centre churches would be needed to make any firm conclusions.

84% of the electoral roll respondents had been attending St James's for more than five years, 20% for more than 15 years. One third of respondents first heard of the church through a friend.

These statistics do not highlight as clearly as I had anticipated the similarities of St James's with the other Christaquarian groups studied. In fact, in some respects, St James's has more in common with the evangelical control group than the other New Age Christian groups. For example, the age spread at St James's is more congruent with the control group than with the other groups; the opinion of varying types of spirituality was similarly congruent; there was a similarly weak emphasis on meditation and a low level of reported paranormal phenomena. These similarities between St James's and the control group may well be because both are churches, whereas the other groups are a community and a network, and both are Anglican, whereas the other groups are non-denominational and inter-denominational.

One in five respondents at St James's visited Alternatives before attending a Christian service at St James's, backing up Revd Reeves' claim to the effectiveness of the project in getting people back to church. 43% of respondents at St James's indicated that they had adopted New Age ideas or practices, and for nearly half of these this had been for ten years or longer. Over three quarters of the electoral roll respondents could give a definition of New Age, compared to a national average in the US of 23% (Heelas 1996a:109). When asked for an example of New Age, the most common example given was Alternatives, followed by Creation Spirituality, Findhorn, healing, crystals and green issues.

Over one half of respondents have participated in over ten of the New Age practices listed by Stuart Rose in his thesis on New Age[28]; no member of the evangelical control group had participated this much in New Age practices. The most popular practices among St James's respondents were hypnotherapy, recycling, T'ai Chi Ch'uan/yoga, psychotherapy, homoeopathy, aromatherapy, acupuncture/shiatsu, creative visualisation, green politics, healing workshops and vegetarianism – all of which had been practised by over four in ten respondents.

In the absence of strict criteria, these are the best indications that a significant number of survey respondents at St James's have some affiliation to the New Age movement. However, based on self-reporting, slightly less than half of respondents saw themselves as having adopted New Age ideas or practices.

Factor analysis of the regularity of attendance and length of adoption of New Age ideas or practices reveals an interesting relationship. Of those respondents who attend the church once a week or more often, 18% had adopted New Age tendencies for five years or more. Of those respondents who attend the church once every few weeks, 42% had adopted New Age tendencies for five years or more. Of those respondents who attend the church less than this, 60% had adopted New Age tendencies for five years or more. Conversely, the three groupings of churchgoers reported increasing denial of New Age tendencies the more frequently they attended the church. The graph on the following page illustrates this, and strongly suggests that the core congregation at St James's tends to be less New Age than those who do not attend as regularly. (Factor analysis of length of membership of St James's church and affiliation to New Age was inconclusive, probably because most members of the electoral roll have joined the church since Revd Reeves' arrival in 1980.)

Figure III.1 New Age affiliation and attendance at St James's

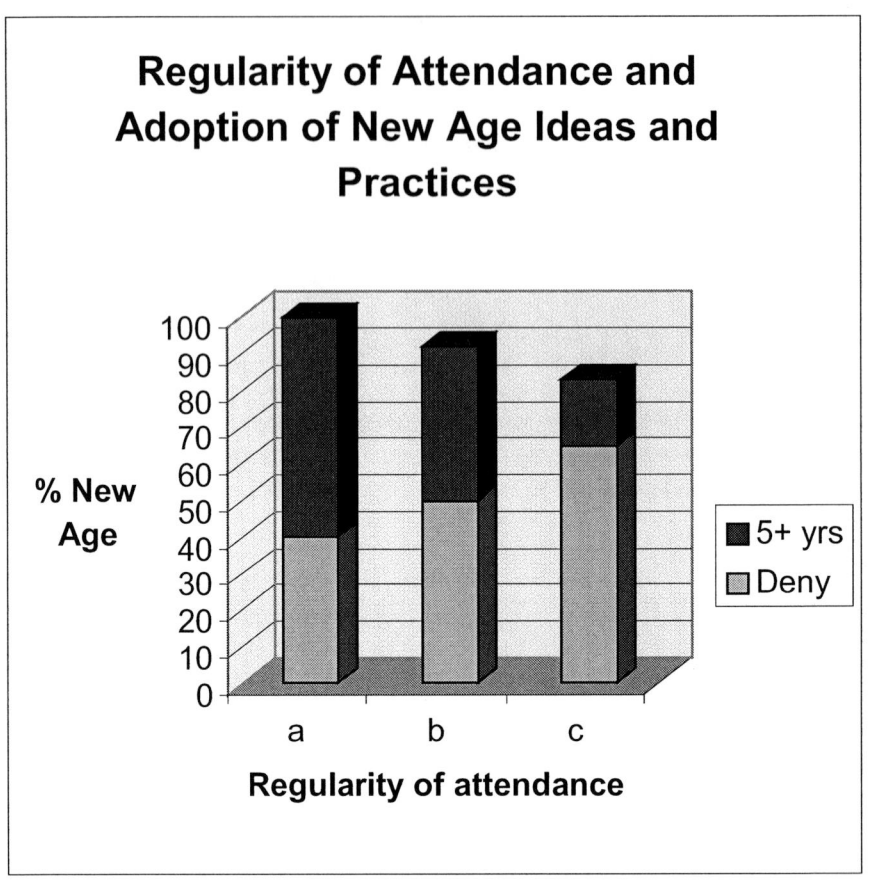

Regularity of Attendance and Adoption of New Age Ideas and Practices

% New Age

Regularity of attendance

- ■ 5+ yrs
- ▢ Deny

Key	Regularity of attendance
a	Occasionally or never
b	Every few weeks
c	Once a week or more
5+ yrs	Respondent has adopted New Age ideas or practices for over 5 years
Deny	Respondent denies having adopted New Age ideas or practices

Interviews

Over the course of my research, I have spoken to a varied section of the congregations at St James's, including people I would consider belonging to each of the three groups of 'regulars', 'associates' and 'occasional visitors'. I have found that New Age is usually mentioned with caveats about avoiding labelling, and avoiding the 'popular' elements such as crystals and pyramids. Nevertheless, there is a general acknowledgement by my informants of the New Age reputation of St James's, and even the more arcane New Age theories – such as the significance of the precession of the equinoxes – have been clearly explained to me.

The 'occasional visitors' section of the congregation are, according to my statistics, those most likely to be involved in the New Age. This may be even more likely among those occasional visitors who are not members of the electoral roll, as the tie with the church is obviously less strong among such people. However, until Professor Barker's survey results are analysed, we have no way of proving this hypothesis with regard to the whole congregation. Many of the visitors I have spoken to come from abroad, and St James's is particularly welcoming of foreigners – asking people where they come from during the service, for example. Some of these foreigners have heard of St James's church through the international Creation Spirituality network[29]. Of course, a certain number are simply passers-by, staying in the nearby hotels, and are no more likely to be New Age than any other Christian tourist.

The floating 'associates' section of the congregation (ie that third of the congregation who attend once every few weeks) seem to have in common an ambiguity about their Christian faith. Inevitably, this section of the congregation is not so well-versed theologically as regulars, and some that I have spoken with have not understood the religious concepts behind, for example, chakra meditation or spiritual healing. The contributions to the open sessions often held with a 'roving microphone' after the sermon tend to be from theologically articulate 'regulars', often demonstrating first-hand knowledge and considerable reading of various religious, philosophical and psychological traditions.

I will give some examples of the 'regulars' I have interviewed at St James's. Some personal details have been changed here in order to protect anonymity. Jane, in her fifties, had been attending Alternatives for two years and Sunday services for about a year. She describes herself as New Age, with qualifications, but the gospels remain the centre of her spirituality. She was brought up Church of England, drifted away, and went back to an Anglo-Catholic tradition in her late 'teens.

> I think from my own experience since a child I always had a sense of innerness, a sense of the spiritual ... but there was a lid kept on it, and it was only in later years, I think my late thirties, that I thought, heh, this is right.
> (Interview, 21 July 1996)

Jane speaks of this 'conversion' in distinct "before" and "after" terms, but thinks it was a "gradual" process. She met Canon Peter Spink, leader of The Omega Order, in 1980, and he has played an important part in Jane's spiritual life. She attended a retreat at The Omega Order during the course of my research. Although Jane is not a member of CANA, she has read Fr Adrian Smith's books and attended some of his lectures, through her interest in Transcendental Meditation and membership of the Christian TM group. Jane is "coming round to the idea of reincarnation" and has been strongly influenced by *A Course in Miracles*, the Gita and the Upanishads. She has done courses on spiritual healing and Reiki. She divides history, like Joachim of Flora, into three periods, the age of the Father, Son and Spirit, the last of which she identifies with the New Age involving "the coming of the cosmic Christ or spirit consciousness".

Another regular, Colin, also in his fifties, first came to St James's in the early 1990s and is now a member of various groups at the church. He would not describe himself as New Age, although he "occasionally find[s] it interesting and illuminating", and jokingly considers himself to be "the most frequently communicant agnostic in the country". He is aware of the huge range of New Age and its "untraditional" nature, and considers that New Age "seems to turn away from important Christian dimensions and visions". He declined to give examples of New Age "because it assumes there is something much more coherent which it can be an example of."

Marianne, one of the several continentals among the regular congregation, first came to Alternatives in 1989 and from there went to the Sunday services. Brought up a Roman Catholic, she has "some problems theologically", and would not call herself spiritually Anglican. She left the church in her late 'teens and joined a coven. However, she avoids categories and does not consider herself a pagan, because it suggests non-Christian – although her friend, Julian, in his twenties, interrupted the interview at this point to defend the term pagan as simply "heathen, non-normal". Julian described the precession of the equinoxes to me as the origin of the term New Age, but Marianne was not sure what New Age means.

Louise, about thirty years old, is unemployed and a vegetarian. She likes the social action of the church – Church Action on Poverty (which she used to belong to), the St Martin's project with the young homeless, and the Asylum Bill lobbying. Alternatives introduced her to the Sufi Order of the West, to which she belongs, although she "would never subscribe to anything as certain." Consequently, she has strong antipathy towards the "certainties of fundamentalism", and although she used to have some evangelical friends, found she was always "treading on eggshells" and no longer associates with them; she said that if some evangelicals knew about the sort of meditation she does, they would "burn her at the cross".

Nilantha is one of the few non-whites among the congregation at St James's. His grandfather was a Methodist minister, and his parents brought him up to think Christianity is superior to Hinduism; Nilantha now doesn't like to label himself. Ten years ago, he embarked on a journey through "Buddhist-New Age" religion, and first heard of Matthew Fox from Elizabeth Kübler-Ross at a workshop in

California. Before coming to St James's, Nilantha was a Baptist for three years.

Surprisingly, although the church does run Sunday schools, relatively few children (compared to the evangelical church studied) attend the Sunday services, and few if any attend alternative religious services or the Alternatives lecture series. It is well-known that if a religious group is to last longer than one generation, it must socialise the young at an early age. At the moment this is not happening at St James's, suggesting that the tradition will die out with the current generation. On the other hand, it may be that the nature of St James's as an inner city church will allow it to continue to attract a variety of fluctuating audiences from the population that passes in and out of the capital.

Beliefs and Attitudes

A number of the congregation have mentioned deep personal experiences facilitated by the ministry at St James's, and the chakra breathing meditation held once a month after the main Sunday service seems particularly open to this. This is a small group led by Revd Mary Robins, one of the assistant clergy, in the chapel at the front of the church, and usually attracts about a dozen people, mostly 'regulars'. However, although 29% of St James's respondents reported experiencing paranormal phenomena, this proportion is closer to the evangelical rate of 30% than Rose's rate of 82% among *Kindred Spirit* readers (1996)[30].

Also held once a month (on a different Sunday) after the main service is a healing ministry. The healers are commissioned by the officiant during the service. One St James's healer has commented to me that a Church of England priest should leave such a blessing to those properly trained in the healing professions. Quite a large queue of people – about two thirds of communicants – builds up after the service to receive spiritual healing from four or five healers. These healers do not use the laying-on-of-hands tradition that has become popular in evangelical and charismatic churches, but the kind of healing used in National Federation of Spiritual Healers centres – that is to say, chakra or auric healing where the healing energy of Christ is channelled down. Outwardly, however, the two varieties of healing appear very similar, especially since laying-on-of-hands has developed the peculiar tradition of holding the hand slightly off the body (a practice which is said to have developed in evangelical circles due to the sweltering heat of one of the first healing halls in the USA (Wimber 1986), but which in spiritual healing circles is to interact with the auric fields and chakra energies).

Respondents to my survey of the electoral roll at St James's were critical of the Church, 74% agreeing that it is too hierarchical and 51% strongly agreeing that Christianity has been too male-dominated; however, only 2% strongly agreed that Christianity is to blame for current environmental problems. 61% do not believe in the literal truth of the Apostle's creed, and 57% strongly disagree that the Bible is literally true. Over twice as many people believe in the resurrection of the dead than do not believe in it, but a third are unsure; similarly, nearly a third are unsure over the question of reincarnation, while 42% do believe in it. Strangely, only 60% of people who believe in reincarnation explicitly reject belief in the resurrection of the dead. While I would not expect these results to be paralleled in an evangelical church, they would perhaps not be too incongruous (apart from belief in reincarnation) in any 'middle-of-the-road' Anglican church.

Attitudes to the occult were mixed, with a generally even spread of belief and disbelief and around a third being unsure. This was the case for astrology, tarot cards, auras, demonic possession and crystals – attitudes tested in both positive and negative questions. The exceptions are homeopathy, which no respondent disagreed with, and hypnotherapy, which 64% denied that it can open the mind to demonic possession.

Similarly, attitudes to the New Age, when explicitly named, were around 60% undecided: on whether we are moving into the Age of Aquarius, and whether New Age travellers are part of the true New Age. However, 53% strongly disagreed that the New Age is part of a conspiracy for a New World Order, and only 10% thought the New Age is dangerous. 55% were unsure whether Dungeons & Dragons Games are occult and dangerous. Although prima facie these results suggest that New Age is not an adequate descriptor of beliefs at St James's, in fact the more probable conclusion to be drawn is that respondents do not associate themselves with the New Age label. This was indeed anticipated and for this reason, the survey was entitled, a "Survey of Spirituality" rather than explicitly mentioning New Age at the outset.

The two spiritual teachings or disciplines that have most self-reported influence at St James's are Christianity and Buddhism, with others such as New Age and Druidry lagging far behind. Influential spiritual writers include Matthew Fox, Donald Reeves, Thomas Merton, CS Lewis, John Robinson and Julian of Norwich, who were all cited by more than five respondents. However, respondents at St James's cited significantly fewer writers who had had some influence in their spiritual lives than respondents from the other two New Age Christian groups.

One Sunday in July 1996, Donald Reeves conducted a straw poll of belief among the circa. 250-strong congregation after a sermon on christology.
Incarnation means that [he asked]:
1. God is with us. It affirms God's involvement in human life.
2. As well as 1. God was involved in the life of Jesus in a particularly powerful and effective way – Jesus was not just an ordinary person but one whose relationship to God has a universal character.
3. Christ existed before his birth in some divine form – eg, the Logos, or the Word (John Chapter 1).
4. There was a total interaction of the divine and human in Christ – qualitatively superior to others, because God "gives himself fully".
5. Jesus has been and will be the only *divine* incarnation in the sense that no other person could be like this again.

6.   The definition of the Council of Chalcedon – Jesus as God and Man
      – is definitive.
(Sermon transcript supplied by Revd Reeves)

The vast majority (perhaps 95%) agreed up to number three, with a small number dropping out at two and then three. Revd Reeves laughed when asking about number six. Only five or six raised their hands. Perhaps put at ease by Donald Reeves' series of sermons questioning traditional christology, a number of members of the congregation have expressed to me especial difficulty in seeing Jesus as God. Without comparative studies outside New Age circles, it is difficult to evaluate the significance of these beliefs.

In my survey, 58% of St James's respondents agreed that Jesus was inspired with the Christ spirit that also inspired Buddha; but at the same time, 57% also thought that Christ is unique, unparalleled by any other human being. 64% agreed with the traditional definition that Jesus Christ was both God and man at the same time, and 66% disagreed that Jesus was simply a very spiritual man and nothing more. Perhaps the reason for these statistics is that, although christology at St James's is fairly conventional, the congregation do not see Christianity as the only path to salvation: 67% strongly agree that there are many paths to salvation, and 63% strongly disagree that Christianity is the only true religion. On the question of the resurrection of Christ, there was an even spread in belief in it as a real, historical fact, and denial of this belief.

Participant Observation[31]

If the centrepoint of Christian ritual is the breaking of the bread, this is not lost in the ritual at St James's, where the fractions are held to the four directions as in some Eastern rites. All communicants gather around the altar in a circle (as in some Catholic churches and at The Omega Order), and receive the bread and wine standing. A note by Revd Reeves sometimes included in the photocopied service sheet explains that the fractions are related to the angels of the North, South, East and West[32]. There is usually a canonised chant before the Eucharistic prayer. The wording as the bread is broken is as follows:

To the East:
This bread is broken in honour of all those who love God – our sisters and brothers who worship the God of the Hindus and follow the path of the Buddha, for our sisters and brothers in Islam and the Jewish people from whom we come.
>   To all these be honour and blessing
>   in the breaking of this bread;
>   and we pray that one day we may be one.

To the South:
This bread is broken in honour of the green blue Earth and all the elements of water, fire and air that surround and support her:
>   Mother Earth, despoiled, plundered and ravaged by our greed

yet alive and green,
To the Earth be honour and blessing in the breaking of the
Bread; and we pray that one day scars will be no more.

To the West:
This bread is broken in honour of the broken and dispossessed
        and for all those who have no bread
        that one day this earth will be a home for all humanity – a room
at the Inn for all.

To the North:
This bread is broken in honour of the brokenness of each one of us:
        the child within us broken by cruelty or coldness
        the adult broken by loneliness or failure
        our health broken by sickness or loss

        To each one here be honour and blessing
        warmth and abundance
        in the breaking of the Bread of Life.
        We pray that one day we will know the wholeness
        that is of Christ.
(Reeves 1996:77-78)

The weekly notices at St James's were, in my experience, unusually long, indicating the range of activities that are centred on the church. They were not collated and announced by the officiating priest, but announced individually by those involved. It is perhaps significant that the notices never mentioned the lectures at Alternatives. There was often some degree of confusion among the various announcers – especially in the case of the so-called 'welcoming committee' which invites newcomers to make themselves known after the service.

Outside of the services, the administration of St James's was in my experience not run as efficiently as that of The Omega Order. This reveals a fundamental difference in the power structures of the two organisations. Canon Spink is most definitely the founder and leader of The Omega Order[33]. In contrast, Donald Reeves describes his approach as more of a facilitator than a leader. His style is 'to provide the inspiration and the starting force behind a project, and then let it muddle along by itself' (Interview, 6 January 1997). Slack administration is a feature of the whole church – for example, there was no parish magazine for several months at the start of my research; the electoral roll was not printed in a usable form until several months after it was compiled in 1996; and a number of my letters to the PCC went unanswered[34]. In his response to a draft of this chapter, Revd Reeves did not deny that the administration was slack, but explained that this slackness was due to the "transitionary" period the church was experiencing at the time of my research in 1996.

In the last couple of years of his incumbency, Donald Reeves began to develop what he called the "beacon ministry" of St James's, that is, its international following. He held workshops in Sweden, but was otherwise careful in considering foreign lecture invitations that he was not neglecting the community at St James's.

St Elisabeth's Open Church in Basel, Switzerland, takes St James's as its role model, although language barriers prevent direct contact between Donald Reeves and the pastor at Basel, Felix Felix. When I visited St Elisabeth's in the summer of 1996, the programme included daily meditation, Zazen twice a week, Vipassana once a week and the Sufi dance of universal freedom once a month. An "experimental service" was held once a month, with dancing, eating and drinking to modern music. Matthew Fox had recently visited the church. The pastor wrote to me that

> ... St Elisabeth's Open Church is very open to the insights and tenets of the "New Age" movement. ... we have no fear of contact with "New Age" and we are happy of the challenge which helps us Christians to read the Bible afresh and discover views in it which the traditional church has for a long time neglected, or indeed forbidden (eg laying on of hands). ... I don't count St Elisabeth's Open Church as a part of the "New Age" movement, but rather would formulate it differently: that this movement has challenged us, that we have learnt from it, that we are in direct contact and ready to go to the edges, or otherwise to show the dangers.
> (Personal communication, 31 July 1996; my translation)

St John the Divine, an Episcopal church in New York City, has also been said to accommodate the New Age (Saliba 1999:108), and its vicar, the Very Revd James Morton, wrote the introduction to David Spangler's *Emergence: The Rebirth of the Sacred* (1984). Although in interview Donald Reeves denies there is any historical connection between the two projects, it is interesting (though far from proving any formal connection) that he attended a formative part of his training under Revd Morton in New York immediately prior to taking up his post at St James's, and describes Revd Morton as a "good friend".

'Leaders'

New Age often presents itself as non-hierarchical and having no leaders. To the extent that New Age is a network of networks, this is true. However, New Agers often speak of 'facilitators' and to the degree that these exert authority over followers, they are acting as leaders. This is especially the case in a church setting, where there are traditional loci of authority in the clergy, the PCC and its officials and the leaders of various groups and sub-committees. At St James's I conducted a series of in-depth interviews with the leaders, having read their many publications.

Revd Donald Reeves (b 1934) was Rector at St James's from 1980 to 1998. After his ordination in 1963 he served at Maidstone (1963-1965), was chaplain to the Bishop of Southwark (1965-1968), and at Morden (1969-1980). His first publication, *For God's Sake* (1988) calls for a "Reformation" of the Church, to listen to the poor and the minorities and to God's spirit. Jesus is depicted to have called for a Kingdom of God that was for justice for the poor – in much the way of the liberation theologians. Revd Reeves also calls for an "Inner Reformation" of the heart, but includes a caveat against the evils of narcissism and the longing for spiritual experiences, quoting Fritjof Capra's experience of the Dance of Shiva as a specific example (Reeves 1988:45).

Making Sense of Religion (1989) opens with questions that are often put to Christians: What about evil? Does God exist? and continues as a sort of compendium of religious teasers. It suggests that idolatry of money prevents true religion today. Like Sallie McFague, Revd Reeves looks for new, relevant metaphors for God, opting in one chapter for creation as the body of God and in others for God as mother and as lover.

Down to Earth: A New Vision for the Church (1996) begins autobiographically with Donald Reeves' childhood visits to Chichester cathedral, undergraduate conversion by Billy Graham and subsequent disillusionment with evangelicalism. As in earlier books, the Jewish holocaust seems to have made a big impression on Reeves' faith. The notion of the 'public', also outlined in Reeves' earlier works, is developed more fully as a forum where community is rediscovered. Again the inner life is championed, as is the importance of ritual. The book ends with the depiction of alternative Christian-based ecological communities.

Things New Age are hardly mentioned in these books – unless we are to count the references to Matthew Fox's *Original Blessing* (1983). Indeed, the phrase "New Age" appears only once, in passing (Reeves 1996:68), as an example of those who are disenchanted with organised religion.

Before leaving St James's, Revd Reeves was appointed Social Affairs Consultant at Rio Tinto Plc, and visited two of their mining operations in South Africa and Namibia. On a voluntary basis, he planned to work for Oikos, a research and communications programme involved with creating debate in the business community about sustainable development. He was also asked to join a small team of social entrepreneurs – *2000 by 2000* – with the aim of extending the work achieved earlier in his career on an Urban Ministry Project. His work with the Church of Sweden continues, with his latest book published in Swedish. In my last communication with him, Revd Reeves was setting up a network of European city churches.

Revd Mary Robins is one of the assistant clergy at St James's, a semi-retired former teacher. Revd Robins holds chakra meditation sessions in the chapel at the front of St James's church after the main Sunday service once a month, and also holds 'awareness through painting' workshops. In 1996 Revd Robins reconstructed the tradition of lamentations within St James's church, including a lamentation for the then current BSE "mad cow" crisis. Revd Robins has had visions and esoteric experiences, and knows of others who have had similar experiences, but she does not try to explain the religious traditions behind these because, in her opinion, this would be too intellectual and impede proper meditation through the body.

Desert Flowers (1990) is a book of Mary Robin's verse which is autobiographical in character. In it she documents her spiritual journey as having included Jungian and Ignatian thought, intuitive massage and Tai-Chi amongst its influences. She describes herself as "an alien in the Tradition of the Church" (Robins 1990:31) and "on the margins of the Church and Society" (Robins 1990:41). A 1992 work, *Still We Rise* is subtitled, *Here and now reflections on the timeless story unfolded through St Mark's Gospel.* Jesus is described as

> pioneer of that Way of enlightenment, illumination, and living creatively from within our human experience. Christ Spirit accompanies us on our life journey, according to our degree of openness. ...
> Our infinite God can only be described through our own experiences. ... We name our own experience, live with as much integrity as we can, discover the message of Christ in our own lives.
> (Robins 1992:v-vi)

Mary Robins has commented (Interview, 11 July 1996) that spirituality since the time of Jesus has been mixed up through the influence of Graeco-Romano culture, especially the dualism between spirit and body; true spirituality can sometimes today be found in New Age things. As an example she cited the witch Starhawk, whose energy she finds compatible with the Jesus story. Revd Robins reports that at least once a week another person visits her on a pastoral basis to talk through difficulties they have experienced with an evangelical church. She has herself experienced some hostility at the Christian summer camp 'Greenbelt', where she was treated as a "witch", and she once gave a talk to a sixth form Christian fundamentalist group on Christianity and the New Age and caused a heated discussion.

Nick Williams (b 1958) was director of the Alternatives project during my research period. Williams' father was a lay Methodist preacher, but his own faith lapsed as a teenager. At about the age of 30, having developed a career as a computer salesman, he came to St James's for an evening on spiritual poetry and then started to volunteer at Alternatives. Williams is also heavily involved in the Course network in the UK. "Part of my return to what I would see as Christian ideals has been through my reading of *A Course in Miracles*" (Interview, 29 July 1998). He runs his own talks and workshops, "about bringing a heart, spirit and soul to our work", with a book, *The Work We Were Born to Do*, published in 2000. He also works as a consultant for various organisations, including local authorities, private companies and the civil service.

As mentioned above, Dr William Bloom (b 1948) co-founded the Alternatives project at St James's. In the early 1970s he published three novels, one novella and four thrillers, and founded the Open Gate imprint to promote counter-culture books, but left this career in 1972. He also co-founded Advise, the first 24-hour immigrant advisory service in the UK. Dr Bloom then studied International Relations at the London School of Economics, where he also taught and gained a doctorate in social psychology (Bloom 1992/1989). However, he did not pursue an academic career and instead gained a Certificate in Education, specialising in communication skills and counselling, and worked for nine years in an inner city community college with special needs adolescents and adults.

Dr Bloom's parents were suspicious of religion and by his early twenties he was spiritually cynical. Like Wade Clark Roof's "baby boomers" (1993), Bloom was involved in the counter-culture movement of the 1960s and took LSD (Bloom 1992/1976:103; cf Bloom 1993:23), but he attributes his 'conversion' to meetings with firstly an American writer, James Baldwin, and secondly, the (then elderly) Freudian psychoanalyst Edward Glover, whom Dr Bloom met through his psychiatrist father, and with whom he was in analysis for three years.

From childhood Dr Bloom had mystical experiences (Bloom 1992/1976:3; 1990:1), and made a strong identification with Jesus as some children do. In his early thirties he was an altar boy in the Liberal Catholic Church, was confirmed and even considered becoming a priest. Dr Bloom is without a doubt that he is Christian and that Christ has been "born again" in his heart[35].
"According to my own lights, I'm Christian. I speak Christology"
(Interview, 26 October 1999)
He also describes himself as Christo-Taoist, but primarily Christian. Although he may honour Buddhism and other traditions, it is the passion event that has "cosmic" siginificance for him. Dr Bloom celebrates Mass from time to time in a family ceremony in his home, and he has no qualms in attending Christian services for social occasions such as his young daughter's harvest service. In early 2000, Dr Bloom held a workshop entitled "Experiencing Christianity" for the New Age Christian group, CANA[36]. Nevertheless, Dr Bloom remains highly critical of the Church, which he says "dumbs down" Christianity.

Dr Bloom first published his autobiographical *The Sacred Magician: a ceremonial diary* in 1976 under the pseudonym Georges Chevalier, reissuing it in 1992 under his own name which was by then identified with such writings. It is an account of a ritual quest he performed in Morocco four years previously over a period of six months, following instructions from SL MacGregor Mathers' (of Golden Dawn fame) translation of the fifteenth century French manuscript, *The Book of the Sacred Magic of Abramelin the Mage*. The original was purported to be in Hebrew, based on the instruction of the Jewish patriarch Abraham to his son, and Judaeo-Christian imagery is used throughout Dr Bloom's 'Operation'. Indeed, Dr Bloom used the Lord's prayer daily (Bloom 1992/1976:54) and read the New Testament – although he also regularly consulted the *I Ching* (Bloom 1992/1976:61).

I was touched at the time by the fact that while I related to myself as being Christian, I could also draw on the wisdom of an Eastern Confucian book of wisdom. I was also touched by the fact that I was a magician – often thought of as heretical – yet completely trusting in Christ. My approach to Christianity, of course, was distinctly outside the formal churches and is what is often called Gnostic or Rosicrucian.
(Bloom 1992/1976:58-59, *original emphasis*)
(By 'Christ I often meant not the historical figure of Jesus, but a cosmic principle of unconditional love which actively seeks to help all of us. I see this cosmic principle in Krishna and in the Maitreya Buddha, for example, as much as in Jesus Christ.)
(Bloom 1992/1976:62, *original emphasis and brackets*)

Nevertheless, there is little in the magical procedures that would be recognized by mainstream Christian mystics apart from the pervasive feeling of "wormhood" or state of sin. Perhaps the nearest parallel is with the occult system of Alice Bailey, whose books Dr Bloom was reading at the time of the ritual. Dr Bloom writes that he "was barely sane through the whole event" (1992/1976:8), and often felt the presence of malevolent forces, but also claims to have approached meditative unity. His daily activities included one-and-a-half hours of prayer, one hour of meditation and five hours of holy reading (Bloom 1992/1976:114). Already, Bloom expresses a desire to popularise the teachings:

> it is my ardent wish that the Mysteries (*the esoteric and magical teachings*) become sufficiently exoteric (*public*) to make it unnecessary for this kind of track [ritual] to be walked in this sort of darkness.
> (Bloom 1992/1976:135)

This has certainly been an effect of his work at Alternatives and Findhorn.

Devas, Fairies and Angels: A Modern Approach (Bloom 1986) provides the logical underpinning for the *Sacred Magician* quest. It is explained exactly what devas are (some overarching sense of 'being' for a particular plant, area or situation) and how to live in alignment with their powers. There are even devas (the seraphim and cherubim) who are invoked in the Christian Eucharist, it is said (Bloom 1986:24). Again there is a debt to Alice Bailey, with a diagram reproduced from Bailey's *A Treatise on Cosmic Fire* (Bloom 1986:34). Strangely, Billy Graham – the charismatic Christian – is also cited in the bibliography: *Angels – God's Secret Agents* (1975). These themes are more fully developed in *Working With Angels, Fairies & Nature Spirits* (1998).

In *Sacred Times: A New Approach to Festivals* (Bloom 1990), Bloom writes that he has

> little – if any – respect for religious organisations or churches. The greater the religious organisation, the more distant it seemed from the essence of its founding inspiration.
> (Bloom 1990:1)

In response to this problem with religions, a "new culture" (Bloom 1990:4) is being created. In the usual (though questionable) New Age fashion, Bloom asserts that the rituals he describes are not prescriptive: "I do not want to tell anybody what to do" (Bloom 1990:i). Nevertheless, we are said to need to celebrate the festivals together for: psychological well-being, ecological harmony, spiritual inspiration and spiritual service to humanity and Gaia (Bloom 1990:8).

The procedure for setting up a ceremonial area is described, and the preparations detailed. These include making the sign of the cross with holy water (Bloom 1990:22); not for any Christian reason but because

> The actual *shape* of the cross resonates in such a way as to place it vibrationally in touch with the archetypal cross and the protective energies that are associated with it.
> (Bloom 1990:23)

Bloom explains that

> If you resonate with a different tradition you may choose to use, for example, instead of the cross, the five pointed star/pentagram or the symbol for OM."
> (Bloom 1990:23).

A naming ceremony is described as "christening" and "godparents" are present (Bloom 1990:32).

Meditation in a Changing World (Bloom 1996/1987) is Bloom's How to Meditate guide. It gives very simple instructions on how to focus on breathing, what posture to assume, and on the process of meditation. An additional section on group meditation is also included, together with an appendix containing mantrams and suggestions for celebrating the festivals.

First Steps: An Introduction to Spiritual Practice (Bloom 1993) is for people who are "not at ease within a particular discipline or school" (Bloom 1993:9) of spirituality – although it is difficult to see how Bloom's method can avoid becoming a discipline of its own. God is defined thus:

> some form of underlying and transcendent connection between everything. ... 'God' is shorthand for an indescribable reality which is experienced in various ways in different traditions and individuals. ... Generally we tend to project onto 'God' ideas that suit our society.
> (Bloom 1993:47)

Throughout the work, there is an almost Gurdjieffian emphasis on remaining aware of the self throughout everyday life, and the importance of a daily review through contemplation, diary-keeping or breathing exercises.

The Christ Sparks: The Inner Dynamics of Group Consciousness (Bloom 1995) may use Christian imagery in its title, but this is not present throughout the book (although see Bloom 1995:43 ["Christed"]; Bloom 1995:50 ["We are sparks working with the Christ"]). The Christ Sparks call themselves so because it is "appropriate for the culture into which we[they] are currently incarnating" (Bloom 1995:15); they are extra-terrestrial units of consciousness that communicate telepathically like bees in a swarm, yet retain their own individual consciousness and can unite with human consciousnesses. Their purpose is to let us know about the energy of group consciousness called the "Avatar of Synthesis" which is said to have arrived on Earth around 1970.

The book purports to be a channelled communication Bloom received in 1987 but did not publish until 1995. Various metaphysical advices are given on, for example, how to relate as a couple or in a group. Although the teaching is generally presented as being within the New Age movement, at times there is criticism of it – for example,

> We are astonished by the number of people within the new age movement who have an awareness of this or that, but it in no way affects their behaviour.
> (Bloom 1995:101)

In *Psychic Protection* (Bloom 1996), Bloom outlines various exercises for creating good vibrationary fields in our everyday lives and homes. A very short section deals with the worries of evangelicals, or "fundamentalists" (Bloom 1996:86; cf 1996:148).

> They might make the accusation that we could just as easily invoke a connection with the devil as with Christ or Mary.
> (Bloom 1996:86)

Bloom assents to this possibility, but assures us that with the correct attitude it is impossible to channel negative energy. Indeed, Bloom does actually invoke Christ (Bloom 1996:90) although with the proviso that,

> (If you do not relate to Christ, then use the connection with another sacred symbol to which you relate.)
> (Bloom 1996:90; cf 1996:87)

And later (Bloom 1996:118-119) Bloom calls upon Christ and uses the Lord's prayer to shield himself from evil energy.

Dr Bloom's most commonly-cited work in New Ages studies is his anthology prepared for the Channel Four television series, *The New Age* (1991), which includes extracts from many of the more important New Age writers. This may be replaced by a new anthology, *Holistic Revolution* (2000). Both works contain useful introductions by Dr Bloom to the New Age movement.

Interpretation: A Postmodern Spirituality?[37]

However different William Bloom and Mary Robins may be, both locate their thought as a *return* to traditional methods of religion. A number of the congregation I have spoken to identify with pagan tradition, and consciously seek to 're'surrect the Old Religion. However, for others the term 'pagan' sounds too anti-Christian, and the PCC reacted strongly against an earlier draft of this chapter which highlighted this interpretation. Neither Revd Reeves nor Revd Robins have ever participated in a pagan circle.

Furthermore, magic as it is used in New Age is not best described as a regression to traditional magical practices, for New Age usually presents itself as allied with the forefront of thinking, especially in neuroscience, cosmology and the so-called New Physics. For example, Marilyn Ferguson's depiction of *The Aquarian Conspiracy* (1980) was a dense résumé of scientific literature, no doubt owing much to her *Brain/Mind Bulletin*. The understanding of New Age as ultra modern science is not just a literary tendency; my fieldwork has strongly suggested that this is also the popular understanding. A hypnotherapist attending a lecture at St James's told me that she emphasises to new clients that she receives referrals from psychiatrists and dentists. A participant at an enneagram course explained that crystal energy is just a power like electricity which can be used for good or bad. Even an evangelical Christian has told me that reflexology must be a "science", because she had felt her solar plexus "tweek" when her foot was massaged. Yet while arguing in scientific terminology for the New Physics, New Agers typically denigrate 'mainstream' science and its dualism as the root of contemporary ecological and spiritual crises. New Age science is presented as having gone beyond the limitations of mainstream science.

Wouter Hanegraaff describes a Hegelian 'dialectic tension' between *New Age Religion and Western Culture* (1996), arguing that New Age frequently allies itself with reason and science, and therefore has to demarcate itself from rationalist and scientific ideologies. The solution to this dilemma is, Hanegraaff suggests, the affirmation of a "higher perspective" (Hanegraaff 1996:515) in which religion and science are one. This is one valid way of seeing New Age appropriation of earlier traditions. An alternative academic perspective on such appropriation, which I prefer, is the perspective of postmodernity.

Postmodernity refers to the conditions created by the globalized, post-industrial, information society that replaces the national, industrial, mechanistic culture of modernity. Knowledge is increasingly available but increasingly subjective, dependent on perspective. The image replaces the text. 'Grand meta-narratives', broad structures of thought that interpret reality, are said to be part of history. Local networks and situation-specific ideas replace tradition – hence the dictum, "Act locally, think globally". The differences between and merits of various commentators on postmodernism – including Foucault, Baudrillard, Deleuze, Guattari, Lyotard, Jameson, Laclau and Mouffe – need not concern us here, and the reader is referred to the introductory works of Best and Kellner (1991) and Lyon (1994).

One point of contention in discussion of postmodernity is whether the recognisable exaggerations of modernity that are present in the contemporary world constitute simply a quantitative extension of modernity or rather a qualitative leap into a new era of postmodernism. I believe that New Age and Christaquarianism may be seen as a response to the peculiar conditions of the contemporary world – whether we wish to describe this as postmodern, late modern or by any other similar term.

Postmodern theory often intersects with new social movement theory. The student movement of May 1968 led many thinkers to abandon the grand metanarrative of Marxism for new political movements such as feminism, environmental movements and homosexual groups. In some ways, the new social movements may be said to have anticipated later postmodern theory in their emphasis on decentring political control away from the proletariat, and their concern with issues of difference and cultural relations. Touraine sets out to locate the paradigmatic new social movement that will become the central movement of the "programmed society", assuming the position of the labour movement in industrial society. He considers Solidarity (Touraine et al, 1982) and the anti-nuclear movement (Touraine et al, 1980) among others. While I would question whether the search for a *single* central movement was not a peculiarly modernist search, I suggest that the New Age movement and Christaquarianism might be considered as typical movements of postmodernity.

Ironically, it is a scholar who denies that New Age is postmodern, Paul Heelas, who provides (1996b:65-66) the most comprehensive summary of the case for their identification. First, Heelas says that both are "de-differentiated", with distinctions between high and low culture being eroded. With the replacement of the printed text by html, culture is accessible to all. Second, both are examples of consumer culture. New Age therapies are paid for just as much as access to the Internet requires possession of a PC. Third, both collapse the subject-object distinction. New Age calls for a merging with Gaia, the Earth spirit; postmodernists argue similarly in a more philosophical fashion. Fourth, both emphasise the disembedded, de-situated nature of the self. New Age is often accused of being 'older' than its name suggests: a rediscovery of a historical tradition, sometimes known as the 'perennial philosophy', but without the historical ties of identity. Postmodernism has a similarly 'pick-n-mix' approach to history. Fifth, and connected to the last point, is that both movements are expressivist, valuing 'authenticity', 'love' and 'freedom'. Finally, both treat history in terms of periods.

David Lyon also gives a list of similarities, arguing that both postmodernity and New Age may be seen as responses to a perceived 'crisis of modernity'; both refer to a new era; both abandon old truths; both centre on self and consumption; neither are much interested in politics; both adopt new organizational structures; both are implicated in globalization; and both may be understood in terms of the fin de siècle (Lyon 1993:117).

Aldo Terrin subtitles his work on *New Age: La religiosità del postmoderno* (1992), and writes that
> ... the real problem that New Age poses is the *rapport between religion and the postmodern.* ... [New Age] *appears simply as the spirit of the new postmodern culture.*
> (Terrin 1992:245-246, my translation[38], *original emphasis*)

D'Andrea asserts that,
> just as Protestantism was the "spirit" of modernity, the NAM [the New Age movement] is the "spirit" of late modernity (or of post-modernity)[39]
> (D'Andrea 1997/1996:69, my translation[40])

Anna Kubiak (1999) treats New Age as a "postmodern conspiracy" (cf Knoblauch 1989:504).

Paul Heelas in fact rejects the characterisation of New Age as postmodern because he denies that postmodernism is distinct from modernism. Rejecting the oft-proposed motifs of differentiation for modernism and dedifferentiation for postmodernism, Heelas (Heelas 1998:1-18) argues that both differentiation and dedifferentiation are present in both modernism and postmodernism. He claims that postmodernism is merely an extension of trends already present in modernism (Heelas 1996a). Thus New Age is not postmodern, but exemplifies exaggerated forms of modern religiosity, namely of Self Religiosity.

Heelas acknowledges that New Age appears to be postmodern "[o]n the surface" (Heelas 1996b:69), but however not "in any significant or useful sense" (ibid:70). He argues that New Age amplifies an "experiential meta-'narrative'. An inner 'tradition', that of timeless 'wisdom' …" (idem). Although New Age de-differentiates between high and low culture, on the other hand it differentiates strongly between false consciousness and authentic spirituality. He also claims there is some 'depth' and 'seriousness' to New Age beliefs, contrary to the postmodern idea of 'pick-n-mix'. Finally, he argues that the postmodern 'disintegration of self' thesis is negated by the strong New Age sense of self identity in, for example, the goddess or as a spiritual being.

Lorne Dawson (1998) outlines a new spirituality with a holistic perspective emphasizing inter-connectedness, providing new sources of power and compatible with a range of ideologies. Having defined postmodernism, he acknowledges that its themes call to mind "a few New Age groups" (Beckford quoted in Dawson 1998:149). However, his assessment concludes that the new spiritualities are "redolent of a revised 'Enlightenment project'" (ibid). Likewise, Dawson concurs that NRMs should not be labelled postmodern, a term "still more relevant for the fine arts, architecture, and literature than [it] ever [has] been or likely ever will be for the study of social action" (Dawson 1998:150).

What evidence do we have for suggesting that St James's represents a postmodern spirituality? A large community of post-evangelicals, named after Dave Tomlinson's book in 1995, adopted St James's church *en masse* as their home church in 1996, during the course of my fieldwork at the church. At the time, I regarded this section of the congregation as somewhat of an incongruity, and indeed it was subsequently reported to me that post-evangelicals have stopped attending St James's. However, theoretical reflection has enabled me to understand why the post-evangelicals chose St James's as their base. For both post-evangelicals and Christaquarians are developing a postmodern spirituality.

> My thesis is simple: that post-evangelicals tend to be people who identify culturally more with postmodernity (the culture of the postmodern) than with modernity …
> (Tomlinson 1995:76)

Interestingly, Tomlinson gave a lecture in St James's church while I was conducting my research. Discussion groups were held among the audience (many of whom I recognised from Sunday services), and *The Times* (20 July 1996) reported that a network of self-help groups called 'Fundamentalists Anonymous' would be launched. However, the discussion group I participated in was less radical than this. Tomlinson concludes his 1995 work with a chapter entitled, "Christianity for a New Age". He argues that, while the postmodern world drives some people out of the church to New Age, post-evangelicals continue their search within the church.

Another group of Christians who may be considered postmodern, are members of the Sea of Faith ("SoF"), led by Revd Don Cupitt. Among his many publications (in which his position is developmental rather than fixed) Cupitt has written an article on "Post-Christianity" (1998). The SoF Magazine has advertised a talk given by Revd Donald Reeves (SoF Magazine No. 30 Autumn 1997:28). Fr Adrian Smith, one of the Christaquarian clergy considered in Chapter IV, is a member of the Sea of Faith network, and Fr Diarmuid Ó'Murchú, another Christaquarian, gave a paper at the 11th SoF Conference. The quarterly SoF magazine frequently mentions New Age, but usually in a derogatory way. For example:

> We are not another vacuous New Age spirituality. We do not talk to our
> geraniums, hug trees, or invoke mystical energies (but if some do, they
> won't be expelled for it).
> (*SoF Magazine* No.30 Autumn 1997:2)

Anne Ashworth, the editor of the Quaker *Universalist* magazine (see Chapter VII) is a member of SoF network; conversely, David Boulton, editor of the SoF magazine, is a member of the Quaker Universalists. In a collection of fourteen spiritual autobiographies by SoFties[41] (Wallace ed 1998), only one mentions New Age, and this in a positive light, although others mention interests in Teilhard de Chardin and Jung. I have concluded that SoFties are not fully-fledged Christaquarians, but are Christians who have some difficulty with conventional Christianity. They have not yet adopted new spiritual directions to fill the void left by Christianity.

Undoubtedly, there are other sections of Christianity which may be seen as a response to the postmodern condition. The Nine O'Clock Service ("NOS"), for example, began its radical phase with Revd Chris Brain's research into postmodernism. One NOS handout given to visitors proclaimed "A Search for Postmodern Christianity; Healthy Religion and Healthy Spirituality," asking "Where was the sense of the sacred in a secular, technology-driven society that treats its members as cogs in an industrial era machine?" (quoted in Howard 1996:96).

In the newspaper accounts of the demise of NOS in August 1995, Revd Matthew Fox was depicted as the "sinister guru" who was behind Revd Brain's venture (*Evening Standard*, 24 August 1995). In 1993, Revd Brain and other leaders had been to a conference in Seattle where Revd Fox was speaking. In November 1993, Revd Fox visited the NOS community, returning to give a week of lectures on Creation Spirituality in 1994. Later that year, Revd Brain went to San Francisco to hold a cathedral service with Revd Fox. There were plans for Revd Brain to begin a Ritual Centre at Revd Fox's Institute of Creation Centred Spirituality. With congregations at up to 600, NOS moved in 1993 to an underground rotunda in Sheffield. It was here that the "Planetary Mass" was held, a weekly celebration worship service using music, televisions and projection screens, and body prayer which brought the chakras into line.

Revd Brain stood down as leader of NOS in February 1994, telling his archdeacon that he needed a rest after establishing the Planetary Mass. In August 1995, allegations of sexual abuse by Revd Brain led to the downfall of the community. The press claimed that a large number of women had had sexual relations with Revd Brain, although it was emphasized by insiders that these had never progressed to penetrative sex. Revd Brain spent two weeks at Cheadle Royal Psychiatric Hospital. NOS 'survivors' were assigned to the Revd Philip Allin in April 1996, and the community moved to an Anglican chapel in Attercliffe. Later reports suggest that the community is still moving in a Christian-pagan direction, for example celebrating the Neopagan festival of Samhain (*The Times,* 27 November 1998).

The churchWarden of St James's has requested that I remove any suggestion of a connection between the Nine O'Clock Service and their church, as St James's suffered greatly from 'guilt by association' during the scandal in 1995. She emphasises that it was only after NOS became interested in Creation Spirituality that members had the confidence to expose Revd Brain's abuses. There was some interaction between St James's and NOS, for example during a weekend with Ann Wilson Schaeff on letting go of addictions, but I have been assured that there was never any "ongoing involvement between groups at St James's and NOS"[42], and indeed the different ages and styles of the audiences makes this unlikely[43]. Nevertheless, I remain convinced that both St James's and the Nine O'Clock Service as well as Creation Spirituality are responses to postmodernity. I believe scholars can recognise this similarity without inferring less appealing similarities. It is also interesting to note that the new rector at St James's, Revd Dr Charles Hedley, was involved in the counselling effort in the aftermath of the Revd Brain affair.

There is not sufficient space here to develop an analysis of postmodern religion; my point is that a useful analysis of St James's church is that it represents a response to late modernity or postmodernity. This would not only explain the centrality of New Age to the church, but also its welcoming of post-evangelicals, and the diverse array of other projects and ministries. As mentioned at the outset of this chapter, these include classical concerts, consultations at the Centre for Health and Healing, and the various meetings of the Centre for Creation Spirituality (now GreenSpirit), Church Action on Poverty, the asylum seekers' projects, the small choir, the Blake Society, Bible study groups, Julian meditation groups, the catechumenate, the Taizé group, the lesbian and gay group, Christian Aid, the Vagabonds group and the liturgical dancing group. Again, I emphasise that these projects represent a large part of the work at St James's, but were not considered here because they do not seem to overlap to any significant extent with the New Age project.

Conclusion

What are we to make of St James's and the people it attracts? Certainly, those who are mainly concerned with the Alternatives project are to be considered New Agers. As we have seen, there is some overlap between the Alternatives attendees and the Sunday congregation. The leaders of the church are, however, far from being typical Christaquarians, and the results of the survey of electoral roll members revealed some limitations in considering them as such. Indeed, the survey indicated that more regular attendance at St James's made involvement in the New Age less likely. Nevertheless, the very presence of Alternatives and a number of other 'New Age'-style practices such as the Centre for Health and Healing, the Centre for Creation Spirituality, the chakra meditation and the chakra/Reiki healing are all indications that evangelical critiques of the church as New Age do have at least some basis in fact.

Notes to Chapter III

[1] The original thesis contained an Appendix on German Studies of New Age. This has been withdrawn from the present edition due to difficulties in translation.

[2] An early article by Michael York (1994) is mentioned, but not the 1995 publication of his excellent thesis. Wouter Hanegraaff's (1996) weighty documentary account of New Age beliefs is ignored, as is Christoph Bochinger's comprehensive thesis on the New Age in Germany (1995/1994). Also missing are important, (then) unpublished, accounts by Paul Greer (1994), Stuart Rose (1996) and Steven Sutcliffe (1998).

Perhaps we may excuse Saliba for ommitting Bochinger's account in German. However, he should at least give some indication of the many Christian responses to the New Age movement that have appeared in Germany (see especially Bischofberger et al 1987; Sudbrack 1987; Kehl 1988; Haneke & Huttner 1991; cf also an important early study of New Age by Schorsch 1988). This is particularly the case, since the differing situations in France, Italy and Japan are all covered by Saliba.

Important official documents from churches in the United Kingdom are also ommitted: the Church of England's *The Search for Faith* (MTAG 1996) and the Methodist's "Report to Conference" (Faith and Order Committee 1994).

[3] However, despite the wide fieldwork, the thesis is littered with mis-spellings of names. "Frijof [sic] Capra" appears throughout (Roxburgh 1991:30,31,39,48) although it is correctly spelt once (Roxburgh 1991:37) and in the bibliography. "Maralyn [sic] Ferguson" (Roxburgh 1991:78,174,205), "Neils [sic] Bohr" (Roxburgh 1991:80), "Jurgan [sic] Moltmann" (Roxburgh 1991:174,206) and "Collin [sic] Gunton" (Roxburgh 1991:174) also make appearances, as does a "Piscian [sic] age" (Roxburgh 1991:17,103).

[4] Spangler responds to such demonisation in Spangler (1993).

[5] eg Dominic Corrywright at Bristol University, was researching the concept of New Age spiritualities under Ursula King at the time of submission (Corrywright 2001). In 2002, Jochen Scherer was completing a Masters dissertation on New Age Christianity at Bangor University, and Ruth Bradby was completing a PhD on *A Course in Miracles* at Chester College.

[6] Comment from the chair, British Sociological Association Study of Religions Group conference, 10 April 1999.

[7] Published as Sutcliffe (2003).

[8] Sutcliffe does not discuss at length a doctoral study of Findhorn by Carmen Hendershott (1989), entitled *Stranger than Paradise: Hosts and Guests in a New Age community*, although admittedly the fieldwork in this study is now somewhat dated (1981-1983). Hendershott's thesis is a sound historical presentation of everyday life in the community, though without much sociological analysis. It is interesting to note that guests outnumbered members at this time by at least ten to one, and provided 44% of the income. For this reason, the study focuses on the attitudes of guests. One flaw in the research is that guest members did not know that they were the subjects of research until a leader betrayed Hendershott's intentions after a sharing session. Hendershott also mentions an MA thesis not discussed by Sutcliffe: Rende Zoutewelle, *Attunement to the Vision* (1980) (Hendershott 1989:18).

[9] The fieldwork for these is not extensive. The 14 full-moon meditations of a Lucis Trust Unit of Service were attended between December 1994 and April 1997. 17 individuals were met in all, though usual attendances were much lower. The experience week at the Findhorn Community was first written up in Sutcliffe (1995). Here, a simple questionnaire (few details are given in the thesis) was distributed to 185 residents (out of a total community of 400 to 500), with 37 replies received. This represents a viable response rate of 20% among the sample (which, however, was not selected scientifically), but under 10% of the total population. Although the results of this survey may therefore be questioned, Sutcliffe places little reliance upon them in the text.

[10] The notion of singular seekership was dropped in Sutcliffe (2003).

[11] Completed like my thesis at King's College, University of London, under Professor (then Dr) Peter B Clarke.

[12] In a telephone interview on 12 April 1999, Crockett-Burrows claimed that the paper was wider than the New Age movement and hoped it appealed to everybody. However, the paper is regularly available free at New Age centres.

[13] Private communication, 23 September 1998.

[14] Developing the Verlach/Hine/Ferguson/York SPIN model, which she says is more applicable to secular New Age than religious Paganism, Simes suggests instead the model of a tree. An acronym is suggested, Transglobal Reformist Eclectic Esoteric Shamanism (Simes 1995:507).

[15] For the sake of comprehensiveness, scholars should also consult the following, although little new material will be found: Chandler (1988), Vernette (1990), Porquet (1994), Lacroix (1995), Peters (1991), Carr (1991), Mangalwadi (1992), Tucker (1991/1989), Streiker (1990) and Saliba (1995).

[16] She describes it as "participant observation and 'total immersion'," using a tape-recorder just twice (Prince 1992:30), working in a vegan restaurant and helping produce an 'alternative' newspaper. Weak also is her apostrophisation and spelling - to cite a few examples as they appear: Shirley Maclaine (1992:12,158); Jill Purse (1992:73); Chris Griscon (1992:158); Acquarian Cross (1992:170,171).

[17] The interviewees were volunteers cluster sampled from an annual metaphysical fair in Lafayette, California, and were classed as "service providers" which Roberts admits may cause some methodological problems.

[18] Unfortunately, pertinent as Roof's description of the New Ager may be, it is

difficult to deduce from his survey results. The table below (Roof 1994/1993:81) provides the justification for the demography supplied, and is *annotated by me*.

	%	%	my analysis %	=N
	All others (N=486)	Highly-Active Seekers (N=50)	difference	responses
Over 35 years of age	54	62	8	4
Some college	53	72	9	4.5
White Collar	60	67	7	3.5
Professionals	28	31	3	1.5
Earns $40,000+ annually	45	37	8	4
Married	66	54	8	4
Female	50	54	4	2
Liberal Political Views	26	44	18	9
No Religious Affiliation	7	24	17	8.5

I now assess the validity of the first conclusion from these statistics - that seekers are "older". 62% (=31) of these 50 are over 35 years of age; 54% (=262) of 486 "all others" were over 35. The difference between 62% and 54% of respondents is 8% of 50, or 4 people. These 4 people, who may be aged 34, are the people of whom Roof confusingly says "Compared with others of their generation, they are older ..." This statistic, resting on 4 responses, is hardly significant in a boomer population of 76 million. In a sample of 536, these percentages show nothing more than that 55% of the sample were over 35. As all data provided in the chart rest on the responses of between 1.5 and 9 people, similar difficulties apply to all conclusions.

Roof's haphazard sampling techniques distort the already daunting task of surveying one third of the American population. The 76 million people "arbitrarily" (Roof 1994/1993:266) defined as boomers (born 1946-1962) have less than 1 spokesperson per 60,000 given a basic telephone questionnaire; less than 1 spokesperson per 100,000 given a telephone interview of 25 minutes; and less than 1 spokesperson per million given an interview of one hour. The telephone questionnaire and interview schedules are not outlined. These last 64 interviewees were not selected randomly but to fit "three constituencies of interest to us: dropouts, returnees, and loyalists." (Roof 1994/1993:276) Finally the results of these surveying techniques are presented as 7 individuals - 1 per 10 million - styled "representative boomers" (Roof 1994/1993:60).

So, Roof may be accurate and insightful in his description of the *Generation of Seekers*, but his observations cannot always be supported by his surveys.

[19] See Appendix for details.

[20] After the end of my research, the Centre for Health and Healing moved to another Anglican church in London.

[21] Williams stood down at the end of 1999, being replaced by Janet Watts. Jane Turney was by this time also listed as co-director, having previously been Administrator and Publicity Officer.

[22] I comment later on the administrative inefficacy of the church.

[23] In itself, this is a highly subsidised rate for such a prime location.

[24] In fact, due to the fact that some returns were stolen, only 48 questionnaires were analysed, a return of just below 40%.

[25] Professor Barker has (in a question from the floor at the BSA Study of Religion conference on 10 April 1999) criticised my use of the electoral roll for being unrepresentative of attendees at St James's. My response was that she herself has already researched the congregation at large, and Michael York has already researched Alternatives. Furthermore, my concern is with New Agers who have some Christian commitment - for which membership of the electoral roll at St James's may be an indication.

[26] In fact, because the electoral roll excludes those aged under 16, these results may be misleading.

[27] The *European Values Survey* (Barker et al 1992:43) reports that "core members" of churches (those who attend monthly and are actively involved in church activities) declined from 16% of the population in Great Britain in 1981 to 13% in 1990.

[28] Though the relevance of all practices cited by Rose to New Age must be questioned, such a large degree of participation indicates at least some affiliation to the New Age.

[29] Although a former co-ordinator of the St James's local area networks has commented to me that she has in the past kept records of these connections and has concluded that they are not significant.

[30] Although this question was worded identically in all my surveys, respondents identified their paranormal experiences in different ways. For example, New Age Christian groups identified ESP, coincidences and voices; while evangelicals identified the presence of the Holy Spirit and healing. As no definition of paranormal experiences was supplied by the survey, the results are arguably not comparable. Furthermore, the *Kindred Spirit* question was worded slightly differently, asking about "Psi (paranormal phenomena)".

[31] At the request of the churchwarden at St James's, this section has been truncated of those occasions on which I did not declare to the congregation my research agenda. Obviously, this would have been impractical at every of the many occasions I visited the church.

[32] A similar, but more elaborate ritual is often conducted at Alternatives. Here it is not angels, but the spirits of the four directions that are invoked. However, none of my informants appeared to have noted the similarity between the two rituals.

[33] Indeed, Companions at the Order used to wear habits; they must be invited to become a Companion. Day-to-day missives are sent by Canon Spink on headed memoranda, and weekly rotas are printed.

[34] To give another example, in 1997 the church's finances were in disarray and an

urgent letter was sent to supporters asking for donations. However, by 1998 it was planned that £45,000 would be saved for expected repair expenses, and the church projected an income of approximately £320,000, with over half of this coming from the market operated in the forecourt. The PCC point out that the financial crisis in 1997 was caused by the failure of the Trading Company set up, following legal advice, in 1995, but now disbanded.

[35] It is astonishing that no previous study or publication of or by Dr Bloom has mentioned this profession.

[36] Christians Awakening to a New Awareness, 11 March 2000, see Chapter IV.

[37] See Kemp (2001a).

[38] "... il vero problema che pone in New Age è *il rapporto tra religioni e postmoderno. ... [New Age] appare semplicemente lo spirito della nuova cultura postmoderna.*"

[39] D'Andrea locates his discussion of New Age within the discourse of self and reflexivity as expounded by Giddens, and accordingly does not over-emphasise the term 'postmodern' (although see D'Andrea 1997/1996:68). This is because Giddens, like Jameson (1984), understands what other critics call 'postmodernism' to be a specific development of trends present within modernism. This philosophical and semantic discussion need not concern us here so long as we focus simply on the socio-cultural conditions that give rise to New Age.

[40] "... assim como o Protestantismo foi o "espírito" da modernidade, o MNA é o "espírito" da modernidade tardia (ou da pós-modernidade)."

[41] This is their own sobriquet. Perhaps SoFists would better reflect their cerebral temperament.

[42] Letter from Petra Griffiths, churchwarden at St James's, dated 10 October 1999.

[43] NOS members were typically under 30, while worshippers at St James's tend to be middle-aged.

IV. CHRISTIANS AWAKENING TO A NEW AWARENESS

Christians Awakening to a New Awareness (known to its members as "CANA", as in the wedding of John 2) is a network of 122 people[1], drawn initially from a larger organisation of about 200 people, known as the Bridge Trust[2]. This chapter reports on a telephone interview programme with approximately one third of the members of CANA in November 1997 (used as a pilot study for the questionnaire surveys), a postal survey of the full membership in May 1999, attendance at a day workshop run by CANA, and at a workshop and conference run by Bridge Trust. Additionally, in-depth interviews were conducted with a number of members, and the newsletters and publications of people in the group are reviewed. The chapter begins with a brief history of the groups.

History

Janice Dolley and Michael Josh first met at a Christian retreat weekend and discussed the need to bridge the 'new awareness' with the orthodox 'old'. Revd Peter Dewey, an Anglican priest, acted as a third trustee when Bridge Trust was formed in 1973. Bridge Farming Enterprises was a company set up in 1973, "to start an organic farm, working for community and conservation as a demonstration of the underlying purpose of one-ness"[3]. In 1974, Clift Farm, Dorset, was purchased and Josh and his family, another couple and a single man began to live together in community. After an article was published in *Women's Realm* magazine, so many people were attracted to the Farm, that a house nearby, known as Seniors, was purchased. Around 1980, the farm started to lose money, there were interpersonal problems within the community, and Clift Farm was sold. Seniors was leased to The Omega Trust. Bridge Trust continued its newsletters and gatherings, and the land was retained, comprising a country centre which was used for quiet days and weekends.

In 1987, Kate Money[4], Paul Swann and Janice Dolley formed the Bridge Retreats Group with the aim of promoting retreats. Dr William Bloom invited them to a New Age Teachers retreat in 1988, and this was an important stage in the programming of retreats. The first Bridge retreat was held on the island of Iona in 1989, entitled "Embodying the Christ Consciousness"; an Easter retreat in 1990 was entitled "Archetypes of Christ Consciousness". CANA was formed in 1992 to address issues that were more specifically Christian, and was originally known as Christians Awakening to a New Age. The group changed its name to Christians Awakening to a New Awareness in 1993, mainly because of the bad publicity that was becoming associated with the term New Age.

Both CANA and Bridge Trust are controlled by 'core groups', which in the case of CANA fluctuates at around eight members. More recently, Bridge Trust has launched Spirit of Learning ("SOL"), a group deriving much of its energy from Janice Dolley's experience with holistic educational principles including those of Sai Baba; Dolley was also a professor at the Open University. One of SOL's aims is to "promote Spirit as a dimension of learning in mainstream education and beyond" (promotional literature 1998).

Although not institutionally connected to Bridge Trust or CANA, The Grail Retreat Centre[5] in Abergynolwyn, mid-Wales, must be mentioned as nearly half of the ten facilitators at the Centre belong to Bridge Trust – Fr Adrian Smith, Fr Diarmuid Ó'Murchú, Revd Chris Scott and Janice Dolley. The Grail Retreat Centre was founded in 1997 by Revd Jonathan Robinson. Its promotional literature describes the Centre as "a place for exploring wider spiritual horizons", for "uneasy Christians" who "feel uncomfortable with the Church". The Christaquarian network becomes apparent when we see that Revd Jim Hill, formerly the guest master at The Omega Order, is also a facilitator at The Grail Retreat Centre.

Statistical Surveys

The only prior study of Bridge Trust was an internal postal survey conducted in 1995. Most of the questions in this 1995 survey were concerned with the efficacy of the newsletter and Trust activities. The survey had a 46% response rate from the then 170 members, so it is interesting to note that 36% of the membership had been long-term members – for over ten years, and 21% for between five and ten years. 29% of respondents were male. Kay Allen, who conducted the survey, commented

> that many members, (well over half of the respondents), fully committed locally in their various Bridge-type activities, are happy just to receive the newsletter, as a means of keeping in touch with what others are doing, without any active involvement in Bridge;
> that Bridge nowadays and for the past 10 years or so, is essentially a linking and support 'association', rather than an executive 'doing' organisation. The 'doing' is done by the members, which we aim to support.
> ("Feedback from Bridge Trust Questionnaire," Allen 1996)

The telephone interviews for my study were conducted with a third of the membership of CANA in late 1997, recorded with permission and transcribed for analysis. A structured questionnaire was used, based on Stuart Rose's postal questionnaire for his 1996 thesis. Each interview lasted approximately a quarter of an hour, and the sample was generated according to availability, thus possibly biasing against those in work or leading busy lives, although telephone calls were made at different times throughout the day and on different days of the week. There were two refusals to be interviewed, and one respondent expressed a preference to complete the questionnaire through the post. Experience from the telephone interviews was used to finalise the wording of the postal survey, and the results of the telephone interviews were largely confirmed in this postal survey. The group had almost doubled in size by May 1999, and it is to these latter statistics that I refer below. A response rate of 53% was achieved for the postal survey.

Members of CANA are, as with the Omega Order, predominantly female – 75% –

and elderly – 43% of respondents were over 65. Central Statistical Office figures indicate that only 16% of the population is aged 65 or over, and that 58% of these are female (CSO 1996:39). The professions of respondents – although over half are now retired – were mostly middle-class, such as lecturing, teaching and nursing, with corresponding levels of education. 15% of CANA respondents have postgraduate degrees and 32% have some sort of professional qualification. There are at least five ordained priests (although not all members of the mailing list are listed by their correct title) in CANA, with two more in Bridge Trust, which is perhaps unusual for a group this small.

Again, as with The Omega Order, there is a spread of original religious affiliation from within the mainstream Christian Churches, mostly Church of England and Roman Catholic, with a smaller minority reporting a non-conformist or a spiritualist background. There has been hardly any change (5%) in professed religious affiliation from that into which respondents were born, although 15% of respondents qualified their later faith with terms such as "interfaith", "post-denominational" or "ecumenical". However, although professing mainstream Christianity, when asked for the spiritual discipline or teaching that has had the greatest influence on their life, a significant minority of the telephone sample cited some form of alternative spirituality such as the School of Economic Science, the White Eagle Lodge, the mystical tradition or Creation Spirituality.

A number of members of CANA interviewed over the telephone expressed uncertainty as to the difference between CANA and Bridge Trust, often believing them to be one and the same (although in one case a respondent emphasized that she thought CANA *too* New Agey in comparison with Bridge Trust). CANA was intended by its founders to add a Christian dimension to a non-Christian and more New Agey Bridge Trust. So it may be that people have joined CANA when they may more appropriately have joined Bridge Trust, and that they are not really *Christians* in the New Age, but just normally-religious New Age people. One way to evaluate this potential problem in using CANA as an example of Christaquarianism would be to compare results with a survey of Bridge Trust; in the absence of this, the only indications are that nearly all CANA respondents claimed to be "actively pursuing a spiritual path" and that 74% of respondents pray every few days or more, indicating some degree of religious commitment.

> In the 1991 British Social Attitudes Survey over a third of people described themselves as 'somewhat religious' with a further 7 per cent saying they were 'extremely' or 'very religious'; a third said that they never prayed. In the same year, the British Household Panel Survey asked people how much difference religious beliefs made to their lives; four in ten people said they made no difference.
> (CSO 1996:225)

There are, however, two indications that CANA members are not mainstream Christians. The first is that 72% meditate at least once every few days, with traditions ranging from *The Cloud of Unknowing*, to John Main, mantras and Zen. For comparison, only 23% of the control group surveyed meditate this often. Another indication that members of CANA are not quite regular Christians is provided in their response to the item derived from Michael York's questionnaire,

> *What do you believe God is? A real personality, an impersonal force, a fiction, or something else?*

In York's survey just 6% of respondents at an Alternatives evening in St James's church believed God to be a real personality, while 33% thought God to be an impersonal force. A similar *Gallup* survey in 1993 found that 30% of Britons believe in a personal God, 40% in "some sort of spirit or lifeforce" (Heelas 1996a:166). Nearly one fifth of CANA respondents thought God is a real personality, with around the same number believing God to be an impersonal force. Over half, however, gave some alternative definition. Of the control group, 58% thought God to be a real personality, 17% an impersonal force.

Similarly, there are two indications that CANA members are not typical New Agers. Firstly, although out of the Christaquarian groups studied CANA respondents had the highest level of reported paranormal experiences, at 57%, this compares with Rose's survey of *Kindred Spirit* readers, where 82% reported such experiences. Another indication that members of CANA are not 'hardcore' New Agers, though, is that a number of respondents expressed some reservation as to whether they consider themselves New Age, or to particular parts of the New Age. One telephone respondent could see why people might consider him New Age – he prays with stones and candles, for example – but preferred to see himself as Christian. Another respondent expressed disquiet over witches and the occult, although had adopted other New Age practices herself (such as an interest in 'coincidences').

Nevertheless, 92% of CANA respondents gave a definition of the term New Age, compared to a US national average (probably lower in the UK) of 23% understanding the term (Heelas 1996a:109) – the group was after all formerly called "Christians Awakening to a New Age". A sample of definitions from the telephone survey is listed below. Some examples given of typical New Age groups were: druids, Stonehenge, Glastonbury, hippies, Natural Law Party, ecology, astrology, paranormal, chakras, crystals, American Indians, new therapies. New Age was defined in various ways as:

> A group of people who are travellers who don't live in any particular area, who dedicate their lives to various religious practices, mystic cults of various kinds.

> A turning away from some aspects of where the world is going now to a new ... from the old ways of thinking and acting towards a more spiritual way of living.

> Seeking for meanings which are real for us now in our time with a renewed interest in the spiritual beyond formal religions and science beyond formal science.

> An unfolding age of awakening, not necessarily a new age.

Looking at spiritual things in the context of post-industrial society, trying to incorporate the old with the new, or somehow trying to link up with things that are quite ancient.

Where people are trying to find the spiritual in everything. The spirit is less apparent in churches than it is in nature, and I think New Age people are latching on to that.

A symptom of people's hunger for something more than just material things, and the hunger is not being met by the institutional Churches in this country anyway. It is an emerging of a new awareness maybe you can say of God.

People who don't actually believe in Christ as spiritual, but they believe in something within us, like a soul or spirit, and – I get muddled up with Celtic – and that there is a lot to do with the body that isn't physical, that depends on emotions and outer energies and auras.

I think we are in the New Age. Again, that's a bit like the old dichotomies in trying to turn things into old age and new age. I don't really go for that. I think we are in a paradigm shift, things are happening, and we are all part of it. I don't particularly want to erect another barrier, you know, you're New Age and I go to church. I don't want to do that at all.

New Age is an expression of spirituality which is a departure from orthodox religion into something a little more esoteric than orthodox religion and religious practices.

Some respondents offered the opinion that New Age and Christianity fit quite well together, and that the Church should be more sympathetic to the New Age. One respondent saw New Age and Christianity coming together in healing, being involved in a healing ministry within a church. Another respondent thought the emphasis on wholeness in New Age was particularly in tune with Christianity. Another lady thought New Age rituals and circle dancing are not included enough in the Church.

A 55-64 year-old married female office administrator, who has always been Anglican, wrote the following:

Q33. What is your opinion of Christians who are involved in the New Age?

As one myself, I know it has not been easy. Generally it has been best to keep quiet about my changing beliefs and, for a time, I found it easier to stay away from church where old interpretations began to feel false and empty. But Christianity has been my upbringing and is the one teaching I know much about which shows a way to a closer encounter with GOD. We cannot expect everyone to have a mystical understanding but more and more clergy and layaty [sic] are showing a wider understanding and we can help by remaining part of the church rather than bailing out which some, who have felt so hurt and missunderstood [sic], have felt the need to do.
(Questionnaire 651)

Another respondent wrote,

Since New Age cannot really be defined except in my own personal terms – I cannot answer this. I consider myself Christian and New Age. (Questionnaire 652)

75% of CANA respondents scored between 5 and 8 on Stuart Rose's scale of 'greenness' ranging from 0 to 10. Rose's sample of *Kindred Spirit* readers scored 70% in the 5 – 7 range; Omega Order respondents were 72% in the 5 – 8 range; St James's respondents were 84% in the 5 – 8 range. This indicates that CANA is about as green as other New Age groups (see Pepper 1991). However, the evangelical sample also scored 60% in the 5 – 8 range, suggesting that the general population may also consider themselves to be 'green' to some extent.

Rose's question

Do you believe there can exist the concept of a separate theistic God in New Age ideas and activities?

was generally badly understood in the pilot telephone survey. I do not believe that a meaningful result could have been obtained from this question, and cannot see how it passed the pilot stage in Rose's questionnaire. Similarly, although the question

In your opinion, are there varying types of spirituality, or is spirituality universally the same?

was understood, a large number of telephone respondents agreed with both options at different levels. Thus at the deepest level, spirituality is perceived as common to the whole of humanity, although more superficially it is thought to be manifested in various ways according to differences between cultures and peoples.

There was some agreement as to the writings which had had an important influence on members' lives. Over ten respondents mentioned Bede Griffiths, Carl Jung and Teilhard de Chardin. Teilhard de Chardin was also the most-mentioned influence in Ferguson's survey (1980). Other authors mentioned as an important influence included Matthew Fox, Thomas Merton, Julian of Norwich, Anthony De Mello, Diarmuid Ó'Murchú, Adrian Smith and Gerard Hughes. Influences thus favoured New Age-Christian authors over classical or mainstream influences. Of those who gave an answer, several reported having read over 50 books on the New Age.

Length of membership of CANA spread from one year to those who had belonged to Bridge Trust and CANA since they were formed. The method of recruitment was usually through friends, with exactly one quarter of respondents being recruited in this way, and almost a third recruited through Bridge Trust.

Participant Observation

Various meetings were attended for participant observation. From 20 to 30 members attended a larger meeting, with 9 attending a smaller workshop in which I participated, one of only two men. This "Values and Visions" workshop was held in the house of the then editor of the Bridge Trust newsletter. We were encouraged to examine and share our fundamental personal values, exploring these in discussion of models of human potential and of drawings that we made expressing how we felt. The models were based on material taken from the Human Values Foundation, in turn taken from Sathya Sai Education in Human Values material. Participators in the workshop were variously involved in the Church of England, Lucis Trust Triangle groups, the Friends of the Western Buddhist Order, the Scientific and Medical Network and the Society of Friends. One works as an independent spiritual counsellor.

The Bridge Trust Annual Gathering in 1996 was held in the Quaker International Centre, London. The day consisted of lectures followed by small-group discussion. In keeping with the overall membership, only one quarter of attendees were male, and several people remarked to me (then aged 23) how good it was to have a "young one" among them; I doubt any of them were younger than 45. One of the speakers also holds workshops at the Findhorn Community, and said that Eileen Caddy, the co-founder of Findhorn, had originally seen it as related to Christianity, and that Christianity is increasingly coming to the fore, especially with one former Anglican clergyman, and the use of Taizé chants. Celia and David Storey, who were both at the conference, became interested in matters spiritual through an experience week at Findhorn with their family in the 1970s. They ran a New Age centre from 1982 to 1985, were heavily involved with the World's Parliament of Religions in Chicago 1993, and now run the International Interfaith Centre in Oxford.

Another of the speakers, Eileen Conn, is co-author with James Stewart, also a Bridge Trust member, of *Visions of Creation* (1995), a compendium of the thought of spiritual environmentalists through history. This was consciously written, said Conn, in language that would be amenable to mainstream Christianity. Conn is a former member of the PCC at St James's, Piccadilly, and assisted the current churchWarden in agreeing a draft of the chapter of this thesis on St James's. Stewart teaches a module on Creation Spirituality at Newcastle Upon Tyne University. He set up The Academic Network ("TAN") with Mary Grey and Eileen Conn after a meeting at the Centre for Creation Spirituality at St James's church, Piccadilly. The network was intended to become a sort of para-university, with members exchanging ideas and offering each other accommodation during conferences. The hope was that it would avoid institutionalizing and becoming a bureaucracy, but it failed through lack of support in late 1997. At its height, it had 34 members, including five professors and eleven PhDs.

Jasmine, another of the attendees at the Annual Gathering, had an Anglican upbringing before leaving the church in early adulthood and returning to it aged about 50. After a spiritual experience, she read Steiner in 1985 and soon after came across Bailey and Theosophy. Another psychical experience led her to a spiritual teacher for a year. Recently, Jasmine received a message from her late husband saying it is her mission to bring the intuitive to bear on rational thought. Lisette, a Dutch-born member of Bridge Trust at the Gathering, is a member of Fountain International, founded in 1981 in Brighton to heal communities through light meditation. Working on ideas from Dion Fortune, Lisette extended Fountain's work in the early 1990s to focus on Nazi ley-lines. She saw the culmination of this work in the wrapping of the German Reichstag as a work of art.

Revd Kevin Tingay, although he was not actually a member of CANA or Bridge Trust at the time of my research[6] and has not been present at any of the CANA events I have attended, first introduced me to CANA when I met him at an academic conference. He was vicar of Bradford-on-Tone[7] and its associated parishes from 1990, and is the Bishop's Advisor on interfaith matters for the Diocese of Bath and Wells. He combines his church positions with membership of the Council of the Churches' Fellowship for Psychical and Spiritual Studies, the Theosophical Society (the focus of his doctoral research), and the Scientific and Medical Network. His parents were Roman Catholic converts, and he was brought up nominally Church of England, joining the Theosophical Society youth group and working in the former Theosophical Society bookshop in London during his twenties. He trained at both an evangelical Bible College and an Anglo-Catholic seminary, and complains of being accused by different people of being fundamentalist, high church *and* New Age!

Revd Tingay came across Canon Peter Spink's first book (see following Chapter) shortly after it was published, and used to visit Kent House, Canon Spink's original teaching centre at Tunbridge Wells. He helped in the practicalities of the move of The Omega Order to Winford in 1986 and now visits on average once a year, remaining on the mailing list of *Omega News*. A local evangelical, who caused some fuss in the diocese about The Omega Order, has also heckled at Revd Tingay's own study days on New Age. But having worked in a parish church that was evangelical, Revd Tingay does not make the polarized division between 'fundamentalism' and New Age that is often made. Instead, he sees similarities between the constant need in both movements for something new – more experiences, more members – and judges that evangelicals suffer more psychologically from this pressure than New Agers.

Working near Glastonbury, Revd Tingay often comes across New Age in his ministry. But the specific examples he mentioned during the interview I had with him were his suspicion of Scientology's wealth, and his help with parents worried about mature children involved with 'harmless' New Age teachers; this is not a New Age ministry. More 'New Age' is the discussion group (with a mailing list of 40 and maximum attendance of 24) named "Sophia", meeting four or five times a year at his Rectory. Subjects discussed include Hildegaard of Bingen, Eckhart, Western Esotericism and Blavatsky. The group was discontinued at the end of 1997 due to Revd Tingay's increased work pressures. Revd Tingay also contributed an article on Gnosticism to John Button and William Bloom's New Age resource book, *The Seeker's Guide* (1992:73-74), and has given a lecture at Alternatives on esoteric Christianity.

Literature and Leaders

The Bridge Trust newsletter contains a wide variety of articles ranging from spiritual commentary on current affairs to 'down on the farm' pieces from the dominant ecological element in the group. One strong influence in the newsletter is Alice Bailey – as is shown by the frequent inclusion of World Goodwill leaflets – but this is not necessarily noticeable to those who have not read the words of Djwhal Khul, and is accompanied by other spiritual influences including Buddhism, Steiner and Christianity. The CANA newsletter is published biannually, and is much smaller than that of its mother organisation.

Members of the CANA mailing list are prolific writers. I know of five authors among them (Gillian Paschkes-Bell, Janice Dolley, Fr Adrian Smith, Fr Diarmuid Ó'Murchú and Revd Chris Scott) totalling around 20 publications between them.

Gillian Paschkes-Bell participates in the CANA Core Group meetings. Growing up in a mixed Jewish-Christian household, Paschkes-Bell later joined a house church and then a more liberal church. She first became interested in New Age during an 'alternative' holiday on the island of Skyros in Greece in 1995. In 1998 she completed an MTh degree at Oxford University as a mature student, for which the dissertation was entitled, "Christian Belief and the 'New Awareness' a qualitative sociological study and a theological critique". Paschkes-Bell conducted 24 interviews with people she knew, half with people connected to the Findhorn Foundation, the other half Christian church-goers. Having asked some interviewees about their spiritual history, she asked the others about their concept of the Divine, of good and evil and of self-realisation/salvation. She writes of the Findhorn respondents that

> the points of contrast with Christian doctrine appear to be the monistic and pantheistic world view, the denial of the existence of evil, and the emphasis on self-realisation rather than 'taking up one's cross'.
> (Paschkes-Bell 1998:44)

It would have been helpful if more information had been included on the selection and social backgrounds of interviewees.

The dissertation ends with a short theological discussion:

... every manifestation of God is a manifestation of the second person of the Trinity. The second person precisely *is* God-in-Manifestation.

... God is All-that-Is *in so far* as All-that-Is can be understood as a manifestation of God, the Source of Being. But beyond that manifestation lies the Source, who is not the manifestation.

(Paschkes-Bell 1998:75)

It is concluded, without much argument, that

... it is possible for an individual to be a 'New Age Christian'.

(Paschkes-Bell 1998:84)

A curious epilogue presents her personal 'creed':

Towards a New Age Christianity? or A Christian contribution to the New Age

1. The Divine is perceived in a three-fold way:
* as Divine Cause, Creator and Source of Being, who is not even Being
* as the Manifestation of the Divine, seen in all creation, in potential, seen more clearly in human-kind; seen most clearly when the human will becomes one with the Divine in Christ
* as the Holy Spirit who is non-manifest Divine presence in the world.

2. It is the role of each human being to open his or her-self to find the presence of God within (the third person of the trinity), and to become God (the second person of the trinity), always aspiring towards the God who is utterly other and unknowable, from whom we come and to whom we return (the first person of the trinity).

3. The process and story of creation is a going forth from God and a returning to God. The possibility of evil, which is non-alignment with the will of God, is necessary to enable the going forth to take place; salvation is seen in the returning. This movement of leaving and returning, and the duality good and evil, are characteristics of the created order. However, the created order mirrors the eternal order analogically speaking. The relevant analogy within the Godhead may be seen in terms of the divine processions: the going out which is seen in the kenosis of the First Person who gives God's-self in totality to the Second Person, and the answering kenosis of the Second Person.

4. Salvation is the total alignment of the whole of creation with Divinity. This alignment begins on Earth with humanity, in which the whole of creation is summed up. The point of return is Christ, the Alpha. His work will be complete when his return has been accomplished in the whole of creation, the Omega point. This is an evolutionary process.

5. At the Omega point, the whole of creation will be fully realised, each creature fulfilling its potential for being, in harmony with all others. The evolutionary process involves the duty to aspire towards such fulfilment, but until the Omega point is reached such aspiration cannot be fulfilled entirely, and individual lives will suffer from their lack of completion.

(Paschkes-Bell 1998:85-86)

Janice Dolley was a founder member of Bridge Trust and of CANA, and continues to be a leading influence in the organisations. At the time of my research, she promoted holistic educational programmes including that of Sai Baba as an adjunct to her work as an Open University lecturer. Dolley is also Executive Director of the Wrekin Trust, which continues to promote the work of the late Sir George Trevelyan by furthering the development of adult spiritual education in non-sectarian ways[8]. (Dr William Bloom, who refers to Dolley as a "good friend", is a former trustee of the Wrekin Trust and David Lorimer, of the Scientific and Medical Network, is the current Chair.) Dolley is also a trustee of the Findhorn Foundation.

Dolley wrote two books with the late Lady Ursula Burton, one of which was published. *Christian Evolution* has a foreword by Revd Donald Reeves of St James' church, but by 1996 when I interviewed him, Revd Reeves was not in touch with Dolley. Another interesting connection, as far as this thesis is concerned, is that Lady Burton did some of her thinking for the book at Burrswood in Kent while Canon Peter Spink, founder of The Omega Order, was Warden. Burton and Dolley's starting point is the "clash between the 'orthodox' and 'New Age' streams of thinking" (Burton & Dolley 1984:13). Both felt some unease with their Church[9], its liturgy and creed, looking for affirmation of silence, ESP, rebirth and healing. They document others – all female – with similar feelings of ambiguity and compromise, beginning in the Church but looking for something more. The question is left open as to whether

the Church, as a movement as well as an institution, is to lead this inspiration [by higher values] or whether it is to come from an amalgam of the many small groups now establishing themselves under the vague banner 'New Age'. If the latter comes about, there is a danger that the Church might become overinsistent on outer form and refuse to join forces with them, thereby proving to be a force of reaction heading towards separateness as opposed to wholeness.

(Burton & Dolley 1984:94)

Christianity and the New Age (Burton & Dolley 1990) remained unpublished at the time of Burton's death. The ambiguity of feeling towards the Church remained.

On a structural level what is needed now is re-appraisal, re-assessment and reinterpretation of the old concepts in order to make them relevant today. The Institutional Church would then be a welcome home for the new age seeker.
(Burton & Dolley 1990:chII p12)

A chapter by Fr Diarmuid Ó'Murchú suggests that "bridging the gap" between the Churches and the New Age Movement would be welcomed by most New Agers.

There is quite a wide gap between the New Age movement and the mainstream Churches. In fact, New Age groupings consist of many people who, one time, were closely linked with Christianity, but became disenchanted and disillusioned, and sought bliss and peace elsewhere. Consequently, there exists within the New Age movement quite an interest in religious matters and, basically, an openness to dialogue with official Christianity.
(Ó'Murchú in Burton & Dolley 1990:chIX p2[10])

He suggests the following opportunities for this bridge-building between the Churches and New Age:
   i.   Rediscovering Spirituality.
   ii. Transcending the Mechanistic Consciousness
   iii. Regrounding our Earthiness.
   iv. Neotribalism.
   v.   Broadening the Horizon of Love.
   vi. Coping with Novelty.
(Ó'Murchú in Burton & Dolley 1990:chIX p9)

Fr Diarmuid Ó'Murchú (b 1952) is a Catholic priest, member of the Sacred Heart Missionaries and a social psychologist and counsellor. Having worked in London with people who are HIV-positive or who have AIDS, he now lives and works for eight months a year in a centre that rehouses the homeless. The remaining four months of the year he goes on tour, giving lectures and workshops (Interview, 26 March 1998). These have included, in recent years, a Sea of Faith conference, a Teilhard Society lecture and a Creation Spirituality workshop. Fr Ó'Murchú was a founder member of the Christian Transcendental Meditation Group with Fr Adrian Smith in 1980, having first become interested in TM through an advert he saw the previous year. Evangelical heckling through this venture was an experience which was repeated when he taught meditation in a school and a parent complained to the bishop; he now consciously avoids evangelicals.

Several members of CANA cite Fr Ó'Murchú as somebody whose writings or work have had an important influence on their life. Although he does not situate his own thought within the New Age, many of his themes are consonant with those found in New Age circles, and he declares that every Christian is a New Ager in the sense of expecting the basilea (kingdom). He now prefers the label 'spiritual' to 'Christian'. He met Canon Peter Spink in the mid 1990s at a CANA conference, but has not visited The Omega Order; he has been to St James's church, Piccadilly several times but has not met Revd Donald Reeves.

Much of Fr Ó'Murchú's work is concerned with the Religious Life. *The Prophetic Horizon of Religious Life* (Ó'Murchú 1989) begins by comparing Christian Religious to those of other faiths. He explores the concept of 'liminality' as a defining virtue of the true religious life, and thinks that the focus has now shifted from Religious Orders to

> basic christian communities, *new age movements*, industrial and agricultural cooperatives, spiritual regeneration movements, cults, sects, Green politics, feminism, ecology groups and a host of others.
> (Ó'Murchú 1989:40, *my emphasis*)

Our World in Transition: Making Sense of a Changing World (Ó'Murchú 1997/1992) explains the change in paradigm from the mechanistic to the wholistic, quantum worldview. *Inter alia* it proclaims,

> We need a global government, because contemporary problems are global in nature.
> (Ó'Murchú 1997/1992:66)

The United Nations is seen as the locum of this global government and the answer to current crises. Networks are said to replace institutions. *Reframing Religious Life: An Expanded Vision for the Future* (Ó'Murchú 1995) looks at the changes Fr Ó'Murchú thinks are needed to religious orders. He makes it clear at a number of points that he believes the institutional Church is unnecessary and perhaps hampers religious life (cf 1995:133-135):

> If we Religious are to reclaim our liminal prophetic role ... then a process of disengagement from the institutional Church is both desirable and necessary.
> (Ó'Murchú 1995:71)

Religious life should reclaim the "liminal spaces", "points of intersection between World and Kingdom" (Ó'Murchú 1995:64). The kingdom of God is a sort of utopia that the religious should strive to create in this world, a "new paradigm" (Ó'Murchú 1995:121) (Ó'Murchú uses Thomas Kuhn's phrase (1962) popular in New Age) at the "dawn of a new millennium" (ibid). The kingdom of God is also referred to as the basilea, the New Reign or "*a new world order*" (Ó'Murchú 1995:69). Part of this kingdom theology is Fr Ó'Murchú's affirmation of what he calls "counter-culture" (1995:40f): "ecological and environmental values", the "*recapitulation*" of "modern feminism, which draws a great deal of inspiration from the goddess culture of pre-patriarchal times", shamanic power. This counter-culture, of "today's alternative movements"

> exhibit[s] the liminal challenge much more powerfully and coherently than the formal liminars. Wholistic health movements, alternative technologies, workers' co-operatives, base communities, attempts at ethical investment, and attempts at discerning alternative socio-economic and political strategies are all endowed with liminal potential.
> (Ó'Murchú 1995:54)

Although not directly related to the text, Fr Ó'Murchú includes (1995:86) a diagram of the chakras.

Quantum Theology: Spiritual Implications of the New Physics (Ó'Murchú 1997a) is not a retelling of Capra's *The Tao of Physics* (1976) and Talbot's *Mysticism and the New Physics* (1981); only fourteen pages (Ó'Murchú 1997a:22-36) are devoted to expounding quantum theory itself, with the subsequent two chapters exploring some of its implications. In my estimation, the greatest debt *Quantum Theology* shows to the new physics is the sense of awe at the created world, summed up in an earlier work as *"cosmology* rather than *theology* becomes the queen of the sciences." (Ó'Murchú 1995:64). The work concludes with an appendix that lists the "principles of quantum theology", some of which are remarkably dissimilar from mainstream Christianity. For example, "Notions such as "God" and "divinity" are used sparingly" (Ó'Murchú 1997a:197). A great deal is made of the principle that the whole is greater than the sum of the parts – an insight not new to quantum physics or Christian theology. Matthew Fox's doctrine of original blessing is adopted as a conclusion of the design and purpose evidenced by evolution.

> Revelation is ongoing; it cannot be subsumed in any religion, creed, or cultural system.
> (Ó'Murchú 1997a:199)

The doctrine of the trinity is compared to the theory that quantums can exist only in triads, and this is said to demonstrate God's relational nature.

Some aspects of *Quantum Theology* do not seem to derive from the new physics at all. For instance – the notion that *"Ultimate meaning is embedded in story, not in facts"* (Ó'Murchú 1997a:199), with creation itself as the primary narrator. Elements of liberation theology are affirmed – especially the idea that sin is a structural rather than personal problem. The principles of *Quantum Theology* that most radically deviate from Christian tradition are that "We live in a world without beginning or end" (Ó'Murchú 1997a:201) and

> Resurrection and reincarnation are not facts, but mental/spiritual constructs that articulate both our paradoxical fear of, and yearning for, infinity.
> (Ó'Murchú 1997a:202)

If eschatology, redemption and resurrection are considered central to Christian soteriology, these alterations to the tradition seem fundamentally difficult to reconcile. The conclusion to *Quantum Theology* is rather trite: God is love.

Reclaiming Spirituality: A new spiritual framework for today's world (Ó'Murchú 1997b) revolves around the observation that human spirituality has existed for at least 70,000 years, whereas formal religion is an invention of the patriarchal Agricultural Revolution. The book is therefore aimed at

> the growing spiritual consciousness ... in the lives of those who have either veered away from (or abandoned) the practice of formal religion, or may never have had a religion in the first place.
> (Ó'Murchú 1997b:1-2)

Fr Ó'Murchú sees this spirituality as a "counter-culture" that is driven by evolution (1997b:12), much in the de Chardin tradition. Fr Ó'Murchú has some nostalgia for a matriarchal society, referenced to Marija Gimbutas' works *The Goddesses and Gods of Old Europe, 7000-3500 BC* (1982) and *The Civilisation of the Goddess* (1991). However, the notion of a matriarchal religion has recently been brought into question by Ronald Hutton (1991) among others.

In *Reclaiming Spirituality* (Ó'Murchú 1997b) occurs one of Fr Ó'Murchú's few explicit references to the New Age movement: Fr Ó'Murchú plays down the Christian reaction against New Age, claiming that it is more attractive to those without any religious affiliation, and urging us not to judge it by its excesses. Again with de Chardinian overtones, Fr Ó'Murchú makes the unusual suggestion that New Agers are

> 'acting out' subconsciously what millions across the world are experiencing, rather than consciously perpetuating a philosophy of their own making.
> (Ó'Murchú 1997b:26)

He concludes that New Age "could rock the foundations of Christendom, but not the central challenge of Christianity" (Ó'Murchú 1997b:27).

Fr Adrian Smith (b 1930) is a "good friend" of Fr Ó'Murchú, and is also a Catholic priest and a missionary, of the White Fathers. He was a missionary in Africa for over 15 years, writing his earlier works in this context (Smith 1977; 1978a; 1978b; 1982). In addition to belonging to Bridge Trust since the early 1980s and to CANA, Fr Smith also convened for a time in the mid 1990s one of the study groups at the Centre for Creation Spirituality at St James's Piccadilly and was a founder member of the Christian Transcendental Meditation Group in 1980. He has also visited The Omega Order several times, twice when they were still in Tunbridge Wells (ie prior to 1986), and has been a member of the Churches' Fellowship for Psychic and Spiritual Studies since about 1993. Since 1990 he has run with a Quaker marriage counsellor-and-ex-Lutheran spiritual healer regular "non-religious retreats" which aim to be spiritual without mentioning God[11]. This "More-to-Life Partnership" has advertised with the CANA newsletter, with *Miracle Worker* (*A Course in Miracles* magazine in the UK), and Cygnus bookclub (which is run by the leaders of Lectorium Rosicrucianum, a neognostic organisation).

Fr Smith's African work was written before his 'New Age' period, and thus offers little of interest to this study. Of note, however, is that he values the charismatic experience (Smith 1978a:8-12) and is open to new means of communicating the gospel such as through a cassette course. A fundamental shift in his thought occurred in 1976 when he learnt Transcendental Meditation in Nairobi, coming to it through an Indian sister he had met, and learning the more advanced Sidhi techniques from 1978. In 1980 Smith was to found with Fr Diarmuid Ó'Murchú the Christian TM Group, amid some controversy in Ireland. Fr Smith still uses TM meditation daily (Interview, 21 November 1996), and there is some cross-attendance between CANA and Christian TM events.

TM: An Aid to Christian Growth (Smith ed 1983) presents TM as a "purely human technique" (Smith ed 1983:8) which one can pursue while continuing to practice Christianity. At this time, Smith wrote

I believe many new insights can be given to Christian revelation by understanding it in Eastern metaphysical terms, provided that this is accepted as an alternative insight and not as a replacement explanation. (Smith ed 1983:115)

TM was therefore to be seen as a parallel to the Church, not even as an agent of reformation, although Fr Smith acknowledged that it sought to usher in a New Age (Smith 1983:114). *A Key to the Kingdom of Heaven: A Christian Understanding of Transcendental Meditation* (1993) repeats the 1983 volume in Fr Smith's own words: TM is a "natural, human exercise" invented before any of the religions (Smith 1993:9); it is spiritual but not religious. Meditation gives us an "intuitive knowledge" (Smith 1993:16) of the "interconnectedness of everything" (Smith 1993:21).

In 1986 Fr Smith first writes more explicitly about the New Age, equating it to the Kingdom of God (Smith 1986:14f). In some ways, the New Age began when the Messiah came as the first "new-age person" (Smith 1986:34f). On the other hand, this "great evolutionary step forward" is still to happen in the Age of Aquarius (Smith 1986:87). *God and the Aquarian Age: The New Era of the Kingdom* (1990) is Fr Smith's most explicitly New Age work. His understanding of New Age is under four headings: a "bursting forth of human potential", that the "universe is shot through with living intelligence" and is one living system, that we are to be in harmony with creation, and that "the consciousness of human beings is tapping into the global consciousness of our planet, bringing about a spiritual awakening" (Smith 1990:34). New Age is traced to Teilhard de Chardin, Jung, Maslow, Rogers and Huxley (Smith 1990:35). As Fr Smith writes, "The big question is whether this change [the emergence of the New Age] will result in a breakdown or a breakthrough for the Church." (Smith 1990:73). His answer to this question is that there will still be a need for a church as a 'focus' for the Kingdom (Smith 1990:89f). However, Christianity will not continue as a religion, as it has heretofore been understood; Christians should be more concerned with experience than doctrine, less concerned with formal moral rules, more concerned with mystical prayer and meeting for Eucharist, and less bound by hierarchical structures.

The reason why I am a Christian is because that particular form of religion, for which Jesus as the Christ is central, is the path that appeals to me most, being a child of Western culture. (Smith 1990:85)

The God Shift: Our Changing Perception of the Ultimate Mystery (1996) argues that, with contemporary cultural changes, it is time for a change in the conception of God: "for too long we have over-emphasised the transcendence of God at the expense of appreciating God as immanent." (Smith 1996:10). Ultimately, "our deepest physical, psychological and spiritual experiences are the same" (Smith 1996:10), but "this can never give rise to one universal religion because each of these religions was born within a particular culture" (Smith 1996:21). At the mystical level, there is simple unity.

Fr Smith prefers the term "era of new consciousness" to "New Age". His concept of New Age is unusual in that he does not see it as a movement, but as an event.

> It is not a specific philosophy or a specific doctrine, or promoted by anybody or group – it is just an occurrence, an evolutionary step I believe in consciousness that is taking place. And you can only talk about all the manifestations of that. You can't tie it down to a material example.
> (Interview, 21 November 1996)

The mention of evolution reveals a debt to Teilhard de Chardin which is acknowledged with the caveat that his cosmology is now passée.

Another member of CANA, Revd Chris Scott, was for four years in the 1970s a Franciscan brother, and is now a counsellor and part-time Anglican chaplain to a small almshouse community in Surrey, and a facilitator at The Grail Retreat Centre in Mid-Wales. His wife is also a minister in the Church. His 1996 publication, *Between the Poles*, is subtitled "*creative living between atheism and religion*", and aims to present a "secular spirituality" (Scott 1996:4), but the poles are defined as subjective and objective experience, with the 'between' called "cojectivity" (Scott 1996:17).

> Cojectivity can become the meeting place where peoples of different religious understandings or none, can come together in a common understanding of their humanity.
> (idem)

Nothing in any religion is necessary, says Revd Scott, unless it is helpful.

> Whilst I am highly critical of religion, especially in its institutionalised form, nevertheless there remains at its core a wisdom, a fundamental truth which is ageless, because it expresses the fundamental truths of what it means to be human.
> (Scott 1996:125)

Although his book is promoted by CANA, Revd Scott distances himself from the New Age movement, claiming it presents a one-sided view of the truth (Scott 1996:50). Nevertheless, he discusses the possibility of Christians believing in reincarnation, karma, out-of-the-body experiences, and the importance of the spiritual over the religious (Scott 1996:94f). It is perhaps not a coincidence that he writes,

> To understand Jesus in contemporary society we need not to strip away the myth, for myth is the essential medium in which truth is contained, but rather to create *new myths for a new age*.
> (Scott 1996:128, *my emphasis*)

Beliefs and Attitudes

These writings, and the interviews and surveys conducted, reveal what June Anne English (1985) (see Chapter VIII) has located as the starting point for a new social or religious movement: there must be a problem, a set of difficulties to be resolved. CANA members have concluded that conventional Christian beliefs do not provide the answers for the challenges to their faith that the contemporary world poses. Their response is to articulate these conflicting beliefs explicitly. Once articulated, this agenda provides the identity of an alternative worldview, which can become distinguished as an incipient movement.

In 1998 CANA produced and discussed at a conference in London a draft paper entitled "Exploring Ways Forward for Christianity into the Twenty-First Century"[12]. A final version of the paper was distributed the following year more widely among Christians and spiritual groups, although it was produced too late to distribute at the Lambeth Conference as was first suggested.

The first section of the paper outlines some personal "frameworks of Christian beliefs", comparing traditional expressions of Christian belief with contemporary alternatives. The beliefs listed include a liberal approach to the Bible and revelation, a definition of God as the Ground of Being with an emphasis on 'becoming', a Christology which emphasizes the humanity of Jesus, humans as still evolving, the church as one religious community among many perspectives on the One truth and theology as tentative. This section is followed by some "personal creeds" by members of CANA. These vary greatly in content, style and length. Another section outlines personal "visions for the Church". Jill Gant suggests that churches should become "Open Pastoral Centres" for the spiritual life of whole communities, not restricted to Christians, and offering some welfare assistance. Adrian Smith suggests that the church must "downshift" and become "non-powerful, non-clericalist, [and] de-centralised" (CANA 1999:23).

The paper includes a list of helpful books. The first on this list is Robin Amis' 1995 *A Different Christianity: Early Christian Esotericism and Modern Thought*, which is a dense study of Eastern Orthodox spiritual techniques. Amis holds seminars for his Praxis Research Institute (based in the New Age town of Totnes, Devon) at such New Age venues as the Golden Square Bookshop[13], London and Dartington Hall, Devon. His seminars have also been advertised by CANA. However, his wife wrote to me that

> In his view, there is not much connection between mainstream new age thought and the tradition of Christian thought.
> (Personal correspondence, 10 February 1998)

Other authors on the list include Ken Carey, Matthew Fox, Bede Griffiths, William Johnston, Adrian Smith, Keith Ward, Fritjof Capra, Diarmuid Ó'Murchú, Peter Russell, David Spangler, Eileen Caddy, Peter Spink, George Trevelyan and Ken Wilber.

In the *Paper* (1999), CANA members list 41 alternative beliefs, printed opposite the conflicting traditional beliefs. A sample of these beliefs is listed in *Table IV.1* below:

Table IV.1 Some Expressions of Christian Belief

Familiar Traditional	Contemporary Alternatives
1. God has given us a full and final Revelation of Himself, to be guarded against	Humanity is still evolving so our understanding of God is always in the process of developing.

corruption.

12. God is the all-powerful, all-knowing Lord of all creation; the loving Father who sent his Son to reveal the mysteries of Divine Grace.	God is the Divine presence in, and creative energy of, this world whom we discover through our relationships with people, things, events and concepts.
19. Jesus equals God, a Divine Being who took on human nature.	Jesus, in his humanity, does not equal God, but is a human being who is transparent to the Divine. God was as fully present and active in Jesus as is possible in human form.
25. Redemption is an act of rescue by an external, Divine agent.	Redemption is the transformation process by which the life-giving Spirit within us moves us from human-centredness to Divine-centredness.
28. Sin is an offence against God.	Sin is a failure to grow in wholeness, within ourseveles, with others and in relation to the whole of creation. It is to ignore the Divine within us.
34. Christianity alone holds the true Revelation and key to Salvation. All other religions are false or inadequate.	Christianity is the religion in which the role of Christ is most clearly understood. Other religions have different perspectives on the One Truth. Each is a path to ultimate union with God for their followers.
41. Matters of the spirit are more sacred, of greater significance and value than matters of the flesh and the material, and must be given greater reverence, respect and care.	Spirit and matter are equally sacred. Therefore we must revere, respect and care not only for the spirit but also for the temple of the spirit – the human body, the body corporate, the Planet and its biosphere and the whole of material creation.

(CANA 1999:2-6)

There was some consternation in the conference[14] to discuss the draft of the *Paper for Dialogue*, that CANA should not be seeking to establish a new dogmatic credo – this was the kind of religiosity that CANA was seeking to supersede, it was suggested. However, the leaders of the group decided to go ahead and publish the *Paper*. This now provides us with an unparalleled exposition of typical Christaquarian beliefs – always with the caveat that individual Christaquarians may have somewhat different beliefs. I shall now present this theology in more detail, highlighting the contrasts with conventional Christian beliefs and producing evidence from my postal survey that CANA members actually hold these beliefs.

Underlying the theology is an acknowledgement that Truth is never final; Revelation is ongoing and developmental. 84% of CANA respondents did not think the Bible to be literally true. Furthermore, the sources of Truth are not limited to the Bible, but extended to outer reality and, importantly, inner experience. The Truth is thus not limited to any one religious tradition such as Christianity (88% of CANA respondents thought there are many paths to salvation), and indeed must be reinterpreted for each new generation. Literal belief in the Gospel record of Jesus, for example, is merely one interpretation of his life provided by his contemporaries. Each resulting reinterpretation of Truth provides a framework of faith by which we should lead our lives.

There are thus many ways also of understanding God, which need not be limited to the model of the Holy Trinity. The Holy Spirit is not limited to the Church, but "inspires all people of good will in different ways" (CANA 1999:2). Paul Tillich's phrase, God as the 'Ground of Being', is adopted in the *Paper*. God did not create the world at some distant time, but is continually holding all things in existence as the creative energy of this world. We must understand God in the context of this ongoing story of Creation, CANA says.

Similarly, there are many ways of understanding Jesus. Four in five CANA respondents proclaimed Jesus as their only Lord and Saviour. Nearly three quarters thought Jesus was inspired with the Christ spirit that also inspired Buddha. 57% thought Christ is unique, 62% that Christ was both God and man at the same time. 58% disagreed that Jesus was simply a very spiritual man, nothing more. The CANA *Paper* says that through Jesus, we may begin to know something of the mystery of God – Jesus is the "icon" of God who encouraged us to live by the higher values of the Kingdom of God. Humanity is called to "At-one-ment" with the divine nature through these higher values. Jesus was conceived and born naturally, and the emphasis should be on his humanity rather than his divinity – he is a human being transparent to the divine, and we do not worship Jesus himself but rather, God through Jesus. Jesus was not omniscient and omnipotent, but limited by his humanity. He acted as a human being, although his supernatural powers came from his awareness of his unity with God.

This manifestation of God in Jesus is the most appropriate Way for Christians, but followers of other faiths need not follow the same path, CANA argues. At-one-ment with the Divine is the goal of human evolution – this is at conflict with conventional accounts of atonement for sin, ransom or reparation. Redemption is to be understand as part of this process of moving towards the divine. The resurrection of Jesus was the Gospel writers' way of showing that the spirit of Jesus remains among us – he did not physically come back to life after he had died on the cross. 43% of CANA respondents strongly believed in the resurrection of the dead, and 53% believed the resurrection of Christ to be a real, historical fact.

Creation is essentially good and the story of the fall is a representation of humanity's evolution in consciousness of the self. 92% of CANA respondents strongly believed that the Earth is one interconnected whole. According to the *Paper*, sin is ignorance of the divine within, not an offence against God, and obedience to the Ten Commandments will not lead to everlasting life. Rather, living a loving life will lead to our own and others' fulfilment. Humans are not the Lords of Creation, but merely the most evolved species yet to appear – for evolution continues, says CANA.

The Church should be an example of life lived by the values of the Kingdom of God, suggests the *Paper*. It should not be hierarchical organization, but a community of fraternal relationships. 81% of CANA respondents thought the Church is too hierarchical. Christians alone will not bring about the Kingdom of God, but together with all who act unselfishly for others. Christianity is not the one key to salvation, but simply the religion which uses the perspective of Christ. After death, we continue on a journey of union with God. Only 24% of CANA respondents rejected belief in reincarnation, and of those that explicitly accepted it, half also believed in the resurrection of the dead. In this life, it is loving service for others that leads to union with God. Jesus showed this way, and Christians should follow his example, says the *Paper*.

Nearly two in three CANA respondents claim to have adopted New Age beliefs for three years or longer, half of these for over ten years. Over nine in ten could give an explicit definition of New Age. The most common examples given of New Age were Findhorn and healing, in broad agreement with examples given by the other Christaquarian and evangelical groups surveyed. CANA respondents participated more than either the *Omega News* respondents or St James's respondents in Rose's (1996) list of New Age practices. With an average of 39% of respondents participating in each 'New Age' practice listed, CANA respondents are not far behind Rose's *Kindred Spirit* respondents level of 47%. Furthermore, 42% of CANA respondents have participated in more than 15 of the 'New Age' practices, nearly double the level of *Omega News* and St James's respondents.

Interpretation: Cognitive Dissonance

It will be seen that many of these beliefs and practices directly confront conventional Christian understandings. Leon Festinger et al (1956; cf Festinger 1962/1957) famously studied an example of 'cognitive dissonance', or conflicting beliefs, in their study of a millenarian flying-saucer group whose prophecies were not realized on the predicted date. The group was said to have responded to the uncomfortable mental situation by preaching their doctrine more forcefully. As a general principle, Festinger stated that,

> The larger the number of people that one knows already agree with a given opinion which he holds, the less will be the magnitude of dissonance introduced by some other person's expression of disagreement.

(Festinger 1962/1957:179)

However, Hardyck and Braden (1962) were unable to replicate Festinger's results with a millenarian group which expected a nuclear holocaust, and there remains some doubt over the concept of cognitive dissonance. It is probably safer to retain unspecific notions of conflicting beliefs, as in English (1985), rather than to delineate a specific theory of cognitive dissonance. Nevertheless, the suggestion remains that these conflicting beliefs may cause CANA members to proselytize their worldview more forcefully than if they held conventional beliefs.

Festinger et al defined 'dissonance' as follows:

> Two opinions, or beliefs, or items of knowledge are *dissonant* with each other if they do not fit together – that is, if they are inconsistent, or if, considering only the particular two items, one does not follow from the other.
> (Festinger et al 1956:25, *original emphasis*)

On this definition of dissonance, New Age beliefs such as those held by CANA members are clearly dissonant with conventional Christian beliefs, and we may expect such Christaquarians to exhibit cognitive dissonance should they retain their commitment to Christianity (as they do by my understanding of Christaquarianism). Festinger and his co-authors went on to outline

> ... the conditions under which we would expect to observe increased fervor following the disconfirmation of a belief. There are five such conditions.
> 1. A belief must be held with deep conviction and it must have some relevance to action, that is, to what the believer does or how he behaves.
> 2. The person holding the belief must have committed himself to it; that is, for the sake of his belief, he must have taken some important action that is difficult to undo. In general, the more important such actions are, and the more difficult they are to undo, the greater is the individual's commitment to the belief.
> 3. The belief must be sufficiently specific and sufficiently concerned with the real world so that events may unequivocally refute the belief.
> 4. Such undeniable disconfirmatory evidence must occur and must be recognized by the individual holding the belief. ...
> 5. The individual believer must have social support. It is unlikely that one isolated believer could withstand the kind of disconfirming evidence we have specified.
> (Festinger et al 1956:3-4)

Christaquarians do not exhibit all of these tendencies: (1) although they hold deep convictions, these do not usually have some relevance to action; (2) although the Christaquarian has often committed him or herself to a Christaquarian group, this action is not difficult to undo; (3) the beliefs are not usually specific and concerned with the real world; (4) and are therefore not subject to undeniable disconfirmation in this way; (5) but nevertheless, the believer sometimes has social support amongst other Christaquarians. On balance, Festinger's theory is not directly applicable to Christaquarianism.

However, the definition given of dissonance remains useful in discussion of Christaquarian beliefs, which are clearly dissonant with commitment to conventional Christian beliefs. Disconfirmation of Christaquarian beliefs occurs with every recital of the Nicene creed and in conversation with other, more conventional, Christians. Over three quarters of CANA respondents denied that they believe in the literal truth of the Apostle's creed. The individual Christaquarian is, within the groups studied, supported by social networks which may bolster attempts to withstand this kind of disconfirming evidence.

The cognitive dissonance involved in accepting typical Christaquarian beliefs while remaining a Christian may seem great, but is similar in degree to the dissonance involved in accepting a liberal version of the faith while remaining a Christian. For example, traditional Christian creeds demand belief in the virgin birth of Christ; liberal theologians deny this but do not thereby deny their Christian faith. Similarly, Revd Don Cupitt may at times approach a Buddhist version of Christianity without belief in an objective God – how is this reconciled with Christian faith? Yet thousands of Christians (including some respondents to my surveys) read Revd Cupitt's many books as part of their spiritual diet. To take another instance, the miracles reported in the Gospels were, until the nineteenth century, taken at face value as part of Christian faith; how was the scientific approach to textual criticism reconciled with faith in miracles? These are just three examples, but sufficient to show that the liberal assault on conventional Christian beliefs is equal to, if not more revolutionary than, Christaquarian challenges to orthodox Christianity.

An alternative resolution of cognitive dissonance among Christaquarians has been put forward. Professor Peter Byrne[15] has suggested that Christaquarians perform a convoluted form of mental compartmenalization in retaining their Christian affiliation while believing in such things New Age as reincarnation. But this is not appropriate. Christaquarians usually integrate their New Age beliefs in full with their Christian confession. I shall demonstrate this by considering *Christianity and Reincarnation* (Frieling 1977/1974), a book by a leader of the Anthroposophical Christian Community Church, Rudolf Frieling[16].

Frieling does not compartmentalize his Christianity from his belief in reincarnation. Instead, reincarnation is modified from Western traditions of rebirth, and from Buddhist notions, to fit in with Christian teachings of life after death. Thus Christ is excluded from reincarnation, as he is said in the Gospels to have ascended to heaven soon after death. Other humans, though, will have their souls reincarnated after a period in the spirit world in which they face judgement of God and angels. At the end of time, there will be a final Last Judgement in accordance with Christian tradition. In this way, reincarnation is fully integrated into Christian teachings, and Frieling is able to cite scripture to support his views.

Becoming a Christaquarian

Given this initial mental conflict of belief, how does one become a New Age Christian? Although my fieldwork did not concentrate on the process of becoming a Christaquarian (mainly because I did not study the field for a long enough period to follow 'conversion' through to full 'membership') I did make some *ad hoc* observations which I shall now briefly discuss.

There are few if any Christaquarian evangelists out preaching to shoppers in the street, and many Christaquarians, especially 'lone' New Age Christians in more orthodox congregations, keep their Aquarian preferences to themselves in order to avoid criticism from fellow Christians. Furthermore, it is questionable whether we can speak of 'conversion', which is such a one-off event, in relation to New Age and Neopagan religion. Tanya Luhrmann[17] has introduced the notion of "interpretive drift" which is more processual:

> the slow, often unacknowledged shift in someone's manner of interpreting events as they become involved with a particular activity.
> (Luhrmann 1994/1989:12; cf ibid:312,322)

New Agers often speak of 'coming home' to an understanding of religion, which they have always felt subconsciously. Matthew Fox reports that

> many persons, on hearing me lecture on creation spirituality over the years, have said to me, "Now you have articulated what I live and have experienced."
> (Fox 1983:22)

Nevertheless, Eugene Gallagher asks if Neopaganism is "A Religion without Converts?" (1994) as Margot Adler (a Neopagan author) claims (1986), and concludes that it is meaningful to talk of conversion in this context, its denial being a function of apologetics.

Starhawk, a witch who teaches at Matthew Fox's educational institute, described in a public lecture at St James's this process of interpretive drift, in which she moves from a psychological understanding of magic to a realist belief in it:

> ... over all these years of practising ritual and magic, ... I have actually come to believe it [laughter]. When I started I was really a rationalist, and it was all very wonderful but it was all very psychological, and I could have a lot of good explanations of the Goddess as, you know, this archetype or that energy. I think in some ways I was a more effective speaker at that point because I could talk to people rationally about it, it would make sense and it would be not threatening. But over the years I have really come to, not so much believe, but my experience has been that if you work with the Goddess in a particular aspect something happens.
> (Starhawk: Alternatives, 30 April 1996)

In this way, the scientistic presentation of New Age can facilitate its reception in the modern world. From here it is a short step to using the suggestive techniques exemplified in *A Course in Miracles* and the slogan "You create your own reality." The final step in the adoption of a New Age worldview is a realist understanding of the efficacy of magical invocations or shamanistic journeys.

Some Christaquarians do actively proselytize, and there is a definite trend among New Age Christians for conversion – or interpretive drift – from a prior Christian orthodoxy to a later Aquarian bias. Few Christaquarians are either born into their faith or are straight converts from secularism or non-Christian faiths – most have converted from some form of Christianity, usually Church of England or Roman Catholicism. Perhaps this is because for the age category of which we are speaking – ie 47%, 76%, 77% and 78% over the age of 55 in the four groups studied – Christianity was the dominant cultural influence during formative years.

Fr Adrian Smith's "More-to-Life Partnership" has inserted leaflets into Bridge Trust newsletters, the Course in Miracles' UK newsletter and brochures of the Cygnus Book Club which is run by members of Lectorium Rosicrucianum. One half of the proceeds from his courses are run back into advertisement; with such a high cost, there is little if any profit left for him and his partner, indicating the importance they attach to such proselytization[18]. The Omega Order also advertises its retreats, not just in its own newsletter, *Omega News*, which is mailed to over 300 recipients, but also in local event magazines and in publications such as the *Church Times, Vision* and *The Tablet*. Alternatives lecture programme at St James's Piccadilly has the most dynamic advertisement programme, distributing its schedule of lectures at major New Age festivals such as Mind-Body-Spirit and having a quarterly colour mailshot to previous enquirers which is now also available via e-mail. Advertisements for CANA have to date only been for events such as conferences; there have been no membership drives.

While direct advertisement may be the most noticeable pathway to conversion, it is not necessarily the most effective. My statistics show that over one third of first contacts with Christaquarianism are through people known to the convert. Often, the first contact with Christaquarian groups is a chance meeting – say at a conventional Christian retreat – with other New Age Christians. Occasionally, these contacts are contrived – such as the member of CANA whom I first saw at St James's Piccadilly, who was actively trying to "convert" a certain vicar in her home town.

A number of visitors to The Omega Order first came across Canon Peter Spink through a chance encounter with one of his books. Christaquarians are highly literate, and can often name a dozen spiritual writers or more who have had an important influence on their lives.

Table IV.2 'Conversion' to Christaquarianism

First contact with group %	Omega Order	St James's	CANA
Friend	36	45	25
Bridge Trust	0	0	32
Other church ministry	0	10	0
Seminar	4	2	15
Met leader	14	0	13
Advert	15	0	4
Passing by	0	16	0
Book	11	0	0
Lived nearby	2	4	0
Media	0	4	0
Other	7	4	6
No answer	11	18	6

These figures show that existing social networks are the most important means of recruitment to Christaquarianism. Not only must we consider contact through friends, which accounts for between 25% and 45% of first contacts. Also to be taken into account is recruitment through social networks such as other organisations (eg Bridge Trust) and events (eg seminars) or meeting the leader of a movement, usually in a public place. Direct advertisements, whether in magazines or books (accounting for 26% of *Omega News* first contacts) or in the form of adverts in the street outside the church (accounting for 16% of first visits to St James's church), are of relatively lesser importance. Indeed, only 4% of CANA members are recruited through such advertisement.

We can immediately relate this to the conclusions of Matthew Wood's thesis on spiritual possession in the New Age. Wood suggests (1999a, 1999b) that New Age networks develop through existing kinship ties and therefore do not merit being called a 'movement'. My research confirms that a large percentage of Christaquarians first came into contact with the movement through somebody with whom they were already acquainted. Similar results have been obtained by Keishin Inaba (1999) in his research on the Jesus Fellowship and the Friends of the Western Buddhist Order. Earlier studies, such as that by Diani (1995) and Snow et al (1980) have found that people recruited to various movements through pre-existing social networks regularly exceeded three quarters of members. Unfortunately, Wood's research is limited to an ethnography and does not attempt to evaluate the percentage of New Agers recruited through kinship lines. He may be over-interpreting this general trend of recruitment in NRMs, and we may safely retain the definition of New Age as a movement on these criteria.

Frederick Lynch (1977) has proposed a theory of conversion and commitment to the occult which summarizes some of the factors involved (see *Figure IV.1*). His model divides conversion and commitment into four phases, as shown below, starting with intellectual curiosity and/or reading in the occult, followed by emotional conviction promoted by a personal psychical or mystical experience. Tension and stress can contribute at this stage. The crucial phase III is when the convert meets a charismatic occultist and/or attends an occult group with friends or relatives. Social support in the occult community, collective rituals and a sense of individual growth and development keep up commitment to the occult.

The early, largely unsuccessful campaigns of conversion of the Unification Church in America (Lofland & Stark 1965; Lofland 1977) centred on casual "pickups" in public places and bombarded them with the doctrine of the movement. From about 1972, however, new, more successful methods were employed. Conversion was begun at the emotional rather than the cognitive level, for example through inviting potential convertees to dinner. It continued in an 'encapsulated', controlled setting such as a farm, where affective bonds could be developed without interference from outsiders. The core of the process was to create the perception of being loved. Finally, once a significant social relationship had been established, a commitment was asked for.

Figure IV.1 Conversion to the Occult

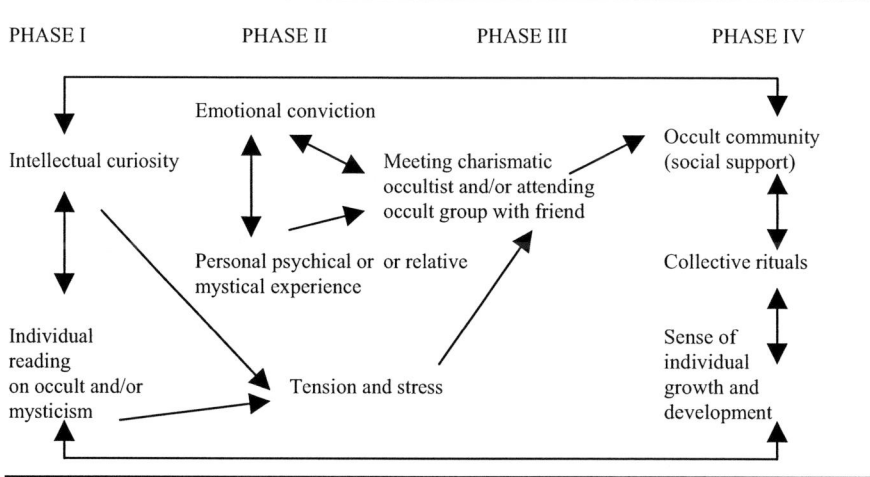

(Lynch 1977:895)

While Lofland's analysis may prove useful to an understanding of some of the more structured and institutionalised NRMs, it is less applicable to the New Age movement and Christaquarianism. After all, there is no structural authority to demand the all-important final step: commitment to the movement. However, some of the factors may be at work in the process of becoming a Christaquarian. For example, the importance of a network of religious retreat centres, and the development of affective ties between participants at Christaquarian events.

Lofland and Stark, in a well-known article entitled "Becoming a World-Saver: A Theory of Conversion to a Deviant Perspective" (1965), enumerated seven conditions for conversion derived from study of one millenarian group:

> For conversion a person must:
> 1. Experience enduring, acutely felt tensions
> 2. Within a religious problem-solving perspective,
> 3. Which leads him to define himself as a religious seeker;
> 4. Encountering the D.P. ["Divine Precepts", in the particular group they studied] at a turning point in his life,
> 5. Wherein an affective bond is formed (or pre-exists) with one or more converts;
> 6. Where extra-cult attachments are absent or neutralized;
> 7. And, where, if he is to become a deployable agent, he is exposed to intensive interaction.
>
> (Lofland & Stark 1965:874)

Later work by Lofland and Skonovd (1981) identified six further "Conversion Motifs": intellectual, mystical, experimental, affectional, revivalist and coercive. Of these, the experimental motif is explicitly related, even at this early date, to New Age (Lofland & Skonovd 1981:378). However, my statistics show that New Age Christians also have significant levels of intellectual and affectional conversions. For example, 11% of the Omega Order respondents first heard of the Order through a book (intellectual motif), while 45% of St James's respondents first heard of it through a friend (affectional motif).

Not all Christaquarians remain Christaquarians: there are apostate Christaquarians. The silent majority of such apostates are very difficult to locate, as they disappear from mailing lists and do not turn up to festivals and seminars. However, there is a strong body of apostate Christaquarians who are not silent, within the New Age 'counter-cult' movement and within evangelical congregations. Roy Livesey, whose campaign against the New World Order of the New Age movement is examined in a later chapter, is such an ex-New Ager; Elliott Miller (1989) and Vishal Mangalwadi (1992) are others.

Conclusion

Although Bridge Trust has been in existence for over 25 years, and CANA for a decade, the movement is still in developmental infancy when compared to other movements. Membership of CANA is increasing at geometric rates, from 46 members in March 1997 to over 100 in March 1999 and 122 in March 2000. Nevertheless, it has not institutionalized to a great extent, apart from a well-maintained mailing list and occasional meetings of members. Indeed, early attempts at institutionalization in Clift Farm and Seniors failed through interpersonal conflict and lack of resources, and Janice Dolley claims that, "It has never been our intention to create a cult or sect"[19]. There is a core of leadership material, but the leadership does not exercise a charismatic or totalitarian control of the membership. Again this hampers consolidation of the movement into a cult or sect.

However, with the production of the *Paper for Dialogue* (1999), came the possibility for further consolidation. Geoffrey Nelson (1969) has argued that cults based on the affiliation of individuals with similar interests may develop in association with other cults with similar interests. This is exactly what the *Paper* envisages. Although copyrighted, CANA is allowing copies of the *Paper* to be made "for purposes of furthering discussion". A Round Table of like-minded organisations[20] was held on 13 November 1999, with the hope that in the longer term, a "collaborative, informal Steering Group will be established, involving CANA, other interested groups and representatives from the mainstream Churches" (CANA 1999:34). A web-site was proposed[21], together with a further conference in Autumn 2001 or Spring 2002.

Notes to Chapter IV

[1] CANA membership directory, March 2000. Membership in 2002 exceeded 150.

[2] The associated charitable arm, Bridge Environmental and Educational Trust, does not have members.

[3] Janice Dolley, personal communication, 17 May 1999.

[4] Now Kate Porteus and leader of Quiraing Lodge retreat centre, Isle of Skye.

[5] The Grail Retreat Centre closed in 2001.

[6] Revd Tingay has subsequently become a member of CANA.

[7] In 2002, Tingay was Rector of Camerton.

[8] The Wrekin Trust closed in November 1991, and re-constituted in 1997 after Trevelyan's death. The first Sir George Trevelyan Memorial Lecture was given in October 1998.

[9] Dolley was Anglican, while Burton was Catholic.

[10] Now available at www.Christaquarian.net.

[11] These retreats ended in 2002.

[12] Now published as Smith (2002).

[13] By the end of 1999, this bookshop had closed down.

[14] 28 November 1998. I was unable attend this conference through illness and my observations come from a telephone conversation with Gillian Paschkes-Bell shortly after the event.

[15] Tutorial, 26 April 1999.

[16] cf MacGregor (1982).

[17] It is interesting to note that Luhrmann has herself since experienced a conversion to Anglicanism.

[18] Fr Smith comments, "I really take exception to your using the word *proselytization* in connection with the More-to-Life retreats. That is exactly what they are not. They are completely non-directive. We provide a service, a space, for people to work out their own journey. If we were suspected of proposing any one particular line they would not have continued to attract so many people. This is precisely why they are unique" (Personal communication 1 December 1999). I would question the possibility of non-directive retreats but as the More-to-Life retreat I was booked to attend was cancelled through lack of interest, I cannot comment from experience.

[19] Janice Dolley, personal communication, 6 January 2000.

[20] The following organisations were represented: Alister Hardy Society, Association of Christian Communities and Networks, Association of Creation Spirituality, Bede Griffiths Sangha, British Teilhard Assocation, CANA, Catholics for a Changing Church, Christian Transcendental Meditation Group, Contact 2000, Cultural Country Retreats, The Grail, Grail Retreat Centre, Living Spirituality Network, Modern Churchpeople's Union, Omega Trust, Sea of Faith Network, ONE for Christian Renewal and We Are Church. See www.Meta-Net.info.

[21] The idea for a web-site was abandoned by February 2000, and resurrected in 2002. See www.canaweb.info.

V. THE OMEGA ORDER[1]

Several miles into the Bristol countryside lies a large, eighteenth-century manor house, just outside the village of Winford. It had fallen into a bad state of disrepair by 1986, when an energetic group of Christaquarians moved in and began a total renovation, converting the coach house into bedrooms and adding over the course of the years several new residential wings and a purpose-built chapel. One of the outhouses has recently been converted into a conference centre, and there is a long-running project to build another centre with a small swimming pool to be used for hydrotherapy.

These New Age Christians are members of The Omega Order, a small residential religious community led by Canon Peter Spink. For the last few years, the community has fluctuated from about a dozen to twenty residents. Over 300 people currently receive its newsletter, *Omega News*, around 150 of whom help support the Order through additional donations, and many more New Age Christians have paid visits to the manor for a quiet, spiritual retreat or to attend one of the regular workshops.

The material in the first half of this chapter derives from four residential participant observation visits at the Order. A total of 14 days was spent as a visitor of the community on four separate occasions. During the second visit a semi-structured interview programme was conducted with most of the residents, and others were followed up on the later visits. The Order maintains a large collection of cassette recordings of talks it has held, and many of these were listened through during my stays, although there was not enough time to listen to all of them. The community has published a fairly large amount of the work of Canon Spink, and this is also analyzed below. A questionnaire survey was sent to all those who receive *Omega News* magazine, that is, friends and subscribers, a total of 322. 182 analyzable responses were received prior to the cut-off date for analysis, representing a healthy return of 57%.

The second half of this chapter presents one possible version of the intellectual history of New Age Christianity. As will be seen, The Omega Order uses a historical tradition of mystics, and some heretics, to legitimate their use of contemplative thought. According to June Anne English (1985), the presence of a legitimating tradition is an important part in the consolidation of a new movement. New social movement theorists speak of the importance of cultural framing in the formation of social movements.

History

Peter Spink (b ca 1925) was brought up in a nominally Anglican family and had an evangelical conversion experience at the age of 17 (Spink 1991a:93). He trained at an evangelical bible college from 1946-1949 before embarking on a mission to India, holding what he later described as "fundamentalist attitudes to the non-Christian world" (Spink 1983:37). A daughter, Kathryn, was born in

India in 1953, who today writes spiritual biographies. Ordained as an Anglican priest in the 1950s, Canon Spink spent part of his career as chaplain to the British Embassies in Bonn, Vienna, Prague and Budapest. Canon Spink has retained the title "Canon", granted for his services at Coventry Cathedral, despite his move in 1997 to the Roman Catholic Church.

The roots of Canon Spink's interests in decidedly unevangelical spirituality may be traced to 1972, when he was sent by his bishop to the island of Iona for a conference, organized by Sir George Trevelyan's recently-founded Wrekin Tust, on "Spiritual Awakening in our Day" (Spink 1991:1). One of the speakers, Ludi Howe, so impressed Spink that she led him through a kind of conversion experience (Interview, 2 October 1996). While on the staff at Coventry Cathedral, Canon Spink ran a spiritual centre called Hill House, and a meditation group which attracted the interest of the young James Fahey[2], a Roman Catholic who is still with him. In 1972 Canon Spink received an inheritance which allowed him to convert the cellars of Hill House to a crypt. In 1975 Sister Joyce[3] was 'borrowed' from the Community of St Laurence, Belper, and remained with Canon Spink until her death in 1997.

Invited to become Warden at the Burrswood Home of Healing near Tunbridge Wells, Kent, Canon Spink kept this post from 1977 to 1980. With some opposition from within the Home, he established a centre for the teaching of spirituality at a local near-derelict house, which came to be known as Kent House. From 1980 Kent House welcomed guests through advertisements in spiritual publications, and this remains one of the main means of proselytisation for Omega. The tradition of healing derived from Dorothy Kerin (1889-1963), the founder of Burrswood, remains important to Canon Spink, and is discussed in a later chapter. A number of the present residents in The Omega Order had come under the influence of Canon Spink by now. Around this time, a small retreat house was started at Brighton, but was soon sold.

The Omega Order was founded in 1980, and was to remain based at Kent House for six years. An early event in the history of Omega that broadened its appeal to the Antipodes was Canon Spink's speech at a "One Earth" festival in New Zealand in 1983. He returned to New Zealand with a group of Omega people in 1985. These links renewed in 1996 when Canon Spink spent several months of convalescence over there. The initial links had been made when a friend of the Order had sent a meditation tape to relatives in New Zealand. In 1997 a therapist known to the Order through these New Zealand links spent several months living and working at Winford.

Bridge Trust (see Chapter IV) approached The Omega Order in the early 1980s to ask if they could take on the management of a house in Semley which Bridge Trust could no longer afford to run. Sister Joyce took on the project, as she had with the house at Brighton. However, having restored the house, The Order recuperated its money from Bridge and concentrated their resources at Kent House.

Group Structure

Like other New Age Christian groups[4], about 70% of subscribers to *Omega News* are female. They tend, however, to be considerably older than the average New Ager, according to Rose's survey (1996) of *Kindred Spirit* readers where 76% of respondents were aged 54 or under: nearly 60% of *Omega News* respondents are over the age of 65. *Omega News* has recently carried obituaries for residents aged 95 and 91 (1995: vol 58; 1994: vol 52), and Sister Joyce died after my third visit to Winford. Of the 16 residents in October 1996, six were male. Three ordained men had left by 1999 and Canon Spink had become a lay Catholic. Although males were over-represented in positions of authority, many of the women lead the daily services and conduct some of the retreats held for the public.

There is a structural hierarchy in place at The Omega Order. Canon Spink, as the founder, is accorded most respect and heads his written communications "From the Prior", although this title is not generally used in the community. Since his conversion to Roman Catholicism, a Roman Catholic chaplain, Fr Richard McKay, has been appointed to the House. Revd Jim Hill, who has now left the Order, was also highly respected by residents for his wide knowledge on religious – and other – matters. James Fahey takes responsibility for much of the day-to-day affairs of the community, and also conducts retreats.

Below this tier of authority, are the "Companions" of the Order. These are full-time residents who have been accorded a special status. To qualify for Companionship, an applicant has usually been resident for at least a year. Then they must lead the worship for several services. Finally, they may be asked if they want to become a Companion. In October 1996 there were 9 Companions out of a total of 16 residents. The remainder have no special name and are referred to by the office secretary as "long-term residents" to distinguish them from occasional visitors.

The Order derives much of its income from paid contributions by the residents, although in some cases the community makes a net contribution to the needs of residents. A small amount is raised in donations from the circa 150 'friends' of Omega, which range from £10 to £1000. The remainder of the income is from residential retreats offered to the public. There are a large number of guest suites in the house for this purpose. The 1997 programme of retreats offered 21 events, 14 of which were to be conducted by Companions. These included Canon Spink's "Insight retreat" (which I attended), James Fahey's enneagram course and Revd Hill's look at mysticism in contemporary films, with similar events having been advertised for following years.

There is a routine of daily offices at the Community which are attended usually by from a third to half of the residents. Offices are currently held at 0800, 1200, 1800 and 1915 hs and are part of the daily routine along with the communal meals. The liturgy is printed for the congregation on cards, and is quite traditionally Anglo-Catholic, with some innovative meditative additions such as the "Omega Invocation":

> May the Light that shows the Way illuminate the mind,
> May the Love that knows the Truth unfold within the heart,
> May the Power that gives true Life arise within the soul,
> Let Light and Love and Power raise all in Christ to God.
> Amen.
> (*The Omega Offices* 1994:14)

Based on John 14:6, this replaced previous use by the Order of the invocation written by Alice Bailey and promoted by Lucis Trust. A bell is rung to indicate the beginning and end of silent meditations. Many chants are also used, including some from Taizé.

Liturgies used to be conducted in a small chapel in the original manor buildings, and until recently an early morning watch was conducted here, but was discontinued due to the ill health of a number of the Community. This chapel remains open for private use. Most liturgies and workshops are, however, now held in the Michael Chapel. This is a spacious, purpose-built carpeted hall with modern ash chairs around three sides and an oval ash altar at the far end together with a large free-standing candelabrum for seven candles. To either side of the altar are chairs for the presiding leader and, if in attendance, Canon Spink.

Recordings of popular classics are played at the start and end of services, and are used by most worshippers for meditation. Some adopt conventional meditative postures for this and at other times during the services: straight back, feet firmly on the floor, hands facing palm upwards on knees or gently crossed in the lap. Sunday services are usually attended by some members of the local village community, and include a circle dance to music. Communion, which cannot now be blessed by Canon Spink, is distributed in a circle around the altar table, and prefaced by words which the community recites by rote. Short readings are often included in the services, selected by the leader of the service and not always by Christian authors.

Statistical Surveys and Interviews

This section summarizes some of the results of the questionnaire survey and the structured interview programme with residents at the Order.

Over 95% of *Omega News* respondents had a Christian background, with nearly 80% retaining this affiliation today. By far the largest denomination represented is Anglicanism. This is reflected in the residents of the Community, where all professed Christianity at the time of the fieldwork and the majority had a mainstream Christian upbringing, the most common being Anglican. It would appear that Canon Spink had the least religious family background among the residents – a "non-churchgoing", "nominally Anglican family", although he was converted to evangelicalism in his 'teens and preached his first sermon at a Methodist church at the age of 18. Fahey has been a Roman Catholic since what he calls childhood "inculturation" in the Republic of Ireland, and became interested in the Interfaith movement while at school. Revd Hill came from an

Anglican family and "got involved with evangelical Christians" at 16, having a "charismatic experience" in the late 70s and still styling himself evangelical until the early 80s, when the 'narrowness' of the tradition stopped him mixing in evangelical circles.

The shift from these relatively conventional religious backgrounds displays no obvious pattern. Canon Spink had a second conversion experience following a discussion with a speaker at a conference in Iona in 1972. Fahey was ironically introduced to meditation when he opposed Canon Spink's meditation group at Coventry while a student nearby. Revd Hill's interest in wider cultural issues was the context in which he was encouraged by a friend to read books on mysticism. Two of the elderly female residents had less conventional religious backgrounds on the maternal side, Mollie Nettleton[5] with a Christian Scientist and Lillian with a "psychic" mother, who was not connected to any group. However, neither strongly connected their mother's interests with their own spirituality at Omega, Nettleton having become interested in light meditation and healing through friends (see Pixley 1978/1957), and Lillian having been involved with radionic healing, and the Churches' Fellowship for Psychic and Spiritual Studies.

It is interesting that nearly one in five *Omega News* respondents have dropped their affiliation with Christianity. The largest gainer in this switch has been the "no religion" category, although phrases such as "universalist" and "beyond religion" also crop up. Nearly 40% of respondents had adopted New Age ideas or practices for over 10 years. 55% had experienced some form of paranormal phenomena, usually specified as telepathy, visions, clairaudience, coincidences or ESP. 75% had practised five or more activities included in Rose's thesis as indicators of New Age practice. Each of the following practices had been practised by over 40% of those responding: acupuncture/shiatsu, creative visualization, flower remedies, healing workshops, herbalism, homoeopathy, massage, reflexology, recycling, T'ai Chi Ch'uan/Yoga and vegetarianism.

Over one third of *Omega News* subscribers first heard of the Order through a friend. The next most common way of introduction was from an advertisement, and the Order pursues a thorough advertising campaign in spiritual journals including *Science of Thought*, *Vision*, *The Church Times*, and *The Tablet*. Other common ways of introduction were through meeting Canon Spink at a seminar or reading one of his books. 38% of respondents have received *Omega News* for over 10 years.

Approach to the New Age

In the questionnaire survey, 88% of respondents gave a definition of New Age, the most common examples given being The Omega Order, healing and Findhorn. One of the most remarkable responses shared by most Omega residents in the interview programme was the inability to give concrete examples of New Age groups, authors or individuals; and even when examples were given, knowledge was often second-hand. Revd Hill, who was by far the interviewee at Omega most well informed about New Age, mentioned Findhorn, Dartington Hall, William Bloom, Douglas (sic) Spangler, and paganism; his knowledge is largely gleaned from long-term subscription to *Resurgence* magazine, and Michael Perry's *Gods Within* (1992). In 1997, Revd Hill was granted a six-month sabbatical to investigate the New Age and 'update' the knowledge of the Order in that area. Fahey mentioned Findhorn and the Alternative Technology Centre. Lillian could cite no particular groups, although she had met some New Agers who came to Omega, and listed some speakers at a Christian Spiritualist church she once attended – Arcane, Rosicrucian, Qabbalah. Nettleton: "If you said to me, Will you go out and find a New Age group, I don't know where I'd go quite."

Canon Spink spoke in abstract terms about a Christ Impulse underlying spiritual renewal in church and New Age:

> Well there are tremendous movements within the Church, the charismatic movement has loosened the structures a great deal, the contemplative movement is increasing within the Church. If that is New Age, then there is a correlation between the two. I see one movement of the Spirit manifesting in different ways, in the Church in one way and in what you call New Age circles in another. It's the same impulse.
> (Interview: 2 October 1996)

However, "this recognition of the Christ cannot be encapsulated within the ecclesiastical system".

Canon Spink had made an early criticism of the use of New Age techniques within the Church:

> Methods commonly employed in the Churches and those imported from the East by so many so-called 'new age' groups fail to fulfill this threefold requirement. They are either intellectually orientated, or their efforts through lack of knowledge, do no more than release the lower emotions.
> (Spink 1983:78)

At this time, Canon Spink saw New Age as "part of the growing one-world consciousness" (Spink 1983:81).

New Age is classed by Canon Spink as a psychic phenomenon, not on the higher level of the spiritual.

> A spontaneous change of consciousness may occur in a sensitive person when exposed to a situation where psychic energy is generated. An example of this is that which not infrequently takes place in revivalist-type gatherings, whether New Age or religious. A build-up of intense emotional energy through repetitive singing precipitates participants into a sudden and acute awareness of the astral world with all its pressures. This is often confused with spiritual experience.
> (Spink 1991:20)

Also of note here is the equation of New Age with "revivalist" – elsewhere "charismatic" – phenomena.

Revd Hill gave a more down-to-earth definition of New Age:
> Aspirations to see a non-rational element in humanity, a certain awareness of the divine in and about creation, an awareness of the mystery of things; interconnectedness of the universe. Usually New Age means an interest in ecology, and it seems to me that it is a product of the western world in the late 20th century, with the global village aspect of the western world, with ideas spreading all over the world from all over the world. Travel being so easy, people draw from all kinds of traditions. I think that has great dangers especially that it can be rather trivial, you draw a bit from Buddhism, a bit Hinduism, a bit from Christianity, a bit from Islam, so that you can be just really too eclectic. The result is triviality. That's one of the things that bothers me about New Age. I think it's best to stay with one tradition, and to be careful how the other traditions or ideas apply to it. That's why I see you staying within a tradition, either the one you've grown up in, or one that you feel happy with embracing.
> (Interview, 3 October 1996)

Fahey gave a picture of a sinister leaderless network which is at the moment a spiritual rather than religious movement. He implied that if it became more organized this would not only provide a centre for addressing questions and complaints, but could also 'get it back on track' spiritually. New Age is a search by people to make their life "meaningful", as the Church has not kept up with the religious questions people are asking. He expressed surprise at the type of 'New Age' retreat now conducted in some diocesan houses.

Lillian, like Canon Spink, thought the Universal Christ central to New Age, but further thought this was within the church, and saw Omega's mission as to renew the church by teaching the Universal Christ. On the other hand, she spoke of "weird" and "strange" things, such as devil worship, which she thinks are part of New Age. Nettleton also referred to Canon Spink for her definition of New Age, and actually showed me which chapters of his book answered the question. She had earlier described her pre-War light meditation group as "what we'd now call New Age", although the term was then unknown to her.

If New Age was to have institutionalized within the Church of England, it should have been at The Omega Order. It has not.

Since the middle of the last decade (1980s) there has been a significant development within the context of New Age spirituality. ... Many are now returning to their own spiritual and cultural roots, searching for ways in which they can relate to Christianity. Yet it would be a mistake to see them as looking for quick incorporation into exclusive ecclesiastical frameworks, or as ready to receive package deals of doctrine and dogma.
(Spink 1991:69)

Institutions for Spink preclude true knowledge. Salvation is Christ consciousness that can only be attained beyond barriers and outside structures. This is what Canon Spink calls the new ecumenism or unity.

... there is no salvation other than through Christ, for outside this level of consciousness and operation the laws of death and mortality hold sway. This reality operates far beyond all man-made barriers or articles of belief. Indeed, we see today a great paradox: Structures erected over the centuries to enshrine 'truths' which, understood from the perspective of a true Christ consciousness, cannot be contained within them.
(Spink 1983:16)

Barriers between the religions are ... artificial and ultimately of no significance. The people of the Way (i.e. the Christ centred) are seen to be confined within no one pattern of beliefs.
(Spink 1983:44)

For Canon Spink, Christ consciousness, inner knowledge – gnosis (Spink 1991a:37) – is the true experience that is salvation. Faith is the crystallization and preservation of this ineffable experience (Spink 1983:28). Canon Spink sees value in cultic faith in so far as it has preserved the possibility of the Christ consciousness.

Canon Spink (1993) contrasts cult (fixed religion) to dynamic (fluid religion), perhaps aware that other Christians may characterize The Omega Order as a cult – for he explicitly asserts Omega's complete orthodoxy. Canon Spink turns the debate around, using the word "cult" not in the normal sense of what he calls "the cults" (and he adds that there are many of these in the Church), but in its etymological sense as a system of worship. The New Age, he says, tries to reject the cultic Church completely, but for Canon Spink this is a vain hope: he believes it is not possible to escape cult (ie institutionalisation).

At times, Canon Spink's rhetoric almost goes so far as to disassociate Omega from Christianity.

We are working with Christian images, Christian archetypes, Christian myths and mirror images, because that's where we happen to be. ... today I had a long letter ... saying Omega is far too immersed in Christianity ... churchianity. ... This is where history has put us for good or ill. ... We start where we are.
(Talk at Co-Worders' Weekend, 17 February 1990)

Canon Spink goes on to say that "non-religious" (by which he probably means non-institutionalised) spirituality is "the ideal" but we are in a society and have to work within familiar forms.

The Omega Order affords many insights into the mechanisms of Christian-New Age relations. Nevertheless, there must be some qualifications in consideration of it as a purely New Age group. Omega residents have only minimal knowledge of the New Age and their understanding of it is largely theoretical; but nevertheless they are clear that they do not wish to be considered New Age.

Residents are almost totally unaware of specific contemporary New Age groups, unable to cite any except the most obvious examples such as Findhorn and "Douglas" (sic) Spangler and largely unaccustomed with major instances of New Age Christianity, for example as at St James's Piccadilly, although Matthew Fox has visited the Order[6]. Knowledge of contemporary New Age is largely derived from secondary sources. The programmes offered at Omega are more similar to those offered by diocesan retreat houses[7] than to those that used to be offered by, for example, Neal's Yard[8] or other centres offering more recognizably New Age workshops.

Omega's residents do not now accept New Age as a description of their Community, but see their work within a classic Christian tradition of contemplative meditation. While this orthodox mystical tradition is represented[9], I would suggest that Omega owes more to a larger, twentieth-century tradition of mysticism of which Theosophy, Alice Bailey and Rudolf Steiner are central exemplars. This tradition includes more that is akin with the British Christian healing movement as outlined by Claire Gartrell-Mills (1991), and with the Churches' Fellowship for Psychic and Spiritual Studies. This can be seen in a visit to the Omega library, apparently stocked mainly in the 1970s with noticeably fewer additions since. It is no doubt to be explained mainly by the advanced age of the residents, whose spirituality formed outside mainstream churches before typical New Age spirituality was formulated.

Yet, as recently as 1991 when he published *A Christian in the New Age*, Spink actively evangelized under the New Age banner, and acknowledges[10] that Omega used to consider itself New Age until the meaning of the term, in his opinion, changed. In a question that did not directly ask whether the respondent was New Age, 56% of respondents to the *Omega News* survey indicated that they had adopted New Age ideas or practices, while in answer to another question just one respondent explicitly identified their current religious affiliation as New Age. This is consistent with the general Omega view that the term has been bastardized in the popular media by association with "strange" things, from crystals to New Age travellers.

The disavowal of the New Age label was not only explicit (a response that could possibly have been provoked by a researcher such as myself) but also revealed implicitly in references to New Age visitors to the Community in "them" and "us" terms. Only one interviewee expressed serious concern about the Movement, depicting a powerful, leaderless network with no central authority to which questions may be addressed. But even this respondent shared the outlook with other residents that while they may not understand or accept New Age therapies themselves, all is well if the therapy works for the New Age recipient. This generous sentiment is typically accompanied by a comment that people who resort to New Age therapies must be desperate.

Several factors may have contributed to this change in self-definition, which may also be applicable more widely to other Christaquarians. The most simple explanation is that given by respondents, that New Age actually did change in meaning over the last decade. My impression is that in Britain the term "New Age" was indeed current in spiritualist, theosophical, healing and fringe-Christian circles for several decades before it received adverse media attention in the late 1980s and early 1990s[11] with the simultaneous influx of new, American-inspired additions to its repertoire (such as crystals, channelling and new therapies) and of originally-American bible-based opposition to these practices. This would be similar to Hanegraaff's distinction between a New Age *sensu stricto* and New Age *sensu lato* (Hanegraaff 1996:97). Many hitherto New Agers may also have shared Spangler's well-known expression (1984, 1987) of this disaffection with what he called attention-seeking, "glamour" New Age. These factors were probably compounded by the sympathy that many New Agers, Spangler included (see Spangler 1984:19-20), had with their evangelical Christian critics: hitherto New Agers did not want to be separated from the charismatic revival in spiritual gifts and healing; on a more practical level, neither did they want the bad publicity from people they considered potential allies.

Literature

Canon Spink's early works were privately published by Michael Link Press, Tunbridge Wells. These include *Religion in the New Age* (nda), *Christ in the New Age* (ndb) and *The Third Way, or The Christian in a New Age* (ndc). Later pamphlets, such as *The Sevenfold Call* (1988/nd), *A Time for Knowledge* (1984) and all of his tapes, are published by Omega Trust. Other works are published by Darton, Longman and Todd and, more recently, the New Age publisher Piatkus.

Canon Spink's first book-length works form a trilogy. *Spiritual Man in a New Age* (Spink 1980) interprets the contemporary spiritual search. *The Path of the Mystic* (Spink 1983a) outlines a practical way of relating to this search. (Both these books were published by Darton, Longman & Todd, as was Spink's introduction to and reader of Bede Griffiths, *The Universal Christ* (Griffiths 1990)). *The End of an Age* (Spink 1983b) (published by Omega Trust), the third in the trilogy, applies these thoughts to the question of the relation of Christianity to other religions.

Each chapter of *The Path of the Mystic* (Spink 1983a) ends with a meditational exercise. Spink emphasises that mysticism

> resonates completely with orthodoxy of belief, and experiences no difficulty with the definitions of Christian theology.
> (Spink 1983a:1)

Nevertheless,

> The purpose of ... [this] meditation is union with the Source – or God."
> (Spink 1983a:81)

Mysticism is specifically related to the New Age movement (eg Spink 1983a:78)

The End of an Age (Spink 1983b) defines salvation as "wholeness" (Spink 1983b:12). Evil is defined as the absence of good – to believe in evil as an essence is to create it (Spink 1983b:13). Evil cannot exist as an essence for the world is to be realized as a monistic unity. The physical world is but an illusion, seen as inter-related energies through the eye of the contemplative (Spink 1983b:53). Psychic investigation, a lesser skill than contemplation, can reveal energies as elemental forces of nature or 'devas' (Spink 1983b:55). These energies are ordered in a hierarchy from mineral through vegetable, animal, human to spiritual. Transformation through the raising of the level of energies is the same process as the attainment of Christ consciousness.

The final chapter asks how New Age philosophy relates to Christianity, and gives three possible answers. The first is the way of "complete departure" where "the new appears to supersede the old" (Spink 1983b:83). The second way, "contained contradiction" is a kind of "spiritual schizophrenia" where "There is no serious attempt to bring the two together" (Spink 1983b:85). "[T]hose who follow the Third Way are able to comprehend the uniqeness of the Christian revelation, not in terms of the old exclusiveness but with a new understanding" (Spink 1983b:86-87).

A Time for Knowledge (1984) answers forty commonly-asked questions about the spiritual journey. Each question ends with a "seed thought" for meditation, as in the Alice Bailey material. Spink defines the New Age as a period of change and transition beginning in the early 1950s.

> In religion there is now the great transition from devotionalism to interior awareness with the growth of intuitive knowledge of 'the God Within'.
> (Spink 1984:10)

He goes on to say,

Because the starting point of the search has had no credal form the [New Age] movement has from its early beginnings been generally suspect or rejected by institutional Christianity. There is now however a significant new development. For the change of consciousness is being felt by many within the churches. ...

... The rejection of Christianity is giving way to a growing appreciation of the essence behind its forms and the dynamic which gave birth to its credal definitions.

... Those who are thus drawn and who in this manner see and hear are truly 'New Age Christians'.

(Spink 1984:11)

In 1991, Canon Spink published under the title, *A Christian in the New Age*. New Age was broadly defined, said to have begun in the late 1950s with the secularization represented by John Robinson's *Honest to God* (1963), the disillusionment with science and technology, and the new "journey inward" and the turn to the East (Spink 1991:6). Anthroposophy, theosophy, the Arcane School, Teilhard de Chardin and FC Happold are important influences. Canon Spink highlights the importance of "Open Centres", especially Findhorn. The "validity of the New Age phenomenon", he says, must be tested according to the uses to which it is put (Spink 1991:13).

A Christian in the New Age (1991) still employs the motif of the New Age, which was then becoming associated with New Age travellers and what David Spangler called 'glamour' New Age. However, there is some evidence of a subtle distancing from the motif of the New Age. For example,

What is now apparent is that where experiential wisdom ceases to be the criterion of rebirth into the age of Aquarius, then a new dogmatism arises. The pattern of this dogmatism is not difficult to discover, and at the beginning of the 1990s it is fast assuming credal shapes.

(Spink 1991:72)

Canon Spink outlines this credal shape of Aquarius as belief in reincarnation, vegetarianism, astrology, communication with the dead, an apocalyptic note, and evolution (Spink 1991:72f). Three types of meditation are defined by Canon Spink, corresponding to use of the imagination, the intellect and the intuition: creative meditation, reflective meditation, and contemplative meditation (Spink 1991:36).

This emphasis on meditation prepares the way for Canon Spink's 1996 presentation of his thought, *Beyond Belief: How to develop mystical consciousness and discover the God within*. Here Spink's object is to take the reader "'beyond belief' into direct knowledge" (Spink 1996:5). Each chapter ends with a meditation exercise, and the process is said to awaken the heart [chakra] and lead to the way of the contemplative.

Legitimating Historical Tradition

Apart from those of Canon Spink, the spiritual teachings and disciplines that have had most influence on *Omega News* readers are Christianity (cited by almost half the respondents in my survey), The Omega Order itself, Buddhism, prayer, meditation, the mystics of the church and GI Gurdjieff. Spiritual writers that have had an important influence include the Bible, Alice Bailey, Paul Brunton, Fritjof Capra, Anthony de Mello, Matthew Fox, Bede Griffiths, Teilhard de Chardin, Joel Goldsmith, GI Gurdjieff, FC Happold, Martin Israel, John of the Cross, CG Jung, William Johnston, Krishnamurti, CS Lewis, John Main, Thomas Merton, Maurice Nicole, Henri Nouwen, PD Ouspensky, John Robinson, Sai Baba, Rudolf Steiner, George Trevelyan, Evelyn Underhill, Leslie Weatherhead, Ken Wilber and Laurens van der Post – who all received six or more citations by the 190 respondents. After Peter Spink, Bede Griffiths and Teilhard de Chardin were the most popular writers, with 32 and 27 citations respectively. To judge by this question, *Omega News* readers are far more widely read in spirituality than members of St James's church or CANA.

The second half of this chapter considers these and other possible historical influences on The Omega Order. It is suggested that this is a viable tradition which can be used by the Order and other New Age Christian groups in order to legitimate their own thinking. Histories of the New Age movement (eg Sutcliffe 1998a, Introvigne 1994) detail a wealth of influences upon the contemporary movement, but it would be an exaggeration to pretend that the multifarious trends of thought represented in such histories are perceptible in any one strand of today's New Age movement.

It must be clarified that the possible presence of a Christaquarian tradition does not give the groups I am studying objective legitimation. The concept of a legitimating tradition, as discussed by June Anne English (1985), does not claim that the presence of a historical tradition verifies that tradition philosophically as the Truth. Rather, it is used sociologically to understand the internal process of consolidation within the movement. Thus, my argument is that the possible presence of a longaeval Christaquarian tradition may be a decisive factor in the unification of diverse groups. I do not mean to consider whether this historical tradition is objectively valid.

It is not claimed here that the historical movements covered are part of an existing tradition, but rather that the potential of a legitimating historical tradition is available to Christaquarians. The tables below give a rough-and-ready indication of the extent to which Christaquarian and New Age authors legitimate their writings with reference to this historical tradition, and the extent to which well-read[12] respondents are influenced by this tradition. It is to be used as nothing more than a crude guide which suggests that there is a rudimentary legitimating historical tradition as outlined in the second half of this chapter.

Table V.1 Historical legitimators cited by contemporary Christaquarian and New Age authors

	Spink	Fox	Johnston	Smith	Ferguson	Conn & Stewart
Dionysius	✓		✓	✓	✓	
Hildegard of Bingen		✓	✓	✓		✓
Francis of Assissi	✓	✓	✓	✓	✓	✓
Eckhart	✓	✓		✓	✓	✓
Dante		✓		✓	✓	✓
Julian of Norwich	✓	✓	✓			✓
Teresa of Avila	✓	✓	✓	✓		
John of the Cross	✓	✓	✓	✓		
William Blake	✓				✓	
Teilhard de Chardin	✓				✓	
Carl Jung	✓	✓		✓	✓	✓
GI Gurdjieff	✓			✓	✓	

Table V.2 Number of respondents who cited historical legitimators as an important spiritual influence.

	Omega Order	CANA
Teilhard de Chardin	27	15
GI Gurdjieff	15	0
Carl Jung	14	12
Matthew Fox	10	9
William Johnston	9	6
John of the Cross	7	2
Other church mystics	7	13

One of the earliest groups to influence Christaquarians predates Christ. The Essenes were a Jewish religious group in existence from c167 BCE to c70 CE. In 1947 the so-called Dead Sea scrolls were discovered in a cave near the remains of a community at Qumran, and the popular conclusion was that these were the texts of the Essenes. However, although probable, this is not conclusive. Their beliefs were dualist, distinguishing between those under the New Covenant and the rest of the Jews; between the power of God or light and the power of Belial or darkness. There was a strong eschatological element to their thought, with belief in the imminence of the coming of two, three or four messiahs, of the final judgement and of a global conflagration. The community followed the law more strictly than the Pharisees, and was ascetic in character. (See Vermes 1981).

Reender Kranenborg (1998) has compared this historically verifiable information on the Qumran/Essene community with the presentation of the Essenes in Western Esotericism. He traces the influence of this presentation to Helena Blavatsky (1831-1879), founder of the Theosophical Society (see below), who wrote that Buddhist missionaries under emperor Asoka founded Egyptian hermetic fraternities, converted Pythagoras and that the Essenes taught Jesus. Blavatsky describes a strict monastic order where members are initiated after a trial period and live the life of a religious wanderer. Furthermore, Blavatsky claims that Jesus was part of a subgroup of the Essenes, the Nazarenes, but broke away from them to revert to the original Buddhist teachings.

Possibly interwoven[13] with the Essene movement are the Gnostics[14]. Gnosis was a term of Christian heresiologists popularised in the second century CE, used to refer to various institutionally unconnected groups of both Christian and non-Christian orientation. Gnostics' unifying characteristic was the importance of knowledge (*gnosis* in Greek) for salvation. This knowledge was an understanding of the real nature of the self, the divine spark that resides within us. It was a knowledge revealed by this spark itself, which among the spiritual elite (*pneumatics*) was predestined to return to its divine source; less fortunate, material (*choic* or *hylic*) souls were condemned to remain in the material cosmos. In between these two anthropological categories Gnostics posited the existence of a third group, the psychic, orthodox Christians. The material body and the world was an obstacle to the development of the spiritual: Gnostics were fundamental dualists.

The journey a soul had to take after death to rediscover its true divine self was arduous. In a fascinating spiritual experience, during its ascent the soul had to recite magical formulae, learnt while trapped in the cosmos, to the rulers or *archons* of each of the seven planets before returning to the original *pleroma* (fullness). This conforms to the ancient cosmology wherein the earth was at the centre, surrounded in concentric circles by the moon, the planets, the fixed stars and the heavens. The material world had originated in a divine catastrophe in the pleroma. The pleroma contained all attributes of the archetypal androgyne, and emanated these in a limited number (which varies in different texts) of aeons, pairs of mythological hypostases existing at increasing distance from the centre. In some gnostic systems, the last aeon, Sophia (wisdom), generates the Demiurge (creator). Christians and Jews (psychics) put their faith in the creator of the world, whereas Gnostics knew the original source.

Gnostic Christianity died out in the Roman Empire by the fifth century, through the efforts of the Christian heresiologists. Its spirit however remained and resurfaced periodically throughout history, for example in the Cathars and Bogomils. Just as some scholars question the validity of the idea of a New Age movement, so has the validity of the Gnostic category been questioned (Williams 1996).

Neoplatonism in the ancient world was a current of thought based on Platonic and pseudo-Platonic ideas. Ammonius Saccas (b 242 CE) is generally attributed as the founder of Neoplatonism. He is said by Eusebius to have been born in a Christian family. However, he left no writings and so it is from his pupils Plotinus and Origen[15] that we have knowledge of his teachings.

Plotinus[16] (205-270 CE) travelled with the Emperor Gordian to Mesopotamia in 242 CE, and oriental ideas are discernible in Plotinus' doctrine. Plotinus posits the existence of the One, the Absolute, the Infinite – God, the true source of reality who is above us. God may only appropriately be described as Good and One. Because there are two qualities, God does not remain one, for goodness tends to diffuse itself. Intellect (*nous*) emanates from the One, from Intellect emanates the World-soul, and from World-soul emanates the Forces, one of which is the human soul. These emanations are in a hierarchical order of degradations, the final of which is Matter, the antithesis of God and the source of all evil. Humans are partly spiritual and partly material, and have the goal of returning to God by purging matter from their being. This is achieved through a process of purification (*katharsis*) in which the soul retires itself from the material world. Contemplation of the Intellect within leads to contemplation of the Intellect and, through the free revelation of God, to contemplation of the One. This is ecstatic union, the destiny of the human soul.

Later Christian philosophers, like Nemesius (fl. 450 CE) and Synesius Bishop of Ptolemais, appropriated Neoplatonism for Christianity. Augustine details his period as a Neoplatonist in a famous passage of the *Confessions*, and does not entirely abandon the philosophy after his conversion to Christianity.

> No science can better convince us of the divinity of Jesus Christ than magic and the Kabbalah
> (Pico della Mirandola quoted in Scholem 1974:197)

Giovanni Pico della Mirandola (1463-94) presented this proposition among his famous 900 theses in Rome. He had started researching Qabbalah (there are various spellings of this word) in 1486, and around him and the Medicis in Florence grew a circle of Christians who thought the Qabbalah represented the restoration of the original revelation of God to humanity. The Qabbalah is often described as the Jewish system of mysticism, just as Sufism is the Islamic system, but it also contains theosophical and gnostic trends. The most common pattern for the qabbalistic *Sefirot* ('spheres') is known as the 'tree' and consists of a number of triangles with pathways between them. There are countless systems of symbolism with the tree, with each *Sefirah* having a complex of attributes including family relationships, the four elements, the four winds, the four metals, the sun and the moon. There were a number of important works by Christians explaining the Qabbalah and its relation to their faith[17].

While the Qabbalah is a Jewish influence on the New Age, the New Age movement is often also associated with a Celtic revival (eg Button & Bloom eds 1992), in both its Christian and non-Christian forms. CANA held a conference on reclaiming the Celtic tradition in 1997; Revd Gordon Strachan[18], a Church of Scotland minister, gave a paper at a conference on "Exploring our Celtic Spiritual Roots" organised by the Centre for Creation Spirituality in St James's church in 1991. Amy Simes, although concentrating on Wicca[19], has commented that "some Druid groups *are* Christian, rather than Pagan" (Simes 1995:216). However, as Ronald Hutton (1991) has shown, modern revivals of paganism are often based on dubious interpretations of historical evidence. This is certainly the case with the Celtic tradition, as most surviving sources are at the earliest medieval and often owe much to eighteenth century revivals as in the case of Iolo Morgannwg (Edward Williams). Despite this, Marion Bowman has pointed out that there are now many people who might be classified as 'Cardiac Celts' for whom spiritual nationality is a matter of elective affinity (Bowman 1993). *The Invention of Tradition* has been described in another context by Hobsbawm and Ranger eds (1983). These comments on the objectivity of the historical tradition of the Celts are applicable to the notion of a historical tradition of Christaquarianism as a whole. It does not matter that this tradition is constructed, so long as it is affirmed by those involved.

It is, nevertheless, possible to reconstruct some objective elements of pre- and post-Christian Celtic traditions. The druid's centre at Anglesey was sacked by the Romans in 64 CE, extinguishing any possibility of a historical continuation of their knowledge to modern-day revivals. Re-enactments by latter-day druids since at Stonehenge ignore the fact that the first henge was built there two millennia before the arrival of the Celtic peoples, although the site was undoubtedly adopted by them. The druids told of an Otherworld (rather than an Underworld), where life on earth is perfected to the utmost degree, while retaining all its worldly qualities. Modern traditions celebrate eight 'Celtic fire-festivals', although Hutton (1991) has again demonstrated that there is no surviving evidence that ancient Celts actually celebrated these festivals. They are calculated according to the summer and winter solstices, the spring and autumn equinoxes, and the mid-points between them: Oimelc on 31 January, Beltain on 30 April, Lughnasadh on 31 July and Samhain on 31 October. The Celtic New Year was celebrated on Samhain, now known as Hallowe'en. These festivals are today celebrated by most pagans, not just those deriving from Celtic traditions.

St Columba (b c521 CE) left Ireland in 563 CE to found the missionary monastery on the island of Iona. The contemporary Iona Community, based on the restored Iona Abbey, was founded in 1938 by Revd Dr George MacLeod. The Community has over 200 full members living all over the world, 1000 associates and 2000 friends. Members share a five-fold rule of prayer and Bible study, economic sharing, the planned use of time, meeting together and working for justice and peace. The Community is ecumenical from within the Church of Scotland. Christian New Agers, as well as others, often visit the island for retreats – as did CANA in 1997 and Bridge Trust in 1989.

The Rhineland is another area that experienced a flourishing of mystical activity influential to Christaquarianism. Hildegard of Bingen (1098-1179) was placed with an anchoress at the age of eight by her parents, members of the local nobility. She had her first visionary experience when she was five, and continued to experience them throughout her life, often accompanied with an illness which some have suggested was severe migraine attacks. They resulted in three visionary books: *Scivias* (Know the Ways) with illustrations of her visions, *Liber Vitae Meritorum* (Book of Life's Merits) and *Liber Divinorum Operum* (Book of Divine Works). She also wrote about natural history and medicine, and composed music and songs which have recently been reinterpreted and released as chart-topping CDs (eg *Vision: The Music of Hildegard of Bingen*, Angel Records 1995).

Meister Eckhart (c1260-c1327) had entered the Dominican order at Erfurt in his mid-'teens before holding various top-level positions within the order. In 1326 an inquisitional tribunal met at Cologne to examine Eckhart's works, attacking a large number of his propositions for being antinomian and pantheistic. The following year, Eckhart appealed to the pope who was then residing in Avignon. As a result, 28 propositions from the original lists were declared 'heretical as stated', but the pope did not condemn Eckhart himself as a heretic and Eckhart died before the proceedings were finalized. Robert Forman (1991) argues that Eckhart taught a developmental progression of transformative experiences. Attachment (*eigenschaft*) to worldly objects is the condition of the fallen state. Transformation can be achieved through letting go (*lâzen, Getâzen*) of these attachments, resulting in a condition of detachment (*Abegeschedenheit*), wherein one is not troubled by the affairs of the world. The rudimentary mystical experience, rapture (*gezucket*) Forman describes as "the dynamization of silence" (Forman 1991:95f). Eckhart deemphasizes visual and auditory mystical experiences. The intermediate mystical experience is described as the birth (*geburt*) of the Son (or Word) of God in the soul. This expression was one of those judged heretical, for Eckhart says there is no distinction between God and the soul if God is born in it. The final mystical stage, which is permanent and pervades all experiences, is called the breakthrough (*durchbruch*) of the soul to the Godhead. Throughout, Eckhart emphasises that mystical techniques should not be used, but the process is a passive one dependent on God.

Jacob Boehme's (1575-1624) first book, *Aurora* (1612), was not intended to be published, but when it was, Boehme was jailed and forbidden by the church authorities to write[20]. Boehme was influenced by the 'holistic' nature philosophy of Paracelsus (1493-1541), and other, mystical writings, alchemy, astrology and the Christian Qabbalah. He also had a number of spiritual experiences. He taught that God first created an eternal, supra-natural heaven or celestial earth, before creating this Earth. Human beings embrace both natures, heavenly and earthly. The first nature gives rise to the second nature which is initially in chaos, is ordered into the body of God and will eventually be destroyed, revealing the primordial nature in its glory. Boehme was not, however, a pantheist; he called the pure deity the *Ungrund*, the nothingness that sends forth Being to reveal itself. God is born in darkness, in hell even, and unveils himself to us in his works. This revelation is achieved in a seven-part cycle. God does not reveal himself, but has a perfect twin, Sophia (Wisdom) by whom God is known. Humans are born according to the third, earthly principle (the first two principles are light and darkness), and will be reborn in the celestial realm in a second birth equal to the resurrection of Christ. Boehme prophesied the dawning of a new age where the celestial nature would be realised on earth. In England his followers were Anglicans and did not consider themselves heretics, but called themselves 'behemists', gathering around John Pordage (1608-1681) and his Philadelphian Society. Arthur Versluis has documented a little-known *Christian Esoteric*

Tradition (1999) deriving from Boehme.

Emanuel Swedenborg[21] (1688-1772) was the son of a Lutheran bishop. He made his name as a mineralogist before he learned dissection, publishing his results in *The Economy of the Animal Kingdom* (1740). His famous work, *Arcana Caelestia* or *Heavenly Secrets* (1749) is a detailed analysis of the symbolic meaning of the first two books of the Bible. *Heaven and Hell* (1758) is an account of the spiritual realms Swedenborg directly experienced. *Apocalypse Revealed* (1766) is an analysis of the last book of the Bible. *The True Christian Religion* (1771) is a collection of his central theology published the year before he died in London. Swedenborg taught a theory of spiritual dispensations, of which there have been four with a fifth New Age of the New Jerusalem about to begin. Each age begins with divine revelation and ends in spiritual corruption. The Universal Human is the summation of all life, which has an underlying unity with hierarchical levels. The human spirit is part of the Universal Human and the soul is the form of the divine human or Son of God – Christ. Christ is not the second person of the Trinity, but the one God. Redemption is the overcoming of temptation from all the hells by the divine human.

The Swedenborg Society was instituted in 1810 and still publishes all Swedenborg's works. Membership is open to those of any religion, and the Society advertises in the Mind-Body-Spirit exhibition magazine. The New Jerusalem Church, or the New Church, holds the theological works of Swedenborg as divine revelation. In Britain there are two branches of the church, the General Conference of the New Church and the General Church of the New Jerusalem.

The problems of interpretation of Christaquarianism are provided a vignette in the example of William Blake (1757-1827). Like modern-day New Age Christianity, Blake's poetry betrays the influence of what scholars have called "the tradition" (Raine 1968) or "the hidden stream" (Hirst 1964) of Boehmenist, hermetic, Neoplatonist and Qabbalistic thought. Yet was he truly part of a living tradition, or did he simply stand at an obtuse angle to a Dissenting sectarian milieu in which he may have been brought up? Had he read Porphyry, Proclus, Boehme and Swedenborg or had he merely picked up their ideas second-hand in the discussions and journals of his period? EP Thompson argues (1993) that Blake's mother brought to him the influence of an antinomian sect, possibly the followers of Ludowick Muggleton. Certainly at one time Blake was a member of a Swedenborgian church. Muggletonians were unorthodox Christians in the Ranting, Quaker, Boehmenist milieu. Anti-clerical and anti-hierarchical, they met in public houses and sang hymns to the popular melodies of the day. Their doctrines included Satan as the God of Reason; the impregnation of Eve by the Serpent resulting in Cain and his evil, material offspring; Christ as the only God; and Mary giving Jesus his fallen, material body. Similar – though not identical – ideas may be found in Blake. Although now famous for his poetry, Blake was not so well-known in his life-time, and etched out an existence as an engraver.

Bochinger (1995:520-524) traces the origin of the term "New Age" directly to

Blake. This is theoretically possible, as Blake does use the term occasionally, although unlikely as New Agers place more emphasis on the astrological origins of the term in the Age of Aquarius. Additionally, the term is a natural phrase, occurring for example in the Bible. One of Blake's poems, "London" (1790-1792), betrays the fact that Blake was a Londoner. In fact, he was baptised in St James's church, Piccadilly and lived near Golden Square for much of his life. In recognition of this heritage, St James's church hosts a Blake Society; it is perhaps merely coincidence that Blake espoused the sort of unorthodox Christianity for which St James's now has a reputation.

The historical influences on Christians in the New Age movement which we have considered so far do not have much direct continuity with modern groups. It would be difficult to prove, for example, that there is a continuous tradition from the ancient Gnostics to modern-day Christian movements which claim a gnostic allegiance. The historical influence is by analogy and mimicry rather than causal. It is only in the nineteenth century that we can begin to discern groups which have a causal historical influence on present New Age Christians. The most important of these are the Theosophical Society and Christian Science.

The Theosophical Society[22] was founded in New York in 1875 by Helena Petrovna Blavatsky (1831-1891). Blavatsky produced under inspiration from the Mahatmas letters of instruction for her followers, and the monumental works *Isis Unveiled* (2 vols 1877) and *The Secret Doctrine* (2 vols 1897-1898). The Mahatmas are a spiritual group of adepts at whose head lies the ex-Venusian Lord of the World, who lives at Shamballa in the Gobi desert. His helpers include Buddha, Jesus, Confucius, Plato, Manu and Maitreya; the latter two have assistants known respectively as Master Morya or Master M, and Master Koot Hoomi or Master KH, both of whom often figure in Theosophical Society transmissions. Jesus is master of all religions, not just Christianity.

> Though it [Christianity] was certainly not excluded from the synthesis of the theosophical wisdom religion, there was a clear move against it apparent in the colonel's [Olcott's, the co-founder of Theosophy] drift towards Buddhism, HPB's [Blavatsky's] indifference to all religions except her own personality cult, and their joint cultivation of everything native [Indian].
> (Washington 1993:79)

The Society's motto is "There is no religion higher than Truth" and its aims are

1. the formation of a universal human brotherhood without distinction of race, creed, sex, caste or colour,
2. the encouragement of studies in comparative religion, philosophy and science, and
3. the investigation of unexplained laws of nature and the powers latent in man.

(Washington 1993:69)

Blavatsky had a number of influential followers. Evelyn Underhill (1875-1941) is the author of a large and influential volume on *Mysticism* (1993/1911), which is often to be found on the bookshelves of Christaquarians. She was a Theosophist before being led to Anglicanism by Friedrich von Hügel (Jones et al 1992/1986:18).

Anna Kingsford (1846-1888) was married to an Anglican clergyman but became a Roman Catholic in 1870 before founding the Hermetic Lodge of the Theosophical Society (later renamed the Hermetic Society) in 1884 with Edward Maitland (1824-1897), her close companion. With Maitland, an educated medium, she read the Bible allegorically as an account of the destiny of the soul. Christ's crucifixion was described as a spiritual experience for us all prior to regeneration; in Christ the soul of the regenerated person unites with the Divine Spirit. Jesus had merely incarnated the Christ spirit to a unique extent. They were introduced to Levi and Boehme by the Spiritualist Lady Caithness (1830-1895), a Christian who believed in reincarnation. Having produced a complete system of esoteric Christianity, Kingsford and Maitland then read Blavatsky's *Isis Unveiled* (1877). In 1881 they gave lectures on the "new gospel" which proclaimed reincarnation, published as *The Perfect Way; or, the Finding of Christ* (1882).

Annie Besant (1847-1933), also the wife of a clergyman, wrote *Esoteric Christianity* in 1901, championing the ideas of Maitland and Kingsford. Before she became President of the Theosophical Society in 1907, Besant was already well known as a campaigner for the National Secular Society, birth control and other atheistic causes, but had to recant on these issues when she became a Theosophist after meeting Blavatsky in 1889.

Revd Charles W Leadbeater (1854-1934) was a younger associate of Besant. In 1916 he was ordained (and assumed the title of Bishop) in the Liberal Catholic Church ("LCC"), a recently established offshoot of the Old Catholic Church which had been formed in 1870 in protest against the proclamation of papal infallibility. Leadbeater received a new hymnbook and liturgy under dictation from Master the Count. According to Leadbeater, he and Besant had had a child in 40,000 BC who was now reincarnated as the Indian boy, Jiddu Krishnamurti. In the present age, Besant mothered Krishnamurti as the World Teacher or Maitreya and future Mahatma, founding with George Arundale in 1911 the Order of the Rising Sun, later styled the Order of the Star in the East, for his followers. In the 1920s Leadbeater fell prey to a LCC sex scandal including claims of pederasty, and Krishnamurti rejected his proclaimed position as Maitreya, to the disappointment of his Theosophical followers.

Leadbeater's idea that Krishnamurti was a reincarnation of Christ had already caused Rudolf Steiner, leader of the German Theosophists, to break away from the Theosophical Society in 1909 and form in 1913 his Anthroposophy movement. Steiner believed in the uniqueness of Jesus Christ, but also believed Christ was a spirit who entered the human body of Jesus for the last three public years of his life. The descent of the Christ spirit became necessary because humankind had become overdependent on the material realm and had lost contact with the spiritual realm. To prevent the complete 'fall' of humankind into the material realm, the Christ incarnated into Jesus so that from there he could enter the etheric earth, and thus alter people's spiritual nature. The spiritual Christ transferred into the etheric earth at the crucifixion. Now the Christ seeks to 'mass incarnate' into all humankind, in the real 'Second Coming'.

The Christian Community is a Christian church with its roots in Anthroposophy, formed with Steiner's assistance but independent from his movement. Evelyn Capel is a retired priest of the Christian Community Temple Lodge of Hammersmith, London. Her 1989 publication, *An Introduction to Counselling from a Spiritual Perspective* is almost indistinguishable from the standard pastoral advice an Anglican vicar could give. While explicitly acknowledged (Capel 1989:24), her Steinerian background rarely surfaces. The current priest of the Community, Mrs Shepherd, corroborated this approach to me. Her Community is not especially concerned with psychotherapy, it just happens to be a personal interest of hers, as it was with her predecessor. Mrs Shepherd only mentions spiritual ideas if the clients ask, and then does not speak as a priest of the Community, but as an individual counsellor with spiritual beliefs. She considers her counselling technique to be "ordinary", her own "way" developed from her previous training with Befrienders International in South Africa (the name for The Samaritans[23] outside the UK).

Anthroposophical and Theosophical works are available in The Omega Order library, and they are often referred to in the taped lectures by Canon Spink and others. Alice Bailey's works, also available in the library, are even better known and more frequently cited. Alice Bailey (1880-1949), is credited by Dr William Bloom with inventing the modern meaning of the term "New Age"; we may agree that she did much to popularise it. In her autobiography (Bailey 1994/1951) she describes her transition from "a dyed-in-the-wool Fundamentalist" (Bailey 1994/1951:50) to a well-known occult teacher. Some beliefs were retained through the transition:

> I believed in the power of Christ to save then and I believe in it a thousandfold more today. ... I know that Christ lives and that we live in Him and I know that God is our Father and that, under God's great Plan, all souls eventually find their way back to Him.
> (Bailey 1994/1951:60-61)
> ... though I am recognised all over the world as a teacher of meditation I have at the same time never relinquished my habit of prayer.
> (Bailey 1994/1951:179)

She worked as an evangelist with the British army in India, moved from Britain to the United Sates and married Walter Evans, an Episcopalian rector in California, having three children which she later brought up by herself on a shoestring budget, working in a factory. After a period of questioning her Christianity, she came into contact with Theosophy through friends, and soon began to hold classes in Theosophy. In 1919 she met Foster Bailey, who that year became the National Secretary of the Theosophical Society and whom she later married. It was also this year that she first contacted the spiritual entity known as The Tibetan, or Djwhal Khul ("DK") from whom many of her 24 lengthy books are channelled. Bailey became disenchanted with the Theosophical Society around the time of the Krishnamurti episode, but did not yet resign. She started her Secret Doctrine class in 1921 among Theosophical people, and the popularity of this was the roots of the Arcane School, founded in 1923 and still active.

The Arcane School is non-sectarian, and runs a correspondence course for which there is a spiritual examination paper before entrance is granted. I have met one New Age Christian who has been refused entrance to the Arcane School, and was a member myself (for research purposes) for three years from 1993. The course consists of readings from Bailey's/DK's works with questions. There are "seed meditations" for personal work. Regular reports are sent to the headquarters and a secretary assigned to each student, often located in South Africa or some other distant place, who replies with comments on the work. Bailey also started various other groups, including the New Group of World Servers, which is those people who, whether conscious of it or not, are working to further the Plan for a new world of goodwill. World Goodwill is an organisation which has its headquarters in the United Nations plaza. Triangles is a worldwide network of meditation cells consisting of three people. These groups are all run by Lucis Trust, originally known as Lucifer Trust. The financial summary for 1997 showed income of £396,110, over a third of which was from legacies. Expenditure was £317,064, with over a third going on salaries and administrative services.

Bailey's "Great Invocation" (below) is well-known among New Agers and Christaquarians. It was used by The Omega Order during the course of their worship, until replaced by a specially-written invocation for Omega.

From the point of Light within the Mind of God
Let light stream forth into the minds of men.
Let Light descend on Earth.

From the point of Love within the Heart of God
Let love stream forth into the hearts of men.
May Christ return to Earth.

From the centre where the Will of God is known
Let purpose guide the little wills of men –
The purpose which the Masters know and serve.

From the centre which we call the race of men
Let the Plan of Love and Light work out.
And may it seal the door where evil dwells.

Let Light and Love and Power restore the Plan on Earth.

At around the same time as the burgeoning of The Theosophical Society, Christian Science emerged, also in the United States of America. At least one current residential member of The Omega Order has some prior connection with Christian Science. It might, however, be argued by practitioners of Christian Science that they should not be dealt with as part of the historical tradition, but in the contemporary scene. Certainly, Christian Scientists have held a stall at the

Mind-Body-Spirit festivals in Alexandra Palace, London recently. The idea of outreach at the festival came from Maria Gonzalez from the First Church, Bromley[24]. However, when I visited the Bromley church, it did not prove to be a hot-bed of New Age activity; in fact the impressive structure was almost empty for the main Sunday service[25], although the Wednesday evening testimonies were quite lively considering the age of participants. The Christian Science Committee on Publication for London answered my written enquiry about the New Age in the following way:

> Most of the current philosophies, therapies, and religious practices that are part of what we understand of the New Age movement do, it is true, have spirituality and healing at their heart. But these words can have different meanings. When Christian Scientists think of spirituality and healing, we mean *Christian* spirituality and *Christian* healing, as found in the New Testament.
>
> To answer your question on how our church relates to the New Age. It may be that Christian Scientists do not relate to the changing religious views and practices of New Age, etc.. It [sic] fact, it may be that our church has remained much less affected and influenced by these changing religious values and practices than others because of the stability of the Christian Science textbook, *Science and Health* ...
>
> (Pam Chance, personal communication 24 June 1996)

Mary Baker G Eddy (1821-1910), the founder of Christian Science, was brought up a strict Calvinist Congregationalist, and remained in this church for some time after discovering Christian Science, always considering her new sect a part of mainstream Christianity. Indeed, she exhorted Christian Scientists to retain belief in the historicity of the gospels (Gottschalk 1973:21). Eddy had visited the so-called "Dr" Phineas Parkhurst Quimby (1802-1866) in 1862 and received healing for her nervous condition. During Eddy's lifetime, and continuing afterwards, there was controversy as to how much Christian Science owes to Quimby, but there is no contention that Quimby did not first use the phrase, "Christian Science". Eddy argues that mental healing was entirely her own revelation, and that Quimby was a mesmerist healer who used direct physical contact with his clients in contrast to her own mental system. However for several years after Quimby's death, Eddy lectured on Quimby's system, used direct physical contact herself; and Quimby's supporters claimed that contact was not an essential aspect of his healing.

In some ways, Christian Science was seen as a return to primitive Christianity where healing was still practised. But more commonly, Christian Science was seen as a continuation and fulfillment of Christian revelation in the modern world. Eddy saw Jesus' promise of a "Comforter" (John 14:26) as a prophecy of her revelation of Christian Science (Eddy 1934/1875:55). Moreover:

> In her autobiography, she [Eddy] declared that "the second appearing of Jesus is, unquestionably, the spiritual advent of the advancing idea of God, as in Christian Science." On the first page of *Science and Health*, the publication of her "new thoughts" is placed parallel to the birth of

"the Bethlehem babe," illuminated by the "daystar of divine Science." Just as the "Virgin-mother conceived this idea of God, and gave to her ideal the name of Jesus," so the latter-day Mary has given birth to the first complete written statement of the divine knowledge of which Jesus was "the highest human corporeal concept" (*Science and Health*, 589). One of her students recalled Eddy's direct statement that "Christian Science is indeed 'the Christ, the Saviour of the world."

... The first issues of the *Journal of Christian Science*, published in 1883, also contained enthusiastic testimonials to Eddy's teachings as the fulfillment of biblical promises of salvation.

(Weddle 1991:281-282)

Weddle argues that Eddy did not see herself as the Messiah (Weddle 1991:286), although Stein (1982) presents the case that Eddy broke her autobiography into sections to parallel the gospel stories of Jesus' childhood. In 1894 a picture was authorised by Eddy (though later withdrawn) showing Jesus holding hands with a woman who looked like Eddy, holding a scroll inscribed, "Christian Science". Certainly many of her followers would have considered Eddy in such laudatory terms, and some considered her to have overcome mortality, but Eddy in 1897 wrote that

personal revelators will take their proper place in history, but will not be deified.

(*Miscellaneous Writings* 1897:308 quoted in Gottschalk 1973:174)

Eddy was not *the* Christ but considered herself the greatest woman to have lived because she had received the Christ essence, just as Jesus was the greatest man to have lived but was not *the* Christ. She signed her letters as "Mother Mary"[26].

There is much theology in Christian Science. Divine Mind is held to dwell in all of us, but to a greater degree in Jesus Christ and Mary Eddy. In reality, however, belief in a mortal world is what Eddy termed "error", for only Divine Mind really exists. This is the central revelation of Christian Science which constitutes its healing power – for if only Mind exists, sickness is an illusion. "Mortal mind" itself is merely an incorrect perception of reality. Once this faulty belief is overcome, as Jesus achieved in the resurrection, existence on the material plane will cease. At the same time, the existence of evil has logically to be denied, despite Eddy's paranoid fears of Malicious Animal Magnetism, an evil force perpetrated by her enemies. MAM, or hypnotism as it was also known, was simply the attraction to belief in the real existence of things other than the one Principle – and Eddy was sometimes so afflicted by its effects that Christian Scientists were called upon to cure them from her. Another consequence of such idealism is that of immortality – for if the soul is really God, it is infinite.

Most Christian Scientists came from Protestant backgrounds, causing some concern among the clergy, and many pamphlets were produced attacking Christian Science. One of these critics was Mark Twain. Christian anti-Eddy books included Methodist Revd James Buckley's *Faith Healing, Christian Science and Kindred Phenomena* (1892), William McCorkle's *Christian Science Examined* (1899) and HF Haldeman's *Christian Science in the Light of Holy Scripture* (1902). At one point, Eddy offered free classes in Christian Science to

the clergy so that their critiques could be well informed. As the movement
became more mainstream, the common request from converts to Christian Science
for letters of recommendation from their old churches was often granted. A
number of orthodox clergy left their churches for Christian Science – including
Revd Severin Simonson, a Methodist, and Revd Andrew Graham, an
Episcopalian. Liberal Protestants were generally more open to Christian Science,
and there even emerged a movement, the Emmanuel Movement from the
Emmanuel Episcopal Church, Boston in 1906 that practised psychological faith
healing.

Claire F Gartrell-Mills (1991) has written on the acceptance of Christian Science
in British society from c1895 to 1940, including some detail on its reception by
the Anglican church. The Roman Catholic clergy regarded Christian Science as ·
heresy (Gartrell-Mills 1991:177). Initially the Anglican response was also hostile.
However, Gartrell-Mills claims that the clientele of the new sect, namely middle
to upper class, was instrumental in the formation of healing movements within the
church, citing as an example the Guild of Health which was founded in 1904. It
was claimed in the British Medical Journal that the Church and Medical Union's
purpose was to "beat Christian Science on its own ground" (Gartrell-Mills
1991:152).

Revd Leslie Weatherhead's 1951 volume, *Psychology, Religion and Healing*, was
reasonably positive in its approach to Christian Science. The role of Christian
Science in the development of this more "holistic" approach is acknowledged to
have been paralleled with other influences, such as Freudian psychology.
Nevertheless,
> ... Christian Science appeared to move towards some reconciliation of
> the old faith and the new science in which many were inclined to repose
> their faith.
> (Gartrell-Mills 1991:21)

In this respect, Christian Science's bridging action between Christianity and
science is paralleled by New Age popularisation of the new physics. Gartrell-
Mills in her conclusion goes so far as to say that Christian Science is a precursor
of the human potential movement (1991:284), which is in itself a precursor or
constituent of the New Age movement, although she adds that Christian Science
stresses the spiritual more than human potential, and thus remains closer to
traditional Christianity.

Christian Science was paralleled in its emergence by the rise of the so-called New
Thought movement. This was a disparate collection of mental healers practising
in ways similar to Christian Science, but who either derived their teaching from
Quimby and other mesmerists, or were one of the many students who had broken
from Eddy. In 1914 the International New Thought Alliance (INTA) was created
in London, a very loose association of mental healers that today holds c350
institutions. At the Cincinnati Congress in 1919, the following paragraph was
added to the Declaration of Principles, showing the original Christian bias of the
Alliance:

We affirm the Christian standard in all things. The world has never yet had a real Christian movement. This gives us a good opportunity to have one now. We will build our house upon this rock and nothing can prevail against it. This is the vision and mission of the Alliance. (Bulletin of INTA No. 17 quoted in Braden 1966/1963:194)

But New Thoughters, if they may be so called, did not place as much emphasis on Christianity as Eddy showed – they considered Christianity as one valid religion among many. Nevertheless they still saw value in Christianity – Revd Warren Felt Evans (1817-1889), for example, a successor and former patient of Quimby, numbered *Esoteric Christianity and Mental Therapeutics* (1886) among his six publications on mental healing or phrenopathy. *Esoteric Christianity* identifies the core of Christianity with Hinduism, Buddhism, Platonic, Hermetic and Kabbalistic philosophy. Revd Evans was a Methodist minister until 1863, when he joined the Church of the New Jerusalem (Swedenborgian). *The Mental Cure* (1869) was the first book to be published on mental healing, and affirms, "in all men the Divinity becomes finitely human" (quoted in Braden 1966/1963:107). In *The Divine Law of Cure* (1881) he describes himself as a Christian pantheist (Braden 1966/1963:105).

Various new movements emerged under the New Thought umbrella. These included the Unity School of Christianity founded by Charles Fillmore (1854-1948) and his wife Myrtle, who had been taught by Emma Curtis Hopkins (1853-1925), a former student of Eddy's – one of the New Thought movements to retain claims to be Christian. There are now about 525 Unity churches. Charles began *Modern Thought* magazine in 1884, and in 1890 his wife began a new section called, "Society of Silent Help", later "Silent Unity", which promoted absent treatment through co-ordinated "silent soul communion" (Braden 1966/1963:235). In the sixties, Silent Unity received annually in excess of 600,000 requests for prayer, employing about 150 workers to respond to requests (Braden 1966/1963:237). All Unity services are offered free of charge. Unity maintains a conception of the unity of Truth revealed through Christ. Charles Fillmore is said by Braden (1966/1963:260) to have believed he was a reincarnation of St Paul, but belief in reincarnation is not a Unity doctrine.

Other New Thought groups include the United Church of Religious Science (c175 churches), Religious Science International (c100 churches) and the International Divine Science Association (c40 churches) (figures from Melton et al 1991:343). The cofounder of Divine Science, Revd Nona Brooks (1861-1945), was, like the Fillmores, first brought to New Thought when Emma Curtis Hopkins healed her serious throat infection. Her sister, Fannie James, was the other cofounder. The first Divine Science Sunday morning church service was held in 1899. Brooks' contemporary, Malinda Cramer, claimed to have come to the teachings of Divine Science through her own experience, publishing *Divine Science and Healing* (1904) after 17 years of teaching, although the text betrays some knowledge of Eddy's *Science and Health*. Divine Science claims to differ from other New Thought groups in its uniting of Jesus and the Christ. In 1957 Divine Science groups were brought together under the Divine Science Federation International.

One of the main doctrinal differences between Christian Science and New Thought was that New Thoughters did not consider the "flesh" – sickness, sin and death – to be evils, only educational means to greater understanding. Sickness was believed by New Thoughters not to be illusory, as in Christian Science, but as an actual condition that could be healed by the power of the mind. In the 1960s, New Thought circles were among the first to accept New Age ideas. By the 1980s, when New Age had grown in size, New Thought became more parasitic upon New Age's success. However, Melton et al report (1991:347) that some resistance has emerged in New Thought to New Age teachings. INTA and Association of Unity Churches speakers critiqued the New Age Movement at conferences in the late 1980s. Unity members often belong to other churches as well, in contrast to the constricts of Christian Science. Similarly, Unity members use medical doctors, although they maintain that true healing requires more than medical attention. Health is defined as wholeness, oneness with the 'Christ Mind', that is, the part of the Divine Mind that is within each human being. In a way similar to New Age teaching, it is not merely individual mental processes that need transformation, but also global consciousness.

Carl Gustav Jung (1875-1961) is often regarded as the founding psychological guru of the New Age (eg Noll 1996/1994:297; McLynn 1997/1996:487-509), and indeed he was one of the favoured authors in Ferguson's survey of New Agers (1980), Stuart Rose's (1996) survey of *Kindred Spirit* readers and my own surveys[27]. Whereas Sigmund Freud dismissed religion as a neurosis with its origins in infantile sexuality and a 'mythical' primaeval patricide, Jung saw the problem of neurosis in the present: a desperate need for meaning. After analysis of mythology, alchemy, dreams and hallucinations, Jung concluded that meaning could be achieved by means of a myth or a symbol which bridges the gap between consciousness and unconsciousness. His psychology was thus essentially spiritual. Jung is ambiguous as to when the Age of Aquarius is to begin: at one point he dates it to 2813 CE (McLynn 1997/1996:478), at another to 1940-1950 (McLynn 1997/1996:492).

Although Jung was officially agnostic, there is evidently a lot of psychological theory in Jung that is easily developed into a spiritual path, and this has been done by many both inside and outside the New Age (eg Bryant). But Jung has proven especially congenial to Christians, or perhaps more correctly to New Age Christians – for Jung's approach to Christian doctrine was far from orthodox. Before his break with Freud in 1913, Jung had hoped that psychoanalysis might transform Christianity (McLynn 1997/1996:150,235); he had seen that religion needed transforming in the agonies of his father's sceptical doubts as a Protestant pastor. But after this time Jung often set himself up as an opponent of Christianity. Indeed, in a controversial work, Richard Noll (1996/1994) claims that Jung is best seen as the founder of a charismatic occult cult with its roots in the nineteenth century German völkisch tradition that also bred National Socialism (on the link between Nazis and the occult, see further Goodrick-Clarke 1992/1985). These groups, with an important centre at Ascona in Switzerland with which Jung was acquainted, championed solar and Teutonic myths over

Christian and classical traditions. Noll later described Jung as *The Aryan Christ* (1997).

Famously, in 1959 Jung was interviewed for the BBC "Face to Face" programme, answering the question whether he believed in God, "I don't believe, I know," – sounding orthodox but in fact referring to his knowledge of the God image, he explained to his disciples. My impression is that monism, not theism, is the foundation on which Jungian theory is built – the fundamental unity of psychic and physical. Jung was heavily indebted to the Gnostics from 1916 onwards, and the idea of a *pleroma* (or fullness of qualities) was central to his thought, the origin of his idea that the psyche has to balance its opposite qualities by unconscious compensation or by individuation. Jung also believed that all historical events were merely manifestations of the pleroma or its archetypes. Jung's conception of reality is thus mystical and almost pantheistic.

Jung's contemporary, Edgar Cayce (pronounced 'K-C') (1877-1945) presents an unusual mix of an orthodox, quasi-fundamentalist Christian and a trance-channelling, reincarnation-believing proto-New Ager; York calls him

> expressive of what might be termed "New Age Christianity" or "Christian New Age."
> (York 1995:61)

Hanegraaff, however, comments that

> Over the years, Cayce's conservative Christian beliefs seem to have been increasingly ignored while the esoteric aspects of the material have been emphasized.
> (Hanegraaff 1996:35-36)

Cayce grew up in a Christian church – Disciples of Christ (Melton et al 1991:42) – and rejected occultism (York 1995:60) but popularised belief in the existence of multiple supernatural dimensions within a monistic worldview. Silent meditation was advocated for the attainment of spiritual guidance – Cayce regularly placed himself into hypnotic trances to provide "readings", or diagnoses, for people whom were often not present. Cayce's reading no. 3528-1 proclaims

> the Master, Jesus, even the Christ, is the pattern for every man in the earth, whether he be Gentile or Jew, Parthenian or Greek. For all have the pattern, whether they call on that name or not; but there is no other name given under heaven whereby men may be saved from themselves.
> (Cayce quoted in York 1995:61-62)

One of the attendees of a retreat at The Omega Order spoke to me of his earlier involvement in Dion Fortune's magical groups. Dion Fortune was the pen-name of Violet Mary Firth (1890-1946). Her mother was a Christian Scientist, and Violet published a poem entitled "Angels" in the *Christian Science Journal* of April 1908. In 1925 Fortune was involved with the Theosophical Society and its Christian Mystic Lodge, of which she was president. Daisy M Grove was the first president of the Lodge in 1923. Grove wrote *The Apocalypse and Initiation* (1926) and *The Mystery Teaching of the Bible*. After some aborted discussions with the Liberal Catholic Church under Fortune's direction, the Lodge split in 1927, with Fortune's non-Theosophical faction known as the Fraternity of the

Inner Light. Sunday rituals were held with a mixture of Grail and eucharistic imagery. Fortune wrote some meditations on the collects of the Church of England. During the Second World War, Fortune gave lectures at the Marylebone Spiritualist Association and contributed to the spiritualist newspaper, *Light*. Fortune practised as a medium, describing the technique of trance mediumship in an article in her *Inner Light Magazine* of April 1938. One of the spirits she channelled was known as the "Master of Medicine".

Fortune also wrote weekly letters to the Fraternity of the Inner Light, which for 1941 are available in the British Library. Although these are understandably quite jingoistic, it is clear that Fortune was talking in the Fraternity in terms of a New Age of Aquarius that would begin after the War.

> Religion must be re-stated in the new age, not because truth has changed, but because the manner of its expression has become atavistic and in consequence is not only incomprehensible but definitely leads astray a new age with a new destiny.
> (Fortune 1941: no.67, 30 March)

After the War, the Society of the Inner Light dropped the Guild of the Master Jesus which performed the quasi-Christian ceremony, but one member wrote that

> a very powerful Christian dynamic burst into the group in 1960/1 and one which was sufficiently powerful to cause many sparks to fly and various members to disperse and go their separate ways.
> I had a very powerful experience of this myself whilst by myself in the Library. Suddenly, out of thin air, it seemed that Jesus, the Risen Christ, simply walked into the room. ...
> The group as a whole took a new turn as a consequence of all this. The old graded structure was abandoned and all reverted to the 1st Degree again. Members were encouraged to wear plain clothes or ecclesiastical cassocks instead of magical robes.
> (Knight nd)

Gareth Knight is the pen-name of Basil Wilby. Knight left the Society of the Inner Light and met Revd Anthony Duncan, an Anglican clergyman who prepared him for confirmation. Duncan was to publish *The Lord of the Dance* (1972), *The Christ, Psychotherapy and Magic* (1969), and Knight *Experience of the Inner Worlds* (1975) and *Practical Guide to Qabalistic Symbolism* (1965). Together with WE Butler, another former member of the Society of the Inner Light, Knight formed the esoteric organisation Servants of the Light. Luhrmann (1994/1989) refers throughout her study to Knight's "Western Mysteries inner circle", consisting of about a dozen people. There is a study group lasting five years, and students are initiated after about a year. Luhrmann also describes an open annual May weekend that Knight holds at a converted manor house in Wiltshire, called Greystone (Luhrmann 1994/1989:211-217). One of the purposes of Knight's rituals is, she says, "uniting Christian and pagan spiritual currents" (Luhrmann 1994/1989:317).

Finally in this extended presentation of a legitimating history of Christaquarianism, I shall consider the writings that are most frequently quoted by

Canon Spink: those of Pierre Teilhard de Chardin (1881-1955). Teilhard de Chardin was the writer most frequently cited in Ferguson's survey of 'Aquarian Conspirators' (Ferguson 1980:463); the third most frequently cited in my survey of *Omega News* readers; and the fifth most frequently cited in my survey of the electoral roll at St James's church, Piccadilly. From the facts of de Chardin's life, this popularity is surprising, since he was a biologist, palaeontologist and a Jesuit, spent much of his life in China, and was prohibited from publishing his spiritual works by his Order. Long in circulation in manuscript, these were however published after his death. The most popular are *The Phenomenon of Man* (1955/Eng trns 1959) and *Le Milieu Divin* (1957/Eng trns 1960). As a scientist, de Chardin centres his thought on the concept of evolution – genesis, cosmogenesis – and extends this to include psychic evolution into a global consciousness – the noogenesis of the noosphere. The final goal of creation is Christogenesis, the Omega Point of convergence and unification under God. De Chardin's evolutionary schemata has been repopularised in the New Age by Peter Russell's *The Awakening Earth: The Global Brain* (1991/1982). However, from the library records at The Omega Order, it is clear that many residents and visitors to the Order have read de Chardin's own works rather than later popularisations. From the interview programme, it is clear that what appeals is the idea of teleology in the world, and the immanence of psychic intercommunication in a global consciousness.

It must be reiterated that this is just one possible presentation of a legitimating historical tradition that could be used by New Age Christians. At The Omega Order, as we have seen, much of it is in current use, though not all aspects of it receive the same degree of attention. The Gnostics and the Celtics, for example, are barely mentioned; while de Chardin is the most common influence. In a later chapter, we will see that June Anne English (1985) cites the presence of a legitimating historical tradition as an important factor in the consolidation of a movement.

Notes to Chapter V

[1] From the early 2000s, The Omega Order was rebranded as Winford Manor Retreat and the newsletter similarly renamed. In January 2003 James Fahey reported to me that The Omega Order had in fact disbanded, due to a perception of the problems with insitutionalised hierarchies. He also strongly objected to any association of Winford Manor Retreat with New Age.

[2] It would be impossible to mention Fahey without identifying him, and I have therefore not used a pseudonym. Fahey may also be classed as a leader, since he takes retreats and manages much of the day-to-day affairs of the community.

[3] Not a pseudonym.

[4] St James's electoral roll: 69%; CANA membership: 73%.

[5] I have not supplied a pseudonym for this Companion, as she publishes her own material advertising a light meditation group (Nettleton nd).

[6] A number of interviewees have expressed to me reservations about Revd Dr Fox.

[7] As advertised in, for example, *Vision* magazine. See Chapter VII.

[8] Neal's Yard operated as a forum for New Age groups in central London, distributing many brochures from its small shop. This has now closed, although the meeting rooms are still available for use by New Age groups.

[9] In the library and liturgical use of, eg St Francis' prayer.

[10] Conversation in the Teilhard Centre, Winford, 3 October 1996.

[11] Articles include "Hocus-pocus with a golden focus", Rachel Storm, *Sunday Times* 13 October 1991; "New Agers spell end for science", Martin Ince, *Times Higher Education Supplement*, 8 May 1992; "Today's New Agers", Jonathan Hughes, *The Times*, 6 June 1992; "The selling of the New Age", Bryan Appleyard, *The Times*, 17 June 1992; "Turbulent priest ministers to New Age soul", Martin Wroe, *The Independent*, 14 July 1992; "Professionals fall prey to New Age gurus", Ray Clancy, *The Times*, 21 July 1992; "God and the New Age", *The Times*, Russell L Ackoff, 6 August 1992; "'Dark side' of New Age heresies condemned", Ruth Gledhill, *The Times*, 16 June 1994; "Dreamers are taking over the asylum", Roger Hutchings, *The Guardian*, 11 February 1995; "Just say no", Linda Grant, *The Guardian*, 3 June 1995; "In thrall to New Age thrills", Pat Kane, *The Guardian*, 4 January 1995.

[12] Respondents from St James's and *Kindred Spirit* are not as widely read as respondents from The Omega Order, and do not elicit helpful results in such an analysis.

[13] This is a common New Age idea.

[14] See Filormao (1992/1990); Pagels (1992/1975); Pagels (1982/1977); Rudolph (1987/1977).

[15] See Trigg (1998).

[16] See Gerson ed (1996).

[17] Johannes Reuchlin (1455-1522) published *De Verbo Mirifico* (1494) and *De Arte Cabalistica* (1517). Francesco Giorgio (1460-1541) published *De Harmonia Mundi* (1525) and *Problemata* (1536). Cornelius Agrippa von Nettesheim's (1486-1535) *De Occulta Philosophia* (1510-1533) associated Qabbalah in the minds of many with black magic. Guillaume Postel (1510-1581) translated the

Zohar and the *Sefer Yezirah*, the main Qabbalistic texts, into Latin. Knorr von Rosenroth published *Kabbala Denudata* (1677-84).

[18] For Revd Strachan's New Age approach, see also Strachan (1985).

[19] Lurhmann (1994/1989) studies Wicca in the context of the New Age. I have no experience of Wiccan groups and could not comment on the validity of including Wicca within New Age, although this is often done by the evangelical Christians I have studied.

[20] *Beschreibung von dem drey Prinzipien* however appeared in 1618, *De Signatura Rerum* was written between 1621 and 1623 and *Der Weg zu Christo* in the year of his death.

[21] See Stanley ed (1988).

[22] See Godwin (1994).

[23] It is interesting to note that the founder of The Samaritans, Revd Chad Varah, is a believer in reincarnation.

[24] In April 1996 according to Shirley Nicholston, who was manning the Christian Science stall at the Mind-Body-Spirit festival on 8 September 1996.

[25] Stark (1998) has suggested reasons for the meteoric rise and decline of Christian Science. The decline is attributed to the over-emphasis of recruitment on older women with low fertility rates, ineffective socialization of recruits, compromises in its distinctive doctrines relating to healing, a decline in the effectiveness of its placebo effects in relation to the rise in general health and well-being of the population, and to the improvement in career opportunities for women. Taking his figures from the *Christian Science Journal*, Stark reports that there were in 1995 just 116 practitioners in England, compared with a peak of 1,104 in 1940.

[26] Eddy was 'ordained' by her students in 1881 as the pastor of the First Church of Christ (Scientist), which had been founded in 1879, and signed herself "Reverend". "The Mother Church" in Boston was founded in 1892, after the First Church was disbanded by Eddy in 1889 when she was centralising her authority in the movement that had thereto been more democratic. From 1885 to 1890 her literary advisor (or ghost-writer) was Revd James Henry Wiggin, a Unitarian minister. As early as the 1890s, hostile comments on other Christian denominations were discouraged (Gottschalk 1973:195f). The cross is featured on the cover page of *Science and Health*, and forms part of Christian Science's official emblem.

[27] 14% of *Kindred Spirit* respondees cited Jung as an important influence; 14 people in my survey of *Omega News* readers cited him.

143

VI. Evangelical Responses to New Age

Any statistical survey must have a control group before the results can be properly analysed. This is the major drawback with Stuart Rose's (1996) otherwise admirable survey of *Kindred Spirit* readers, as, until my survey repeated some of his questions, it could not be seen how typical or atypical his results were. For my study, in addition to using Rose's results as a control group on the New Age side of Christaquarianism, I have selected a control group on the Christian side. This group has been chosen for contrast rather than comparison: an Anglican evangelical congregation. The choice has also proven convenient, since the congregation in question is well known to me, being the church in which I grew up, and was married during the course of the research.

The benefice in question splits its congregation between two churches, SS Peter and Paul, Cudham, and St Mary's, Downe. This is a rural area on the edges of greater London, with the vicarage located in Cudham, the larger congregation. However, the two churches regularly meet for joint services and hold joint PCC meetings. In all, 114 questionnaires were sent out to members of the two electoral rolls and 53 were returned, a return rate of 46%. It was not found meaningful to represent the results of the two churches independently, and so I have treated them as one joint benefice. Formal interviews carried out among the congregation lasted from three-quarters to one-and-a-half hours. Additionally, a healing ministry course run by the vicar over nine weeks was attended, and I went to the main Sunday service about once every other month during the period of study, chatting over coffee after the service. The names of the clergy are genuine, but those of the congregation have been changed.

Statistical Surveys

The age of the population closely matches that of St James's, Piccadilly, also an Anglican church, that is to say, those over 44 are over-represented. Compared with Rose's *Kindred Spirit* readers, the control group is older, and compared to *Omega News* respondents and CANA respondents, the control group is younger. All groups studied had a male female ratio of approximately 3:7. Any differences between the control group and the other groups studied is therefore unlikely to be due to general characteristics of age or sex.

The Anglican evangelicals had the highest rates of partnership of the groups studied (from fieldwork, most of these are married) at nearly 70%. This may therefore have some effect on the results, although it is difficult to say why or in what way. They were also those most reticent about their income, with nearly 20% declining to answer, possibly because I was better known to them personally than in the other groups studied. Of those who answered, nearly 50% reported incomes below £5,000, with all higher categories of income being significantly under-represented compared both to the national average and to the Christaquarian groups studied. 36% were retired, similar to the 29% at St James's, but lower than at The Omega Order and CANA, whose members tend to be older. The educational level of Cudham and Downe respondents approximates that of The Omega Order respondents, that is to say, the congregation is less well-educated than St James's or CANA, with only 17% reporting a degree as their highest level of qualification. This may account for the relatively low level of income at Cudham and Downe.

58% of Anglican evangelicals surveyed defined God as a real personality, The Omega Order being the next highest on this question at 21%, CANA at 19% with only 14% at St James's. Thus Christaquarian groups studied tend, on this measure, to have less personalist pictures of God than Anglican evangelicals. Asked whether there are varying types of spirituality or whether spirituality is universally the same, the evangelicals responded in a way that was more similar to the other Anglican church in this study than to the other New Age -oriented groups, ie 72% of the evangelicals thought spirituality to be of varying types. This is significant in that Christaquarians will tend to view differing traditions of spirituality as of one source, facilitating their appropriation of these traditions.

Again, the rates of meditation in both Anglican churches were similar with around half only meditating occasionally, while around half of the other groups generally meditated once a day or more. The rate of prayer for the evangelicals was nearly as high as that at The Omega Order, which has daily offices including prayer; and significantly higher than at St James's and CANA. The final similarity with St James's was the level of experience of paranormal phenomena at the control group, three in ten. However, these experiences were described in different ways by evangelicals, who spoke of feeling the Holy Spirit move within them rather than specifying telepathy, visions, clairaudience or coincidences. From these statistics, then, it can be seen that although the evangelical grouping may be contrasted with the Christaquarian grouping, in fact there are a number of similarities between the two Anglican churches, the evangelical and St James's. This was perhaps to be expected.

Evangelicals are about as green as other groups studied, according to Rose's measure. Additionally, 55% of evangelicals have recycled their waste, indicating that this practice is not limited to a New Age population and should be rejected from Rose's list as an indicator of New Age beliefs[1].

In my evangelical sample, 62% gave a definition of New Age, compared to 75% at Alternatives, 78% at St James's, 88% at the Omega Order and CANA, and only 23% in a national US survey (Heelas 1996a:109). Although the Christaquarian groups studied are therefore more *au fait* with New Age, the evangelicals appear to be significantly better versed with New Age than the general public. The most common examples given of New Age by the evangelicals studied were healing, crystals and astrology, tarot and the occult. These examples rarely named specific groups, however, in contrast to the results obtained in Christaquarian groups, indicating perhaps that this knowledge of New Age among evangelicals is second hand. Interestingly, over one in five evangelicals surveyed had practised homeopathy, nearly the same number had practised aromatherapy and 11% had been to a reflexologist, again indicating that Rose's list of New Age practices for measuring involvement in the New Age must be used with care. However, overall, the evangelicals participated significantly less in Rose's list of New Age practises, at an average of 7% compared to 47% among Rose's *Kindred Spirit* readers. No evangelical had participated in more than ten of these practices, whereas over half of St James's electoral roll respondents and nearly two-thirds of CANA resopndents had. Therefore, Rose's list of New Age practices may be retained provided we do not use it too simplistically.

The churches of SS Peter and Paul and St Mary preserve a stable congregation, with over half having been a member for 15 years or more. Just over a quarter of The Omega Order respondents and one fifth of St James's respondents had been affiliated to the respective groups that long. However, this is not a strict comparison as the church has been in Cudham for over one thousand years, while the Christian New Age groups studied are all less than 20 years old[2]. Interestingly, 8% of evangelicals surveyed had been to St James's, which is a journey of only about three quarters of an hour away. This again indicates that the bipolar divide between evangelicalism and New Age may not be as clear as is often thought, although it may also be for 'non-faith related' reasons such as weddings, christenings or funerals.

Interviews

The vicar, Revd Tim Hatwell (b 1953), defines the New Age (1) by its pantheism, including "those who are Green"; (2) by its moral monism, "there is no concept of evil, no concept of sin"; and (3) by its "anything goes" approach, "if it works". Examples he gives of New Age are White Eagle Lodge, Transcendental Meditation, crystals, astrology, and Tarot cards. However, he has never had a serious discussion with a New Ager about their beliefs, and these ideas are mainly garnered from Christian writings including *What is the New Age* (Cole et al 1990) and a booklet by Philip Seddon (1990). Revd Hatwell speaks of "grey areas such as acupuncture and reflexology or even aromatherapy" for which he is unsure of the correct Christian approach. In general, though, he thinks a Christian should be open in friendship to New Agers and engage in dialogue with them.

Revd Nigel Hinton (b 1950), the curate, cannot give any examples of New Age groups or practices, but is nevertheless quite happy to define it as (1) self-centred and subjective; (2) pantheistic; and (3) all-embracing. Two of these three characteristics are thus identical to those given by his vicar. Again, he thinks Christians should be open to New Agers and engage them on common ground, but ultimately the purpose of any dialogue would be to convert them to "objective" religion. Revd Hinton has few qualms about alternative medicine, and has seen some success in the homeopathic treatment of his daughter for ME. However, he "would certainly look very hard to see what if anything was laying behind" any alternative therapy and "would be very wary of yoga, there is a whole philosophy, spirituality tied up with that. ... my suspicion is that it wouldn't necessarily be God's healing. It might work, but there is a danger it would be [satanic]." Revd Hinton has had one experience of satanic power, after friends used a ouija board that named him.

146

The church Reader declared himself unable to comment on the New Age as he knew absolutely nothing about it.

Richard, a long-term member of the congregation, thinks that New Age, by definition, has "the devil ... behind it because it is not of Christ." Again, he mentions pantheism as a defining characteristic of New Age. He has come across New Age in a management course at work, and although he participated on some of this course, he talked to other participants about what he perceived as the dangers of New Age and handed out evangelical tracts. He has also rejected some homeopathic healing for his son when he discovered that the remedies were tested by their energy fields. The approach that Christians should take to New Age, he thinks, is "love the person, hate the sin."

Janice has had some exposure to New Age at work: where a colleague is a member of the School of Economic Science, sometimes attends St James's church, Piccadilly and whose wife is a Reiki initiate and druid. This colleague knows Janice is Christian, and often talks to her about New Age exhibitions he is going to. Janice is not interested, but she has been on an aromatherapy course and is impressed by the efficacy of reflexology.

Surprisingly, there is a tangible link between Cudham Church and The Omega Order, for two ladies of the congregation visit from time to time Burrswood Home of Healing, where Canon Peter Spink, now leader of the Order, was formerly Warden – although it must be emphasised that Burrswood has now moved away from its quasi-Spiritualist roots to a more evangelical base. In fact, the link is quite close to home, because one of these ladies, Jasmine, was introduced to Burrswood by a talk at a Woman's Institute meeting by Revd David Flagg, now the vicar of Knockholt, the parish adjoining Cudham, who is a former chaplain to the Home and co-author of a book on healing (Tuckwell & Flagg 1995). Jasmine placed a video advertising Burrswood on the Cudham church bookstall, where it remains for borrowing. Jasmine has two sons who have been on a Silva Method course and benefited from it, she says. She has also had her hair analysed by a pendulum, becoming quite worried at the predictions that were given. "Before you know what you've done, you are oppressed, caught by it," she said.

Val is something of an anomaly within the congregation for, although attending the parish church, she distances herself from what she calls the "happy-clappy fundamentalists". But despite her interest in alternative forms of Christianity and spirituality, she still also distances herself from New Age which "lays such emphasis on self." What attracts her to reading about New Age is the idea of reincarnation, which she knows "is a Christian heresy" but still finds fascinating. Val also receives reflexology healing regularly and does John Main meditation on the *maranatha* mantra with a local group, which is also attended by another member of the congregation. She often had arguments with the previous incumbent and his churchWarden, a doctor, about using acupuncture, which they said was evil.

147

A common theme among most of the interviewees was that of possession by demonic spirits. This is said to happen during meditation unless the object of meditation is Christ, and can also happen if you channel healing from powers other than Christ. Revd Hinton sums up the fears, "I get a little worried about anything that has a loss of control. Once you start losing control, there is a risk of the satanic side coming in." Richard spoke of the dangers of "laying yourself open to things that are unhealthy ... and as far as I am concerned if it's not Christ it's the devil." Jasmine named this process as being "ensnared" or "oppressed" by an evil force.

Literature

It is impossible to include in this section all evangelical literature on the New Age; there is just too much of it[3]. What has been included below has been that most easily available in evangelical bookshops and on church bookstalls during the period of study. Indeed, many of the texts were actually bought by me at a bookshop owned by a Christian couple who lived for many years in Cudham village. Although the themes expressed in these books are evidenced by evangelicals in the field, in my interviews and surveys there were few actual instances of the works having been read first hand. Nevertheless, they must be mentioned in this thesis as their critique of the New Age has filtered down to the congregation, probably through the clergy and other evangelical leaders, and through religious magazines and other literature.

The *Leitmotiven* of much evangelical Christian analysis of New Age were first vividly painted for a wide readership by Constance Cumbey in 1983 in *The Hidden Dangers of the Rainbow*: the rainbow as the hypnotic calling sign of the movement, the Antichrist as its leader, connections with neo-Nazism and the coming of the "Fourth Reich", the conspiracy directed by followers of Alice Bailey, the heresy of finding God within the self.

> According to New Age sources, the New Age Movement is a worldwide network. It consists of tens of thousands cooperating organizations. Their primary goal or the secret behind their "unity-in-diversity" is the formation of a "New World Order". The Movement usually operates on the basis of a well-formulated body of underlying esoteric or occult teachings. ...
> Carefully structured along the lines set forth in the Alice Bailey writings, it includes organizations teaching mind control, holistic health, esoteric philosophy; scientific workers, political workers; and organizations dedicated to peace and world goodwill. It also includes many consumer, environmental and nutritional organizations as well as religious cults of every shade and description.
> (Cumbey 1983:54)

Although Cumbey claims to have read extensively on New Age, it is difficult to take her scholarship as anything but paranoid propaganda when, for example, she casts Peter Berger as a New Ager (Cumbey 1983:157), and lists as a symbol of New Age the humble circle (Cumbey 1983:262).

148

Roy Livesey is a British anti-New Age campaigner. Beginning in 1984, his regular prayer letters became the subscription-free *New Age Bulletin* in 1988, reporting in bi-monthly densely printed volumes on the development of New Age in forwarding what he calls the New World Order. These are now available in spiral-bound back issues. In many ways, Livesey has progressed from writing simply about New Age to writing about a grand conspiracy theory that involves pretty much every group except his own.

It is difficult to locate Livesey in any religious category, but he describes himself as: ex- and anti- occultist, ex- and anti- pentecostal, ex- and anti- charismatic, ex- and anti- socialist; and a self-professed conspiracy theorist. Until 1982 he was in Moral ReArmament, and from then until 1986 in an Elim church. In 1990 he saw pentecostalism as a "deception" and moved to a Brethren-type church. He distances himself from evangelicals, whom he says are "mostly embracing the world's deadliest religion – Rome," (*New Age Bulletin* V.4 1994:3), and one volume of the *Bulletin* is devoted to the false revival of charismatic experiences in the Toronto blessing as a means of introducing the New Age (*New Age Bulletin* V.5 1994). Speaking in tongues 'blankens the mind' "and blanking the mind is basic to getting started in the occult, whether introduced in the Church or outside it." (*New Age Bulletin* V.5 1994:4). Two volumes of the *Bulletin* at the end of 1994 summarise Livesey's approach to New Age, being an address he gave to the Lewes Bible Conference that year. New Age is presented as a new Gnosticism[4], concentrating on "the unseen aspects of life" rather than both the material and spiritual as Christians should.

Dave Hunt and TA McMahon wrote best-selling volumes on *The Seduction of Christianity* (1985) by *The New Spirituality* (1988). Theirs is a hostile critique of New Age within Christianity. They particularly look at the crossover between the positive thought tradition and evangelical Christianity in the United States. We are warned that spiritual discernment is needed in these days approaching the Second Coming of Christ, and a number of prominent Christians are named. Mention is made of St James's church, Piccadilly and St John the Divine, New York (Hunt & McMahon 1985:71).

Angels of Light? The Challenge of New Age Spirituality (1992) by Lawrence Osborn[5] acknowledges that

> An increasing number of Christians are prepared to call themselves New Age Christians or Christian New Agers. Many more have been influenced consciously or unconsciously by aspects of the New Age.
> (Osborn 1992:153)

In particular, Osborn discusses St James's Piccadilly, The Omega Order and Creation Spirituality. Asking why the New Age is perceived by many Christians as a threat, he suggests that this is because it is a successful rival in that it is similar to Christian renewal, and for fear of the occult (Osborn 1992:174). The approach that is recommended is Paul's approach in Athens, "Confrontation in Love: The Way of Dialogue" (Osborn 1992:ch12). *Guardians of Creation: Nature in theology and the Christian life* (Osborn 1993) also considers the work of Matthew Fox.

Douglas R Groothuis's series on New Age (*Unmasking the New Age* [1986], *Confronting the New Age* [1988], *Revealing the New Age Jesus* [1990]) is explicitly constructed in order to facilitate resistance of its incursion. New Agers, whom he often refers to as "the One for all", are presented as being distinguishable by their beliefs:

Table VI.1 New Age and Evangelical beliefs according to Groothuis

		New Age	Christian
1.	Metaphysics	God is the world, pantheism God is impersonal/amoral All is spirit/ consciousness, monistic	Creator/creation distinction God is personal/moral Creation of God upheld by God, interconnected but not monistic
2.	Epistemology	Man is all things, truth within	Truth revealed in the Bible
3.	Ethics	Autonomous and situational (relative)	Based on the revelation of God's will, absolute
4.	Nature of Humans	Spiritual being, a sleeping God	Made in the image of God, now fallen
5.	Human problem	Ignorance of true potential	Sin – rebellion against God and his law
6.	Answer to Human Problems	Change of consciousness	Faith in and obedience to Christ
7.	History	Cyclical	Linear and providential
8.	Death	Illusion, entrance to next life (reincarnation)	Entrance to either eternal heaven or hell
9.	View of Religion	All point to the One (syncretism)	Not all from God, teach different things
10.	View of Jesus Christ	One of many avatars ...	The unique God-Man, only Lord and Savior

(Groothuis 1991/1986:167)

However, while acknowledging the power of some Christian conspiracy theories about the New Age, Groothuis urges caution over them (Groothuis 1991/19876:35). Groothuis describes New Age as a development of secular humanism, that former bugbear of evangelical Christianity (Groothuis 1991/1986:53). He also points out that New Age may influence those who remain Christian. Ways in which some Christians have "compromised" their faith in this way are: mixing it with psychology such as Jungian therapy; reading mystics who speak of union with Christ; emphasising positive thinking; being interested in ecology (Groothuis 1991/1986:171f). To be effective, Groothuis suggests that evangelizing to New Agers should "look for legitimate common ground," admitting "We can agree on some things." (Groothuis 1991/1986:173)

Caryl Matrisciana in *Gods of the New Age* (1985) gives a readable autobiography of her involvement in New Age from the sixties in London, her childhood experiences in India, conversion to Christianity in America and anti-New Age campaigns run for a time at Bromley, Kent – Cudham and Downe's borough town. Matrisciana's work throws some insight on those evangelical campaigns which accept much of the New Age worldview (eg spirits, healing) while questioning its goodness in comparison with Christian spirits and Christian healing.

Walter Martin, the late founder of the Christian Research Institute and author of *The Kingdom of the Cults* (1985) devoted his last work to *The New Age Cult* (1989). He describes it himself as "theology in newspaper language" (Martin 1989:9); this is perhaps an optimistic evaluation of the style. Again, the defining features are ten doctrinal differences with orthodox Christianity (Martin 1989:25-34); these can all be answered by the patristic answers against ancient heresies. Martin believes the Jonestown deaths can be directly related to Jim Jones' New Age teachings (Martin 1989:55). Regarding Christian-New Age relations, Martin writes:

> Since New Agers use many Christian words, confusion seems likely because many Christians are unaware that good words have been radically redefined with bad meanings.
> (Martin 1989:81)

Nevertheless, he urges Christians to

> Praise the zeal, dedication, and (wherever possible) the goals of the New Age movement, because its basic nature is both messianic and millennial. The New Age Cult is seeking the right things, but with the wrong methods and with wrong reasons, sometimes merely because their vision is impaired by sin.
> (Martin 1989:102)

Elliot Miller, employed by Walter Martin at the Christian Research Institute, writes:

> The New Age movement then is an extremely large, *loosely* structured network of organizations and individuals bound together by common values (based in mysticism and monism ...) and a common vision (a coming "new age" of peace and mass enlightenment ...).
> (Miller 1990:15)

Miller describes the movement as a "metanetwork" (Miller 1990:15). All New Agers are monists and pantheists, he claims (Miller 1990:17), who proclaim enlightenment through gnostic evolution. The major examples he explains are holistic health, ecology and channelling.

> ... some New Age groups identify themselves as "esoteric Christians," and most New Agers think highly of Jesus ...
> (Miller 1990:29)

Miller questions the authenticity of the fundamental New Age experience:

But what if mystical "enlightenment" is really delusion?
(Miller 1990:44)

He further believes that mysticism engenders civil apathy, whereas the Christian worldview provides a basis for social concern and action (Miller 1990:80).

What is the New Age Saying to the Church? asks John Drane (1991), an evangelical who is also lecturer in religious studies at the University of Stirling, Scotland, and was the supervisor for Paul Greer's thesis on New Age. His approach to New Age is therefore more open than that of other evangelicals to the lessons that the church can learn from the New Age. The central examples Drane uses to define New Age are the actress Shirley MacLaine, JZ Knight who channelled Ramtha – a 35,000 year old warrior, crystals, and a management course. In sweeping up common threads, Drane emphasises the importance of consciousness and its transformation leading to social transformation, as a compensation to modern frustrations. Drane's PhD in Gnosticism enables him to draw some parallels (Drane 1991:84f), and further chapters include discussion of channelling, the environment and life-style management courses.

Drane accepts the New Age critique that Christians

... have gone spiritually off-course by viewing things in a mechanistic and reductionist frame of reference ...
(Drane 1991:214)

This is the reason, he thinks, that 80% of New Agers were once church members and have now left (Drane 1991:238). He sees several parallels between the New Age and Christian agendas:

Concern for personal freedom and maturity, for the environment, for peace and justice, for self-discovery, for a holistic view of life ...
(Drane 1991:214)

The main difference between Christianity and the New Age is that

Whereas the New Age outlook identifies the basic problem as an alienated or undeveloped consciousness, Christians take evil and suffering seriously, and affirm that the basic problem is a moral one, not a metaphysical one.
(Drane 1991:214)

The way forward, thinks Drane, is for the church to become less intellectual and cerebral, and to give people the kind of spirituality they want, with the emphasis on the supernatural. In the final analysis, Drane's approach is still to 'win New Agers for Christ' (Drane 1991:239).

Paul Vitz's *Psychology as Religion: The Cult of Self-Worship* (1994/1977) is cited by a number of Christian anti-New Age works as a scientific authority[6], and in due course the second edition included a new chapter on "Psychology and the New Age Movement" (Vitz 1994:113-125).

... psychology was one of the major intellectual and social forces that brought today's [New Age] movement into cultural prominence.
(Vitz 1994:117)

Vitz critiques "Selfism as Bad Science" (Vitz 1994:32-46), citing against New Age use of Abraham Maslow lack of empirical support, overestimation of the importance of physiological needs before motherly love, and the application of self-actualization to children rather than adults as Maslow intended. He notes that because some psychologists reject the scientific paradigm (Vitz 1994:40), it is difficult to argue with them. The intrinsic goodness of human nature is rejected in an analysis of Erich Fromm, which raises the philosophical question of the origin of evil – individual or social – and the scientific question of the representativeness of his data. Further chapters criticize Selfism for transforming descriptive psychology into moral exhortation (Vitz 1994:54), being more concerned with the individual than the family (Vitz 1994:57f) or society (Vitz 1994:84f).

Frank Peretti's works present the evangelical critique of the New Age in the form of the novel, and are available from the small library in Cudham church. The cover of *This Present Darkness* (1997/1986) proclaims that it has sold over one million copies. It is the story of

> '... a decisive and powerful tool of the Universal Consciousness Society, the Omni Corporation ... establish[ing] still another foothold for the coming New World Order and the rule of the New Age Christ.'
> (Peretti 1997/1986:348)

This is the only time New Age is mentioned explicitly, but it is clear that this is his main target.

The Omni Corporation is secretly infiltrating the town of Ashton, purchasing property, securing its members in influential positions, and achieving this through blackmail and fraud. Behind Omni Corporation is the Universal Consciousness Society, and behind that are a multitude of demons. As in all Peretti's works, the human plot is paralleled and affected by an angelic-demonic plot of spiritual warfare. The captain of the Angelic Host is called Tal, while the demon controlling Ashton is Rafar. Although the demons outnumber the angels, in the end it is the angels who win by stealth, hiding under a protective cover of prayer provided by churchgoers in Ashton.

Piercing the Darkness (1997/1989) is the sequel, with Marshall Hogan and Bernice Krueger brought in as the investigative heroes who collect the evidence to stop a lawsuit that was potentially damaging to the religious freedom of Christians in America. The American Citizen's Freedom Association ("ACFA") was championing a test case against the Good Shepherd Academy, a small "fundamentalist" (1997/1989:351) Christian school whose teacher had administered corporal punishment to and exorcised a demon from a child, Amber Brandon. But behind the ACFA lay a secret organisation, the Royal and Sacred Order of the Nation which initiated male members with a secret name and gargoyle-shaped golden ring. A derivative of the Nation is LifeCircle, a small meditation group. Also connected is the Omega Center for Educational Studies and the Summit Institute for Humanistic Studies.

It must be repeated that there are many more evangelical critiques of the New Age, although their rate of publication does seem to have peaked by the early 1990s.

Having reviewed the literature that provides the backdrop for evangelical attitudes to the New Age as revealed in the survey material and interview programme, I now make a tentative analytical suggestion. It was my assumption when I began my fieldwork that New Age is at the opposite end of the spectrum from evangelical Christianity. However, a number of commentators have detected similarities between New Age and evangelical Christianity. I will now consider some of these parallels. It must be remembered in this analysis that I have not done extensive fieldwork in evangelical Christianity, my data being limited to one church, and thus the description of evangelical Christianity is undoubtedly oversimplified.

One of the most authoritative insider commentators on New Age, David Spangler, notes the similarity.

> In fact, in some of its expressions, the idea of the new age (certainly as I first encountered it) is identical in spirit if not always in language to many of the current millennial expectations of evangelical and fundamentalist Christian groups.
> (Spangler 1984:19-20)

Sheena Govan, one of the original inspirations of Eileen and Peter Caddy and thus of the Findhorn Foundation (which Spangler made famous), was the daughter of John Govan, the founder of the Faith Mission, an evangelical Protestant movement (Sutcliffe 1998a:50).

Damian Thompson (1997/1996:208-212) summarises the "odd similarities" between New Age and fundamentalism, including the apocalypticism, the emphasis on disembodied voices rather than visions, the stress on health and healing, the recognition of material prosperity as a sign of blessing, individual experience of the spiritual leading to personal transformation, and a "DIY" organisational structure. Thompson attributes these similarities to similar responses to changes in Western culture, and describes both New Age and fundamentalism as "the religion of the outsider" (Thompson 1997/1996:210) which defines itself in opposition to the mainstream.

Catherine Albanese (1988) presents New Age as an ethnic American response to secularism which may be similar to Christian fundamentalism in a number of emphases. Albanese articulates here two central reasons for Christian fundamentalist antagonism against New Age: boundary maintenance in the face of (1) common origins and (2) common practices. For both traditions, personal transformation and direct spiritual experience are central. This transformation affects in both cases the family or society at large. In their experiences, both fundamentalists and New Agers are said to hear voices more than see visions. Both also stress healing. A form of ontological positivism is said to predominate in both: God is matter, in effect, and embracing God means embracing the world. This positivism embraces in both cases science, whether creation science or quantum physics. Finally, both groups are said to be celebrators of a spiritual

154

democracy where everyone has access to the mystical state.

Taking his cue from Albanese, Philip Lucas (1992) suggests that the New Age movement and the Pentecostal/charismatic revival are distinct yet parallel phases of a fourth 'great awakening' in American history. He outlines four parallel trends: first, both movements emphasise the importance of the experience of the sacred in everyday life; second, both movements value community; third, both movements use healing and inner transformation; and finally, both movements see themselves as part of a planetary spiritual transformation with power in individual rather than institutional hands.

Roof first emphasizes the divide between New Age and evangelicals, then notes significant similarities. The differences are fourfold:

Table VI.2 New Age and Evangelical beliefs according to Roof

New Age	Evangelical
Self-fulfillment	Submission to divine will
Truth within	Authority in external God
Mystical	Theistic meaning system
Spiritual styles: letting go	Mastery and control

(adapted from Roof 1994/1993:121)

The similarities are finally attributed to Emersonian conceptions of self and God, increased currency of psychological language, the move from print to television and image, and the large numbers of people now entering the reflective time of mid-life. No figures are offered for these observations.

Chrissie Steyn (1994)[7], in her survey of New Age in South Africa, remarks several times on the similarities with charismatic Christianity (Steyn 1994:7,50,166,312). However,

> On the whole there appears to be a rejection of the Christian tradition, or rather of the Christian churches, since some participants claimed that it was New Agers who have preserved the essence of Christianity while the churches are said to have distorted the original message of Jesus.
> (Steyn 1994:167)

I shall now summarise the phenomenological similarities between evangelical Christianity and New Age. Personal transformation is central to both, whether being born again or coming to Enlightenment. Transformation centres on experience, either speaking in tongues and being slayed by the Spirit or through altered states of consciousness. Another central experience is healing through the laying on of hands – the power coming through Christ or the auric fields.

Both evangelical Christianity and New Age are ontologically positive – God is seen to embrace matter either through the doctrines of Creation Science or

155

application of Quantum Physics. Both have a spiritual democracy with the traditional priesthood of believers or the idea that everyone is God. The sacred is continually present in the everyday lives of evangelicals and New Agers, who live in Christ or live as God. Both value the community. The attitude to the outside world in both is to transform it, either building God's kingdom or preparing for the New Age. Both share a similar attitude to money evinced in prosperity consciousness. The attitude to the future is also similar, both showing varying shades of millennialism.

The form of worship among evangelicals and New Agers is also similar. For example, evangelical choruses are similar to New Age chants and Taizé chants are used in both contexts. Prayer or meditation is often a group exercise in both congregations. Evangelicals cut across traditional institutional divides among the Churches; New Agers are similarly outside of traditional institutions. Both have significant origins in the late nineteenth century. The typical member of both is a middle-class, middle-aged woman.

I shall now present various examples of the similarities between conservative Christianity and the New Age movement. The most surprising result of my interview programme is the discovery that *all three* leaders of the Christaquarian groups studied had an evangelical conversion experience in their youth. Both Janice Dolley and Revd Donald Reeves had been converted by Billy Graham, the American evangelist, and Canon Peter Spink also had a conversion experience in his 'teens. Revd Jim Hill and another Anglican priest staying at the Order had similar experiences. All had later repudiated this experience, expressing much dissatisfaction with the evangelical tradition, mainly due to its 'dogmatism' and over-reliance on an authoritarian approach to the Bible. The significance of this double conversion to and from evangelical Christianity is difficult to evaluate. It may well be that many leaders of religious groups today had similar experiences in their youth – similar to the "baby boomer" spirituality suggested by Roof (1993). In the absence of a wider survey, I cannot tell whether it is common for leaders of religious groups now in their late middle age (or older in the case of Canon Spink) to have had an evangelical conversion experience. I suggest, however, that it is highly significant, because of the similarities in the style of religion as outlined above.

Some residents at The Omega Order were also former evangelicals. The relationship between charismatic Christianity and New Age was often perceived as one of lower and higher levels of spirituality rather than a bifocal for/against. Despite the small sample of interviewees at The Omega Order, the relatively high incidence of contact with evangelicalism at the Order must surely be significant. Unfortunately, the questionnaire survey to *Omega News* did not include a question about previous involvement with evangelicalism. However, when the possibility of a relationship became apparent to me, I added a question to the survey and so CANA members were asked whether they had ever had any contact with evangelical Christianity. Exactly two thirds of respondents, a surprisingly large number, indicated that they had had some contact. Asked to expand on the nature of this contact, 37% of these respondents indicated that this was a negative experience. The true figure of negative experiences may well be somewhat higher. Canon Peter Spink's published works go so far as to claim a historical link between the Pentecostal healing movement and the holistic healing movement (Spink 1991a:45). While not denying its efficacy, Canon Spink considers charismatic-style healing to be on a lower, more "psychic" plane than the holistic healing he aims to offer at Omega[8].

At Winford, the diocese was forced to issue a conciliatory statement on The Omega Order, due largely to a campaign orchestrated from their arrival in 1986 by a local evangelical. Charismatic Christianity was not generally rejected at Omega, but perceived to have some value and some similarities with contemplative meditation and New Age.

> In its [the Charismatic movement's] emphasis on the psychic gifts it bears a remarkable resemblance in all but language to the New Age phenomenon.
> (Spink 1991a:47; cf ibid:76-77)

James Fahey described this similarity best with the idea of turning down the volume on a television set showing a Gospel preacher, and putting a rainbow in the background to find a New Age speaker. He was in fact referring to "psychic energy", a concept that Canon Spink used to delineate between the charismatic and contemplative movements – psychic is seen to be on a level lower than spiritual. To this concept was added Fahey's critique of the leaderless network: neither New Age nor "Gospel" Christianity have authorized bodies which can be addressed, and rely instead on vague legitimations and the authority of personal experience. The understanding of healing by Revd Roger had not significantly changed since his evangelical parish ministry; and Revd Hill's understanding of healing while he was evangelical was essentially Jungian. This having been said, Lillian and Nettleton, two of the more elderly residents, did perceive the relations between New Age and evangelicalism as a simple bipolar divide. Others were aware that evangelicals also usually see the divide this way.

Burrswood, "A Christian Centre for Medical and Spiritual Care" founded by Dorothy Kerin (1889-1963) near Tunbridge Wells, Kent, came to my attention at The Omega Order where several residents and Canon Peter Spink mentioned it as one of their historical influences (Spink 1991b). Yet their suggestion was that Burrswood was no longer in tune with the Omega vision, and had turned "more evangelical". In fact, Canon Peter Spink was Warden of Burrswood from 1977 to 1980, when the foundation of The Omega Order took priority. After Kerin's death in 1963, Dr Edward Aubert, author of *Faith, Medicine and Healing*, directed Burrswood until 1975, replaced on his death by colleague Dr Kenneth Cuming, author of *God and the New Age* (1975) until his retirement in 1977 (Farr 1986/1970:107-108).

Dr Cuming's pamphlet, published by Michael Link, gives a detailed astrological explanation of the New Age and uses the vocabulary of Alice Bailey. Cuming's conclusion reveals a tension similar to that expressed at The Omega Order, although interestingly at this time the Charismatic movement is included within the New Age movement:

The two lines of approach should not be regarded as mutually incompatible, but rather as complementary and not antagonistic. For the Charismatic and Pentecostal movements are the spiritual-emotional wing and the new schools of philosophy, science and psychology represent the spiritual-intellectual wing. Both together are thus the Wings of the Holy Spirit, and both have their allotted function in the New Age movement. (Cuming 1975:19)

Dorothy Kerin's ministry of healing began with a spiritual healing experience in 1912 which has since been described as an out-of-body and near-death experience. During a serious illness, she saw a woman with a lily, understood by others as the Virgin Mary, telling her to return to earth and heal others (Kerin 1987/1914:18). Kerin believed the world in 1912 to be "on the threshold of a great Revelation from the Spirit that is Infinite" (quoted in Farr 1986/1970:11). On the last page of Kerin's last published work, an associate describes her as standing "on the threshold of this New Age as God's signpost" (Kerin 1960/1952:166). Kerin thought the Second Coming would be "soon" (1987/1914:43), within the lifetime of her friends (Chavchavadze 1995:x). As late as 1961, Kerin accepted an invitation to talk in New York from Dr Norman Vincent Peale of positive thought fame (Chavchavadze 1995:69). This suggests a continuity of thought between her and the Wardens that managed Burrswood after her death until 1980. But a confused tension between 'evangelical' and 'esoteric' is also apparent. As early as June 1912, 22 year old Kerin published an article distinguishing her healing, which came direct from Christ or God, from

> any of the established systems of healing, such as healing by hypnotism, suggestion, the help of "friendly spirits", "faith healing", Christian Science, suggestive therapeutics, etc.
> (quoted in Farr 1986/1970:12)

Bishop Maddocks reports her favourite description of her healing mission was to be an instrument, "a bit of pipe" (Maddocks 1991/1981:89). From 1913 to 1916 Kerin spoke in Theosophical and Spiritualist meetings, until a friend arranged a two-hour discussion with Kerin's cousin and thereafter Confessor, Revd Dr R Langford-James (Farr 1986/1970:23). Kerin later healed a lady "suffering from tormenting spirits as a result of attending spiritualistic seances" by "cutting the psychic links that had been forged" in what is described as "possession by demonic or earthbound spirits" (Chavchavadze 1995:61). The current Order of Service at the Church of Christ the Healer in Burrswood prays for delivery from oppression by evil. Chavchavadze distinguishes Kerin's clairvoyancy (direct from God), from Spiritualism (via spirits) (Chavchavadze 1995:20).

Gareth Tuckwell and David Flagg, doctor and former priest respectively at Burrswood, discuss in *A Question of Healing* (1995) the use of 'alternative' therapies and the New Age. Whilst recognizing the effectiveness of some of these therapies, and acknowledging (Tuckwell & Flagg 1995:38-40) "grey" areas of differing opinions among Christians on, for example, yoga, they find "'New Age' concepts" "[u]nderlying many of the alternative therapies".

> 'Spiritual healing' is often a fashionable front for
> spiritualistic/mediumistic practice. The latter always leads, in our
> experience, to some kind of oppression or bondage.
> (Tuckwell & Flagg 1995:37)

Healing and Wholeness, a magazine that incorporates the earlier *Burrswood Herald* but with a wider target audience, is antipathetic to New Age healing. It includes articles such as one discussing whether orthodox medicine is "tied up with pagan religion" and whether "any doctor would try to steer you towards New Age religion" (*Healing and Wholeness* 1996.2:38-39). It advertises a conference at Holy Trinity Brompton and offers "Saints for Healing" to new subscribers. "Saints for Healing" forms the basis of an evangelical course in the Ministry of Healing I attended at Cudham church during the period of research.

Another example of the overlap between New Age and evangelical Christianity is the Nine O'Clock Service. What is particularly interesting about this group is that it started out in evangelical Christianity before moving on to the New Age through postmodernism. Revd Chris Brain (b 1957) was converted in his late 'teens to evangelical Christianity and baptized in 1975 at a Baptist church. Soon after his marriage in 1977 he moved to the Anglican church. Revd Brain's first rock band was called "Candescence", formed in answer to a divine command, and aimed at converting the young to Christianity. Following a large donation, the band was put on a secure financial footing and the Brains lived in a Christian community household with the donor. By the early 1980s, this had become the Nairn Street Community, an evangelical group of about 30 people living in a number of community houses in Sheffield, sharing their incomes and having weekly community meetings, concerned with social justice and the development of the rock band.

After a visit from the American charismatic healer John Wimber in 1985 to St Thomas' church, Sheffield, the Nairn Street Community was asked to begin a service for non-Christians aged 18 to 30 at 9pm every Sunday evening – whence its name, The Nine O'Clock Service ("NOS"). The church was made to appear like a night club, with video loops projected onto the church walls, but they used Wimber's style of service. Within a year they had a regular congregation of 150 and by 1988 there were 400 members. In 1989, nearly 100 people were confirmed. NOS Community became a separate congregation within St Thomas's church, and in 1990 the Nine O'Clock Trust was founded to promote experimental worship, a body that was independent from the church. New members of NOS were asked to make a three-year commitment and, if single, to remain celibate. Revd Brain was ordained six months early in 1992, omitting the usual period of curateship as it was felt he had enough pastoral experience and NOS needed him quickly so that they could celebrate communion.

So well was Brain regarded by the church in his pioneering worship, that he was commissioned by George Carey, Archbishop of Canterbury, and John Habgood, Archbishop of York, to write a chapter for *Treasures of the Field*, a book produced by the Church of England for the Decade of Evangelism (an inter-denominational campaign to increase evangelism in the 1990s). A 1992 article by

Brain shows his original attitude to Matthew Fox's Creation Spirituality:

> Whilst there is a desperate need to recover the creation traditions, Fox's apparent proposal that they should actually replace the redemption tradition is unacceptable because, for one thing, it dangerously belittles the reality of evil.
>
> (Brain in *Anglicans for Renewal* magazine, 1992, quoted in Howard 1996:90)

The story of NOS' move into New Age circles has been told in the chapter on St James's.

Thus we have detailed many examples of an overlap between evangelical Christianity and the New Age. A recurring problem with the methodology of this thesis is that there is no way of telling how representative of wider trends within Christianity and New Age are the groups actually studied. Thus we have no idea whether it is common or unusual for evangelical groups to spawn New Age groups, or vice versa, or rather whether the overlap is infrequent but noticeable. The only conclusion that we can draw, in line with Thompson, Albanese and Lucas, is that there is a definite similarity and overlap between evangelical Christianity and the New Age movement. This is surpising given the nature of evangelical literature on the New Age, but may actually explain the hostility between the two groups. Far from acting merely as a control group, then, my limited study of evangelical Christianity has provided further insight into the relations between Christianity and the New Age.

Notes to Chapter VI

[1] Eckberg and Blocker (1989) found, in a random sample of people in Tulsa, Oklahoma, that the best predictor of lower levels of concern for the environment was belief in the literal interpretation of the Bible. Greeley (1993) used the national General Social Survey to refute this correlation, claiming that it disappears when religious imagery and political moral rigidity are taken into account.

[2] Even St James's church, though built by Christopher Wren, may date its New Age leanings to the arrival of Revd Reeves in 1980.

[3] For a comprehensive list (which, however, is now quite dated) see Lewis (1991); see also Saliba (1999).

[4] New Age as a version of Gnosticism is not just an evangelical critique; cf Raschke (1980) and Zoccatelli (1998).

[5] Osborn's study was funded by the evangelical Whitefield Institute, which declined to support my research on Christianity and the New Age.

[6] eg Livesey 1988/1983:86; Groothuis 1991/1986:84

[7] For *Worldviews in Transition* (1994) Steyn conducted 30 interviews in 1990, with a limited amount of participant observation, and presents the results thematically under the headings "The New Age Vision; God and the Cosmos; Anthropology and Theodicy; Knowledge, Healing and Transformation" (Steyn 1994:passim). The definition of a New Ager is as follows:

> They would not even have to identify with the movement as such. If they (a) concurred with the notion of humanity being at a crucial point in its history, *and* (b) agreed that presently there are indications of a transformation of consciousness, they were considered eligible for inclusion.
> (Steyn 1994:11)

This is a very broad definition, and the most detailed analysis Steyn gives of the New Age "grid" is as follows:

> The four tributaries (the alternative tradition, the Eastern philosophies, humanistic and transpersonal psychology, and the new physics) that have converged in the mainstream of the New Age movement give us a vertical distinction, while the four levels identified by Spangler (the commercial, the New Age as glamour, personal and social transformation, and the New Age as the incarnation of the sacred) ... provide us with a horizontal distinction, which together form a framework or grid in which each individual phenomenon within the movement can be situated and the spectrum of beliefs plotted.
> (Steyn 1994:125)

[8] Interview, 2 October 1996.

VII. CHRISTIAN RESPONSES TO NEW AGE

Christians have responded in a variety of ways to the challenges posed by the New Age movement. Those I am most interested in – those I dub Christaquarians – have adopted many New Age beliefs and practices while retaining their Christian faith. The Churches as institutions have been less accommodating, and have issued warnings against the New Age, while other individuals have set up Christian outreach groups to convert New Agers. Previous chapters have considered group case studies; this chapter gives an overview of the many and varied Christian responses to the New Age.

The Responses of the Churches

The Churches as institutions have been generally less than positive in their corporate responses to the New Age. The Catholic, Anglican and Methodist churches have all issued official reports which almost totally condemn the New Age and warn Christians against it.

Pope John Paul II wrote in 1994,

> We cannot delude ourselves that this [the so-called New Age] will lead toward a renewal of religion. It is only a new way of practising gnosticism – that attitude of the spirit that, in the name of a profound knowledge of God, results in distorting His Word and replacing it with purely human words.
> (*Crossing the Threshold of Hope* 1994:90 quoted in Heelas 1996a:221)

There is no extended discussion of New Age by the Vatican[1]. It was the Irish Theological Commission that published in 1994, *A New Age of the Spirit? A Catholic Response to the New Age Phenomenon*. The analysis begins positively, saying that the New Age

> challenges the Church to look at the way she serves people. ... not everything in the New Age is evil or bad.
> (Irish Theological Commission 1994:5)

It then lists several contributions the New Age has made: its concern for a healthy lifestyle and environment, for spirituality, for psychology. But these positive aspects are not given further consideration. The Commission claims that "vast numbers" (ITC 1996:26) of Christians have tried to Christianise New Age practices. However, the report claims that Christianity has failed in the eyes of New Agers who think that it should be

> either transformed by NAM [New Age Movement] teaching or 'dealt with' ... That transformation lies in mixing Christianity with eastern religions initially, then with the occult.
> (ITC 1994:27)

With reference to Benjamin Creme and Alice Bailey, the Commission writes

> What is afoot is the reconstruction of a new World Order. ...
> Part of this plan is also a One World Church, which these writers refer to
> as the New World Religion. ...
> What would happen to the Church is she resisted this take-over? There
> are subtle hints in these NAM books that resistence [sic] will be crushed.
> (ITC 1994:50-52)

Although some primary sources have been consulted in preparation of the report, such as Marilyn Ferguson, William Irwin Thompson, David Spangler, Benjamin Creme and Alice Bailey, much of the analysis comes from evangelical critiques. For example, with reference to Texe Marrs, it is claimed that the Lucis Foundation and the Association for Research and Development in Virginia "appears to be the brain centre for the NAM" (ITC 1994:34). Another claim, this time unreferenced, is that New Agers maintain contact through an international computer system called "Peacenet" (ITC 1994:54).

The Commission concludes with a chapter discussing certain New Age practices: reflexology, acupuncture, TM, yoga, astrology, New Age music and books, crystals and management courses. For reflexology, it concludes that it is effective if carried out by a nurse but Christians should be wary of being offered New Age philosophy at the same time; for other therapies, the judgement is less conciliatory.

The Search for Faith, a report published by Church House in November 1996, received wide publicity[2] as the Church of England's agenda against an ascendant New Age religion[3]. In fact only one chapter of *The Search for Faith* is explicitly concerned with New Age: Chapter 3, "The world is my oyster" (Mission Theological Advisory Group 1996:74-109). This is prefaced like other chapters with a character sketch – here, Adam "has done cards, pyramids, stones" and says "I don't need Church." Under the heading "How contemporary spirituality challenges the Church", imaginary examples of "generalised belief" (MTAG 1996:75) are given and explained as post-materialist individualist articulations of the numinous. In particular, the need to control one's destiny, to feel good, to have hope for the future and concern for nature – are considered "component elements of contemporary spirituality ... which are open to Christian" appropriation in evangelism (MTAG 1996:78).

Although it is considered that 'New Age practices' become ends in themselves rather means to a closer relationship to God (MTAG 1996:82), the report recommends acknowledgement of these "elements" or "aspects" in the Christian tradition. The final test for the "label 'incompatible with Christianity'" (MTAG 1996:82) appears to be "the amount of distraction from the Christian occupation of working for and in God's kingdom" (MTAG 1996:83). Suggested responses to "New Age practices" are: liturgies that address peoples' experiences; commissioning of artwork; use of the metaphor of pilgrimage for Christian faith; praise of God as creator; recognition of the community of Christian believers; seeing the wholeness of the earth; and rediscovery of 'spiritual' language such as that of 'angels'. The concluding paragraphs view New Age in terms of Christian mission.

Judging from the references within the Methodist Faith and Order Committee's *Report to Conference* (1994), there appears to have been little if any original or field research for the document, with quotations coming from accessible works on New Age by Ferguson, Bloom, Fox, Chandler, Drane, Seddon and Perry. Thus although some New Age authors are consulted, these are overshadowed by hostile analysis provided by mainly evangelical critics – even though the charismatic movement is criticized in the *Report* as coming "very close to many New Agers in its fervency" (Faith and Order Committee 1994:9). Examples the *Report* gives of New Age are Findhorn, Glastonbury, Marilyn Ferguson, George Trevelyan and David Spangler. It claims that New Age ideas "are becoming all-pervasive" (Faith and Order Committee 1994:3) but acknowledges that there is no organizational structure or established doctrinal agenda, and its "socio-political ambitions" are regarded as "negligible" (Faith and Order Committee 1994:10). Four features are identified as typical: the emphasis on the spiritual rather than the material, especially belief in reincarnation; the ideas of harmony, unity and wholeness, including the doctrine of pantheism; the emphasis on the individual and their right to chose their own religion; and the "hopefulness" at the dawning of a New Age (Faith and Order Committee 1994:5).

The attitude taken by the *Report* to New Age is generally negative, but

> Its theological content is to be taken ... seriously, as both a challenge and a stimulus to orthodox Christian teaching.
> (Faith and Order Committee 1994:10)
> ... critical dialogue by Christians is what is needed.
> (Faith and Order Committee 1994:17)

Two doctrines in particular are examined in this regard: creation and Christ. It is noted that theocentric Christian accounts of creation are not accepted in New Age, which places more emphasis on a pervasive cosmic force with nature. Secondly, Cartesian, mechanistic thought about the environment is rejected in New Age, it is stated, for holistic thought. A third tradition from which New Age derives its view of creation is, it is said, Eastern religion: the concept of all in one, of maya ("illusion"), of divine emanation, of Earth Mother, of karma, of avatars and of cyclical history. These New Age views on creation are seen as a challenge to Christians to become more "pro-earth" (Faith and Order Committee 1994:16), but the *Report* does not go all the way in seeing nature as sacred.

The penultimate section outlines various missiological and pastoral questions raised by the New Age movement. The general tone is to learn from the New Age movement.

> It may be important ... to affirm the search for enlightenment which the New Age represents, and to acknowledge how real is the hunger for the divine out of which it emerges. What we may be more cautious about is the context of consumerism and instant gratification in which this quest is set today.
> (Faith and Order Committee 1994:24)

The concluding section gives three "starting points" for dialogue:

i)   the Spirit as an expression of the divine life
ii) the process of continuous spiritual development towards self-transcendence
iii) the presence of the Spirit in people throughout history (although retaining the uniqueness of Christ)
(paraphrase of Faith and Order Committee 1994:26-27)

Whilst the corporate responses of the Churches to the New Age movement are therefore largely negative, individual Christians who have a negative response to the New Age have formed constructive responses in the form of outreach groups. For example, Glastonbury boasts two Christian outreach organizations to the New Age. The Quest Community, after several years of activity, was dedicated on 6 June 1993 in Glastonbury Abbey at a service conducted by the Bishop of Bath and Wells. Its leader is Revd John Sumner, and there is a Core Community of six people with a mailing list of between one and two hundred. A Christian prayer presence of up to 20 pray-ers is maintained daily at noon for all who pass through Glastonbury, and members of the Quest Community are on hand for pastoral or ministerial guidance to seekers.

Revd Mark Bond, vicar of Highbridge in Somerset, is a trustee of the Quest Community, but also runs another outreach programme called The Coracle at the annual Glastonbury festival. Although Glastonbury is widely known for its music festival held on farmland, there is also what is called a "Healing Field" at the festival where various spiritual healers offer their wares. Michael Eavis, the organizer of the festival, is Christian and gives 20 free entrance tickets to members of The Coracle for their outreach stall. The approach taken is non-aggressive, and members take part in the daily discussions held in a marquee in the field. Revd Bond reports that he has never been heckled at Glastonbury – such as some evangelical outreach programmes might expect. Revd Bond predicts that New Age will become institutionalized like any other religion (Telephone interview, 21 March 1998). In an article in *Chrism* magazine, Revd Bond (1998) argues that the Church must adapt its sacraments to the needs of the New Age, suggesting development of the ritual of the shared meal, the sacredness of meeting, use of New Age music in churches and the public response to the death of Diana, Princess of Wales.

Fountain of Life is an outreach group (not to be confused with the Spiritualist group Fountain International) that is run by Simone Pentel under the umbrella of the Kensington Temple, a large evangelical church in London. Kensington Temple also runs outreach teams for various areas of London, for OAPs, the homeless, prisoners and Jehovah's Witnesses. Pentel was brought up in a Jewish family, and was involved with such things New Age as crystals before becoming a Christian. She has held an outreach stall for several years at the Mind-Body-Spirit festival in Alexandra Palace, and at the Healing Arts festivals. I have also met Pentel 'moonlighting' with another Christian outreach group at a Mind-Body-Spirit festival. A number of the New Age stall-holders at the Mind-Body-Spirit festival in May 1996 complained to me about the aggressive methods of outreach used by some evangelicals[4]. Tracts handed out by Fountain of Life contained apocalyptic conspiracy theories about the New Age movement, prophesying a one-world government led by the Antichrist. The European Union was said to be working towards a New World Order with President Clinton.

In the summer of 1996 Fountain of Life ran a lecture programme entitled "The Alpha and Omega Course", with evenings including "The spiritual realm: Angels, demons, UFOs, spirit guides", "Meditation and Healing", "The Divine Plan and the Global Crisis". Some of these evenings did not attract a single New Ager, and the lecture I attended, "The spiritual realm", had just one other attendee. These lectures are obviously designed to attract New Agers, as is Pentel's general dress-style, but their success rate may be questioned.

Reachout Trust, based in Richmond and with a homepage on the Internet, offers evangelical Christian outreach to the occult and New Age. Monthly prayer-letters are distributed in churches, detailing the efforts of local outreach programmes and asking for prayer over specific individuals. The Trust also distributes leaflets and a glossy booklet warning of the dangers of the occult and the New Age, and explaining how to evangelize. A booklet produced in 1995 traces the roots of New Age to Theosophy, secular humanism, paganism, sixties culture and the Gaia hypothesis. Common beliefs said to be held by most New Agers are monism, pantheism or panentheism, gnosticism, relativism, transformation, the Cosmic Christ, and the coming of the New Age. The World Council of Churches is said to serve as a focal point, although conspiracy theories are explicitly rejected. St James' church Piccadilly is mentioned as an example of the New Age, as is "William [sic for Michael] Perry" and the Churches' Fellowship for Psychical and Spiritual Studies.

Ecological and Metaphysical New Age

This thesis will not consider further the responses of the Churches to New Age. Likewise, the thesis is not particularly concerned with evangelical or fundamentalist responses to New Age, except as a control group against which to measure positive Christian responses to the New Age movement. What particularly interests me is the group of Christians who interact positively with the New Age movement, apparently reconciling the difficulties which other Christians find there. I ask, somewhat boldly, whether these Christians may be considered as part of a movement, which I have dubbed Christaquarianism.

Probably the vast majority of Christians who accommodate the New Age into their faith are loners – if they were Neopagans we would call them "hedge witches" after Rae Beth's felicitous term (1990). They are very difficult to study objectively, as there is by definition no central record of the people involved. Occasionally it is possible to meet a lone Christaquarian at a New Age exhibition, for example, but there must be many Christians interested in the New Age who do not venture outside of their own churches and may never mention their interest to anyone else. Perhaps the easiest way to meet lone Christaquarians today is over the Internet. With this in mind, I set up a website inviting people to respond to a synopsis of my thesis (now updated and expanded at www.Christaquarian.net).

An example of the responses I received is from lrp@aol.com[5]. He has never really shared the full extent of his Christaquarian beliefs – except over the Internet – despite being a Methodist Local Preacher for nearly 30 years. A sermon mentioning Creation Spirituality received positive reactions, but a mention of Taoism provoked a hostile response. Lrp@aol.com is 51, married with two daughters, and first heard of Matthew Fox when he (ie, my correspondent) was a member of the Green Party. His interest in New Age is derived from his father's interest in British Israelism, and to begin with lrp@aol.com was fundamentalist in his Christian beliefs. An Anglican curate, however, introduced him to the writings of Bede Griffiths, William Johnston and the Julian Meetings. These modern mystics led him to William Law, Jacob Boehme and Pseudo-Dionysius. He currently receives the GreenSpirit magazine on Creation Spirituality and *Kindred Spirit*, the New Age magazine.

Following Greer (1994), I believe that the two lone Christaquarians considered below represent two tendencies within New Age: the 'ecological' tendency which affirms 'green', 'feminine' 'earthiness'; and the 'metaphysical' tendency which emphasizes non-physical, 'masculine', hierarchical values. Henrietta is an ecological Christaquarian, Vicki a metaphysical Christaquarian.

Henrietta is a biodynamic psychotherapist who offers therapy and workshops in central London. Her flat is part of an extended New Age/Neopagan community run on co-operative lines and operating a vegetarian café, and she is happy to describe her work as New Age. In 1997, as in previous years, she offered a series of workshops entitled "Energy in Balance: A cosmic journey via various stations of our body" – 12 evenings related to the signs of the zodiac. She usually uses massage in her work, as she believes psychological blockages attract fluid, which solidifies as a crystal, preventing energy moving out. These crystal blockages can be removed by massage. Flower remedies are also used. Henrietta is also a spiritual healer, and in this work she uses the concept of chakras.

A table of leaflets in Henrietta's therapy room includes a leaflet for the Alternatives lectures at St James's church. Henrietta is an Anthroposophist, sometimes goes to a Christian Community church, and the Christ forms an important part of her belief structure. The Christ force helps us to be free spiritually, she believes. Henrietta describes herself as Christian and has had visions and dreams of Christ – as well as of Rudolf Steiner. She sees herself as slightly different from most of the community in which she lives, and tries to bring a Christian emphasis into it: Rudolf Steiner told her through automatic writing that she should be the link to Christianity for the rest of the community. A medium has told her that in a past life she was a Christian orator who was thrown to the lions in a Roman amphitheatre. In this life, she was brought up as a Protestant and in her early twenties became interested in von Däniken, left the church and went to India.

Vicki is an eclectic hypnotherapist working in greater London. If she had to use one label to describe her religion, she would say, "Church of England", and she attends her local Anglican church. Her bookshelves are lined with New Age books including Shirley MacLaine, Silva Mind Control, Eileen Caddy, Gestalt books, and older works such as Levi Dowling's *The Aquarian Gospel of Jesus the Christ* (1987/1907), Florence Scovel-Shinn's *The Game of Life and How to Play It* (1925) and Baird J Spalding's *Life and Teaching of the Masters of the East* (vols 1-5 1924).

Vicki first came to hypnotherapy through her own nervous condition in about 1980, and trained in hypnotherapy before attending courses in polarity therapy, Reichian therapy, bodywork, reflexology, NLP and various other therapies. At the time of research, she was involved with Chuck Spezzano's "Psychology of Vision" group, attending various workshops and seminars and using his *Awaken the Gods* (1991) every morning in her self-hypnosis. Vicki describes God as Energy or sex energy (Spezzano teaches Tantric mastery). Everything is made of Energy; or, to put it another way, we create objects ourselves. If you change your thought, reality starts to change around you: Vicki believes in miracles. There is a hierarchy of circles of Energy, she believes, from the Earth to the higher selves and God. The higher selves are the Masters. Vicki does not believe in evil, the devil or hell. The Energy is good. Vicki also gives evening classes in hypnosis, and many of her private clients have first been her pupils. Spiritual ideas are never mentioned to clients or the beginner classes in self-hypnosis that she runs; these are reserved for the advanced classes where participants are usually into spirituality in any case. Christianity is never discussed, as it can put people off, she said.

A Course in Miracles

Having given three sketches of lone Christaquarians, I now move on to consider various Christaquarian groups. Vicki has also studied parts of *A Course in Miracles* ("the Course"), a huge text – over 1,000 pages with the workbook for students and manual for teachers – of spiritual instruction channelled by the late Dr Helen Schucman and first printed in 1975.

> The purpose of the workbook is to train your mind in a systematic way to a different perception of everyone and everything in the world.
> (Anonymous 1985/1975 vol II:1)

The underlying philosophy is idealist: the world does not exist except in our minds. Salvation is achieved through the perception of this fact, when we become one with God and are able to perform "miracles", or rather, become aware of the true nature of things.

The Course has been used in mainstream Christian study groups, for it claims to be channelled from Jesus and uses Christian vocabulary such as Christ, Son, Holy Spirit, Love. Many of those who read the Course continue to profess Christianity. But as a promotional leaflet for the book explains,

Although it uses Christian terminology, it deals with universal spiritual themes. It is a restatement of the perennial philosophy in a form that is practical and applicable to our everyday lives.
(Advertisement inserted in Anonymous 1985/1975)

Around the Course have grown various exegetes, the most famous of whom are Gerald Jampolsky, Marianne Williamson and Kenneth Wapnick. Marianne Williamson, whose works are often available on the bookstall at Alternatives lectures, asserts (in a series of taped lectures) that attuning ourselves to powerful words like "Christ" can heal us "magically", but according to the Course, a complete change in belief is needed to effect a lasting cure. Williamson has undertaken ordination training with the Unity Church in Detroit (*Miracle Worker* 1998 Vol 23:3). Similarly, The New Seminary, founded in 1986 by Miranda Holden, teaches a curriculum of the major spiritual traditions, including the Course, alongside spiritual counselling, ceremonies and healing rituals. After two years, graduates are ordained as Interfaith Ministers and Spiritual Counsellors. Interfaith services are held by Holden on the first Sunday of each month at the Centre for Inner Peace in Worcester, and on the third Sunday in the Temple of All Faiths, Reading.

In the United Kingdom, there is a "Miracle Network", which publishes a bi-monthly newsletter, *The Miracle Worker*, to support students of the *Course*. The newsletter lists nearly 100 Course study groups in the UK, some of which offer telephone counselling. Dr Chuck Spezzano's works are distributed by The Miracle Network. Dr Spezzano told an audience at St James's church Alternatives (12 February 1996) that he had seen cancer and haemorrhoids cured in people using his Psychology of Vision. An important technique to *Awaken the Gods* (Spezzano 1991) is the magic of miracles:

To have a miracle know who you are and share that knowledge.
To create a miracle change your mind.
Creating a miracle is not believing an illusion through affirming the truth.
(Spezzano 1991:86-87)

The Miracle Network also distributes the work of Kenneth Wapnick. Wapnick distinguishes between magic which does work on the illusory plane of physical reality, and real miracles which heal the sick and raise the dead through destroying the illusion of reality. W Norris Clarke, a Jesuit, notes the tension:

[Clarke:] On one hand, I am hearing you say that it does not make any difference if you project a parking space or what you do as long as you do not attribute that to the Holy Spirit. But now you are saying the opposite, which is do not project parking spaces or any such thing, they are all in the mind.

[To which Wapnick replies:] Right, I am saying both things. I am saying that the best thing is not to use magic at all, but most of us are not up to that all the time. The best thing would be to ask the Holy Spirit, "What should I do?" rather than to project the parking spot.
(Wapnick & Clarke 1995:81-82)

For some time, Kenneth Wapnick designed his exegesis of the Course to appear Christian. This involved extensive quotation of scripture and, as in the *Course*, adoption of a pseudo-Christian terminology. However, he no longer professes Christianity, and also expresses an antipathy to the New Age (eg Wapnick 1994:94,144). In the 1992 preface to the fourth edition of *Forgiveness and Jesus*, which is subtitled *The Meeting Place of A Course in Miracles and Christianity*, Wapnick explicitly states that his teaching has moved on from bridging Christianity and the New Age (Wapnick 1994:xiv). He outlines the distinctions as follows:

> 1) the Course's metaphysical teachings about the fundamental illusory nature of the world; 2) the striking contrast between the biblical God who believes in sin, separation, and specialness and the absolutely non-dualistic God of the Course; 3) the inherent sameness between ourselves and Jesus; and 4) the non-sacrificial and non-suffering death of Jesus – render impossible any attempts to parallel these two spiritual approaches.
> (Wapnick 1994:xiv-xv)

The association of the Course with what I have called metaphysical Christaquarianism becomes clearer when we examine another of Wapnick's works, *Love Does Not Condemn* (1990/1989). This is subtitled, *The World, the Flesh, and the Devil According to Platonism, Christianity, Gnosticism and A Course in Miracles*.

Neognostic Christaquarians

Many of the patriarchal/metaphysical New Age groups in Greer's ecological-patriarchal continuum are Neognostic in character[6].

The Ecclesia Gnostica claims to be "the oldest public Gnostic sacramental body in the United States" (http://www.gnosis.org/ecclesia/ecclesia.htm), moving there in 1959 under the late Bishop Richard, Duc de Palatine. It had previously been known in England as the Pre-Nicene Gnostic Catholic Church. Dr Stephen A Hoeller is the current Regionary Bishop of the church, and ordination is open to both men and women. The Los Angeles parish of the Ecclesia Gnostica holds eleven church services and four lectures each month; there is a second parish in Portland, Oregon, a mission in Salt Lake City, a seminary in Arizona and a mission in Norway. It incorporates the Gnostic Society, founded by James and John Pryse in 1928, and is in "fraternal alliance" with the Eglise Gnostique Catholique Apostolique of France, recognising its holy orders. Also in California is the New Age Bible and Philosophy Center, based on the 1930s works of Theodore and Corinne Heline, which include a seven-volume explicitly "New Age" interpretation of the Bible (eg Heline 1992/1935).

The Universal Christian Gnostic Movement of the UK (New Order), currently with centres in London, Manchester, Birmingham and Edinburgh, is a splinter group of the Gnostic Movement UK. As an undergraduate, I researched this latter group as a reporter for Cardiff's student newspaper (see Kemp 1992). It was part of the International Gnostic Federation, co-ordinated by JE Amortegui Valbuena, also known as VM Rabolu. Samael Aun Weor (1917-1977) founded the movement in the 1960s in Colombia, and wrote six books: *Revolutionary Psychology, The Great Rebellion, The Mystery of the Golden Blossom, Perfect Matrimony, Fundamental Education* and *The Three Mountains.* The Cardiff neognostic group also advertised its courses under the names Esoteric Psychology and The Inner World, and taught beginners a conventional relaxation technique. It is interesting that the Christian element in the teachings is now being emphasised.

On the continent, the Eglise Gnostique Universelle was founded in 1890 by Jules-Stanislas Dionel, the Gnostisch Katholische Kirche in 1908 by Theodor Reuss (Hanegraaff 1992b:21). Max Heindel (Carl Louis von Grasshoff) (1865-1919), originally a Theosophist, founded the Rosicrucian Fellowship in Los Angeles in 1907, of which Jan Leene (1896-1968) and his brother Zwier Wilhelm Leene (1892-1938) became the most important leaders in the Netherlands in the 1920s. These brothers dated the founding of Lectorium Rosicrucianum ("LR") to 1924, but they only formally split from the Rosicrucian Fellowship in 1935 and adopted the name LR in 1945. Catharose de Petri (pen-name of Mrs H Stok-Huyser (1902-1990)) also wrote influential texts for LR at this time. Antonin Gadal (1871-1962), a mastermind of the Cathar revival, was president of the LR branch created in France in 1957.

I have completed a small amount of participant observation, informal interviews and a cursory review of literature with LR. One member of LR I spoke to thought their movement predated New Age, but another agreed that, in the absence of anything else, it was the best category under which to class it. In 1996, LR began holding introductory lecutres at the Neals Yard meeting rooms in London, a popular New Age location. Leaders of the British branch of LR also organise, on a separate basis, the Cygnus mail order book club, which markets New Age books such as *The Celestine Prophecy* (1994) by James Redfield and the works of Kahlil Gibran. The Cygnus brochure includes a small number of reviews of works for sale, for example of a talk given at the 'Mystics and Scientists' conference in 1994.

Greer (1994) has studied LR as an example of New Age. Introvigne (1997) claims that there are currently over 15,000 pupils and members of LR, but does not cite evidence of this claim. Introvigne describes LR as "a dualist and gnostic Christianity" but denies that it is part of the New Age movement, despite acknowledging that it has, often deliberately, recruited members from the New Age movement. His reasoning is that LR considers New Age and occult techniques to be "typical of the dialectical field ... LR pupils are looking for esoteric models regarded as more "pure" and closer to a genuine ancient wisdom" (Introvigne 1997). Yet surely this is a simple case of one New Age organisation

171

seeking to elevate itself above other, less cohesive, parts of the milieu.

In many ways, LR may be similar to the Order of the Solar Temple. Few scholars had heard of the Order of the Solar Temple (but see Mayer 1993) prior to the deaths of 53 members in Switzerland and Canada on 4 October 1994. Fourteen more bodies were found near Grenoble in France after the winter solstice in 1995. Even now, the academic literature on the Order is far from satisfactory (eg Hall & Schuyler 1997:285-312; Introvigne 1995; Mayer 1999). However, it has been possible to reconstruct some of the doctrines and beliefs of the Order from the accounts of surviving members and the available literature, although I will not discuss the various allegations of persecution by the authorities that are said to have contributed to the deaths.

Both leaders of the Order were among the dead. Luc Jouret (1947-1994) had been ordained a priest in a French independent church, and thus was able to celebrate a version of the Catholic mass called the "Essene ritual". He was also a trained doctor, and his entry to the New Age movement appears to have been through alternative medicine, particularly homeopathy. In the early 1980s he formed the Amenta Club (later "Atlanta") to consolidate his conferences and workshops on the New Age circuit. One of the groups he often addressed was the Golden Way Foundation in Geneva, led by Joseph Di Mambro (1924-1994).

The International Order of the Chivalry Solar Tradition, from about 1990 known as the Order of the Solar Temple, was an inner circle of the Archédia Clubs, founded in 1984 by Jouret and Di Mambro, in turn an inner circle of Amenta. The Order derived from a schism in 1984 in the Renewed Order of the Temple ("ORT"), a neo-Templar group connected for a while with the large Rosicrucian organisation AMORC (Ancient and Mystical Order Rosae Crucis) founded by Harvey Spencer Lewis (1883-1939). Jouret had joined the ORT in 1981, and after the death of the leader, Julien Origas (1920-1983), campaigned without success to replace him. Di Mambro had also been influenced by Origas, as well as by Jacques Breyer, a French alchemist who with Maxime de Roquemaure founded the Sovereign Order of the Solar Temple, based on doctrines about the end of the world and a "Solar Christ".

The Order of the Solar Temple traced its roots to the Order of Poor Knights of the Temple of Solomon, a knightly Catholic monastic order founded in 1118-19 by Hugues de Payens (or Payns) and dissolved after considerable persecution by the King of France in 1307. The myth of the underground persistence of the Templars has been kept alive among Freemasons, with its Templar degrees of initiation, but is certainly fantastical. The 53 dead of the Solar Temple (plus one survivor) were to have contacted the 54 spirits of some of the original Templars burnt at the stake in 1310.

In the 1980s there were about two to three hundred members of the Solar Temple in Switzerland, Canada and Australia, though a move to communal living reduced this to about one hundred by 1993. There were three major degrees in the Order – Brothers of the Court, Chevaliers of the Alliance and Brothers of Former Times.

Enlightenment to these degrees was achieved through elaborate ritual, dressed in the traditional Templar costume of white robes with a red cross. The rituals were assisted with special electronic and holographic effects.

Jouret and Di Mambro received apocalyptic revelations that the last guardians of the Earth would leave by the beginning of 1994. At this time, human bodies were to be discarded for "solar bodies" operating in a superior dimension in the "Great White Lodge" on Sirius, the Dog Star – this was referred to as a "Transit". Jouret's eschatology probably originally derived from his interest in ecological apocalypse, and his interest in environmentalism in turn derived from his interest in homeopathy. Pollution was seen as

> an exterior reflection of a pollution much deeper inside Man – mental pollution, emotional pollution, and, at the extreme, an authentically spiritual pollution.
> (Jouret quoted in Hall & Schuyler 1997:293)

A universal conflagration was to accompany the transition from the Age of Pisces to the Age of Aquarius. The Solar Temple may be located on the extreme fringe of the Christaquarian circuit. Had they not committed suicide, they would probably have remained largely unknown.

Heaven's Gate

Another NRM that committed mass suicide, and had similar debts to Christianity and extra-terrestrial mythology, is Heaven's Gate. Appropriately, most of my research on Heaven's Gate was done on the Internet (see also Thompson 1997/1996:346-350), for Heaven's Gate was a highly Net-literate religious movement, leading some scholars (eg Clarke 1998) to present it as one of the first NRMs to recruit over the Web[7]. Although Heaven's Gate's own homepages have now been taken down, a number of sites provide full mirrors with extensive journalistic comment.

Heaven's Gate's homepage proclaims "Red Alert: Hale-Bopp brings closure to Heaven's Gate". Followers of Marshall Herff Applewhite and his wife Bonnie Lu Trousdale Nettles – known variously as "The Representative", "Do and Ti", "The Two", "Bo and Peep" and "Tiddly and Wink" – believed that the comet named Hale-Bopp was a "marker", a sign that a spaceship from the Level Above Human would come to take them home to "their" world. On 26 March 1997, 39 members of the group took their own lives in San Diego, believing that they would be transported to the spaceship.

Applewhite was the son of a Presbyterian minister and attended a seminary himself. In March 1975 he and his wife sent their "First Statement" to ministers around the world. This claimed that Jesus was the first human to metamorphose into a higher form. A lecture tour with over 130 meetings in the US and Canada followed. By April 1976 there was a group of around 100 followers, when recruitment was stopped because "the 'Harvest' is closed". The students met in the Medicine Bow National Forest, Wyoming, and their numbers soon halved. There followed a long period of "seclusion".

In 1988 an "Update" was sent

> to various New Age Centers, Health Food Stores, writers, preachers, ufologists, monasteries, and so on. ... Reports of government cover-ups of UFO crashes, alien technology being acquired and tested by the military, and rumors of underground bases housing joint alien/government projects circulated widely.
>
> (http://www.levelabovehuman.org/book/3-1.htm)

From late 1991 to early 1992, the group was known as Total Overcomers Anonymous, expressing their desire

> to overcome all aspects of the human kingdom, while remaining at the same time, both separate and anonymous.
>
> (http://www.levelabovehuman.org/book/4-1.htm)

In 1993 the group published an advertisement in *USA Today* and over 20 other alternative newspapers in the US, Canada and Australia. In the next year followed another series of public lectures.

Heaven's Gate taught that humans were a transitionary stage between the animal kingdom and the Kingdom of God, the Evolutionary Kingdom Level Above Human. Earth's present civilisation is about to be recycled onto this next level. Followers of the group were to overcome all "human-mammalian behavior" which tied them to this level, such as sex, drugs, alcohol, possessions and past relationships with family and friends. Many alien races had previously presented themselves to humans as gods, and were known as the "Luciferians", for they had fallen away from the true Kingdom of God. Two thousand years ago, the true Kingdom of God appointed an Older Member to send His Son and some students to incarnate on the Earth. The humans under the control of the Luciferians killed the Captain and his away-team crew, and perverted his teachings.

Organized religion, especially Christianity, was presented by Heaven's Group as the "Great cover-up". The information brought to earth by Jesus the Representative had been ignored or obscured, they said.

> **The Christians have unwittingly even become their own dreaded *Anti-Christ*.**
>
> (http://www.levelabovehuman.org/book/6-6.htm, **original emphasis**)

Nevertheless, Heaven's Group continued to quote scripture in their teachings. One web-page (http://www.levelabovehuman.org/book/b-2.htm) contains seven A4 pages of supporting quotations from the Bible. Similarly, although Heaven's Gate adopted the New Age language of UFOlogy, they also distanced themselves from the movement.

> ... the true antichrist is now here and has taken several faces, one of which is the New Age "Ye are Gods" concept, or "I have only to become aware of my own 'Christ consciousness within'" while continuing to practice the ways of the world.
>
> (http://www.levelabovehuman.org/book/3-3.htm)

Despite these protestations against both Christianity and the New Age, it is fair from a sociological point of view to label Heaven's Gate as Christaquarian, for they contain all the hallmarks of New Age beliefs (eg extraterrestrials, transformation, end of the age) and Christian beliefs (eg reference to the Bible, respect for Jesus).

Creation Spirituality or GreenSpirit

So far we have been discussing the metaphysical or patriarchal Christaquarians of whom Vicki is typical – those who are interested in traditions claiming legitimacy from Platonic and Gnostic traditions such as Christian Science and New Thought (see Chapter V). Henrietta is typical of what we may call ecological Christaquarians who are more inclined towards Neopaganism and feminism. An important grouping of Christaquarians in this ecological tradition is Creation Spirituality, now known in the UK as GreenSpirit (to distinguish it from fundamentalist Creationism), which is concerned with the theology of Revd Matthew Fox. GreenSpirit was also in early 2000 setting up an e-mail list.

Timothy Fox (b 1940) became Brother Matthew when he began his training as a Dominican in 1958. One of his doctoral supervisors was Père MD Chenu, whom Revd Dr Fox often quotes in his publications – it was he who first made explicit for Revd Dr Fox the division of Western spirituality into two traditions: "fall/redemption" and "creation-centered spirituality" (Fox 1996:69). A theme that runs throughout *Whee! We, Wee All the Way Home: A Guide to Sensual, Prophetic Spirituality* (1981/1976) is that of the transition from the Piscean Age of Christians to the new spiritual Age of Aquarius. Nevertheless, Revd Dr Fox strangely emphasises that
> (I do not *believe* in astrology)
> (Fox 1981/1976:30)

Sensual spirituality as Revd Dr Fox sees it should allow "natural ecstasies" to "get [us] high all the time on nature, friendship, sex, the arts, sports, thinking, travel, and involuntary deprivations" (Fox 1981/1976:45). He then lists some "tactical ecstasies", or methods of attaining ecstatic experiences, including chants, fasting, drugs, celibacy, yoga, Zen, TM and biofeedback. "[O]ur experience of ecstasy *is* our experience of God" (Fox 1981/1976:73). "[W]hen we spend time with ecstasies of creation, we become like the Creator and take on the Creator's characteristics" (Fox 1981/1976:79). The final part of the book deals metaphorically with the "dragons" that prevent us experiencing ecstasy: such as bloated egos, moralizing and institutions.

Creation-centered spirituality was first expounded at length by Revd Dr Fox in *Original Blessing* (1983). Here he rejects the tripartite model of mysticism in the Christian tradition for a fourfold paradigm: "Befriending Creation: The Via Positiva", "Befriending Darkness, Letting Go and Letting Be: The Via Negativa", "Befriending Creativity, Befriending Our Divinity: The Via Creativa" and "Befriending New Creation: Compassion, Celebration, Erotic Justice, The Via Transformativa". The Via Positiva is about celebrating the original blessing that God gave us in Creation. Part of this is the avowal of panentheism over theism – God is in everything and everything is in God – which Revd Dr Fox distinguishes from pantheism, a heresy.

The Coming of the Cosmic Christ (1988), subtitled, "*The Healing of Mother Earth and the Birth of a Global Renaissance*" restates creation spirituality in terms of a mysticism based on the spirituality of Christ as the cosmos. Revd Dr Fox locates biblical support for belief in the cosmic Christ in the Old Testament, the Pauline epistles, Revelation, and throughout the Gospels and Acts. He then continues with the tradition of the cosmic Christ in the Middle Ages with Hildegard of Bingen, Francis of Assisi, Thomas Aquinas, Mechtild of Magdeburg, Dante, Meister Eckhart, Julian of Norwich and Nicolas Cusa.

> Embracing the Cosmic Christ will demand a paradigm shift, and it will empower us for that shift:

A shift from

from anthropocentrism	to a living cosmology
from Newton	to Einstein
from part-mentality	to wholeness
from rationalism	to mysticism
from obedience as a prime moral virtue	to creativity as a prime moral virtue
from personal salvation compassion	to communal healing, i.e., as salvation
from theism (God outside us)	to panentheism (God in us and us in God)
from fall-redemption religion	to creation-centered spirituality
from the ascetic	to the aesthetic

(Fox 1988:134-135)

The Institute in Culture and Creation Spirituality ("ICCS") was founded by Revd Dr Fox at Mundelein College, Chicago in 1977, with the ambitious aim of training mystics and prophets, and its successor college today in Oakland, California, now confers postgraduate degrees. In Britain, the Centre for Creation Spirituality was until 2002 based at St James's Church, Piccadilly, and there are 52 groups countrywide. They produce a journal, *GreenSpirit* (prior to 1999 known as *Inter*change) which comes out three times a year, and hold various meetings in the halls next to the church. Their trading company is now also known as GreenSpirit.

Revd Dr Fox distances himself from both fundamentalist Christianity and New Age as "pseudo-mysticism" (Fox 1988:45). The former he often calls "Christofascism" after Dorothee Soelle (Fox 1988:175). The latter he once saw in a slightly more positive light:

> The contemporary mystical movement known as 'new age' can also dialog and create with the creation spiritual tradition.
> (Fox 1983:16)

Indeed, Revd Dr Fox is commonly viewed as a typical example of New Age by Christaquarians, with Creation Spirituality being the most common example (after the Alternatives lecture series) of New Age given by respondents to my survey of the electoral roll at St James's.

176

Members of the Creation Spirituality network in the UK often, though not always, consider themselves to be Christian. A Notre Dame sister who runs a programme of Creation Spirituality workshops in the Liverpool area writes in *Inter*change journal,

> I experience creation spirituality as springing directly from my commitment to the gospel and to gospel values. Although it demands a major shift in spiritual awareness, I do not see creation spirituality as separate from our culture's Christian (and in my case specifically Catholic) heritage, but as growing directly out of it.
> (June Raymond in *Inter*change Summer 1998:10)

Revd Dr Fox was received into the Episcopal church in 1994, following a year of silence imposed by his order in December 1988. In his autobiography, *Confessions: The Makings of a Post-Denominational Priest* (1996), Fox gives his reason for switching allegiances as an attempt to assist the development of the Anglican rave church community, the Nine O'Clock Service ("NOS") (Fox 1996:8-14).

Neopaganism

Most Christian critiques of New Age (eg Cumbey, Groothuis, Livesey) include Neopaganism under the New Age umbrella. Yet most Neopagans I have met abjure the New Age label, with significantly more vehemence than non-pagans who are merely distancing themselves from the commercialisation and trivialisation of New Age. Should a study of New Age include reference to paganism? Michael York distinguishes even in the title of his work the "Sociology of the New Age and Neo-Pagan Movements" (1995), although noting the overlap (1995:1 et passim). His motivation for maintaining this distinction appears to be the claims of mutual exclusivity made by New Agers and Neopagans towards each other (eg York 1995:99), and in York's analysis these eclipse the similarities he notes between the two movements.

Tanya Luhrmann's sympathies in *Persuasions of the Witch's Craft* (1994/1989) alternate from academic distance to personal involvement, enabling both an empathetic and objective look at Neopaganism and perhaps suggesting to her the useful concept of "interpretive drift" (Luhrmann 1994/1989:12 et passim). An isolated sentence comments:

> In whatever form magicians practise magic, they situate it within what is proclaimed the 'New Age'.
> (Luhrmann 1994/1989:32)

While Luhrmann evidently locates her study within New Age, her subsequent reticence on – purposeful avoidance of? – the New Age movement itself is disquieting. She does not consider the possible distinctions between New Age and Neopaganism.

Amy Simes' 1995 thesis, *Contemporary Paganism in the East Midlands* criticises both York and Luhrmann in their analyses of Neopaganism. York is criticised for

177

restricting his fieldwork to one small group, Shan's House of the Goddess. Luhrmann is criticised on the count that, as she did not know the individuals prior to her research, she could not legitimately claim to have observed the diachronic change in style of reasoning that led to her concept of interpretive drift (Simes 1995:512). The concerns of pagans encountered in Simes' fieldwork are also aired, specifically that Luhrmann was unethical in publishing an account of a closed coven, and unethical in being initiated in a coven for purely academic purposes (Simes 1995:129).

Simes includes a section on "Why Paganism is distinct from the New Age" (Simes 1995:489f), citing a number of answers. Firstly, she defines shamanism within Paganism as "a religious act", while within New Age it is "a secular activity" because New Agers

> ... may as commonly carry out shamanic activities in order to 'heal the child within' or 'contact a higher self' which is not necessarily believed to be divine in nature.
> (Simes 1995:490-491)

Secondly, New Age spirituality is said to be more 'vague' than Pagan spirituality. Thirdly, New Age interpretations of reincarnation are said to emphasise karmic law and judgement and hierarchical planes, whereas Pagan interpretations are said to have a simpler view of natural cycles and the spiral dance that is more suggestive of the eternal round than vertical planes. Fourthly, it is claimed that New Age prefers the spiritual to the material, while for Pagans the reverse is the case. Fifthly, New Age is described as patriarchal and Paganism as democratic. Sixthly, New Age is said to have less ritual activity than Paganism. Seventhly, Pagan groups are claimed to evidence more commitment and community than New Age groups. Finally, New Agers are said (questionably) to construe their movement as modern, while Pagans emphasise historical continuity. Simes concludes that

> It is therefore not particularly accurate to suggest that any sort of significant crossover of identity exists between these two movements.
> (Simes 1995:497)

Nevertheless, there are problems of validity with Simes' research. Most seriously, one of her major groups of study, the Empyrean discussion group in Nottingham, was organised under her own influence in the summer of 1993, with no more than 25 regular attendees and expanding to a mailing list of 40 by the end of the research period. This obviously provided much fieldwork material, but we must ask to what extent Simes created by her own leadership the very phenomena she claims to have observed. In addition to this group, which was by far the largest, Simes observed three Pagan groups: an open working group based in Lincolnshire with 10-20 members; a Druid grove in Derbyshire with five members; and a group deriving from this grove with an unspecified membership. In total, she completed 18 two-hour interviews, and complains that this required 72 (sic) hours of research and transcription[8]. She claims a total "population" for her study of approximately 70 (Simes 1995:51), believing this to represent the majority of pagans existing in her study area of the East Midlands. Questions must be asked, then, as to the numerical significance not only of her fieldwork, but also of the national phenomenon of paganism in general.

Despite the *prima facie* distinction between Neopaganism, New Age and Christianity, some groups have mixed two or three of these traditions. A number of self-identifying pagans regularly worship at St James's church, Piccadilly. The Covenant of Unitarian Universalist Pagans ("CUUPS"), an independent affiliate of the Unitarian Universalist Association based in Cambridge, Massachusetts, is the only Christian-Pagan organisation of which I am aware, unless one is to count Creation Spirituality. Its journal, "Pagan Nuus", first produced in 1987 when CUUPS was founded, reported a mailing list of 2,350 in 1990 (York 1995:137). "Circle Network News", the journal of Selena Fox's broadly-based Circle Network located in Mt Horeb, Wisconsin, reports that

> An annual observance of Samhaim has become part of the worship cycle at a few Unitarian Universalist (UU) churches in Ohio. This began in the late 1980's as part of the growing awareness of Earth-centered spirituality in the Unitarian Universalist Association (UUA). This led in 1995 to adoption of a formal denominational resolution embracing such traditions as a source of UU religion.
> (David Burwasser in *Circle Network News* Spring 1996 vol 59:21)

Revd Richard E Kuykendall, minister of the Community Congregational Church of Tehachapi, California, adopted neopagan rituals as a "contemporary worship experience" called "Spiritwind", in a drive to attract young people to his church in the late 1980s, having begun to study witchcraft in 1983 (Kuykendall 1996). Pagan festivals were 'demythologized' to exclude references to non-Christian deities and used as celebrations of the Earth's changing seasons. Some of these Earth liturgies were published in 1992 as *Liturgy of the Earth*.

Frederick R Lynch (1977, 1979) documents the rise of what I would, with hindsight, consider a Christaquarian group that moved in to Neopaganism. He gives it the pseudonym the Church of the Sun[9], and it was begun in 1957 by Harold W Hall, who channelled *The Wisdom of Archangel Seven*. This small book overlaid a basic Christian mysticism with occult and magical beliefs.

> In practice, Christian mysticism was more pronounced in the Sunday morning devotional services; occultism was the dominant interest in the week-day evening classes taught by Hall.
> (Lynch 1979:283)

In the early 1960s, the group studied Levi's *Aquarian Gospel of Jesus the Christ* (1907). It grew from a small 'family' of 15 to 20 members to a larger church of 75 to 80 members. One of the evening classes offered at this time was entitled, "The Meaning of the New Age" (Lynch 1979:286). Increasingly, the church was emphasizing the occult over the Christian. But as the group moved from simple study of the occult to practice of magic in the early 1970s, the original membership began to fall away. This was especially the case after the arrival of a new leader who was heavily interested in the occult. In 1973 the First Order of the Inner Circle of Isis was formed within the church. Lynch calls "evolutionary drift" the move from "a mystical, pan-Christian cult ... not unlike those of the so-called "New Thought" organization" (Lynch 1977:892) to a more pagan orientation. This may be a corporate version of Luhrmann's "interpretive drift".

Despite the above evidence of overlap, Neopagans usually distance themselves from Christianity, citing the tradition of Christian-inspired witch-hunts. They are also sceptical of relations with Christians due to the hostility of some fundamentalist (and, often, more mainstream) Christians. A notable example of such Neopagan hostility to Christians is Zsuzsanna Budapest, the Hungarian witch who founded the feminist Dianic tradition in North America.

Having considered 'ecological' and 'metaphysical' versions of Christaquarianism, I shall now move on to more central versions of the phenomenon which do not exhibit the identifying traits of these two contrasting poles of the movement. Many central Christaquarians are Catholics – including Paulo Coelho, John Main, Laurence Freeman, Bede Griffiths, William Johnston and Thomas Merton. However, denominations such as the Quakers and various other denominations also have their own Christaquarians. There is further an ecumenical movement of retreat centres which often hold New Age style retreats, and many of these are based on the teachings of what we may call Christaquarian psychologists, often drawing from Carl Jung – for example Morton Kelsey, John Sanford, Christopher Bryant, and M Scott Peck.

Catholic Christaquarians

This research project did not carry out an in-depth study of a Catholic-based New Age group, unless we are to count The Omega Order whose leader moved late in life to Catholicism (see Chapter V), but many Catholics were encountered in the field. Some of them attended the Anglican church, St James's, Piccadilly. None of the Catholics mentioned in this current section adopt the term "New Age" to describe themselves. However, they all exhibit tendencies towards a New Age interpretation of Christianity and, although there are few sociological links between them, should be considered a thematic group.

> "... What does magic have to do with the Catholic Church?"
> Petrus said just one word:
> "Everything."
> (Coelho 1997/1987:44)

At a public lecture[10], in response to my question concerning the relationship between his Christianity and the New Age imagery in his books, the best-selling author, Paulo Coelho (b 1947), distanced himself from the New Age. Initially he had been interested in the movement, he said, but now finds it "airy-fairy", lacking roots and grounding, and also "fundamentalist" in that it dictates to its followers the attitudes they should have regarding vegetarianism, the environment, etc. Coelho describes himself as Catholic and his novels abound with Christian imagery and quotations from the Bible (eg Coelho 1997/1987:101,107,120,134,etc). He has been a member of various esoteric groups, including Aleister Crowley's Magick. However, he was educated in Catholic schools and cites the Bible and the *Spiritual Exercises* of Loyola as the most important books he has read (D'Andrea 1998).

180

The book that made him famous was *The Alchemist* (1988), which details the spiritual journey of a shepherd in search of the philosopher's stone. Autobiographical, *The Pilgrimage* (1997/1987) details another spiritual journey, within the Order of RAM, of which Coelho is now a Master, a 500-year old group of esotericists that works within the Catholic Church.

> R for rigor, A for adoration, and M for mercy; R for *regnum* [rule], A for *agnus* [lamb], and M for *mundi* [world].
> (Coelho 1997/1987:2)

The Order of RAM is part of what Coelho calls "the Tradition", in other words the esoteric tradition which is now open to all.

> The road of the Tradition is not for the chosen few. It is everyone's road.
> (Coelho 1997/1987:3)

The Valkyries (1996/1992) is also autobiographical, and describes a journey Coelho makes at the command of his spiritual master. This time the trip is to the Californian desert in order to meet a young man called Gene whom Coelho's master said could teach him to see his angel. Paulo is accompanied by his wife, Chris.

> "I've always respected your spiritual search, but I have mine, too," Chris said. "And I'm going to go on with it. I want you to understand that. I'm going to continue attending mass."
> "I go to church, too." [said Paulo]
> "But what you're doing here is different, you know? You chose this way of communicating with God, and I've chosen a different one."
> (Coelho 1996/1992:87)

Although Coelho in this way distinguishes between his esoteric religiosity and his wife's more traditional Catholicism, in fact Chris joins him on his spiritual search. They spend much of the book in the company of a group of female bikers, called the Valkyries. Their leader, appropriately named Valhalla, finally leads Paulo through a ritual which enables him to see his angel.

By the River Piedra I Sat Down and Wept (1997/1994) is a fictional romance, the story of Pilar who falls in love with a childhood friend who has entered a monastery and has the charismatic gift of healing and talking with the Virgin Mary. There is much respect shown for the charismatics:

> These people are very close to the original truth of Christianity, when everyone was capable of performing miracles.
> (Coelho 1997/1994:110)

The monk teaches an immanent goddess theology (Coelho 1997/1994:66) and that all religious paths lead to God (Coelho 1997/1994:90). Pilar makes a conscious attempt to regain her former Christian faith in order that her friend might leave the monastery, and eventually succeeds on both counts, but only after her friend has renounced his vocation and healing abilities, because "The church is not yet ready for that [teaching]." (Coelho 1997/1994:156).

There is quite a long history of Catholic approaches to Eastern thought, which may be seen as similar to Catholic approaches to New Age thought. JM Déchanet, a Belgian Benedictine monk, promoted *Christian Yoga* (1960), although he dissociated the techniques he taught from other Hindu teachings. Hugo Lassalle (1898-1990), a German Jesuit, became Enomiya Makibi after taking Japanese citizenship, and is often referred to as Enomiya-Lasalle. He first practised Zen during the Second World War, and sought to achieve enlightenment and teach it to others. *Zen Meditation for Christians* (1974) and other works sought to bring Zen practices to members of his faith. He argued that Zen could be separated from Zen Buddhism and grafted onto Christianity. Dom Aelred Graham wrote about a hybrid *Zen Catholicism* in 1963.

Before becoming a Benedictine monk, John Main (1926-1982) was a diplomat in the Far East where he learnt meditation from an Indian monk. In 1975 he opened the first Christian Meditation Centre in London. Main's meditation is focused on Christ, and he recommended the use of the mantra "maranatha", which means "Come Lord" in Aramaic. Two periods of meditation at the beginning and end of the day are recommended by the Centre, each of about 20 to 30 minutes. Main's books include *The Inner Christ* (1987), *The Way of Unknowing* (1989) and *The Present Christ* (1985).

In 1977 with his student, Dom Laurence Freeman (b 1951), Main founded and became Prior of the Benedictine Priory of Montreal, Canada, a contemplative urban monastery. Freeman now continues the tradition of Main's Christian Meditation, writing his own books including *Christian Meditation: Your Daily Practice* (1995), *Light Within* (1986) and *The Selfless Self* (1989). There is a quarterly newsletter. The Centre's distribution company, Medio Media Ltd, also produces tapes and videos by Main, Freeman, Griffiths, Johnston and others.

An annual John Main Seminar has been held by the Christian Meditation community every year since his death in 1982. Bede Griffiths met Main only once, in 1979, but led a seminar on him in 1991, at which time The World Community for Christian Meditation was formed, to be based in London. According to promotional literature, there are now Christian Meditation groups in 40 countries, and 22 Christian Meditation Centres in cities around the world. A Christian Meditation group run by a student in Lancaster University that I attended in 1996 began with a short excerpt from a tape of John Main. We listened to some choral music for several minutes before half an hour of silent meditation on the maranatha mantra, followed again by several minutes of music. Most of the half a dozen meditators were female students, but the group had been founded by a local nun.

The Golden String (1979/1954) is Bede Griffiths' (1906-1993) autobiography, taking its title from a poem by William Blake. The autobiography reads like a compendium of his reactions to literary classics, from the Romantic poets which replaced Christianity for him in his youth, to the philosophical and theological readings of later years. By family background an Anglican, Griffiths was received into the Roman Catholic church in 1931, and entered a monastery just one month later. He took his final vows in 1937 (Griffiths 1979/1954:132)[11]; he was ordained in 1940.

In 1955 an Indian Benedictine monk asked him to found a monastery, and in 1958 they founded Karisumala Ashram in Kerala, South India, which belonged to the Syrian rite given the allegiance of local Christians. In 1968 he went to Shantivanam Ashram. These ashrams were small, almost self-sufficient communities of no more than a dozen monks, often only two or three and at times consisting solely of Griffiths. Jill Purce and Rupert Sheldrake – both prominent Christaquarians who are now married to each other[12] – numbered among the more famous visitors in 1982-1983.

A New Vision of Reality: Western Science, Eastern Mysticism and Christian Faith (1992/1989) was proof-read by Sheldrake, and is consonant with his vision. Griffiths also pays homage to Fritjof Capra and Ken Wilber (Griffiths 1992:7). The book opens,

> The world today is on the verge of a new age and a new culture.
> (Griffiths 1992:9)

The final chapter (Ch 13 1992:276f) is entitled "The New Age" which is defined as:

> a new relationship to the world of nature …
> a sense of communion with an encompassing reality will replace the attempt to dominate the world. …
> a new type of human community … a decentralised society …
> an integral education of body, soul and spirit …
> there will be a turn to alternative [medicine] …
> (Griffiths 1992:281f)

Given Griffith's interest in Blake and the mysticism of the Romantics, it is not surprising that he calls in this chapter for a return to ancient wisdom.

> The only way of recovery is to rediscover the perennial philosophy, the traditional wisdom, which is found in all ancient religions and especially in the great religions of the world. But those religions … have each to be renewed … so that a cosmic, universal religion can emerge, in which the essential values of Christian religion will be preserved in living relationship with the other religious traditions of the world.
> (Griffiths 1992:296)

However, most of his works (eg *Vedanta and Christian Faith* (1973), *The Marriage of East and West* (1982)) are concerned with the translation of Hindu thought into Christian terms, and do not mention the New Age. In 1990 Griffiths suffered from a stroke in which he discovered the feminine, receiving an inspiration to "Surrender to the Mother".

Thomas Merton (1915-1968) became Brother Louis in 1941, a Cistercian at the Abbey of Gethsemani. He had gone to Cambridge but transferred to Columbia University and completed his Masters in "Nature and Art in William Blake" in 1939, being ordained in 1949. Once hoping to be a novelist, Merton published his autobiography, *The Seven Storey Mountain* (1947) (an allusion to Dante's *Purgatorio*). His only systematic theological treatise, a study of John of the Cross, *The Ascent to Truth* followed in 1951, but his numerous spiritual works are very popular among Christaquarians, New Agers and orthodox Christians.

The Christian Meditation Centre also advertises the work of William Johnston, a Jesuit born in Northern Ireland who went to Tokyo in 1951. Johnston is well-known among Catholics interested in spirituality for his use of Zen meditation. *Christian Zen* (1979) went so far as to proclaim,

> I believe that the Christian West needs a touch of this so-called monism. Modern people are looking for it, and most of it can be understood in a Christian sense.
> (Johnston 1979:38)

Johnston mentions often the modern hunger for things spiritual (eg Johnston 1978/1974:15,22), and while this is a common Christian diagnosis, the suggested cure of monism is not commonly understood in a Christian sense.

Johnston introduced *Silent Music* (Johnston 1974) by observing the "rise of a great meditation movement" which includes Zen, Yoga, TM, biofeedback, visualization and psychic healing, and a later chapter in the same work entitled "Cosmic Healing" speaks of an "age of planetization", "our movement towards a new cosmology and a new consciousness", and the "cosmic implications" of meditation. The earliest reference to the New Age movement by name comes in a letter dated 1 June 1989 (Johnston 1991:51-59), and it sounds like a recent discovery for Johnston:

> One thing that has caught my attention, however, is the New Age movement which has now spread to the whole world.
> (Johnston 1991:51)

This letter goes on to outline Johnston's attitude to New Age: the need for dialogue and discernment of the occult and demonic, while concurring with the analysis that the world is entering a "new age". Johnston often uses this uncapitalised phrase to mean something different from the New Age movement, and when I asked Johnston, at a lecture in the Benedictine Centre for Spirituality in London in April 1996, to clarify what he meant in his references to new age, he explained he hadn't been referring to the New Age movement. "new age" seems to refer to the response of the "new religious consciousness" (Johnston 1989/1988:11) or "new mysticism" (Johnston 1991:1) to the crises in the modern world. Johnston describes this "meditative movement" as a *"tertium quid"* (Johnston 1991:1f) with five characteristics: its appeal to the laity, its holism, emphasis on posture and breathing, emphasis on faith rather than reason, and on enlightenment. Johnston is mentioned with respect by Jacob Needleman as one of the few Christians who are teaching "intermediate Christianity".

Father Anthony de Mello (1931-1987) was mentioned by eight subscribers to *Omega News* as somebody who has influenced them by their writings. In 1998 the Congregation of the Doctrine of the Faith presented a Notification which declared that some of de Mello's positions "are incompatible with the Catholic faith and can cause grave harm." In the explanatory note, the document acknowledged that his earlier writings, while influenced by Buddhism and Taoism, remain within Christian boundaries. Later writings, however, are said to develop themes which go beyond this. In particular are cited his theory of contemplation as an awareness which can be achieved through human effort; his reduction of the personal nature of God to a vague cosmic reality; his dilution of the divine sonship of Jesus into the notion of the divine sonship of all men; his use of the cross as the symbol of interior liberation; his idea that humans will dissolve, "like salt into water", into God; his indiscriminate criticisms of the institutions of the Church; and his equation of evil with lack of enlightenment. De Mello's best-known books are *Sadhana: A Way to God* (1978) and *Wellsprings: A Book of Spiritual Exercises* (1984). Furthermore, some collections of anecdotes were published after his death, including *Awareness* (1990) and *Contact with God: Retreat Conferences* (1990).

Quaker Christaquarians

While there are many lone Catholic New Agers, the Quakers are one of the few established Christian denominations to have developed a co-ordinated corporate positive response to the New Age: they advertise in *Kindred Spirit*, the New Age magazine. Their practice of individual meditation and emphasis on personal inspiration is obviously congenial to many New Agers. A small section of the Quaker movement, The Quaker Universalist Group, has a membership of around 300 with a much smaller affiliated group in the United States. It runs annual conferences, publishes a magazine *Universalist* and pamphlet-size works of members.

> The Quaker Universalist Group is based on our understanding that spiritual awareness is accessible to everyone of any religion or none, and that no one person and no one faith can claim to have a final revelation or monopoly of truth.
> We acknowledge that such awareness may be expressed in many different ways. We delight in this diversity and warmly welcome both Quakers and non-Quakers to join with us.
> (Back cover of *Universalist* magazine)
> It is true that the universalist sensibility tends to clash with those members of the Christian communion who insist that people who do not recognize Jesus of Nazareth as their Lord and Saviour are ipso-facto inferior in spiritual realization.
> (Seeger 1986:7)
> The terms *universalist* and *universalism* in the sense that they are now used by Quakers worldwide, were almost certainly first employed by John Linton in 1977 when he addressed members of the Seekers Association ... The Quaker Universalist Group, founded in 1979[13], adopted the term ...
> (Hetherington 1993:3)

The theologian John Hick is an honorary member of the QUG, and they publish a sermon of his entitled "Christ in a Universe of Faiths" (1983). Ralph Hetherington, a founder member of the QUG, lists the defining marks of Quaker Universalism as belief in the reality of the Inward Light, of direct spiritual experience, the primacy of the Inward Light over the Bible and the belief in "That of God" in everyone (Hetherington 1993:28). He outlines the influence of John

Robinson on panentheism and Matthew Fox on creation-centered spirituality in developing Universalist ideas.

> ... there are Universalists who look forward to the development of a new world religion arising out of an emerging world culture, a religion which would enshrine the truth of all religions.
> (Hetherington 1993:5)

Adrian Cairns, author of a Quaker Universalist pamphlet and member of the Scientific and Medical Network, writes in the *Universalist*,

> Perhaps we need to re-express ourselves as something like 'new Quakers' or 'Post-Quaker' Quakers for the 21st century.
> The bottom line of all this seems to be that we have to rid ourselves of all institutional religious authoritarianism, including 'official' Christianity ...
> (Cairns in *Universalist* 54 October 1998:6)

Dr Jean Hardy trained in psychosynthesis before joining the Society of Friends, becoming administrator for the Centre for Health and Healing at St James's church, and editor of *GreenSpirit* magazine. Dr Hardy has written a brief review of the CANA *Paper* (1999) for *GreenSpirit* magazine (Winter 1999:26), commenting that *GreenSpirit* members would like more about the development of new rituals. *A Psychology with a Soul: Psychotherapy in Evolutionary Context* (Hardy 1996/1987) details Dr Hardy's own interpretation of Assagioli, and Christianity plays no important role; this is seen best in her writings for *Universalist*, the journal of the Quaker Universalist Group, which

> has helped make for far greater respect towards those with other than firmly Christian views in the Society. ...
> Many people see [wrongly, according to Hardy] a recognition of the aliveness and sacredness of the natural world as pantheism, as paganism, as the basis of a religion that Christianity defeated.
> (Hardy 1996b)

Dr Hardy is used by Fr Legere in his *Popular Book* (1993:3) to bridge Christianity and New Age (see Chapter II). Dr Hardy nevertheless denies that there is a movement of New Age Christians, and declares that her faith is not 'Christian' in the conventional sense[14]. Dr Hardy has contested my description of Quaker Universalists as Christaquarian. However, in a survey[15] by Josephine Teagle in late 1999, of the 289 members of the group (with a remarkable 75% response rate) 11% said New Age had influenced their spirituality. These respondents further defined their interest in New Age as including spiritual healing, fairy-tales workshops, Goddess spirituality, White Eagle, Findhorn, TM, *A Course in Miracles*, Celtic Christianity, Gaia, Sai Baba, Starhawk and Margot Adler.

Having considered Catholic and Quaker responses to the New Age, we may now move on to the less cohesive responses in other denominations. These include Verney (1976), Whaling (1996), Perry (1992), Anglarès (1992), Millikan & Drury (1991), Moore (1992) and Palmer (1993a, 1993b).

Into the New Age (1989/1976) by Revd Stephen Verney (b 1919) is an example of the earlier tradition of New Age in Britain, before it acquired its American flavour. Verney became bishop of Repton in Derbyshire in 1977, and had written the book after the experience of his wife's death from cancer. Three insights were gained in this period:

> *Good and evil interlock within ourselves. ...*
> *All things are one. ...*
> *The end of our searching is the presence of the risen Christ.*
> (Verney 1989/1976:42, *original emphasis*)

The New Age is for Verney an "evolutionary leap forward in the realm of the spirit" (Verney 1989/1976:13).

> What do we mean by the new age? ... First to describe any historical era, such as the Renaissance, which follows upon an 'evolutionary leap' ... Secondly, to describe the new era which Jesus declared to be 'at hand' and which he called the kingdom of God. We can never say of this kingdom, 'Such and such a group of people, or I myself, have finally entered this new age.' It is a way to be walked each day.
> (Verney 1989/1976:149)

Nevertheless, Taizé is considered by Verney as an example of the new age life (Verney 1989/1976:87).

Frank Whaling (1996), in a paper produced by the Religious Experience Research Centre in Oxford (which investigates mystical experiences), gives a brief, broadly positive overview of New Age. He writes that

> Christians can largely affirm ... the new science, holistic thought, a concern for ecology, a concern for women's [values, a] focus on global issues, and a recognition of the power of healing, human potential, and inward spirituality. Vibrant Christians can ally with New Age thought and sometimes are new age in these matters.
> (Whaling 1996:5)

However, he goes on to outline three areas in which Christians should be cautious about New Age thought: channelling; its interpretation of psychic and spiritual power without discernment; and the challenges made by some New Age thought to Christian doctrines, for example in Christology.

Revd Michael Perry's (1992) understanding of the New Age as a transmutation of the human potential movement is narrow, and somehow manages to exclude his considerable personal interest in psychical research. The "basic concepts" Perry lists are:

... the human spirit must be free ...

... reappropriate a more ancient wisdom ...

... we are responsible for our own spiritual progress ...

(Perry 1992:21-27)

Revd Perry (1992:33-37) quotes William Bloom's definition of New Age from *Sacred Times* (1990).

A similarly ambiguous rejection of New Age is achieved by Michel Anglarès in *Nouvel Âge et Foi Chrétienne* (1992). He does not question the orthodoxy of belief in the influence of energies at a distance (Anglarès 1992:106), or in the influence of the stars (Anglarès 1992:109), or of the use of New Age therapies as techniques for relaxation (Anglarès 1992:61). Indeed, he shares the New Age criticism of the Greek philosophy that is said to have bastardised Christianity (Anglarès 1992:55). Yet still the call is for "discernement" (Anglarès 1992:36), with much reference to the Bible (Anglarès 1992:78f).

Worlds Apart? Christianity and the New Age (1991) is by David Millikan, "an orthodox if curious Christian" and Nevill Drury, "a devoted and articulate New Ager" (Millikan & Drury 1991:1). The work is a true dialogue between the two, with each giving an exposition, followed by a conversation between them. Drury describes the New Age as

> the most recent spawning in a series of subordinate [to Christianity] belief systems that have trickled along as part of a spiritual undercurrent through the centuries. Not that these belief systems have necessarily seen themselves as anti-Christian, simply as not wholly Christian.
> (Drury in Millikan & Drury 1991:10)

David L Moore, a Presbyterian Sunday school teacher, writes that he has accepted some New Age practices and rejected others. *Christianity and the New Age Religion: A Bridge Toward Mutual Understanding* (1992) reads as the work of an auto-dictat. He writes,

> The parallels between the advent of Christianity during the time of Judaism and the advent of New Age Religion during the time of Christianity are striking. And just as Judaism survives today without an overlay of Christianity and Christianity survives in the complete absence of Judaism, a similar relationship will be developed between Christianity and New Age. However, just as Christianity becomes more meaningful within the continuance of the Judeo-Christian heritage as bridged by Hebrews, so will New Age become a more meaningful religion within the continuance of the Christianity-New Age heritage. As Hebrews teaches us, the good of the old need not be discarded when accepting the advances of the new.
> (Moore 1992:22)

Coming of Age: An Exploration of Christianity and the New Age (Palmer 1993a) is mainly a critique of New Age for being nothing new, and of fundamentalist reactions to New Age, but does offer some pointers to a form of revitalised Christianity.

... I want to posit the radical changes that Christianity needs to make within itself; the new way of visioning the world and the movements already underway which might mean a dramatically re-viewed Christianity plays a significant role in the community of faiths and beliefs of the future. For I believe there is a new form of Christianity arising.

(Palmer 1993a:13-14)

This revitalised Christianity pays much more attention to the diversity of faiths. As outlined in *Living Faiths* (Palmer 1993b), Palmer is interested in non-Romano-Hellenic forms of Christianity for their diversity of approach.

Retreat Centres

Having considered various positive Christian responses to the New Age movement, I now consider mainstream Christian retreat centres. Most Christian denominations run retreat centres, from official diocessan centres, to religious communities which open their doors to "the non-religious" (as those who have not taken vows are known), to centres run by private individuals. Retreat centres are by no means necessarily New Age or even New Age Christian; the majority are orthodox centres of spirituality. However, a number of retreat centres, even the more traditional, hold New Age Christian courses and are known in the Christaquarian network.

Examples of New Age Christian courses at Christian retreat centres are myriad: "Deep Ecology" at The Abbey, Sutton Courtenay; "Rediscovering the Child Within"[16] at The Grange, Ellesmere; "Spirit in Movement, Mind in Matter – workshop based on the ancient Sumerian myth of Inanna" at The Community of the Sisters of the Church, St Michael's Convent, Richmond; "Christian-Buddhist retreat" at the Priory of Our Lady, Hassocks, West Sussex; "Holistic Retreat" at the Assissi Retreat and Prayer Centre, London. Below I will relate some participant observation conducted at an enneagram retreat, a form of personality exploration common among Roman Catholics and New Agers.

There are various groups that promote retreats. The National Association of Christian Communities and Networks[17] (distinct from the Steinerian Christian Community Churches) is an ecumenical organisation whose membership includes individuals, religious orders, 'new' communities and other groups from a variety of Christian traditions. NACCAN publishes a magazine and a directory of communities, which is particularly helpful for researchers as it lists the number of members and the year of foundation.

Open Centres is a non-Christian newsletter established in 1977 which
> links Centres, Groups, Private Houses and Friends who share the aim to be open to the TRUTH through MEDITATION, MOVEMENT, HEALING and INTERFAITH work.
> (*Open Centres* Summer 1996:3)

Findhorn, the National Federation of Spiritual Healers, the College of Psychic

Studies, Lucis Trust and the Scientific and Medical Network are among the groups mentioned in the magazine. Groups discussed in this thesis also appear – The Omega Order, Bridge Trust and Christians Awakening to a New Awareness, The More-to-Life Partnership, and The Christian Meditation Centre.

The National Retreat Association ("NRA") is a federation of six retreat groups – Association for Promoting Retreats, which is mainly Anglican; National Retreat Movement, which is mainly Roman Catholic; Methodist Retreat Group; Baptist Union Retreat Group; United Reformed Church Silence & Retreat Group; and the Quaker Retreats and One-to-One Ministry. The NRA publishes an annual journal in December, *The Vision*[18], which lists the yearly programme of over 200 retreat centres in the British Isles. The first NRA conference was held in 1992.

I attended a Christian enneagram workshop at a Catholic retreat centre in the course of my research. The enneagram, which is often used by Christaquarians and New Agers as well as mainstream Christians, is an interconnected nine-pointed diagram whose origins are obscure, but may be Sufi, Gurdjieffian, or from Oscar Ichazo, founder of the Arica Institute. Each point is numbered and said to represent personal characteristics. Karen Webb conducts enneagram workshops by invitation at the Emmaus Retreat Centre, West Wickham, Kent. I attended a course entitled, "Enneagram I – Wholeness on the way to Holiness: spiritual growth using the Enneagram as a tool". The Emmaus Centre "welcomes people from any denomination" (promotional literature 1996) but is run by the Daughters of Mary and Joseph, an originally Belgian Catholic community first formed in 1817 and formerly known as the Ladies of Mary. I had the impression Webb was making an effort to use Christian vocabulary, at the same time as being quite critical of Christianity. For example, she declared during an open session "I believe in God"; the Cloud of Unknowing was quoted at length; nirvana or meditation was described as "a state of grace"; she described Jesus as "the most important" and thought that the "bottom line" is Jesus' words, "Love your neighbour as yourself"; redemption is seeing your type and working through it.

On the other hand, Webb said that there were originally nine deadly sins (as in the enneagram), but two were excluded by the church because it is itself built on fear and deceit; the church has forgotten what the confession is for – rather than emphasise how bad you are, it should emphasise how loved you are; sin is not something evil in your personality, just something that doesn't work, causes friction with other people, and is 'nasty'; and there is a great difference between spirituality and religion.

Webb thought most people interested in the enneagram are presently Christian. The Emmaus Centre ask her to teach the enneagram, although she has also booked an unsolicited course on relationships with the enneagram. Christ is a "spiritual master" for her, but her upbringing had caused her to react against Christianity. She said wasn't Christian in the church sense, although she was in the spiritual sense. Therefore, it would be incorrect to describe Webb as a Christaquarian, although her workshop was aimed at people I would class Christaquarians.

Spirituality and Psychology

New Age-style retreats at Christian centres often blur the distinction between spiritual and psychological. Indeed, Hanegraaff (1996:224-229) has described a trend in New Age for the "psychologisation of spirituality" and the "spiritualisation of psychology". A number of Christian psychologists have penned works that are influential in the New Age fringe of Christianity.

For John Sanford, Christ is indistinguishable from the "Center" of the personality (Sanford 1992:126), the "God within" (Sanford 1992:57). Christianity is true in so far as it is an anticipation of Jungian psychology, and Jesus Christ was a prototype of the Total person (Sanford 1987/1970:171). Sanford describes the "split between paganism and Christianity" as "unnatural" (Sanford 1987/1970:127), for according to his Jungian analysis both Christianity and paganism are manifestations of deeper psychological truths, but Sanford's Christian profession is retained in his description of Christianity as a "consummation" of myth which "grew out of paganism but also goes beyond it" (Sanford 1987/1970:127-128).

Morton Kelsey is a friend of John Sanford and reveals a similar debt to Jung. He attributes the unpopularity of his healing ministry in the church to the influence in the West of the Aristotelian paradigm of rationalist materialism, compared to the Platonism of the East and the early church (Kelsey 1973:ch3). Modern science shows materialism to be untenable (Kelsey 1991:47), and Jung allows for a revaluation of psychoid reality to an importance equal to that of physical reality (Kelsey 1991:74). Kelsey has described five methods of meditation: entering as a player into the biblical myth; inner dialogue with saints; guiding moods through creative imaging; analysing dreams; becoming quiet (Kelsey 1991:77-80).

Christopher Bryant wrote *The River Within* (1978) "in the hope of making a contribution to the working out of a spirituality for the late twentieth century" (Bryant 1978:i). Christ is identified with the centre of the personality (Bryant 1978:27), although Jesus' life and death was a historical event, not just an ideal (Bryant 1978:26). Jungian individuation parallels and can facilitate Christian salvation because of "an overlap of meaning", but individuation is not as universal as salvation (Bryant 1988/1983:52).

Philip St Romain explains his *Kundalini Energy and Christian Spirituality* (1995) on the ground that there was no Christian vocabulary for his personal experiences (St Romain 1995:11), and the best explanation he could find was in a New Age catalogue of books and tapes (St Romain 1995:35). St Romain fully accepts the Hindu description of his experiences and acknowledges a Jungian interpretation of *kundalini* (St Romain 1995:66f), but does retain a Christian distinction between God and the soul (St Romain 1995:106). The book draws to an ambiguous conclusion:

Having read and reflected much on this topic, I am now prepared to say that the kundalini process may or may not give testimony to the work of the Holy Spirit.
(St Romain 1995:124)

M Scott Peck was baptised a nondenominational Christian in 1980 (Peck 1993:165) two years after the publication of *The Road Less Travelled* (1978). He acknowledges the similarity of his work to New Age (Peck 1993:218), and defends what he calls the "symboline" aspects of the movement that encourage integration (Peck 1993:194-218). His criticism of "diaboline" aspects of the New Age movement obviously alludes to the demonic oppression model he mentions as common to the "satanic conspiracy" theories of "Christian fundamentalists" (Peck 1993:195), yet in actual fact Scott's criticisms centre rather on "heresy" (beliefs contrary to his own) (Peck 1993:205f) and brainwashing cults (Peck 1993:212f).

The Holy Order of MANS

As a coda to this chapter, I offer the unusual case of The Holy Order of MANS, which transformed from a New Age group into an Orthodox sect (Houston 1994; Lucas 1995). Earl Wilbur Blighton (1904-1974) founded the Science of Man Church in California in 1961, opening an office and chapel in San Francisco in 1966. He had been raised a Free Methodist and was influenced by the Roman Catholicism of his first wife. Prior to his founding his own religious organisation, Blighton passed through the Ancient and Mystical Order Rosae Crucis (AMORC), the Freemasons, spiritualist churches, a Christian Yoga Church, read the Science of Mind writings of Ernest Holmes, and was prosecuted for treating patients without a license with a light machine. Blighton's Church targeted the hippies of the Haight-Ashbury district of San Francisco, hoping to redirect them back to mainstream life through offering a social project of food vouchers, temporary accommodation and a careers service, combined with spiritual counselling. He held evening classes and Sunday services, and dressed his students in second-hand black suits with dog collars. The group adopted a non-proselytizing stance despite their "street missions" in dangerous areas which sought to radiate light onto the troubled communities by evening patrols.

Presenting himself as a reincarnation from the White Brotherhood of Paul of Tarsus, being addressed as "Master Paul", and receiving revelations – sometimes channelled to his congregation – from Jesus Christ, Blighton viewed the order's purpose as the restoration of the "universal Law" of mental dynamics to mainstream Christianity. Blighton had been ordained in 1946 by the Universal Church of Psychic Science, and quickly ordained his students, including women disciples, starting in 1967 with his second wife Ruth. The Science of Man Church transformed from a church organisation to a religious brotherhood by 1967, and in 1968 the Holy Order of MANS received the California State charter.

MANS is a secret acronym revealed only to disciples who have taken life vows into the brotherhood, although an exoteric explanation was given in 1978 by the movement's director general: the acronym means "The mystery of love through the Christ-mind grants wisdom", from the Greek words *mysterion, agape, nous*, and *sophia*. The Order was situated at this time thoroughly within the New Age milieu of the late 1960s counterculture, overlaid with a Christian vocabulary such that one priest referred to it as "New Age Christianity" (Lucas 1995:232). It was avowedly non-sectarian and non-political, "universalistic" in the sense that it taught the coming of a new world religion revealed by "the next Christ" avatar.

Highly ritualistic, the Order distributed the sacraments of communion, baptism, illumination, realization, ordination and marriage. The sacrament of illumination planted a body of light, attuned to the finer vibrations of the New Age, into the disciple's physical body. Self-realization was

> a neoshamanic "rending" of an "etheric veil" that was perceived to surround the indwelling "spark" of divinity in a person (called the "SELF"). Once this veil had been removed, a person was believed able to see a luminous globe or "point of light at the center of their being."
> (Lucas 1995:59)

By 1969 there were 210 vowed members of the brotherhood, and it had begun to establish mission centres outside of California. Lucas reports their religious backgrounds as approximately 50% Roman Catholic, 35% Protestant and 15% Jewish (Lucas 1995:69). There were three sections of the Order: the Renunciate Brotherhood, which took life vows, the Christian Communities which were lay groups, and the Discipleship movement, which was a correspondence course. Members took jobs in the outside community and pooled their incomes in a common fund at the centre in which they resided – thus accumulating large assets for the Order.

The Order professed ecumenism, and usually tried to meet with the local churches, although there was sometimes resistance from Roman Catholic churches. In the early 70s, use of Christian vocabulary in Blighton's sermons pushed out use of Rosicrucian discourse, and sermons started with a reading from the New Testmament. The Order's journal, *HOOM*, increasingly used Christian imagery. In 1971 Blighton wrote to his followers to ban the use of Eastern meditations except the Aum, asking them to restrict their observances to those of the Western tradition. The Order promoted a developed Mariology. Mary also revealed to Blighton the idea for two suborders, the Immaculate Heart Sisters of Mary and the Brown Brothers of the Holy Light.

Initially when Blighton died in 1974, his place was taken by Master Raeson (Anthony) Ruiz, who became interested in Erhard Seminars Training (est) and eventually left the Order to form the Society for Christ's Disciples, which remained loyal to Blighton's original New Age conception of a Christian initiatory school. Masters Philip and Marthelia McCaffery took over the leadership for a year, followed by Masters Andrew and Patricia Rossi. These transitional years represented a period of internal power struggles.

After the Jonestown suicides in 1978, the Order was subject to hostile press reports and attention from the anti-cult movement, being listed as a cult by, among others, the Christian Research Institute and the Spiritual Counterfeits Project. The privy council of the Order questioned the viability of their nondenominational stance – how was it possible to be universal without belonging to any particular denomination? Some of the leaders of the Order joined the growing ecumenical movement. Esoteric Christian publications were removed from the order's booklists, replaced with CS Lewis and Bonhoeffer. The leaders began to refer to themselves as "Christian Masters".

> Members would no longer view themselves as part of a New Age Christian "mystery school" administering "solar initiations," but rather as an independent Christian community whose roots were firmly planted in the normative apostolic tradition.
> (Lucas 1995:171)

A 1979 brochure proclaimed the movement

> "Christian in its essence, in its form, and in its practice.".... Although the group existed "as an independent community, outside the authority of the major denominations," it recognized and submitted itself to "the authority of the Body of Christ on earth, the living Church." The order promulgated no new forms of Christianity, the booklet avowed, and accepted the basic doctrines of Christianity as expressed in the Apostle's Creed."
> (Lucas 1995:179)

Andrew (né Vincent) Rossi, director of the Holy Order of MANS 1978-1990, had once attended a mainstream Catholic preseminary for four years with the hope of becoming a priest. His leanings towards mainstream Christianity were reconfirmed during his period of directorship. It was apparently his readings of Symeon the New Theologian during this time that drew him to Eastern Orthodoxy over Catholicism. He also discovered the journal *The Orthodox Word*, devoted to traditional Russian monasticism, in which vociferous articles by the late Seraphim (né Eugene) Rose made a deep impression on Rossi. These articles were strongly anti-ecumenical in a millenarian fashion that suggested the charismatic gifts were forebodings of the Antichrist.

From 1983, elements of Orthodox Christianity were gradually introduced into Order affairs, beginning with the Nicene creed. Also in this year, Rossi met with Abbot Herman (né Gleb) Podmoshensky, co-founder with Seraphim Rose of the Saint Herman of Alaska Brotherhood and publisher of *The Orthodox Word*. Orthodox prayers were now used by the Order of MANS, a sermon by the Constantinople patriarch John Chrysostom was read at an Easter service in 1984, and Orthodox iconography was printed in the Order's publications. Podmoshensky began teaching at Renunciate communities of the Order.

> By November 1986, the only parts of the worship service bearing any resemblance to Blighton's original rite were the gospel reading and the office of the "transmutation" of the bread and wine. Apart from these, every element was now a borrowing from the Eastern Orthodox Divine Liturgy.
> (Lucas 1995:207)

In 1985, Rossi was secretly baptized by Podmoshensky, but this was not revealed to the Order in case it revolted before Rossi was able to bring it *en masse* into Orthodoxy. This was finally achieved in 1988 when the Order changed its name to Christ the Savior Brotherhood ("CSB") and merged with the Archdiocese of Vasiloupolis through the Metropolitan Pangratios Gerasimos Vrionis, archbishop of the Greek Orthodox Archdiocese which has its headquarters in New York. Many former members of the Holy Order of MANS left the new organisation, including Blighton's widow Ruth, who revived the Science of Man church in 1987 with other Blighton devotees. Other former members were on the contrary so true to their new Orthodoxy, that they could not endure the non-canonical status of Metropolitan Pangratios with the Standing Committee of Orthodox Bishops in America and the Russian Orthodox Church Abroad – and indeed, the Metropolitan is not recognized by any other mainline Orthodox jurisdiction. These apostates objected to Podmoshensky's unfrocking in 1988 by the Russian Orthodox Church Abroad, and Pangratios' unfrocking in 1970.

The St Herman of Alaska Brotherhood is now a branch of CSB, and has renamed the former headquarters of the Holy Order of MANS in Forestville, California as St Paisius Abbey. Podmoshensky has all but taken over the charismatic role of Blighton in the Order. In 1991 Revd Stevan Bauman was elected chair of the new "Brotherhood Council", and Rossi was given $250,000 to study for a PhD in patristics at Oxford. Finally, the Renunciate Brotherhood was dissolved as an autonomous unit with CSB.

The Holy Order of MANS is unusual in the completeness of its transition from New Age to Christianity. In my experience, far more common is the integration of New Age themes into Christianity. It is this that I have named Christaquarianism.

Conclusion

We have seen, then, that Christian responses to the New Age movement vary from constructive attempts at outreach and official condemnation in church reports, to positive adoption of New Age beliefs and practices by both lone Christaquarians and associations of individuals. Groups with a positive response to the New Age movement include *A Course in Miracles* study groups, the Creation Spirituality network, the Quaker Universalists, various neognostic groups and the Christian Meditation Centre in London. Earlier chapters developed in-depth case studies of three further Christaquarian groups: St James's church, Piccadilly; Christians Awakening to a New Awareness; and The Omega Order. There may, however, be a great number of individual authors and lay Christians who are involved with the movement without belonging to any of these groups. Finally, it must be noted that there have been some unusual outcomes of Christian involvement in the New Age, including the scandals of the Nine O'Clock Service and the suicides of the Order of the Solar Temple and Heaven's Gate, and the unusual case of The Holy Order of MANS. Having given here an overview of Christian involvement with the New Age movement, the next chapter moves on to give a sociological interpretation of the phenomena.

Notes to Chapter VII

[1] *Fides et Ratio* ("Faith and Reason") is an encyclical issued by the Pope in October 1998. It does not refer explicitly to the New Age, but contains a message particularly relevant to consideration of New Age Christianity, developing the Vatican's critique of the relationship between faith and reason. It is warned that

> In tracing Christianity's adoption of philosophy, one should not forget how cautiously Christians regarded other elements of the cultural world of paganism, one example of which is gnosticism.
> (Pope John Paul II 1998:IV.37)
> The Church has no philosophy of her own nor does she canonize any one particular philosophy in preference to others.
> (Pope John Paul II 1998:V.49)

There is strong recognition by the Pope of the validity of non-Christian philosophies.

> Every people has its own native and seminal wisdom which, as a true cultural treasure, tends to find voice and develop in forms which are genuinely philosophical.
> (Pope John Paul II 1998:I.3)

Nevertheless, at root it is emphasised that Christianity is the only Truth.

> ... beyond different schools of thought, there exists a body of knowledge which may be judged a kind of spiritual heritage of humanity.
> (Pope John Paul II 1998:I.4)

[The above was the footnote in the original 2000 edition. In February 2003 Pontifical Council for Culture and the Pontifical Council for Interreligious Dialogue of the Catholic Church issued a preliminary report, *Jesus Christ the Bearer of the Water of Life: A Christian reflection on the "New Age"* which is unprecedented (for a Church) in its objective and well-researched approach to New Age. For a considered evaluation of the report, see Smith (2003).]

[2] Eg *The Times* 12 and 13 November 1996.

[3] An alternative C of E view on the New Age was expressed in a paper entitled "Anglicanism and the New Age" (Kemp 1994b) delivered to a group of mainly Anglican clergy at a conference on "The Future of Anglicanism" held at Christ Church College, Canterbury, at which the chair of the Church House report, Rt Revd Dr Michael Nazir-Ali (Bishop of Rochester) also presented a paper.

[4] The following year I heard the same complaint from Christian Scientists at the Mind-Body-Spirit festival – and they were there in the same capacity as the evangelicals, proselytizing in the name of Christianity!

[5] I also received an e-mail request from the bestselling Christaquarian author, Paulo Coelho (see below), for a copy of my thesis.

[6] For a brief overview of ancient gnosticism, see Chapter V – there can be no historical connection between Neognosticism and its ancient forebear, since orthodox Christianity superseded Gnosticism by the fifth century, through the effectiveness of its hierarchical organization and anti-Gnostic literature campaign.

[7] Heaven's Gate is not the only New Age group to be associated with the Internet. According to the *UK Christian Handbook* (Christian Research 2000), 23% of UK Christian organisations had a website in 1999, while 44% were on-line with e-

mail. Mark Dery, in a popular work entitled *Escape Velocity: Cyberculture at the End of the Century* (1996), devotes his first chapter to what he calls "Cyberdelia" and others have called "Cyberia". Timothy Leary is the paragon of this culture, with his sixties roots, use of psychedelics and openness to New Age philosophies. Dery even reports on an English phenomenon known as the "zippie" ("Zen-inspired pagan professional"), "a combination of sixties flower children and nineties techno-people" (Dery 1996:23).

> What distinguishes the cyberdelic culture of the nineties from psychedelic culture [of the sixties], more than anything else, is its ecstatic embrace of technology.
> (Dery 1996:24)

Cyberdelia is placed by Dery firmly within New Age as a reincarnation of the sixties counterculture, but New Age is not defined. Ronit Yoeli Tlalim has completed an MA thesis on 'Virtual Zen' entitled *On-Line Zen: A Phenomenological and Epistemic Outlook* (1998). She notes several developments in this essentially Western phenomenon: the appearance of cyber-sanghas, cyber rituals, new master-student relations, new concepts of time and space, and various innovations in the forms of freedom.

Many of the groups mentioned in this thesis, including the case studies, have a presence on the Internet. Access these sites through my own website, www.Christaquarian.net.

[8] I am often amazed at the amount of work fellow PhD students expect to get away with. Without wishing to appear conceited, I would like to point out that three years' full-time research should cover far more material, both fieldwork and literary, than is sometimes achieved, even if the student has to juggle the research with employment in an unrelated field, as I did.

[9] This pseudonym must be close to the real name, as he comments that "many outsiders who merely *heard* the name assumed that it was the Church of the S*o*n, not S*u*n, and, hence, simply another Christian organization" (Lynch 1979:293).

[10] St James's church, Piccadilly, 11 May 1998.

[11] cf Griffiths 1997:65 where the date is 1936.

[12] Both visited St James's church during the course of my fieldwork. Dr Sheldrake has co-authored a book with Matthew Fox (1996). In 1995, Dr Sheldrake, Revd Dr Fox and Purce gave an evening together in Grace Cathedral, San Francisco, called "Ritual, Resonance and the Return of the Angels". Jill Purce was involved in the early stages of setting up The Abbey at Sutton Courtenay (a retreat centre) and gave workshops there for Bishop Stephen Verney in 1984. She and her family are "very regular" member of the congregation at Hampstead Parish Church (personal communication, 8 February 1996). Purce was first invited to teach her "overtone chanting" (a form of meditation) in the crypt room in 1983.

[13] The Quaker Universalist Group was established in 1978, with the first *Universalist* appearing in January 1979. *Universalist* 43 Feb 1995:3.

[14] Personal communication, 10 March 1999. Dr Hardy declined to be interviewed.

[15] Personal communication, 22 March 2000. Teagle conducted the research for an MA dissertation at Exeter University, and although she did not complete the

degree, kindly analysed these results for me. 64% of respondents were aged over 70, and 83% over 60.

[16] Course facilitated by a CANA member.

[17] Dissolved in 2002.

[18] Now *Retreats*.

VIII. Is there a Christaquarian movement?

Theoretical Sociological Analysis

The New Age movement and more specifically Christaquarianism, do not readily fit into existing sociological typologies of new religious movements (see Chapter II). Indeed, some commentators[1] have questioned whether New Age does in fact qualify as a new religious movement. And the boundaries of Christaquarianism are not as clear as even the muddy boundaries of the New Age movement. Christaquarianism is definitely not as mainstream as a denomination, nor as institutionalised as a sect. Yet the number of adherents may well be greater than those of some small sects, such as the Quakers[2]. Neither is Christaquarianism a cult (in the sociological sense of the word), for it does not display the unitary cohesiveness of such organizations.

Steven Sutcliffe concludes his thesis (1998a) with the case that the so-called New Age movement itself is no more than a "collectivity" of individual seekers that happen to use the New Age emblem. The argument is that, because it has "no essential purpose or goal", the collectivity cannot be classed as a movement (see Chapter II).

York (1995:324f) and Ferguson (1980:235-236) have argued that the New Age movement is best represented as a SPIN of SPINs, where a SPIN is a segmented, polycentric, integrated network. Christaquarianism, in so far as it is similar to the New Age, may therefore conform to such a sociological analysis. However, in many respects, Christaquarianism is not as well developed as a SPIN; the network is not yet 'integrated' – the polycentric nodes of the network are not in contact with each other to a sufficient extent that we could call the network 'integrated'. To this extent, then, Christaquarianism is more akin to Campbell's (1972) notion of a diffuse 'cultic milieu'. Again, though, there is some discrepancy with this model, as in pockets the field is institutionalized beyond the degree to which we would expect in a cultic milieu. What sociological model are we to use for Christaquarianism, then?

In an extended discussion, York (1995:237-314) points out that sometimes distinction has been blurred between the church-sect typology, which is a definitional construct, and the sect-to-church hypothesis, which is a developmental theory according to which sects develop into churches. Ernst Troeltsch (1931) was the first major theorist of the church-sect-cult typology[3] after Weber. H Richard Niebuhr (1929) modified[4] this definitional typology into a developmental hypothesis where the sect acts as the undeveloped predecessor of the church. Many modifications of these theories have since been promulgated, and some of these are discussed by York (1995:237-314) and Dawson (1997)[5].

It would not be original to repeat such discussion here. Instead, I will try to move the literature on from York's consideration of New Age in the light of the church-sect typology. In studies of the New Age, cultic milieu, alternative spirituality and similar constructs, scholars have to date by and large concentrated on definitional typologies. Surely there is sufficient understanding of the area now to create a developmental theory, analogous to Niebuhr's, according to which the cultic milieu develops into a movement – in the case of this thesis, according to which the New Age fringe of Christianity develops into the Christaquarian movement. Secondly, this discussion should be aware of the insights put forward by theorists of the new social movements, and not be blinkered into consideration only of church-sect type models.

Movements and networks differ from churches and sects in their degree of institutionalization. While both sect and church characteristically centre around a singular organization, movements or networks are disparate, diffuse phenomena. Scott defines the organizational form of new social movements as "parallel [to] their ideological project ...

    (1) locally based, or centred on small groups;

    (2) organized around specific, often local, issues;

    (3) characterized by a cycle of social movement activity and mobilization, i.e. vacillation between periods of high and low activity (the latter often taking the form of a disbandment, temporarily or permanently, of the organization);

    (4) where the movement constructs organizations which bridge periods of high activity they tend to feature fluid hierarchies and loose systems of authority;

    (5) shifting membership and fluctuating members.

    (Scott 1995/1990:30)

This definition of a new social movement is not dissimilar to Gerlach and Hine's (1968) definition of a SPIN and may be applied successfully to New Age. Scott further contrasts new social movements (of which I suggest New Age is an example) with the worker's movement as an example of 'old' social movements:

Table VIII.1 Old and New Social Movements

	Workers' movement	**New social movements**
Location	Increasingly within the polity	Civil society
Aims	Political integration/ economic rights	Changes in values and lifestyle/ defence of civil society
Organization	Formal/ hierarchical	Network/ grass roots
Medium of action	Political mobilization	Direct action/ cultural innovation

(Scott 1995/1990:19)

In his discussion of social movements and contentious politics, Tarrow (1998/1994) emphasizes the importance of changes in political opportunities and constraints for the emergence of social movements. He argues that participants respond to a variety of incentives: material and ideological, partisan and group-

200

based, long-standing and episodic (Tarrow 1998/1994:10). We must consider both opportunities-threats to challengers and facilitation-repression by authorities (Tarrow 1998/1994:18). In terms of the rise of New Age within Christianity, there seem to have been several significant changes in the context of contention. Firstly, for Catholics, the Second Vatican Council (1966) presented opportunities for dialogue with non-Catholic religious traditions which were unprecedented. Secondly, the growth of the Ecumenical Movement within Christianity as a whole must have encouraged Christians to look at the fringe of their tradition. Thirdly, as Tarrow also notes, the 'early risers' of a movement create the context in which others can follow (Tarrow 1998/1994:24). The leadership of people like David Spangler and William Bloom in the New Age from the 1970s has allowed more conventional Christians to express interest in the New Age. Tarrow argues that this change in context is a precondition for the emergence of social movements upon which underlying social networks and action-oriented cultural frames can build.

Tarrow goes on to suggest the development of a movement into a revolution.

> ... when contention spreads across an entire society, as it sometimes does, we see a cycle of contention; when such a cycle is organized around opposed or multiple sovereignties, the outcome is a revolution.
> (Tarrow 1998/1994:10)

While there is some evidence in both hostile evangelical literature and the more idealistic New Age literature that the New Age movement is aiming for a revolutionary New World Order, the more balanced view is that social transformation will be piecemeal and achieved solely through inner transformation.

Three "tipping points" of the cycles of movements are outlined by Tarrow: exhaustion and factionalization, institutionalization and violence, and repression and facilitation (Tarrow 1998/1994:147). Some sectors of New Age have shown exhaustion, for example the value of the economy in attuned crystals, although I would not go so far as Melton (1998) in declaring the death of the New Age movement. New Age has not yet demonstrated factionalization to any great extent, for there are few bodies large or cohesive enough to splinter. Some sectors of New Age have institutionalized (for example, The Omega Order), while others have shown a tendency for violence (for example, the so-called Ecowarriors[6]). Evangelical (and other) Christians have attempted to repress New Age within the church, and may have achieved this with their own followers, but in other areas of the church – such as St James's – New Age is being facilitated by the leadership. Tarrow's analysis of "tipping points" is therefore difficult to apply with any firm conclusions to the New Age movement. In particular, his comments on the tendency of a disaffected core group of members to advocate violence to achieve their aims, is more appropriate for political or fundamentalist religious groups than the liberal religious movement of the New Age. Tarrow's more general comments on the polarization between those willing to compromise with authorities and those who seek continued confrontation after the differential decline of support may be more applicable to Christaquarianism, which is a compromise between the radical demands of the core New Age and the traditional system of Christianity.

Despite the tendency to avoid institutionalization, movements, networks and the cultic milieu do evidence pockets of institutionalization. Consensually recognizable New Age groups exist throughout the spectrum of what Paul Greer (1995) has modelled as a "patriarchal/ecological typology" representing two "poles" of the New Age movement. Thus an individual Christaquarian group may conceivably be institutionalized as a patriarchal church. Christaquarianism as a whole, however, tends at the moment to be characterized by the ecological style of organization which is grass-roots based.

A collection of these pockets of institutionalization working together under a loose umbrella is what we know as a movement. These pockets of institutionalization are what the traditional typology classes as "cults", which are typically small institutions centred around a "mystical" or "alternative" doctrine; their organizational boundaries are fluid. Stark & Bainbridge (1979) distinguish between "audience cults", "client cults" and "cult movements". Bainbridge later (1997) dropped usage of what he considered the pejorative term "cult" in this typology, and added a fourth degree, "private", "at the lowest level of organization, comparable to parallel behavior" (Bainbridge 1997:370). But this is not a developmental hypothesis: private cults may transform into client cults, but equally, cult movements may transform into audience cults.

To adapt another model, John McCarthy (1996) presents a two-by-two matrix of movement-mobilizing structures, as below:

Table VIII.2 Dimensions of movement-mobilizing structures

	Nonmovement	Movement
Informal	Friendship networks	Activist networks
	Neighborhoods	Affinity groups
	Work networks	Memory communities
Formal	Churches	SMOs
	Unions	Protest communities
	Professional associations	Movement schools

(McCarthy 1996:145)

Although McCarthy does not use this matrix as a developmental model, it is easy to see that the informal, nonmovement, kinship networks identified by Wood (1999b) in New Age Spiritualism may develop into affinity groups and *bona fide* movements, which in turn may institutionalize into SMOs (social movement organizations) or finally churches. Hanspeter Kriesi (1996), in the same volume as McCarthy, suggests that SMOs have four options for transformation: radicalization, involution, commercialization or institutionalization. New Age has, in various quarters, manifested all forms of these transformations. For example, Alternatives has institutionalized it, crystal shops have commercialized it, small meditation groups have involuted it, and notorious groups such as Solar Temple have radicalized it.

What I am suggesting is that the *successful* cultic milieu will develop into a broad socio-religious movement and enter the mainstream culture. Peter Clarke (1996) has questioned the meaning of the success of a new religious movement: for instance, in terms of geographical spread and number of converts, Christianity had failed after the first fifty years of its existence. Furthermore, some groups, for example the Shakers and Brahma Kumaris, promote celibacy within a millenarian framework, and therefore do not intend to 'survive' longer than one generation. I am defining a successful cultic movement as a tradition of thought which broadens its social base and disseminates its ideas to a wider public, up to the maximum point of being accepted by the mainstream culture. It must do this without becoming uniformly institutionalized; otherwise it should be regarded as moving along the sect-church continuum. The cult, as traditionally understood, therefore has two options: institutionalization into sect or church as in the sect-church hypothesis; or wider dissemination, probably in association with other cults of a similar nature, through a network or movement. These two options are presented in the table below.

Table VIII.3 Cult development

Traditional model	Alternative model
Cult	Cult
Sect	Association of cults – movement
Church	Mainstream assimilation

Many studies of NRMs define them as alternative in relation to the mainstream. This may preclude objective study of the growth of a new movement into the mainstream, that is, in the present study, the growth of New Age as exemplified in Christaquarianism into mainstream Christianity. Danny Jorgensen[7] argues that

> Since esoteric claims focus on things within the conventionalized domains of medicine, psychology, and religion, they often are viewed by insiders and outsiders alike as rival and marginal, if not entirely deviant, beliefs. It is in this sense that esoteric knowledge generally serves as a source of identity and solidarity for members of the community, and between this community and a larger cultic milieu. In other words, marginality provides the basis for the spirit of a general movement of esoteric thought.
> (Jorgensen 1982:388)

It must be noted that, by implication, as soon as the esoteric community loses its marginal status (ie as soon as it becomes mainstream), it disappears out of existence. In other words, the once marginal community has found a place in conventional society.

In fact, Jorgensen (1982:387) explicitly identifies "New Age Christian" groups to be within this esoteric community, in one of the earliest academic usages of the term. He describes the organization of esoteric culture as "a continuum from collective behavioral audiences to complex groups (Jorgensen 1982:401) and concludes that "there is no 'occult establishment' as such" (Jorgensen 1982:402). Within the esoteric community he distinguishes three distinctive but interconnected segments: a 'psychic' network of cult-like churches, businesses and associations; an 'esoteric' network of small cultic study groups, medical clinics and other associations; and a 'spiritual' network composed of cult-like religious groups (Jorgensen 1983:59).

While scholars of new religious movements are united on the importance of alternality in the identity of the esoteric community, scholars of new social movements have tended to emphasize the overlap with mainstream tradition. As we have seen in our presentation of the cultural framing of Christaquarianism, especially in the chapter on The Omega Order, New Age Christians constantly relate their beliefs to the orthodox tradition.

> [Movements] have to produce identities which are sufficiently specific to provide the foundations for the diversity of the movement, in relation to its adversaries; but at the same time, sufficiently close to traditional collective identities in order to make it possible for movement actors to communicate with those who continue to recognize themselves in consolidated identities.
> (della Porta & Diani 1999:96)

Buttiglione (1988) suggests that

> "Movements" are best understood from their beginnings: they originate in an alienation from the existing institutions (or their concrete form) without already having found a new institutional form.
> (Buttiglione 1988:236)

Similarly, Nelson (1969) has defined cults as

> ... religious movements which make a fundamental break with the religious tradition of the culture ...
> (Nelson 1969:152)

In one sense, this alienation or break from tradition is almost tautologous, for a movement must have features which distinguish it from existing institutions in order for it to be noticed. However, we may note the important criterion that movements have *not yet found a new institutional form*.

Bryan Wilson has pointed out that,

> Because this factor [institutionalization] is culturally limited, classification of religious movements by the extent to which they are institutionalized is a clearly inadequate procedure for movements that have arisen outside the boundaries of established Christianity.
> (Wilson 1975:13)

Analyzing Christaquarianism according to the extent it has institutionalized as a sect or church, then, may reflect a cultural bias. In this vein, Stark makes an analysis of the anti-organizational tendency of New Age doctrinal fluidity (cf Wallis 1975, 1977):

That doctrines can directly cause ineffective leadership is widely evident in contemporary New Age and "metaphysical" groups. If everyone is a "student" and everyone's ideas and insights are equally valid, then no-one can say what must be done or who is to do what, when. The result is the existence of virtual non-organizations – mere affinity or discussion groups incapable of action.
(Stark 1996:139)

There is not much sociological literature available on the formation of new socio-religious *movements* as distinct from individual, hierarchical religious 'cults' or sects. This may be because it is difficult to be in the right place at the right time to observe the formation of fledgling religious movements. However, there are a number of exceptions to this general rule, and these are discussed below (Campbell (1972), Gerlach & Hine (1968), Nelson (1969), Wallis (1979) and English (1985)).

Campbell's notion of the "cultic milieu", goes back to an early stage in the formation of a religious movement. The milieu is united by "a common consciousness", "a receptive and syncretistic orientation" and "an interpenetrative communication" (Campbell 1972:134). Already, however, "seekership institutions" (Campbell 1972:135) have begun to emerge, although these are not yet co-ordinated. Campbell suggests that cultic organizations "face continuing pressure to widen their concerns and explore new cultic regions" (Campbell 1972:127-128), with three end-scenarios: losing its focus of concern; coming under the influence of an individual who lays claim to channeled revelations; or institutionalizing seekership within the organization by "creating several categories of membership corresponding to different degrees of initiation" (Campbell 1972:128).

It is my intention to flesh out Campbell's thesis of the cultic milieu, in combination with the insights of other scholars discussed in this section, into a developmental thesis in relation to the New Age and Christaquarianism. This developmental thesis is essentially as follows: unco-ordinated trends of religious opinion become a collectivity or network of seekers within a cultic milieu of alternative spirituality, before growing into a matrix of fledgling institutions and finally a new religious movement. This understanding of the widely-accepted phrase "NRM" is different from that which uses it as an impartial, academic synonym for the popular term "religious cult". In my conception, an NRM may be both of the singular "religious cult" type, or of a more widespread *socio-cultural* movement. It is in this second sense that Christaquarianism is a NRM. This understanding of NRM is in fact so different from the traditional understanding of NRMs within the sociology of religion, that it may be useful to distinguish it as a new socio-religious movement or "NSRM", to emphasize the wider cultural base and similarity to the new social movements ("NSMs").

Luther Gerlach and Virginia Hine located "Five factors crucial to the growth and spread of a modern religious movement" (1968) (which happened to be the Pentecostal movement[8]). These were:

1.   an acephalous, reticulate organizational structure,
2.   face-to-face recruitment along lines of pre-existing significant social relationships,
3.   commitment generated through an act or experience,
4.   change-oriented ideology, and
5.   real or perceived opposition.

(Gerlach & Hine 1968:123)

All five of these factors can be seen to be at work in the growth of Christaquarianism. Firstly, there is no centralized organizational structure. Secondly, recruitment does not occur 'in the street' or anonymously; it follows pre-existing lines of relationship such as existing church networks (as in St James's) or other networks (as in CANA developing from within the membership of Bridge Trust) (cf Wood 1999b). Thirdly, one of the defining features of the New Age movement and thus also of Christaquarianism is that of an altered state of consciousness or mystical experience. Fourthly, Marilyn Ferguson characterized the Aquarian Conspiracy as a social transformation achieved through personal transformation. Fifthly, there has been vociferant opposition to New Agers within Christianity by evangelicals, in addition to more general societal hostility to alternative spirituality.

Gerlach (1971) went on to develop the model of organizational structure mentioned in the first of his five factors above. Movements were described as

    a.   *Segmentary:* a movement is composed of a range of diverse groups, or cells, which grow and die, divide and fuse, proliferate and contract.

    b.   *Polycephalous:* this movement organization does not have a central command or decision-making structure; rather it has many leaders or rivals for leadership, not only within the movement as a whole, but within each movement cell.

    c.   *Reticulate:* these diverse groups do not constitute simply an amorphous collection; rather, they are organized into a network, or reticulate structure through cross-cutting links, "traveling evangelists" or spokesmen, overlapping participation, joint activities, and the sharing of common objectives and opposition.

    (Gerlach 1971:817)

This is the origin of the SPIN (Segmented, Polycentric, Integrated Network) model that York (1995) and Ferguson (1980) adopted in the SPIN of SPINs model of New Age.

Geoffrey Nelson (1969), described a "cult-religion continuum" whereby all cults originate as "local cults", either through the activities of a charismatic leader or the spontaneous association of individuals with common interests. Charismatic cults generally die with the leader or the loss of her/his charisma. Spontaneous cults generally die when their members lose their original interests or suffer from internal dissensions.

Those local cults that survive do so as the result of a process of institutionalization.

(Nelson 1969:157)

Charismatic cults may develop through establishing branches, while spontaneous cults tend to develop through federation with similar local groups. In this analysis, Christaquarianism is developing as a spontaneous cult: a non-organized association of individuals on the New Age fringe of Christianity, which may die should these members lose their interest in alternative spirituality, but if this spirituality continues, could continue to develop into a broad-based movement through contact with similar groups.

Roy Wallis is one of the few sociologists of religion to give an explicit definition of "movement":

Social movements, then, I shall define as relatively sustained collective efforts to change, maintain, or restore some feature(s) of society or of its members, which employ relatively uninstitutionalized means to promote those ends.

(Wallis 1979:1)

Again, we may note the emphasis on being uninstitutionalized. Wallis' (1979) perception that Christian Science and Scientology emerged initially as secular therapies, transforming to religions due primarily to the need to legitimate authority in the face of hostile public opinion, deserves more attention with relation to the New Age. Conservative Christians speak of secular movements such as environmentalism and psychotherapy as "entry points" to the New Age Movement, and this analysis is not unfounded. IM Lewis (1975:31f) has also remarked in relation to cross-cultural contact with spirit possession that the spirits are first considered of no moral significance, their cultural acceptance being a function of their efficacy. This could be a useful model for understanding the acceptance of New Age practices in Christianity, and I have heard many times the idea that, for example crystals, are neutral powers that are functional, "So what can be wrong with them?"

June Anne English' model of the development of movements in *An Ethnography of Holistic Health Practitioners* (1985) (*Figure VIII.1* below) is an early theoretical[9] account of New Age healers as a social movement[10]. The final paragraph of the thesis should serve as the abstract:

Revealed by their own projections of the future and my analysis of the social constraints, holistic health practitioners face several options. They can invite cooperation with the orthodox medical establishment reforming it, perhaps at the cost of the more esoteric tenets of holistic health. If the future scope-of-work of established medicine permits, a separate profession of empirical medicine might emerge, complementary with rationalist medicine. Some practitioners will choose to remain in decentralized, egalitarian, informal networks, quietly carrying the tourch [sic] of empirical medicine and Aquarian ideals for future generations. It is a matter of individual choice.

(English 1985:329)

Figure VIII.1 The Cycle of a Social Movement

1. *There must be a problem, a set of difficulties to be resolved.*
   ** These can be social, ecological and personal, but must be perceived as having no solution in the status quo.

2. *A catalytic analysis is made. Someone makes a statement about the problem.*
   ** There must be a historical basis - a background to present knowledge
   ** There must be an "analyst"

3. *A crisis occurs, demonstrating the "truth" of the catalytic analysis.*
   ** The crisis must be perceived as such and used to demonstrate the solution that is offered

4. *Members are gathered.*
   ** Individuals must learn how to be members
   ** Groups must unite in ideological networks
   ** The ideology must provide a template for future action and reinforce the need to take action
   Example: A millenarian movement is designed to transform the "real world" into utopia with the help of the supernatural. It depends on a perception of disaster joined with the hope of a new age. The Aquarian ideal is the basis of millenial hopes in the holistic health community.

5. *Secondary analysis* [sic] *are made.*
   ** These form the basis for professional growth and the formation of new groups, insitutionalised and informal.

6. *Policies are formed and institutions are developed.*
   ** The holistic healers must quickly professionalize or be absorbed or destroyed in a [sic] economic conflict with orthodox" medicine.

7. *Informal networks are maintained sub rosa.*

(English 1985:21)

It is claimed that holistic health "is representative of ... decentralized social movements" (English 1985:ix) like early Christianity, and that the thesis therefore focuses on "the [general] problem of continuity and change in an alternative tradition" (English 1985:viii). English provides an unparalleled attempt to provide a non-judgemental[11] schema for defining 'alternative' social movements, which also happens to avoid emphasis on the degree of institutionalization and thereby to redefine the criteria for sociological success.

> The assumption has been that if the social movement has not quickly institutionalized, then it was just a deviant flash in the pan. Institutionalization – the Weberian routinization of individual charisma – has been the traditional baseline for "success" ...
> ... social movements do not spring from a "steady state". No culture is ever "finished and homeostatic." ... If there is no real final solution, then perhaps dissonance is a phenomenon of living systems, not a prime mover.
> I propose that adaptive success should be defined more widely than mere Weberian institutionalization. Social movements can, indeed, be viewed in a different light. Not all stable social movements look like the Catholic Church. After all, the Christian esoteric tradition has coherently existed for an equally long period of time, without necessarily adopting a

cohesive institutional framework. This perspective minimizes the red herring effect of deviance and majority adaptation as definitions of failure and success. Perhaps minority ideas are a "real" part of the complexity of culture – just as manzanita and malodorous mountain misery are a critical part of Yellow Pine forest ecology.

Having tilted at the windmill, I must still provide some redefinition of success. For evaluation alone, I suggest that any system that can reproduce its own primary goals, the ideology that created the movement, and survive under varying conditions is effective. Only the complete extinction of the movement's primary goal constitutes failure. Moderate, but stable survival, is a success as well, differing in scale, not kind.

(English 1985:201-205)

English describes the possible life cycles of the holistic health movement. It is clear from the final analysis discussed above (English 1985:329) that there is in fact a third possible future of the holistic health movement. The diagram then reduces to a continual circle of informal networks and two end-games: professionalization in a plural medical system or absorption into orthodox medicine.

English' model demands that there must be an analyst around which the group can unite. This has been the case with both The Omega Order and St James's church, in Canon Peter Spink and Revd Donald Reeves. However, with the retirement of Donald Reeves in 1998 and the ill-health of Peter Spink since the mid-nineties, we may question whether such charismatic leadership amongst these groups will continue. Canon Spink has expressed to me in interview the wish that Omega does not continue after his demise. Of course, it remains to be seen whether this will actually occur, as a significant number of people have invested their life savings in the Order. Similarly, it is questionable whether St James's church will continue to be led in the same direction by the new Rector. Certainly, the feedback I received from the PCC after the retirement of Donald Reeves was to distance themselves from the New Age. This is a common problem among new religious movements, located already by Max Weber and described by him as the routinization of charisma. My tentative analysis is that the current leaders of Christaquarianism have not routinized their charisma sufficiently to allow the movement to continue in the ways they lead the movement. However, this does not necessarily mean that new leaders with new visions will not emerge.

English' model also demands a crisis to occur in order to demonstrate the "truth" of the catalytic analysis. This crisis may be global or personal. Some people may regard the environmental crisis or decline in the quality of the social environment as confirmatory of the New Age analysis. However, further confirmation would be required in order to crystallise Christaquarianism into a movement. Possible crises which could perform this crystallisation include a 'witchhunt' by conservative Christians in which leaders of Christaquarianism are publicly denounced. This may happen if the CANA *Paper* receives significant media attention, but is in my opinion unlikely. Had the Christaquarian movement crystallised earlier in the UK, when evangelicals were new to the New Age phenomenon, shortly after the publication of Cumbey's incitatory work (1983), such a "witchhunt" may have occurred. But my impression is that evangelical concern with New Age is fading as time goes on and becoming repetitive.

Christaquarianism: A New Socio-Religious Movement?

The model we have developed for Christaquarianism, then, with the assistance of a number of scholars, is as follows. To start with, there is "cognitive dissonance" (Festinger et al 1956): a problem, which cannot be resolved within the existing institutions of Christianity or the New Age movement. A sufficient number of individuals experience this dissonance to form spontaneous local associations with others experiencing similar problems. On a wider spectrum, these local cults may be viewed as part of a cultic milieu. In pockets, they are institutionalised, whereas elsewhere they remain private or audience cults. These nodes of the polycentric network maintain informal contact with each other sub rosa, and are beginning to integrate this contact into a matrix of connections through such documents as the CANA dialogue *Paper* (1999). Indeed, this very thesis may be another push towards integration of the movement.

The prognosis is that these informal networks will be maintained until such time as the policies of groups like CANA become so widely accepted that over-arching institutions begin to form. This has not yet happened, but is likely, given the tendency of any successful movement to institutionalise. Thus the end-game is the same as in the sect-church hypothesis: a wide-ranging, institutionalised, influential worldview. However, the process by which this came about is quite different, with institutionalisation occuring at the final point in the continuum and the intermediate sect stage being replaced by that of a network. I may illustrate this developmental model of New Socio-Religious Movements ("NSRMs") with reference to the groups used as case studies for this thesis.

CANA is the most simply-structured movement studied here to emerge from the cultic milieu. Indeed, it may be argued that it is still firmly within the cultic milieu, existing only as a mailing list for the collection of cult audiences. However, there are signs that the cultural framing of its theology has developed to such an extent that it is self-conscious of its existence as a viable alternative to mainstream Christianity, and is ready to form associations with like-minded institutions. There is already within the history of CANA evidence of its linkage with St James's and The Omega Order, the other two Christaquarian groups studied here.

St James's church has, in its openness to the New Age movement, allowed for a further stage in the development of the Christaquarian NSRM. It is acting as a "host" institution within the mainstream culture for the counterculture group known, appropriately, as "Alternatives". The core competency of Alternatives is its ability to attract regular large audiences to its lecture evenings. The distribution of the lecture programme, through a mailing list, is central to this effort and thus the group has not developed beyond recognition from the audience cult type of NRM represented by CANA. However, with moves for Alternatives to become independent of St James's church, the cycle is beginning to turn and it may be that Alternatives successfully "takes" outside its "breeding ground" in the "host" church.

This final stage in the developmental cycle of the Christaquarian NSRM is apparent in The Omega Order. The origins of this movement are in the circle of contacts Canon Peter Spink built up, first at his meditation group in Coventry Cathedral, and then in the spiritual study centre at Kent House. This can be seen as the audience cult, mailing-list stage of development. His group found a "host" institution when he was invited to become Warden of Burrswood Home of Healing. As seems likely to be the case at St James's, the NRM outgrew its host environment and Canon Spink resigned from his Wardenship in 1980 to concentrate on the foundation of The Omega Order. This institutionalisation was completed on the move in 1986 to Winford Manor.

These developmental stages in the growth of the NSRM of Christaquarianism are only broad indications of what has happened in one particular movement. It may, of course, be the case that other NSRMs develop in different ways. Moreover, even with Christaquarianism, earlier strands of the development are in evidence at later stages. For example, The Omega Order still meticulously maintains its mailing list. Likewise, later strands of development may surface early in the individual NRM's history, as with the experiments in communal living undertaken by Bridge Trust. Nevertheless, it is my analysis that the groups within the NSRM of Christaquarianism have shown a general trend to emerge as a mailing-list from the cultic milieu, adopt a host institution within the cultural mainstream, and finally break free as a NRM in their own right. The collection of these groups, at their various stages of development, is what I take to be the NSRM Christaquarianism.

Conclusion

This doctoral thesis began with a hypothesis – that there exists an identifiable group of New Age Christians who occupy the crossover between Christianity and the New Age movement. I have coined the new sociological label, "Christaquarians" to refer to this group of Christian New Agers.

The critical literature on Christaquarianism has begun to assemble. There are a number of academic theses on the interaction between Christianity and the New Age movement, although most of these tend to be of a confessional nature. Paul Greer (1994), Barton English (1994), Thomas Legere (1993), Alan Roxburgh (1986) and Ron Rhodes (1991) all begin with a stated Christian apologetic bias, with those later in this list becoming less objective. Theses on the New Age movement in general have also considered the overlap with Christianity, although not in as much detail as could be hoped for. We may mention the theses of Anthony D'Andrea (1997), Christoph Bochinger (1995), Wouter Hanegraaff (1996), Michael York (1995), Stuart Rose (1996), Steven Sutcliffe (1998a), Matthew Wood (1999b) and the publications of Paul Heelas (1993, 1996). Both

New Agers and Christians themselves have also written works pertinent to a study of Christaquarians.

It is apparent that this body of literature, although now becoming respectably large and varied, is not yet detailed enough to provide a complete characterisation of Christaquarians. This is the gap that my thesis hopes to begin to fill. But there are some theoretical problems to overcome before this can be achieved. The most pressing problem is that of definition, for most scholars agree that it is very difficult to define the New Age. Accordingly, a family resemblance model of categorisation was proposed that does justice to the diverse aspects of New Age as well as the many similarities between various New Age groups.

Four case examples were considered. These were St James's church in Piccadilly, an Anglican church renowned for its New Age project; Christians Awakening to a New Awareness, a Christian-New Age network and mailing list; The Omega Order, a residential New Age Christian community near Bristol; and, for comparison, an Anglican evangelical church. From survey statistics obtained from these groups, it can be seen that the New Age Christian groups studied share many characteristics with New Age groups such as the readers of *Kindred Spirit* magazine surveyed by Rose (1996) – although typically to a lesser degree – and may be contrasted with the evangelical grouping.

We have seen that Christaquarians have a shared history in various pre-New Age groups. Gnosticism, Christian Qabbalah, the Cathars, Jacob Boehme, Emanuel Swedenborg, William Blake, Theosophy, the Arcane School, Christian Science, New Thought, Carl Jung, Dion Fortune, Teilhard de Chardin – all share similar Christaquarian traits. I do not argue that they have ever formed a self-conscious or continuous movement. Neither do I claim that all Christaquarians necessarily identify with all or even many of the historical movements considered. Rather, their history was presented in my thesis in order to elucidate implicit claims to a historical tradition by contemporary Christaquarians, and in order to show that there is a legitimating tradition available to them.

There is some overlap between the New Age Christian groups studied (see *Figure VIII.2*). Most dramatically, 50% of Omega respondents and 64% of CANA respondents have visited St James's church. A number of individuals were identified during the fieldwork who are members of two and sometimes all three of the New Age Christian groups studied. However, these were a tiny minority. Far more important is the fact that the leaders of the groups studied are part of a dense social network, as depicted below. Fr Adrian Smith, Janice Dolley, Revd Kevin Tingay and Dr Jean Hardy are all leaders of various of the groups studied, and are generally members of each others' groups. However, there is little institutional linkage between the various groups. For example, although Fr Adrian Smith is a member of CANA, co-founder of Christian TM and a visitor to The Omega Order, these remain entirely distinct organisations. Even more obviously, there is no common truck between Canon Peter Spink and Revd Donald Reeves.

So, may we conclude that there is a *movement* of Christaquarians? Many of the characteristics necessary for this conclusion are present among the groups considered. There is a viable legitimating historical tradition, a sizeable body of critical literature, both emic and etic, and a marked similarity of sociological characteristics that was revealed in the statistical surveys. It is even easier to fit these factors into the "movement" label if we are to use the family resemblance model of categorisation, for this allows us to emphasise the differences as well as the acknowledged similarities between the various groups.

But there is one vital characteristic missing from the groups considered: nobody calls themselves a Christaquarian. If we take Wouter Hanegraaff's characterisation of the New Age movement as the cultic milieu having become conscious of itself (Hanegraaff 1996:17), and apply it to Christaquarianism, this should be represented as the New Age fringe of Christianity becoming conscious of itself as a movement. But although there is a sizeable New Age fringe within Christianity, and a hostile consciousness of it from the evangelicals and other critics within the churches, Christaquarians are not yet conscious of themselves as a movement. Furthermore, in my fieldwork I have found that many Christaquarians abhor the term New Age, to the extent that, when Revd Donald Reeves left St James's church in 1998, there was considerable opposition to the continuation of my research.

Figure VIII.2 Leaders and Members *of some Christaquarian groups*

Omega Order
322 receive newsletter
Canon Peter Spink,
Revd Jim Hill,
Janice Dolley,
Revd Kevin Tingay,
Fr Adrian Smith
50% have been to
St James's

St James's Church
179 on electoral roll
c500 at special services
Revd Donald Reeves,
1980-1998

Bridge Trust
c200 members
Janice Dolley.
Revd Donald Reeves
wrote introduction to
Dolley's 1984 book.

Quaker Universalists
c350 members
Dr Jean Hardy

Christian TM
c100 members
Fr Adrian Smith
Fr Diarmuid Ó'Murchú

Sophia
1993-1997
c40 members
Revd Kevin Tingay

More-to-Life
Fr Adrian Smith

Grail Retreat Centre
Revd Jonathan Robinson,
Revd Jim Hill,
Fr Adrian Smith

Creation Spirituality
52 groups nationwide
Dr Jean Hardy,
Fr Adrian Smith,
Fr Diarmuid Ó'Murchú
Centre hosted in St
James's

CANA
c150 members
Janice Dolley,
Fr Adrian Smith,
Fr Diarmuid Ó'Murchú
64% have been to St
James's

This is similar to the problem that many "New Agers" reject the application of that label to themselves. Popularity of the New Age movement may have peaked in the 1980s; there are no available statistics to prove this, and because of the elusive nature of the movement it would in any case probably be impossible to enumerate. By the late 1980s the New Age movement was subjected to severe criticism, both on the secular side for its rabid commercialism, and on the religious side from fundamentalists for its heretical beliefs. Coupled with adverse national press concerning the distinct phenomenon of New Age travellers, this led to widespread rejection of the sobriquet "New Age" by many hitherto New Agers. Although many alternative labels have been suggested, such as New Sprituality and Holistic Consciousness, some New Agers retain their eponymous style and it remains by far the most recognised and useful term.

Despite these qualifications, although only one of the *Omega News* respondents described their affiliation as New Age, 56% claimed to have adopted New Age ideas or practices. At the same time, 79% considered themselves to be Christian. Similarly, although 43% of the electoral roll respondents at St James's claimed to have adopted New Age ideas or practices, 92% described themselves as Christians. Again, while 87% of CANA respondents claimed a Christian affiliation, 64% also claimed to have adopted New Age ideas or practices.

Table VIII.4 Question 8. Current religious affiliation:

Affiliation %	Omega Order	St James's	CANA
None	8	0	2
Christian	79	92	89
New Age	>1	0	0
Universalist/beyond religion	6	0	0
Agnostic	0	0	4
Other	5	8	2

Table VIII.5 Question 16. If you have adopted New Age ideas or practices how long has this been for?

Length %	Omega Order	St James's	CANA	Kindred Spirit
I haven't	31	45	26	N/A
I have for [x years]	56	43	64	78

I consider that sociologists have the authority to label participants Christaquarian, New Age, or whatever else is applicable – even when the subjects do not consider themselves as such, or even when they emphatically deny such a label (see Burke 1984). But I would not argue that sociologists have the authority to identify social trends and similarities, and affix to this the label "movement". For this, the people involved *do* need to be conscious of themselves as a group. This is evident from the definitions of social movement given by Scott (1995/1990) and Tarrow (1998/1994). As shown above, both these sociologists stipulated the need for collective self-identity as a pre-requisite for a social movement. Indeed, Tarrow puts significant emphasis on a shared cultural frame.

There are a number of groups, which may even be smaller in overall numbers than the myriad of disparate Christaquarians, but whose members are aware of each other as part of a movement. For instance, Neopaganism has a number of organisations, many of which are in touch with each other, although the overall membership is small. "Ecowarriors" have become a movement through the publicity of the media, although there are few if any organisational institutions and a questionable number of "true" members. Historically, new social movements such as the civil rights movement in the USA, the anti-Vietnam movement, and the animal liberation movement, have had varying degrees of institutional co-ordination; but all were conscious of themselves as movements.

To take another, hypothetical example, we may consider the (possibly) thousands of individuals who combine their Christianity with an interest in history. It may be that "Christohistorians" have identifiable traditions, literature and sociological similarities. In a number of congregations, they may even form small groups, such as in the many historical societies in village churches around the country.

There may even be regional groups. But they do not identify with each other to a sufficient extent in order for us to ascribe the suffix "movement" to Christohistorianism.[12]

I often sat wondering in English lessons at school, whether some authors had really intended all the literary allusions, metaphors and themes we were "discovering" in their texts. My cynical boast was that, one day, I would write a work loaded with diverse imagery and inter-connecting motifs; but without any over-arching meaning or plot, which was to be supplied solely by the critic's furtive imagination. Are the Christaquarians such a creation of an over-imaginative mind? Has the analysis presented in my thesis read too much into disparate facts, uniting coincidental allegiances into a substantive movement?

What I once thought of as my first original idea was a version of relativism. I took the world to be a heap of facts represented as random dots on a piece of paper. Different philosophies connected these dots in different ways, like a child's pass-time puzzle. Only there were no numbers guiding the artist to the 'correct' picture; all pictures are true to the seer.

My thesis conforms more to this second anecdote of the dot-to-dots, rather than to the first anecdote of the cynical author. What has been done is that social "facts" have been presented in an orderly fashion, creating an overall picture or interpretation. The statistical surveys give credence that this picture is not the product of a furtive imagination. It is rather a valid presentation of observed phenomena.

All the same, this is "only" the picture *I* have seen; others, from different vantage points, must see their own pictures. I strive to retain the relativism I first adopted at school. But I now believe that a consensual picture of reality can be (or *must be*) constructed that gives the semblance of Objectivity. In sociology, this will only be achieved when numerous scholars arrive at similar presentations and a consensus begins to emerge. Such is beginning to be the case with the sociology of the New Age movement (Sutcliffe 1997:100). However, my thesis retains the indefinite article in its subtitle: *A Sociology of Christians in the New Age.*

Christaquarian is a neologism invented by me, the sociologist. It has never been used emically by New Age Christians themselves. It has never been used by other commentators. Is this a valid way of doing sociology? Does a sociologist have the authority to name a social group? Even when the name chosen is not used by the group itself? These questions have been asked about my proposal to call New Age Christians, 'Christaquarians'.

If we are to follow past practice, new social movements have often been named by their detractors. Thus the "Nazarenes", one of the earliest names for the followers of Jesus of Nazareth, were first called "Christians" pejoritavely. The Unification Church was early dubbed the "Moonies" after its leader Revd Moon, and even scholarly studies have been published under this name. The cynic philosophers of ancient Greece were so-named because they lived like dogs.

Often, there are two names for the same group, one coined by its detractors and the other by its supporters. Thus are we more properly to speak of "hunt saboteurs" or "animal rights protestors"; of "terrorists" or "freedom fighters"; of "fundamentalists" or "evangelicals"; of "pro-lifers" or "women's rights activists"?

Only very rarely are groups named in what we might call an objective, scientific way. Perhaps this is because sociologists, arguably in the best position to avoid subjectivity, are paradoxically slow to notice new social trends! The journalists always get there first and create the names that stick in public, and professional, minds. Sociologists usually come in at a later stage to refine already-extant terms. Isn't it time that sociologists actually took the lead, and become the first to discover and name these new social movements? Why should we be content with clearing up the confusions created by other people's sound bites?

No respondent in my survey of over 700 Christians described their religious affiliation as a New Age Christian. Therefore, the heretofore conventional style, "New Age Christian", has no advantage over "Christaquarian" emically. It has, however, been used etically by scholars including Paul Heelas (1996a) and Anthony D'Andrea (1997/1996). Is there any ground for changing the etic term, "New Age Christian" to "Christaquarian"? Has there been a significant change in the referent? The answer to this question is certainly, Yes, because never before has there been an extended academic study of New Age Christians. My study has significantly clarified the nature and extent of New Age Christianity, such that it could be argued to need a new reference. This reference I propose to be "Christaquarianism".

Other critics[13], while not questioning my authority to name the social group I am studying, have raised doubts over the relevance of the term 'Aquarian'. It has been pointed out that this is a dated way of referring to the New Age, which was most popular in the 1970s, and should not be applied to a contemporary New Age group. Two arguments stand against this. The first is that Christaquarians are typically older than most New Agers, and although there is no evidence available on the period in which they formed their beliefs, are likely to have become New Agers in the 'Aquarian period'. The second is that 'New Age' is itself now a dated term, rejected by many 'New Agers', although no replacement term has acquired general currency.

The central hypothesis of my doctoral thesis is the question of whether there is a *movement* of New Age Christians. 65% of respondents at St James's church and 63% of CANA respondents rejected the term Christaquarian as an adequate description of their spiritual position. It may be that surveys of New Age Christian groups with different emphases from St James's and CANA may accept the term, Christaquarian. Indeed, this has been my experience in the field, where a number of people have readily accepted the label. However, in the absence of supporting data – unless we are to rely on the 23% of CANA respondents who thought the term adequately describes their spiritual position – the existence of a self-conscious movement must be rejected for the time-being.

It may well be that my thesis appears at the same time as Christaquarians become conscious of themselves as a movement. If so, this does not necessarily mean that the publication of the thesis has *caused* Christaquarians to become conscious of each other, but rather that the very factors which drew my attention to individual Christquarians and their groups, are also evident to Christaquarians themselves.

The Devils (1971/1871-1872) by Fyodor Dostoyevsky is a psychological treatment of the revolutionary Socialist conspiracies which were underfoot in Russia and Europe at the time he, and his contemporaries Karl Marx and Friedrich Engels, were writing – a generation before the events of October 1917. It depicts the activities of Peter Verkhovensky in uniting a sorry band of five individuals in a provincial Russian town, with the aim of causing mayhem prior to the general revolution which he promised as the result of a huge network of similar groups of five. Dostoyevsky, ignorant of the future, ridicules the idea that such a revolution could be carried out.

> '... I even think that instead of many hundred groups of five in Russia,
> we're the only one in existence and that there is no network at all,'
> Liputin said, panting for breath.
> (Dostoyevsky 1971/1871-1872:551)

Notes to Chapter VIII

[1] Frank Whaling, personal communication 12 April 1999; cf Whaling 1996:5 and Heelas 1996a:9.

[2] At no stage in this thesis do I speculate on the numbers involved in Christaquarianism. My fieldwork does not provide a basis for such an estimation.

[3] Troeltsch actually spoke of "die Mystik" rather than 'cult'. However, as early as 1932, Howard Becker introduced the term "cult" as a substitute for "mysticism", and this designation has been maintained, notably in Yinger (1970).

[4] Troeltsch actually wrote his 1931 model between 1908 and 1911 (York 1995:238).

[5] These modifications include: Yinger (1970), Berger (1954), Nelson (1969, 1987), Glock & Stark (1965), Stark & Bainbridge (1985), Wilson (1970), Martin (1962), Robertson (1970) and Swatos (1976).

[6] I consider many Ecowarriors to be on the Green fringe of the New Age movement, although my evidence is limited to national newspaper reports.

[7] In work deriving from a thesis on tarot card readers for which research commenced in 1975.

[8] The Pentecostal and Charismatic movements may also be better understood as a NSRM than as a NRM.

[9] English' theoretical constructions are unparalleled in their relevance to my study of Christians in the New Age. So it is a great pity that she does not provide an audit trail for us to assess the validity of these inferences from the original fieldwork.

[10] An earlier thesis that considers similar material without such extended analysis is Katherine Brown-Keister's *Legitimation Strategies of an Alternative Health Occupation: the lay holistic health practitioner in the [San Francisco] Bay Area* (1982). This mentions the New Age explicitly only once, uncapitalized (Brown Keister 1982:139), although its conclusions may validly be extended to the New Age movement. "Lay holistic health practitioners" are contrasted with "licensed holistic health practitioners" who hold government-approved licenses "for their more traditional work; there is no license authorizing the use of holistic health techniques." (Brown-Keister 1982:50).
Concentrating on the process of legitimation, Brown-Keister identifies two strategies:

> The first, <u>carving out a territory</u>, refers to efforts by practitioners to define and claim a distinct area for their work. This consisted of defining a domain for themselves that was unclaimed by another professional group. ...
> The other major strategic category is termed <u>cultivating a clientele</u>.
> (Brown-Keister 1982:i-ii, <u>original emphasis</u>)

Four techniques of legitimation are outlined. Firstly, care is taken over the use of language to avoid encroachment upon orthodox medicine. Secondly, the practitioner-client relationship is outlined in contract form. Thirdly, clients are often referred to orthodox medical practitioners. Fourthly, legitimation is borrowed from established sources of legitimacy such as religion, a general business license, and working in association with orthodox medics.

In a brief conclusion, three possible end-game scenarios for lay holistic health are sketched.

> Most likely, attempts by holistic health practitioners to attain autonomous professional status will not succeed due to the near monopolistic control of medical resources by existing medical professionals, the insurance industry and government.
>
> Another possible scenerio [sic] is that both the content of holistic health and the role of holistic health practitioners are legitimated but the control of access to resources is in the hands of other, more established, practitioners. ...
>
> A third possibility is that groups of practitioners representing different alternative techniques but not necessarily espousing holistic principles will break away from holistic health and begin to build separate rationales for their individual therapies and seek professional autonomy for themselves.
>
> (Brown-Keister 1982:175-176)

[11] English departs from her ideal of objective description – giving some subjective advice indicating her preferred outcome:

> The holistic healers must quickly professionalize or be absorbed or destroyed in a [sic] economic conflict with "orthodox" medicine.
>
> (English 1985:21 para 6)

In fact, English favours the very Weberian measure of success that she so maligns: institutionalization.

[12] A further reason for excluding 'Christohistorians' from being a 'movement' is that they do not call for social change.

[13] Stuart Rose, personal communication, 19 May 1998.

AFTERWORD TO THE 2003 EDITION

Three years after completing the text and eight years after beginning the research, my thoughts on the subject of New Age Christianity have inevitably developed. Nevertheless, it is the original text of the doctoral thesis that has been published here, except for a worryingly large number of minor corrections and some footnotes with details of significant changes that have occurred since the doctoral thesis was submitted in 2000.

The research was begun with a certain amount of scepticism regarding New Age versions of Christianity, instilled during my upbringing in an evangelical tradition at the family church if not at home. Certainly, I had a black and white picture of Christianity as compared to New Age. As we have seen, such a simple bipolar picture is not sustainable.

The hypothesis that there may be a movement of New Age Christians, dubbed Christaquarians, was also originally conceived with a certain amount of tongue-in-cheek, partly as a method of promoting the area of my research. I have a suspicion that the success of scholarly concepts depends largely on branding and marketing. Again, this tongue-in-cheek attitude (but not the suspicion) transformed during the course of the research and has continued to do so after completing the doctorate.

What at first seemed a bold claim, that there is a movement of New Age Christians, has come to seem more and more plausible and even desirable. Yet the evidence did not at the time of research support such a claim. Further, actively promoting a tradition in this way would have been out of place in an academic study in the sociology of religion.

Once removed from the strictures of academic research, however, it became possible to employ Alain Touraine's methodology of "conversion" (see Chapter I), whereby the movement under study is encouraged and developed by the sociological researcher. First, when a vacancy arose, I offered to take over as editor of the newsletter for Christians Awakening to a New Awareness.

Then I was asked to report for the CANA newsletter on a Round Table of largely Christian spiritual groups that were seeking to co-ordinate their efforts. CANA was a major player in this network, and for two years I volunteered to serve on the Core Group of the Round Table as secretary. I also designed websites for CANA – www.canaweb.info – and the Round Table – www.meta-net.info. What had been mentioned as a postcript and footnote to Chapter IV of the thesis now, as hinted in the original text, was becoming one of the most exciting areas of development.

Separately, I drafted what I called a New Age Christian Theology. Originally a short essay published on www.Christaquarian.net, this is now being expanded to the length of a short book (Kemp forthcoming b). It gives an idea of what

Christaquarians believe and how they practise their spirituality, from a much more personal perspective than the necessarily dry style of the thesis.

In the three years since completing the thesis, I have discovered a number of omissions. The most serious is that of Unitarianism, which although mentioned in passing in the thesis, was not covered in the depth it deserves. There is even a group that was for sometime known as the New Age Unitarian Network and the Unitarian Pagan Network, now Unitarian Earth Spirit Network (UESN). A second important Christaquarian phenomenon not covered in the thesis is the *Christian*New Age Quarterly*, edited by Catherine Groves and published in New Jersey since 1989.

There are also some material omissions from the literature survey. There is a Masters thesis by Revd Don MacGregor, *The New Age Critique of the Church – what can we learn from it?*, completed at St John's College, Nottingham in 1993, which is now available at www.Christaquarian.net. The Church of Scotland published a critique of New Age in 1993. Bruce Epperly published *Crystal & Cross: Christians and New Age in Creative Dialogue* in 1996.

Since submission of the thesis in 2000, Ross Clifford and Philip Johnson have published two Christian works with a New Age touch: *Jesus and the Gods of the NewAge: Communicating Christ in Today's Spiritual Supermarket* (2001) and *Beyond Prediction: The Tarot and Your Spirituality* (2001) (with John Drane). And of course in February 2003, the Catholic Church issued *Jesus Christ the Bearer of the Water of Life: A Christian reflection on the "New Age"* (Pontifical Council for Culture and the Pontifical Council for Interreligious Dialogue 2003).

The literature survey is also now slightly dated, in that there have of course been new studies of both Christianity and New Age in the meantime. For a more up-to-date and detailed survey of the literature, see my textbook, *New Age: A Guide* (Kemp forthcoming a).

Nevertheless, I remain largely happy with the thesis, which covered a huge amount of material in a way that had not previously been attempted. During the course of the research, I moved from a tongue-in-cheek scepticism to a deeper appreciation of New Age forms of Christianity, in a way that is continuing to grow.

Daren Kemp
Sidcup, Kent
Easter 2003

APPENDICES

A.   Questionnaire

1.   The Omega Order

Survey of Spirituality   King's College London University

This survey is part of a research project into modern spirituality that is personally funded at King's College, London University. Your time in filling out this questionnaire - no more than 15 minutes - would be greatly appreciated. Anonymity will be preserved.

---

1. *What is your age?* ☐ 0-18   ☐ 18-24
☐ 25-34   ☐ 35-44   ☐ 44-54   ☐ 55-64 ☐ 65+

2. *Are you*   ☐ male or ☐ female?
3. *Are you*   ☐ single or ☐ partnered?

4. *What is your approximate annual income?*
☐ £0-5,000   ☐ £5-9,999   ☐ £10-14,999
☐ £15-19,999 ☐ £20-24,999 ☐ £25-34,999
☐ £35,000+

5. *What is your occupation? (Please state)*
....

6.   ☐ retired   ☐ student   ☐ unemployed

7. *Highest level of education:*
☐ None   ☐ O-level/GCSE   ☐ A-level
☐ BA, BSc   ☐ Masters   ☐ PhD
Professional...*(please state)*

8. *Religious affiliation (please state)*
originally...
....
currently..
....

9. *What spiritual discipline(s) or teaching has had the greatest influence on your life? (Please state/list)* ....
....
....
....
....

10. *What do you believe God is?*
☐ a real personality   ☐ a fiction
☐ an impersonal force ☐ don't know
☐ other *(please state)* ....
....
....

11. *Are you actively pursuing a spiritual path?*
☐ Yes ☐ No

12. *In your opinion, are there varying types of spirituality - eg New Age spirituality, Buddhist spirituality, Christian spirituality - or is spirituality universally the same?*
☐ varying types   ☐ the same

13. *How often do you meditate?*
☐ Never   ☐ Occasionally   ☐ Every few days
☐ Once a day   ☐ More than once a day

14. *How often do you pray?*
☐ Never   ☐ Occasionally   ☐ Every few days
☐ Once a day   ☐ More than once a day

15. *Have you had experience of any forms of paranormal phenomena?* ☐ Yes   ☐ No
If yes, please state of what kind..........................
....
....
....

16. *If you have adopted New Age ideas or practices how long has this been for?*
☐ I haven't   ☐ I can't remember
☐ 0-6 months   ☐ 6 months-1 year ☐ 1-2 years
☐ 3-4 years   ☐ 5-10 years   ☐ 10+ years

17. *To what extent do you consider yourself to be "green"? (please circle)*
Not green 0 1 2 3 4 5 6 7 8 9 10 Totally

18. *In a few words please describe what you think the New Age is* ....
....
....
....
....

19. *Please give 5 examples of groups, individuals, books or practices that you think are most typically New Age.*
a...
b...
c...
d...
e...

223

20. *Have you ever participated in or used any of the following. Also, what of the following are you currently engaged in?*

	Yes	No	Currently
Acupuncture/shiatsu	☐	☐	☐
Alexander Technique	☐	☐	☐
Aromatherapy	☐	☐	☐
Buddhism	☐	☐	☐
Channeling	☐	☐	☐
Colour Therapy	☐	☐	☐
Creative Visualisation	☐	☐	☐
Crystals	☐	☐	☐
Dance Therapy	☐	☐	☐
Earth Mysteries	☐	☐	☐
Ethical Investing	☐	☐	☐
Flower Remedies	☐	☐	☐
Green Politics	☐	☐	☐
Healing Workshops	☐	☐	☐
Herbalism	☐	☐	☐
Homoeopathy	☐	☐	☐
Hypnotherapy	☐	☐	☐
Massage	☐	☐	☐
NLP	☐	☐	☐
Past Life Therapy	☐	☐	☐
Psychotherapy	☐	☐	☐
Rebirthing	☐	☐	☐
Reflexology	☐	☐	☐
Recycling	☐	☐	☐
Shaman/Pagan Rituals	☐	☐	☐
Sound Therapy	☐	☐	☐
Spiritualism	☐	☐	☐
Tai Chi Ch'uan/Yoga	☐	☐	☐
Transactional Analysis	☐	☐	☐
Veganism	☐	☐	☐
Vegetarianism	☐	☐	☐
Womens' Studies Groups	☐	☐	☐

Thank you for completing this questionnaire. Please return in the sae provided, displaying in the window the address below:

21. *Would you please name individuals whose ideas have had an important influence on your life by their writings: (please list)*

....
....
....
....

22. *Approximately how many books have you read on New Age or related subjects?*.................

23. *Approximately how many books have you read on Christianity or related subjects?*............

24. *What religious, political and social action groups do you belong to?* ....
....
....
....

25. *How long have you been receiving Omega News?* ....

26. *How did you first hear of the Omega Order?*
....
....
....

27. *Have you ever been to ...?*
☐ A service at St James's church, Piccadilly
☐ An Alternatives lecture
☐ A New Age workshop

28. *What is your opinion of Christians who are involved in the New Age?*
....
....
....
....
....
....
....
....
....
....
....
....

Survey of Spirituality   King's College London University

This survey is part of a research project into modern spirituality that is personally funded at King's College, London University. Your time in filling out this questionnaire - no more than 15 minutes - would be greatly appreciated. Anonymity will be preserved.

1. *What is your age?* ☐ 0-18   ☐ 18-24
☐ 25-34   ☐ 35-44   ☐ 44-54   ☐ 55-64   ☐ 65+

2. *Are you*   ☐ male or ☐ female?
3. *Are you*   ☐ single or ☐ partnered?

4. *What is your approximate annual income?*
☐ £0-5,000   ☐ £5-9,999   ☐ £10-14,999
☐ £15-19,999   ☐ £20-24,999   ☐ £25-34,999
☐ £35,000+

5. *What is your occupation? (Please state)*
....
....

6.   ☐ retired   ☐ student   ☐ unemployed

7. *Highest level of education:*
☐ None   ☐ O-level/GCSE   ☐ A-level
☐ BA, BSc   ☐ Masters   ☐ PhD
Professional .... *(please state)*

8. *Religious affiliation (please state)*
originally..
....
currently..
....

9. *What spiritual discipline(s) or teaching has had the greatest influence on your life? (Please state/list)* ....
....
....
....
....

10. *What do you believe God is?*
☐ a real personality   ☐ a fiction
☐ an impersonal force   ☐ don't know
☐ other *(please state)* ....
....
....

11. *Are you actively pursuing a spiritual path?*
☐ Yes ☐ No

12. *In your opinion, are there varying types of spirituality - eg New Age spirituality, Buddhist spirituality, Christian spirituality - or is spirituality universally the same?*
☐ varying types   ☐ the same

13. *How often do you meditate?*
☐ Never   ☐ Occasionally   ☐ Every few days
☐ Once a day   ☐ More than once a day

14. *How often do you pray?*
☐ Never   ☐ Occasionally   ☐ Every few days
☐ Once a day   ☐ More than once a day

15. *Have you had experience of any forms of paranormal phenomena?*   ☐ Yes   ☐ No
If yes, please state of what kind ....
....
....
....

16. *If you have adopted New Age ideas or practices how long has this been for?*
☐ I haven't   ☐ I can't remember
☐ 0-6 months   ☐ 6 months-1 year   ☐ 1-2 years
☐ 3-4 years   ☐ 5-10 years   ☐ 10+ years

17. *To what extent do you consider yourself to be "green"? (please circle)*
Not green 0 1 2 3 4 5 6 7 8 9 10 Totally

18. *In a few words please describe what you think the New Age is* ....
....
....
....
....
....

19. *Please give 5 examples of groups, individuals, books or practices that you think are most typically New Age.*
a ....
b ....
c ....
d ....
e ....

20. *Have you ever participated in or used any of the following. Also, what of the following are you currently engaged in?*

	Yes	No	Currently
Acupuncture/shiatsu	☐	☐	☐
Alexander Technique	☐	☐	☐
Aromatherapy	☐	☐	☐
Buddhism	☐	☐	☐
Channeling	☐	☐	☐
Colour Therapy	☐	☐	☐
Creative Visualisation	☐	☐	☐
Crystals	☐	☐	☐
Dance Therapy	☐	☐	☐
Earth Mysteries	☐	☐	☐
Ethical Investing	☐	☐	☐
Flower Remedies	☐	☐	☐
Green Politics	☐	☐	☐
Healing Workshops	☐	☐	☐
Herbalism	☐	☐	☐
Homoeopathy	☐	☐	☐
Hypnotherapy	☐	☐	☐
Massage	☐	☐	☐
NLP	☐	☐	☐
Past Life Therapy	☐	☐	☐
Psychotherapy	☐	☐	☐
Rebirthing	☐	☐	☐
Reflexology	☐	☐	☐
Recycling	☐	☐	☐
Shaman/Pagan Rituals	☐	☐	☐
Sound Therapy	☐	☐	☐
Spiritualism	☐	☐	☐
Tai Chi Ch'uan/Yoga	☐	☐	☐
Transactional Analysis	☐	☐	☐
Veganism	☐	☐	☐
Vegetarianism	☐	☐	☐
Womens' Studies Groups	☐	☐	☐

21. *Would you please name individuals whose ideas have had an important influence on your life by their writings: (please list)*

....
....
....
....
....

22. *Approximately how many books have you read on New Age or related subjects?*................

23. *Approximately how many books have you read on Christianity or related subjects?*............

24. *What religious, political and social action groups do you belong to?* ....
....
....
....

25. *How long have you been attending Downe church?* ....

26. *Have you ever been to ...?*
☐ The Omega Order
☐ A service at St James's church, Piccadilly
☐ An Alternatives lecture
☐ A New Age workshop

27. *What is your opinion of Christians who are involved in the New Age?*

....
....
....
....
....
....
....
....
....
....
....
....
....
....

Thank you for completing this questionnaire. Please return in the sae provided, displaying in the window the address below:

Survey of Spirituality   ## King's College London University

Dear Parishioner of St James's Piccadilly,

Please can I ask you to spare twenty minutes of your time to complete this questionnaire. Some of you may remember me from fieldwork I did at your church in 1996. The survey is part of a doctoral research project into modern spirituality that is personally funded at King's College, London University. It has not been sponsored by St James's church. Anonymity will be preserved, but eventually I hope to publish a book with the results of the questionnaire.

Yours sincerely,
Daren Kemp – Doctoral research student, King's College

---

1. *What is your age?* ☐ 0-18   ☐ 19-24
☐ 25-34   ☐ 35-44   ☐ 44-54   ☐ 55-64   ☐ 65+

2. *Are you*   ☐ male or ☐ female?
3. *Are you*   ☐ single ☐ married
☐ divorced ☐ widowed/er?

4. *What is your approximate annual income?*
☐ £0-5,000   ☐ £5-9,999   ☐ £10-14,999
☐ £15-19,999   ☐ £20-24,999   ☐ £25-34,999
☐ £35,000+

5. *What is/was your occupation? (Please state)*
....
....

6. *Are you*   ☐ employed/self-employed
☐ retired   ☐ student   ☐ unemployed

7. *Highest level of education:*
☐ None   ☐ O-level/GCSE   ☐ A-level
☐ BA, BSc   ☐ Masters   ☐ PhD
Professional...*(please state)*

8. *Religious affiliation (please state)*
originally..
....
currently..
....

9. *What spiritual discipline(s) or teaching has had the greatest influence on your life? (Please state/list)*..
....
....
....
....

11. *Are you actively pursuing a spiritual path?*
☐ Yes ☐ No

10. *What do you believe God is?*
☐ a real personality   ☐ a fiction
☐ an impersonal force   ☐ don't know
☐ other *(please state)* ....
....
....

12. *In your opinion, are there varying types of spirituality - eg New Age spirituality, Buddhist spirituality, Christian spirituality - or is spirituality universally the same?*
☐ varying types   ☐ the same

13. *How often do you meditate?*
☐ Never   ☐ Occasionally   ☐ Every few days
☐ Once a day   ☐ More than once a day

14. *How often do you pray?*
☐ Never   ☐ Occasionally   ☐ Every few days
☐ Once a day   ☐ More than once a day

15. *Have you had experience of any forms of paranormal phenomena?* ☐ Yes   ☐ No
If yes, please state of what kind...........................
....
....
....

16. *If you have adopted New Age ideas or practices how long has this been for?*
☐ I haven't   ☐ I can't remember
☐ 0-6 months   ☐ 6 months-1 year ☐ 1-2 years
☐ 3-4 years   ☐ 5-10 years   ☐ 10+ years

17. *To what extent do you consider yourself to be "green"? (please circle)*
Not green 1 2 3 4 5 6 7 8 9 10 Totally

18. *In a few words please describe what you think the New Age is* ....
....
....
....
....

19. *Please give 5 examples of groups, individuals, books or practices that you think are most typically New Age.*
a...
b...
c...
d...
e...

20. *Have you ever participated in or used any of the following. Also, what of the following are you currently engaged in?*

	Yes	No	Currently
Acupuncture/shiatsu	☐	☐	☐
Alexander Technique	☐	☐	☐
Aromatherapy	☐	☐	☐
Buddhism	☐	☐	☐
Channeling	☐	☐	☐
Colour Therapy	☐	☐	☐
Creative Visualisation	☐	☐	☐
Crystals	☐	☐	☐
Dance Therapy	☐	☐	☐
Earth Mysteries	☐	☐	☐
Ethical Investing	☐	☐	☐
Flower Remedies	☐	☐	☐
Green Politics	☐	☐	☐
Healing Workshops	☐	☐	☐
Herbalism	☐	☐	☐
Homoeopathy	☐	☐	☐
Hypnotherapy	☐	☐	☐
Massage	☐	☐	☐
NLP	☐	☐	☐
Past Life Therapy	☐	☐	☐
Psychotherapy	☐	☐	☐
Rebirthing	☐	☐	☐
Reflexology	☐	☐	☐
Recycling	☐	☐	☐
Shaman/Pagan Rituals	☐	☐	☐
Sound Therapy	☐	☐	☐
Spiritualism	☐	☐	☐
Tai Chi Ch'uan/Yoga	☐	☐	☐
Transactional Analysis	☐	☐	☐
Veganism	☐	☐	☐
Vegetarianism	☐	☐	☐
Womens' Studies Groups	☐	☐	☐

21. *How often do you attend a Christian service at St James's Church?*
☐ Never   ☐ Occasionally ☐ Every few weeks
☐ Once a week   ☐ More than once a week

22. *If you have been to Alternatives, did you go there before you had ever attended a church service at St James's?*
☐ I have never been to Alternatives
☐ I went to Alternatives before a St James' service
☐ I went to Alternatives after a St James' service

23. *Would you please name individuals whose ideas have had an important influence on your life by their writings: (please list)*
....
....
....
....
....
....
....
....

24. *Approximately how many books have you read on New Age or related subjects?* ....

25. *Approximately how many books have you read on Christianity or related subjects?* ....

26. *What religious, political and social action groups do you belong to?* ....
....
....
....

27. *How long have you been attending St James's Church?* ....

28. *How did you first hear of St James's?* ....
....
....
....

29. *Have you ever been to ...?*
☐ The Omega Order
☐ A New Age workshop
☐ Findhorn Community

30. *Does the new term "Christaquarian" adequately describe your spiritual position?*
☐ Yes   ☐ No

31. *Please tick the box which most closely represents your reaction to the following statements.*

	-2	-1	0	1	2
A. The resurrection of Christ is a real, historical fact.	☐	☐	☐	☐	☐
B. Christianity has been too male-dominated.	☐	☐	☐	☐	☐
C. The Bible is literally true.	☐	☐	☐	☐	☐
D. The Church is too hierarchical.	☐	☐	☐	☐	☐
E. I believe in the literal truth of the Apostle's creed.	☐	☐	☐	☐	☐

	-2	-1	0	1	2
F. Christianity is to blame for current environmental problems.	☐	☐	☐	☐	☐
G. The Earth is one interconnected whole.	☐	☐	☐	☐	☐
H. There are many paths to salvation.	☐	☐	☐	☐	☐
I. Christianity is the only true religion.	☐	☐	☐	☐	☐
J. I believe in the resurrection of the dead.	☐	☐	☐	☐	☐

	-2	-1	0	1	2
K. Jesus Christ is my only Lord and Saviour.	☐	☐	☐	☐	☐
L. Jesus was inspired with the Christ spirit that also inspired Buddha.	☐	☐	☐	☐	☐
M. Christ is unique, unparalleled by any other human being.	☐	☐	☐	☐	☐
N. Jesus Christ was both God and man at the same time.	☐	☐	☐	☐	☐
O. Jesus was simply a very spiritual man, nothing more.	☐	☐	☐	☐	☐

	-2	-1	0	1	2
P. The stars influence events on earth.	☐	☐	☐	☐	☐
Q. Tarot cards are dangerous.	☐	☐	☐	☐	☐
R. People are deceived when they see auras.	☐	☐	☐	☐	☐
S. Involvement with the occult leaves one open to Satan.	☐	☐	☐	☐	☐
T. I believe in reincarnation.	☐	☐	☐	☐	☐

	-2	-1	0	1	2
U. Spiritual healing occurs only through the power of Christ, the Holy Spirit or God.	☐	☐	☐	☐	☐
V. Hypnotherapy opens the mind to demonic possession.	☐	☐	☐	☐	☐
W. I have experienced spiritual healing.	☐	☐	☐	☐	☐
X. Crystals have special healing powers.	☐	☐	☐	☐	☐
Y. It is OK for a Christian to use homeopathy.	☐	☐	☐	☐	☐

	-2	-1	0	1	2
Z. The New Age movement is part of a conspiracy for a New World Order.	☐	☐	☐	☐	☐
a. We are moving into the Age of Aquarius.	☐	☐	☐	☐	☐
b. Dungeons & Dragons Games are occult and dangerous.	☐	☐	☐	☐	☐
c. 'New Age' travellers are not part of the true New Age.	☐	☐	☐	☐	☐
d. The New Age is dangerous.	☐	☐	☐	☐	☐

32. *How often do you read the Bible by yourself?*
☐ Never   ☐ Occasionally   ☐ Every few weeks
☐ Every few days   ☐ Every day

33. *Do you regularly attend another church as well as St James's?*
☐ Yes ☐ No

34. *How many of your friends would you describe as having adopted New Age ideas or practices?*
☐ 0   ☐ 1-2   ☐ 3-5   ☐ 6-10   ☐ 10+

35. *What is your opinion of Christians who are involved in the New Age?*
....
....
....
....
....
....
....
....
....
....
....
....
....
....

36. *Please add any other comments you think might be relevant.*

Thank you for completing this questionnaire. Please return in the sae provided, displaying in the window the address below:

230

Survey of Spirituality   King's College London University

This survey is part of a doctoral research project into modern spirituality that is personally funded at King's College, London University. Your time in filling out this questionnaire would be greatly appreciated. Anonymity will be preserved. I apologise if I have already asked you some of these questions by telephone, but that was an important stage in the survey design and I beg your indulgence in repeating the exercise on paper.   Daren Kemp

1. *What is your age?* □ 0-18   □ 19-24
□ 25-34   □ 35-44   □ 44-54   □ 55-64   □ 65+

2. *Are you*   □ male or □ female?
3. *Are you*   □ single □ married
                                □ divorced □ widowed?

4. *What is your approximate annual income?*
□ £0-4,999   □ £5-9,999   □ £10-14,999
□ £15-19,999   □ £20-24,999   □ £25-34,999
□ £35,000+

5. *What is/was your occupation? (Please state)*
....
....

6. *Are you*   □ employed/self-employed
□ retired   □ student   □ unemployed

7. *Education (please tick all that apply):*
□ No exams   □ O-level/GCSE   □ A-level
□ BA, BSc   □ Masters   □ PhD
Professional ....*(please state)*

8. *Religious affiliation (please state)*
originally...
....
currently...
....

9. *What spiritual discipline(s) or teaching has had the greatest influence on your life? (Please state/list)* ....
....
....
....
....

10. *What do you believe God is?*
□ a real personality   □ a fiction
□ an impersonal force   □ don't know
□ other *(please state)* ....
....
....

11. *Are you actively pursuing a spiritual path?*
□ Yes □ No

12. *In your opinion, are there varying types of spirituality - eg New Age spirituality, Buddhist spirituality, Christian spirituality - or is spirituality universally the same?*
□ varying types   □ the same

13. *How often do you meditate?*
□ Never   □ Occasionally   □ Every few days
□ Once a day   □ More than once a day

14. *How often do you pray?*
□ Never   □ Occasionally   □ Every few days
□ Once a day   □ More than once a day

15. *Have you had experience of any forms of paranormal phenomena?* □ Yes   □ No
If yes, please state of what kind ....
....
....
....

16. *If you have adopted New Age ideas or practices how long has this been for?*
□ I haven't   □ I can't remember
□ 0-6 months   □ 6 months-1 year   □ 1-2 years
□ 3-4 years   □ 5-10 years   □ 10+ years

17. *To what extent do you consider yourself to be "green"? (please circle)*
Not green 1 2 3 4 5 6 7 8 9 10 Totally

18. *In a few words please describe what you think the New Age is* ....
....
....
....
....

19. *Please give 5 examples of groups, individuals, books or practices that you think are most typically New Age.*
a ....
b ....
c ....
d ....
e ....

20. Have you ever participated in or used any of the following. Also, what of the following are you currently engaged in?

	Yes	No	Currently
Acupuncture/shiatsu	☐	☐	☐
Alexander Technique	☐	☐	☐
Aromatherapy	☐	☐	☐
Buddhism	☐	☐	☐
Channeling	☐	☐	☐
Colour Therapy	☐	☐	☐
Creative Visualisation	☐	☐	☐
Crystals	☐	☐	☐
Dance Therapy	☐	☐	☐
Earth Mysteries	☐	☐	☐
Ethical Investing	☐	☐	☐
Flower Remedies	☐	☐	☐
Green Politics	☐	☐	☐
Healing Workshops	☐	☐	☐
Herbalism	☐	☐	☐
Homoeopathy	☐	☐	☐
Hypnotherapy	☐	☐	☐
Massage	☐	☐	☐
NLP	☐	☐	☐
Past Life Therapy	☐	☐	☐
Psychotherapy	☐	☐	☐
Rebirthing	☐	☐	☐
Reflexology	☐	☐	☐
Recycling	☐	☐	☐
Shaman/Pagan Rituals	☐	☐	☐
Sound Therapy	☐	☐	☐
Spiritualism	☐	☐	☐
Tai Chi Ch'uan/Yoga	☐	☐	☐
Transactional Analysis	☐	☐	☐
Veganism	☐	☐	☐
Vegetarianism	☐	☐	☐
Womens' Studies Groups	☐	☐	☐

21a. How often do you go to church?
☐ Never   ☐ Occasionally   ☐ On special days
☐ Once a month   ☐ Once a week, on average

21b. How often do you read the Bible by yourself?
☐ Never   ☐ Occasionally   ☐ Every few weeks
☐ Every few days   ☐ Once a day

22. Have you ever had any contact with evangelical Christianity? Is yes, please expand.
....
....
....
....

23. Would you please name individuals whose ideas have had an important influence on your life by their writings: (please list)
....
....
....
....
....
....
....
....

24. Approximately how many books have you read on New Age or related subjects?..................

25. Approximately how many books have you read on Christianity or related subjects?............

26a. How long have you been a member of CANA? ....

26b. How did you first hear of CANA?.................
....
....
....

27a. Are you also a member of Bridge Trust?

27b. If yes, how did you first hear of Bridge? .....
....
....
....

28. What other religious, political and social action groups do you belong to? ....
....
....
....

29. Have you ever been to ...?
☐ The Omega Order
☐ A New Age workshop
☐ Findhorn Foundation Community
☐ St James's church, Piccadilly

30. Does the newly coined word, "Christaquarian", adequately describe your spiritual position?
☐ Yes   ☐ No

31. Do you think that New Age may be an outdated term?   ☐ Yes   ☐ No
If yes, what term would you prefer?
....

32. Please tick the box which most closely represents
your reaction to the following statements.

-2	Strongly disagree
-1	Mildly disagree
0	No opinion/don't know
1	Mildly agree
2	Strongly agree

-2 -1 0 1 2

A. The resurrection of Christ is a real, historical fact. □ □ □ □ □
B. Christianity has been too male-dominated. □ □ □ □ □
C. The Bible is literally true. □ □ □ □ □
D. The Church is too hierarchical. □ □ □ □ □
E. I believe in the literal truth of the Apostle's creed. □ □ □ □ □

-2 -1 0 1 2

F. Christianity is to blame for current environmental problems. □ □ □ □ □
G. The Earth is one interconnected whole. □ □ □ □ □
H. There are many paths to salvation. □ □ □ □ □
I. Christianity is the only true religion. □ □ □ □ □
J. I believe in the resurrection of the dead. □ □ □ □ □

-2 -1 0 1 2

K. Jesus Christ is my only Lord and Saviour. □ □ □ □ □
L. Jesus was inspired with the Christ spirit that also inspired Buddha. □ □ □ □ □
M. Christ is unique, unparalleled by any other human being. □ □ □ □ □
N. Jesus Christ was both God and man at the same time. □ □ □ □ □
O. Jesus was simply a very spiritual man, nothing more. □ □ □ □ □

-2 -1 0 1 2

P. The stars influence events on earth. □ □ □ □ □
Q. Tarot cards are dangerous. □ □ □ □ □
R. People are deceived when they see auras. □ □ □ □ □
S. Involvement with the occult leaves one open to satan. □ □ □ □ □
T. I believe in reincarnation. □ □ □ □ □

-2 -1 0 1 2

U. Spiritual healing occurs only through the power of Christ, the Holy Spirit or God. □ □ □ □ □
V. Hypnotherapy opens the mind to demonic possession. □ □ □ □ □
W. I have experienced spiritual healing. □ □ □ □ □
X. Crystals have special healing powers. □ □ □ □ □
Y. It is OK for a Christian to use homeopathy. □ □ □ □ □

-2 -1 0 1 2

Z. The New Age movement is part of a conspiracy for a New World Order. □ □ □ □ □
a. We are moving into the Age of Aquarius. □ □ □ □ □
b. Dungeons & Dragons Games are occult and dangerous. □ □ □ □ □
c. 'New Age' travellers are not part of the true New Age. □ □ □ □ □
d. The New Age is dangerous. □ □ □ □ □

233

33. *What is your opinion of Christians who are involved in the New Age?*

....
....
....
....
....
....
....
....
....
....
....
....

34. *What is your vision for the Christian church in the twenty-first century?*

....
....
....
....
....
....
....
....
....
....
....
....

35. *Please add any comments you think might be helpful.*

....
....
....
....
....
....
....
....
....
....
....

Thank you for completing this questionnaire. Please return in the sae provided, displaying in the window the address below:

234

B.   Survey Results

Qualitative data has provided a good basis for the inquiry into New Age Christianity, but finer detail may be attained by quantitative analysis. To this end, a postal questionnaire survey was conducted upon the Omega Order, St James' church Piccadilly and the evangelical congregation. A copy of the questionnaire mailed to the Omega Order is included in the appendix.

The questionnaire was designed to give results directly comparable to previous surveys of the New Age, in particular to Stuart Rose's survey of *Kindred Spirit* magazine readers. Rose enclosed 5,350 copies of his questionnaire with an issue of the magazine, and received over 900 replies or 17%. Additional questions were derived from Michael York's surveys in *The Emerging Network* (1995).

The Omega Order questionnaire was sent in May 1998 to all recipients of *Omega News* – both subscribing readers and friends of the organisation, who automatically receive the magazine. Thus excluded from the survey are those who have stayed at the Omega Order or participated in workshops without then subscribing to the newsletter. However, although the Order secretary keeps all addresses of course attendees on file, the addresses are not necessarily current and the numbers were in any case too great for a survey of my budget. In total, 322 copies were sent out and 182 returned – an outstanding response rate of 57% which therefore provides excellent representative results.

St James' questionnaire was sent in September 1998 to all members of the electoral roll. Again, this excludes a large section of the congregation at St James' – the less committed or occasional worshippers, as well as those who are attracted to the church by the Alternatives lecture programme but do not have enough Christian commitment to sign up to the electoral role. However, the availability of an up-to-date address list outweighed the benefits of distributing the questionnaire to worshippers one Sunday morning. In any case, this latter approach has already been taken by Eileen Barker in a lengthy survey about 10 years ago which she hopes to repeat soon. In total, 179 copies were sent out and 51 returned – a response rate of 29%.

The Cudham and Downe church questionnaire was sent out in May 1998 to all members of the electoral rolls. The majority of worshippers on any Sunday morning service at Cudham and Downe are members of the electoral roll, so this provides a representative sample. In total, 114 questionnaires were sent out and 53 returned – a good return rate of 46%.

Christians Awakening to a New Awareness were initially not sent the postal questionnaire as their numbers are too small – 53 members would have provided a return number of perhaps 10. Instead, the questionnaire was first conducted in modified form over the telephone. In this way, 32% of the membership were surveyed. By May 1999, however, the group had nearly doubled in size and so a postal survey was possible. A 53% return rate was achieved.

All responses were coded up and recorded on a Microsoft Excel spreadsheet for analysis. Although this format is compatible with the statistical package SPSS, sufficiently detailed analysis for my purposes was possible immediately on Excel. All figures below are percentage points rounded to the nearest integer.

Key to tables

Survey Population	Abbreviation
The Omega Order Omega News readers	OO
St James's church, Piccadilly, electoral roll	SJP
Christians Awakening to a New Awareness, members	CANA
Telephone Survey of CANA in 1997	Tel
Cudham and Downe churches, electoral rolls	Evan
Alternatives lecture evening (York 1995)	Alt
Kindred Spirit magazine (Rose 1996)	KS
National statistics where available	Nat

Sample Size and Return

OO	SJP	CANA	Tel	Evan	Alt	KS
182/322	51/179	53/100[1]	17/53[2]	53/114	48/121	908/5350
=57%	=28%	=53%	=32%	=46%	=40%	=17%

1. Standard Questionnaire

Question 1. What is your age?

Age Range	OO	SJP	CANA	Tel	Evan	Alt	KS	Nat
0-18	0	0	0	0	4		0	}
19-24	0	0	0	0	6	(age 18-34)	3	} 33
25-34	1	14	0	0	13	40	16	16
35-44	6	12	9	6	13	(age 35-49)	30	14
45-54	15	25	13	18	19	50	27	11
55-64	20	22	34	35	15	(age 50+)	14	10
65+	58	25	43	41	25	10	10	16
No answer	0	2	0	0	6		1	-

Question 2. Are you male or female?

Sex	OO	SJP[3]	CANA[4]	Tel[5]	Evan	Alt	KS
Male	29	31	25	27	26	29	30
Female	69	69	75	73	72	71	70
No answer	2	0	0	0	2	-	-

Question 3. Are you single or partnered?

Marital Status[6]	OO	SJP	CANA	Tel	Evan	Alt	KS
Single	47	33	23	59	25	56	36
Partnered	46	35	42	29	68	32	52
Divorced	-	20	15	-	-	-	-
Widowed	-	6	15	-	-	-	-
No answer	8	6	6	12	7	-	12

Question 4. What is your approximate annual income?

Income	OO	SJP	CANA	Evan	Alt	KS	Nat[7]
£0-4,999	16	2	8	36	21	19	17
£5-9,999	21	10	19	9	23	21	33
£10-14,999	22	16	23	9	35	18	23
£15-19,999	13	18	23	6	13	16	13
£20-24,999	6	24	13	6	}	}	}
£25-34,999	7	0	8	11	} 4	} 21	} 14
£35,000+	3	24	6	4	}	}	}
No answer	12	8	2	19	4	5	0

237

Question 5. What is/was your occupation?

Occupation	OO	SJP	CANA	Tel	Evan	KS
Therapist	5	8	11	6	0	20
Retired	-	-	-	-	-	13
Student/teacher/library	15	20	30	41	11	12
Managerial/sales	0	0	0	0	0	12
Nurse/carer/social work	8	10	17	24	4	7
Housewife/parent	7	2	2	0	25	6
Creative	0	24	0	0	2	5
Secretarial/clerical	4	6	8	6	0	5
Professional	9	20	12	6	9	-
Unskilled/skilled labour	2	0	4	0	2	-
Religious	10	0	4	6	0	-
NA/other/unclassified	39	16	9	12	30	20

Question 6. Are you ...?

Status	OO	SJP	CANA	Tel	Evan
Retired	64	29	51	53	36
Student	2	0	0	0	9
Unemployed	2	0	4	12	4
No answer[8]	32	8	2	35	51
Employed/ self-employed	-	63	43	-	-

Question 7. Highest level of education:

Education	OO	SJP	CANA	Tel	Evan
None	10	6	6	0	11
O-level	16	4	13	12	25
A-level	12	8	9	6	11
BA, BSc	18	30	25	41	17
Masters	8	22	15	18	0
PhD	2	0	0	0	0
Professional	30	27	32	18	26
No answer	4	4	0	6	9

Question 8. Original/current religious affiliation:

Affiliation	Original/Current							
	OO		SJP		CANA		Tel	
None	2	8	8	0	2	2	6	12
Total Christian of which …	96	79	91	92	95	89	94	88
"Christian" (not incl below)	5	5	2	2	2	8	6	6
Church of England	65	40	59	80	60	28	47	35
Roman Catholic	10	7	8	2	25	21	29	29
Qualified "Christian"[9]	2	13	4	6	0	15	0	6
Methodist	5	5	4	0	6	2	0	0
Quaker	1	1	4	0	0	11	0	0
Baptist	2	4	0	0	0	0	0	0
Other Christian Denomination	6	4	10	2	2	2	12	12
Omega	0	1	0	0	0	0	0	0
Buddhist	0	1	0	0	0	0	0	0
New Age	>1	>1	0	0	0	0	0	0
Universalist/beyond religion	0	6	0	0	0	0	0	0
Agnostic	0	0	0	0	0	4	0	0
Other	2	3	0	8	0	2	0	0
No answer	0	0	0	0	4	0	0	0

Question 9. What spiritual discipline(s) or teaching has had the greatest influence on your life?[10]

Omega Order

Christianity	91	White Eagle Lodge	5	Anthony de Mello	2
Omega Order	30	Anthroposophy	4	Liberal Catholic Church	2
Meditation	23	Sufi tradition	4	John Main	2
Buddhism	20	Vedanta	4	Thomas Merton	2
Prayer	13	A Course in Miracles	3	Mother Meera	2
Gurdjieff	10	Joel Goldsmith	3	John Wesley	2
Mystics	10	New Age	3		
de Chardin	8	Spiritualism	3		
Yoga	8	Sai Baba	3		
Bede Griffiths	7	Shamanism	3		
Healing	7	Transcendental Meditation	3		
Hinduism	7	Arcane School	2		
CG Jung	6	Celtic tradition	2		

St James's				CANA	
Christianity	24	Iona	2	Christian	32
Buddhism	11	CS Lewis	2	Meditation	11
CG Jung	3	Judaism	2	Zen	4
John Robinson	3	New Age	2	De Chardin	4
Dietrich	2	Donald	2	Buddhism	3
Bonhoeffer		Reeves		Quakers	3
Druidry	2	Yoga	2	Transcendental	3
Hinduism	2			Meditation	
				Yoga	3
				Creation Spirituality	3
				Eastern Orthodox	3

Question 10. What do you believe God is?

What is God?	OO	SJP	CANA	Tel	Evan	Alt	Nat[11]
Real personality	21	14	19	18	58	6	30
Fiction	1	0	2	0	2	0	-
Impersonal force	14	27	17	35	17	33	40
Personality and force	3	0	4	18	2	-	-
Don't know	5	6	4	0	2	13	-
Other	56	49	53	29	17	52	-
No answer	0	4	2	0	2	-	-

Question 11. Are you actively pursuing a spiritual path?

Spiritual?	OO	SJP	CANA	Tel	Evan	KS
Yes	90	73	98	76	75	"majority"
No	8	14	2	6	19	"minority"
No answer	2	14	0	18	6	

Question 12. In your opinion, are there varying types of spirituality – eg New Age spirituality, Buddhist spirituality, Christian spirituality – or is spirituality universally the same?

Spirituality?	OO	SJP	CANA	Tel	Evan	KS
Varying types	30	57	38	12	72	?
The same	57	29	47	47	25	70
Both	9	6	8	12	0	?
No answer	4	8	8	29	4	?

Question 13. How often do you meditate?

Meditate[12]?	OO	SJP	CANA	Tel	Evan	KS
Never	3	16	0	12	21	?
Occasionally	18	45	26	6	53	?
Every few days	15	12	25	24	4	?
Once a day	36	16	28	35	8	}
More than once a day	26	8	19	18	11	} 41
No answer	2	4	2	6	4	?

Question 14. How often do you pray?

Pray?	OO	SJP	CANA	Tel	Evan
Never	3	4	2	6	0
Occasionally	10	24	19	0	13
Every few days	7	33	13	12	15
Once a day	19	16	23	47	26
More than once a day	59	20	38	29	45
No answer	2	4	6	6	0

Question 15.   Have you had experience of any forms of paranormal phenomena?[13]

Paranormal	OO	SJP	CANA	Tel	Evan	KS
Yes	55	29	57	47	30	82
No	41	67	42	12	68	?
No answer	4	4	2	41	2	?

Question 16. If you have adopted New Age ideas or practices how long has this been for?

Length	OO	SJP	CANA	KS
I haven't	31	45	26	?
I have for...[14]	56	43	64	(>78)
0-6 months	1	0	0	?
6 mths-1yr	0	0	0	?
1-2 years	1	0	0	?
3-4 years	3	2	9	?
5-10 years	9	16	21	27
10+ years	38	20	34	51
I can't remember	4	6	0	?
No answer	13	12	9	?

Question 17. To what extent do you consider yourself to be "green"?

Green	OO	SJP	CANA	Tel	Evan		KS
1	0	0	4	0	4		?
2	1	0	2	0	2		?
3	2	10	2	0	4		?
4	2	2	6	6	2		?
5	14	14	11	6	11	}	
6	12	14	9	18	13	}	70
7	20	27	19	24	23	}	
8	26	29	26	24	13		?
9	5	2	6	12	2		?
10	10	2	13	0	11		?
No answer	8	0	2	12	15		?

Question 18. In a few words please describe what you think the New Age is.

Definition Given?	OO	SJP	CANA	Tel	Evan	Alt	US[15]
Yes	88	78	92	88	62	75	23
No	12	22	8	12	38	25	77

Question 19. Please give 5 examples of groups, individuals, books or practices that you think are most typically New Age?[16]

Example	OO	SJP	CANA	Evan
Omega Order	9	2	2	0
Findhorn, Spangler, Caddy	6	8	11	2
De Chardin, Happold, Carey, Wilber, Huxley	4	0	<1	0
Crystals	2	5	3	10
Eastern religion, etc	4	<1	2	2
Healing	8	6	11	13
Green issues	4	5	6	5
Astrology, tarot, occult	2	2	2	8
Theosophy, Bailey, Steiner, Gurdjieff, Trevelyan	4	<1	1	3
Alternatives	0	12	1	0
Creation Spirituality	3	8	3	0
CANA/Bridge Trust	0	0	2	0

Question 20. Have you ever participated in or used any of the following?

Practice	OO	SJP	CANA	Evan	KS
Acupuncture/shiatsu	42	49	64	9	57
Alexander Technique	28	35	36	2	32
Aromatherapy	37	51	62	17	73
Buddhism	38	31	57	0	50
Channeling	10	10	23	0	49
Colour Therapy	20	22	30	2	48
Creative Visualisation	46	45	68	0	80
Crystals	23	12	28	0	71
Dance Therapy	36	27	36	0	30
Earth Mysteries	12	16	9	0	43
Ethical Investing	19	47	34	4	18
Flower Remedies	46	37	51	8	70
Green Politics	26	41	47	8	45
Healing Workshops	55	41	66	13	67
Herbalism	41	31	45	9	57
Homoeopathy	60	59	64	21	39
Hypnotherapy	15	10	25	6	39
Massage	47	71	70	15	73
NLP	9	6	13	2	18
Past Life Therapy	8	6	9	2	39
Psychotherapy	34	57	53	8	42
Rebirthing	8	12	15	0	18
Reflexology	43	37	62	11	64
Recycling	53	71	64	55	74
Shaman/Pagan Rituals	9	20	17	0	35
Sound Therapy	16	14	15	0	34
Spiritualism	21	4	15	6	55
T'ai Chi Ch'uan/Yoga	48	63	57	4	67
Transactional Analysis	16	16	26	8	21
Veganism	4	0	8	0	14
Vegetarianism	48	41	51	11	71
Womens' Studies Groups	16	29	26	11	20
Average of above	29	32	39	7	47

Number of the above ever practised by each individual:

Number Practised	OO	SJP	CANA	Evan
0-4	24	22	15	85
5-9	30	25	23	15
10-14	24	31	21	0
15-32	21	22	42	0

Question 23. Would you please name individuals whose ideas have had an important influence on your life by their writings?[17]

Omega Order

Peter Spink	73	George Trevelyan	7	Dietrich Bonhoeffer	2
Bede Griffiths	32	Alice Bailey	6	Christopher Bryant	2
Teilhard de Chardin	27	Kahlil Gibran	6	Martin Buber	2
The Bible	20	Krishnamurti	6	Wallis Carey	2
Martin Israel	17	Henri Nouwen	6	Carlos Castenadas	2
Gurdjieff	15	Leslie Weatherhead	6	Dali Lama	2
CG Jung	14	Ken Wilber	6	Dante	2
Thomas Merton	14	Deepak Chopra	5	Don Cupitt	2
John Main	13	Mystics	5	Albert Einstein	2
Joel Goldsmith	11	Louise Hay	4	Mircea Eliade	2
FC Happold	11	AB Smith	4	TS Eliot	2
CS Lewis	11	John V Taylor	4	George Fox	2
Evelyn Underhill	11	Gandhi	3	Thich Nhat Hanh	2
Matthew Fox	10	HT Hamblin	3	Richard Holloway	2
William Johnston	9	Aldous Huxley	3	Inayat Khan	2
Maurice Nicole	9	David Jenkins	3	Neil Douglas Klotz	2
John Robinson	9	Jean Klein	3	Eliphas Levi	2
Sai Baba	9	Plato	3	Robert Llewellyn	2
Laurens van der Post	9	Carl Rogers	3	Caroline Myss	2
Anthony de Mello	8	Teresa of Avila	3	Stephen Neill	2
Gerard Hughes	8	WH Vanstone	3	Cardinal Newman	2
Ouspensky	8	HA William	3	Bertrand Russell	2
Paul Brunton	7	A Course in Miracles	2	Rupert Sheldrake	2
Fritjof Capra	7	Roberto Assagioli	2	Mother Teresa	2
John of the Cross	7	Hildegard of Bingen	2	Paul Tillich	2
Rudolf Steiner	7	Lionel Blue	2		

St James's

Matthew Fox	10	Dietrich Bonhoeffer	3	Karl Marx	2
CS Lewis	6	Richard Holloway	3	Mother Meera	2
Thomas Merton	6	John Spong	3	M Scott Peck	2
Donald Reeves	6	HA Williams	3	Carl Rogers	2
John Robinson	6	The Bible	2	EF Schumacher	2
Teilhard de Chardin	5	William Bloom	2	William Shakespeare	2
Julian of Norwich	5	Joseph Campbell	2	John V Taylor	2
Gerard Hughes	4	Don Cupitt	2	Alan Watts	2
Hasrat Inayat	4	Meister Eckhart	2	Oscar Wilde	2
CG Jung	4	Hans Küng	2		

CANA

Bede Griffiths	18	Fritjof Capra	4	Roberto Assagioli	2
Teilhard De Chardin	15	Kahlil Gibran	4	David Jenkins	2
Carl Jung	12	M Scott Peck	4	Leslie Weatherhead	2
Matthew Fox	9	John Spong	4	Deepak Chopra	2
Thomas Mreton	7	Peter Spink	3	John of the Cross	2
Julian of Norwich	7	Teresa of Avila	3	Frank Lake	2
William Johnston	6	George Trevelyan	3	William Temple	2
Adrian Smith	6	Jean Vanier	3	James Robertson	2
Anthony De Mello	5	Ken Wilber	3	Sai Baba	2
Gerald Hughes	5	Hildegaard of Bingen	3	David Spangler	2
O'Murchu	5	Eileen Caddy	3	Chris Scott	2
Rudolf Steiner	5	John Main	3	Danah Zohar	2
CS Lewis	4	Tich Naht Nhan	3		
John Robinson	4	James Redfield	3		

Kindred Spirit (percentage figures)

Louise Hay	14	Jiddu Krishnamurti	4	Ken Carey	3
CG Jung	14	M Scott Peck	4	Ram Dass	3
Shakti Gawain	7	Buddhist Scriptures	4	Sanaya Roman (Orin)	3
White Eagle Lodge	7	Edgar Cayce	4	Sogyal Rinpoche	3
Richard Bach	6	Gill Edwards	4	Yogananda	3
David Icke	5	Betty Shine	4	Carlos Castenada	3
The Bible	5	Sai Baba	4	Paul Brunton	2
Rudolf Steiner	5	Alice Bailey	4	Fritjof Capra	2
Kahil Gibran	5	Stuart Wilde	4	Dalai Lama	2
Shirley MacLaine	5	Taoist writings	3		
Deepak Chopra	4	Julie Soskin	3		

Question 26a. How long have you been [a member]?

Years	OO	SJP	CANA	Tel	Evan
0-4	36	12	58	36	21
5-9	26	40	38	12	9
10-14	12	24	-	29	19
15+	26	20	-	-	51
No answer	2	4	-	24	0

Question 26b. How did you first hear of ...?

How heard	OO	SJP	CANA
Friend	36	45	25
Advert	15	0	4
Book	11	0	0
Met leader	14	0	13
Lived nearby	2	4	0
Seminar	4	2	15
Other church ministry	0	10	0
Media	0	4	0
Passing by	0	16	0
Through Bridge Trust	0	0	32
Other	7	4	6
No answer	11	18	6

Question 29. Have you ever been to ...?

	OO	SJP	CANA	Evan
Omega Order	-	4	36	0
St James's	30	-	} 64	8
Alternatives	40^{18}	67	}	0
New Age Workshop	41	29	58	2
Findhorn	-	6	32	-

247

2. Expanded Questionnaire to St James's and CANA

Question 21. How often do you attend a Christian service at St James's Church?

Regularity	SJP
Never	4
Occasionally	31
Every few weeks[19]	27
Once a week	33
More than once a week	2
No answer	2

Question 22. If you have been to Alternatives, did you go there before you had ever attended a church service at St James's?

Been to Alternatives?	%
I have never been to Alternatives	27
Before St James's	20
After St James's	47
No answer	6

Question 21a. How often do you go to church?

Regularity	CANA
Never	4
Occasionally	17
On special days	6
Once a month	25
Once a week	15
No answer	0

Question 21b. How often do you read the Bible by yourself?

Regularity	CANA
Never	9
Occasionally	45
Every few weeks	6
Every few days	25
Once a day	15
No answer	0

Question 22. Have you ever had any contact with evangelical Christianity?

Contact	CANA
Yes – no comment/ positive encounter	42
Yes – negative encounter	25
No	32
No answer	2

Question 30. Does the newly coined term "Christaquarian" adequately describe your spiritual position?

Adequate?	SJP	CANA
Yes	4	23
No	65	63
No answer	31	15

Question 31. Do you think that New Age may be an outdated term?

Outdated?	CANA
Yes	58
No	32
No answer	9

Question 32. Please tick the box which most closely represents your reaction to the following statements.

	Reaction
-2	Strongly disagree
-1	Mildly disagree
0	No opinion/don't know
1	Mildly agree
2	Strongly agree
X	No answer

	-2	-1	0	1	2	X
A. The resurrection of Christ is a real, historical fact.	16	24	10	22	22	8
B. Christianity has been too male-dominated.	8	6	4	27	51	4
C. The Bible is literally true.	57	27	0	2	4	10
D. The Church is too hierarchical.	4	4	10	35	39	8
E. I believe in the literal truth of the Apostle's creed.	39	22	6	18	6	10
F. Christianity is to blame for current environmental problems.	27	22	22	22	2	6
G. The Earth is one interconnected whole.	0	2	0	14	78	6
H. There are many paths to salvation.	0	0	6	22	67	6
I. Christianity is the only true religion.	63	16	10	4	2	6
J. I believe in the resurrection of the dead.	12	4	33	22	18	12
K. Jesus Christ is my only Lord and Saviour.	24	8	10	33	18	8
L. Jesus was inspired with the Christ spirit that also inspired Buddha.	2	2	29	31	27	8
M. Christ is unique, unparalleled by any other human being.	8	14	14	24	33	8
N. Jesus Christ was both God and man at the same time.	8	2	16	29	37	10
O. Jesus was simply a very spiritual man, nothing more.	35	31	8	4	8	12
P. The stars influence events on earth.	22	16	35	14	6	8
Q. Tarot cards are dangerous.	12	24	35	16	6	8
R. People are deceived when they see auras.	12	24	45	6	6	8
S. Involvement with the occult leaves one open to satan.	18	18	24	25	8	8
T. I believe in reincarnation[20].	8	16	27	18	24	8
U. Spiritual healing occurs only through the power of Christ, the Holy Spirit or God.	16	24	20	18	14	10
V. Hypnotherapy opens the mind to demonic possession.	31	33	25	0	0	10
W. I have experienced spiritual healing.	4	12	27	14	29	14
X. Crystals have special healing powers.	25	8	37	20	0	10
Y. It is OK for a Christian to use homeopathy.	0	0	1	14	76	8
Z. The New Age movement is part of a conspiracy for a New World Order.	53	10	24	0	2	12
a. We are moving into the Age of Aquarius.	6	4	61	8	12	10
b. Dungeons & Dragons Games are occult and dangerous.	12	18	55	4	2	10

| c. | 'New Age' travellers are not part of the true New Age. | 2 | 14 | 57 | 8 | 10 | 10 |
| d. | The New Age is dangerous. | 31 | 20 | 29 | 6 | 4 | 10 |

	-2	-1	0	1	2	X
A. The resurrection of Christ is a real, historical fact.	15	9	21	17	36	2
B. Christianity has been too male-dominated.	4	8	0	11	68	2
C. The Bible is literally true.	62	22	4	2	6	4
D. The Church is too hierarchical.	8	8	2	32	49	2
E. I believe in the literal truth of the Apostle's creed.	51	25	6	11	4	4
F. Christianity is to blame for current environmental problems.	19	30	21	21	6	4
G. The Earth is one interconnected whole.	0	0	2	4	92	2
H. There are many paths to salvation.	2	0	4	11	77	6
I. Christianity is the only true religion.	72	13	8	2	2	4
J. I believe in the resurrection of the dead.	15	6	23	9	43	4
K. Jesus Christ is my only Lord and Saviour.	30	6	15	23	17	9
L. Jesus was inspired with the Christ spirit that also inspired Buddha.	4	4	13	21	53	6
M. Christ is unique, unparalleled by any other human being.	13	17	9	17	40	4
N. Jesus Christ was both God and man at the same time.	13	4	13	26	36	8
O. Jesus was simply a very spiritual man, nothing more.	32	26	11	11	15	4
P. The stars influence events on earth.	9	4	30	28	26	2
Q. Tarot cards are dangerous.	15	13	45	13	9	4
R. People are deceived when they see auras.	42	19	32	2	2	4
S. Involvement with the occult leaves one open to satan.	25	21	21	15	15	4
T. I believe in reincarnation[21].	13	11	32	13	28	2
U. Spiritual healing occurs only through the power of Christ, the Holy Spirit or God.	25	11	13	19	28	4
V. Hypnotherapy opens the mind to demonic possession.	40	28	28	0	2	2
W. I have experienced spiritual healing.	2	0	32	15	49	2
X. Crystals have special healing powers.	4	8	30	23	13	4
Y. It is OK for a Christian to use homeopathy.	0	0	0	9	89	2
Z. The New Age movement is part of a conspiracy for a New World Order.	51	19	17	2	8	4
a. We are moving into the Age of Aquarius.	0	0	34	15	49	2
b. Dungeons & Dragons Games are occult and dangerous.	15	19	55	4	6	2

c. 'New Age' travellers are not part of the true New Age.	6	15	40	19	17	4
d. The New Age is dangerous.	55	19	15	6	2	4

C.   Fieldwork Log

Name/pseudonym	Date	Description	Location
Jonathan Porritt	08.11.95	Lecture	Alternatives
Matthew Fox	21.11.95	Lecture	Alternatives
Paganism and Christianity	02.12.95	Conference	King's College
Jonathon Porritt	04.12.95	Lecture	Alternatives
A Christian astrologer	10.12.95	Telephone interview	London
Rupert	11.12.95	Conversation	St James's
Danah Zohar	11.12.95	Lecture	St James's
Victoria	12.12.95	Interview	Chelsfield
Mrs Shepherd	10.01.96	Telephone interview	London
Val	12.01.96	Interview	Downe
Chuck Spezzano	12.02.96	Lecture	Alternatives
Robert	12.02.96	Conversation	Alternatives
Annie Keller	13.02.96	Lecture	Neal's Yard
Christian Meditation Group	20.02.96	Participant observation	Lancaster University
Canon Peter Spink	23.02.96	Telephone conversation	Bristol
Rupert Sheldrake	26.02.96	Lecture	Alternatives
Karen Webb	01-03.01.96	Enneagram workshop	West Wickham
Service	10.03.96	Participant observation	St James's
Vicki	18.03.96	Interview	Chelsfield
Henrietta	20.03.96	Workshop	London
Janice	03.04.96	Interview	Cudham
Nature Religion Today	09-13.04.96	Conference	Lancaster Uni
Lectorium Rosicrucianum	11.04.96	Taped lecture	London
Paul Heather	15.04.96	Lecture	Orpington Baptist Church
Henrietta	16.04.96	Interview	London
Ervin Laszlo	16.04.96	SMN lecture	Church House, London
Destiny Fayre	20.04.96	Participant observation	Orpington
William Johnston	21.04.96	Lecture	Benedictine Centre for Spirituality, London

Service	21.04.96	Participant observation	St James's
Louise	21.04.96	Interview	St James's
Service	26.04.96	Participant observation	St James's
Starhawk	30.04.96	Lecture	Alternatives
Roger Lovell	02.05.96	Interview	NFSH Bromley
Service	05.05.96	Participant observation	St James's
Magic and Science	11.05.96	Conference	Bath College of Higher Education
Omega Order	12-14.05.96	Participant observation	Omega Order
Mind-Body-Spirit festival	19.05.96	Participant observation	London
Service	19.05.96	Participant observation	St James's
Rosemary Radford Ruether	20.05.96	Lecture	St James's
Betty Shine	21.05.96	Lecture	Alternatives
Service	26.05.96	Participant observation	St James's
Mrs Morris	28.05.96	Conversation	Christian Science Reading Room, Bromley
Dick	29.05.96	Telephone interview	Lectorium Rosicrucianum
Simone Pentel	30.05.96	Telephone interview	Fountain of Life
Arcane School	01.06.96	Participant observation	Annual conference, London
Healing Ministry Course	02.06.96	Participant observation	Cudham
Service	02.06.96	Participant observation	St James's
Marianne	04.06.96	Interview	St James's
Matthew Fox and Rupert Sheldrake	04.06.96	Lecture	St James's
Dick Rosicrucianum	08.06.96	Conversation	Lectorium
Blake Rosicrucianum	08.06.96	Conversation	Lectorium
Service	16.06.96	Participant observation	St James's
Nilantha	17.06.96	Interview	St James's
Jurgen Moltmann	17.06.96	Lecture	St James's
Simone Pentel	18.06.96	Participant observation	Fountain of Life, London

Jill Purce	19.06.96	Lecture	Theosophical Society, London
Simon	21.06.96	Telephone conversation	NFSH Bromley
Zen Meditation	25.06.96	Participant observation	Elizabeth Open Church, Basel, Switzerland
Goetheanum	25.06.96	Participant observation	Dornach, Switzerland
Chakra breathing	07.07.96	Participant observation	St James's
Service	07.07.96	Participant observation	St James's
Revd Donald Reeves	08.07.96	Lecture	Alternatives
Revd Mary Robins	11.07.96	Interview	St James's
Revd Kevin Tingay	17.07.96	Telephone conversation	Bradford-on-Tone
Revd Tim Hatwell	19.07.96	Telephone conversation	Cudham
Service	21.07.96	Participant observation	St James's
Colin	23.07.96	Telephone conversation	St James's
CANA conference	28.07.96	Participant observation	London
Jane	31.07.96	Interview	St James's
Morris Cerrullo	08.08.96	Participant observation	London
Burrswood Healing Centre	10.08.96	Participant observation	Kent
Service	11.08.96	Participant observation	St James's
Leanne	12.08.96	Telephone interview	Bridge Trust
Jasmine	16.08.96	Interview	Cudham
Revd David Flagg	21.08.96	Interview	Knockholt
Sarah	22.08.96	Interview	Cudham
Val	24.08.96	Interview	Downe
Healing Ministry Course	01.09.96	Participant observation	Cudham
Revd Tim Hatwell	03.09.96	Interview	Cudham
Simone Pentel	03.09.96	Telephone conversation	Fountain of Life, London
Revd Kevin Tingay	05.09.96	Telephone conversation	Bradford-on-Tone
Lectorium Rosicrucianum	07.09.96	Participant observation	London
Psychic Fair	07.09.96	Participant	Orpington

		observation	
Mind-Body-Spirit festival	08.09.96	Participant observation	London
Service	08.09.96	Participant observation	St James's
Alternative worship	08.09.96	Participant observation	Nightclub near St James's
Henrietta	20.09.96	Interview	London
Dr Gareth Tuckwell	29.09.96	Interview	Kent
Revd Kevin Tingay	04.09.96	Interview	Bradford-on-Tone
Omega Order	01-04.10.96	Participant observation	Omega Order
Mollie Nettleton	02.10.96	Interview	Omega Order
Lillian	02.10.96	Interview	Omega Order
Canon Peter Spink	02.10.96	Interview	Omega Order
James Fahey	02.10.96	Interview	Omega Order
Violet	03.10.96	Interview	Omega Order
Revd Roger	03.10.96	Interview	Omega Order
Roger's wife	03.10.96	Interview	Omega Order
Jim Hill	03.10.96	Interview	Omega Order
Service	15.10.96	Participant observation	St James's
CANA annual gathering	20.10.96	Participant observation	London
Service	27.10.96	Participant observation	St James's
Alternative worship	03.11.96	Participant observation	St James's
World Goodwill	09.11.96	Participant observation	London
Fr Adrian Smith	21.11.96	Interview	London
Colin	28.11.96	Interview	London
Glastonbury	30.11.96	Day-trip	Glastonbury
Newcomers party	11.12.96	Participant observation	St James's
Service	15.12.96	Participant observation	St James's
Alternative worship	23.12.96	Participant observation	St James's
Omega Order	31.01-01.02.97	Participant observation	Omega Order
Revd Donald Reeves	06.01.97	Interview	St James's
Richard	27.10.97	Interview	Cudham
CANA	21.11-09.12.97	17 Telephone interviews	Various
CANA sharing day	07.03.98	Participant observation	Richmond

Omega Order	22-26.04.98	Participant observation	Omega Order
Revd Nigel Hinton	23.01.98	Interview	Cudham
Revd Mark Bond	21.03.98	Telephone interview	
Fr Diarmuid Ó'Murchú	26.03.98	Interview	London
Nick Williams	29.07.98	Interview	Alternatives
Sea of Faith conference	07.11.98	Participant observation	London
Shaune Crockett-Burrows	12.04.99	Telephone interview	Positive News
Janice Dolley	17.04.99	Telephone interview	CANA
Dr William Bloom	26.10.99	Interview	Glastonbury

In addition, a nine-week Ministry of Healing course was attended, as well as Sunday morning services at Cudham church on average once every five weeks throughout the course of study.

D. Interview Structure

These words must be said at the start of the interview.
"Thanks for letting me interview you. I ought to explain again that I am trying to find out what people think about Christianity and the New Age. This research is for my personal interest as part of my PhD degree. I have prepared some questions so that I ask everybody the same things. The interview will take about 45 minutes. You do not have to answer any of my questions, but the more you do answer, the easier it will be for me to understand the results. Your name will not be connected with the answers you give, but I will be quoting some answers anonymously in the thesis I write for my degree, and I hope to publish the results. So, if you have no questions, shall we begin?"

To begin at the beginning, could you describe your upbringing to me – your educational, religious and family background.
Could you briefly describe your childhood circumstances to me?
Where and when were you born?
What did your parents do for a living, and what was their religion?
Did you go to church or any other religious meetings regularly?
At what age did you finish your education?
If you went to university, what, when and where did you study?
Could you briefly describe your employment history to me?

What religious or other organisations do you belong to?
Have you ever belonged belong to any other religious organisations, or subscribed to any religious magazines – for example, *Do you belong to The Arcane School?* Any others?
Have you ever belonged to any political pressure groups, or subscribed to any campaign magazines, for example Greenpeace? Any others?
Have you ever belonged to any other organisations, or subscribed to any other magazines?

How would you describe your religion now?
Are you Christian?
Are you New Age?

What was your religious background before you came to the Omega Order?
How would you describe your religious affiliation before you came across the Omega Order?
Which church did you go to?
What sort of religious books did you read?
Did you go to any religious retreats, workshops or healing centres?

What brought you to the Omega Order?
When did you first hear of the Omega Order and of Peter Spink?
When did you first come to the Omega Order?
Had you met anyone involved with the Omega Order before you came here?
How long do you think you will stay here?

How important is the Omega vision to you?
What is your daily routine here?
How do you spend the time you are not at the Omega Order?
How many religious books do you read in a typical month?
What do you understand as the main essence and purpose of the Omega Order?

What do you understand by the term 'New Age'?
Could you give me some examples of New Agers and New Age groups?
Have you ever met a New Ager or been to a New Age event or workshop?
Have you ever read any New Age books?
Have you ever read any books about the New Age that were critical of it?

How do you think Christians relate to the New Age?
How would you define the term 'Christianity'?
Describe how you think Christianity and New Age presently and should ideally interact with each other.
How do you foresee the relations between Christianity and New Age will actually change in short, medium and long term, or will there be no change?

What do you think is the Christian view on psychotherapy and hypnotherapy?
Do you agree with this view?
Does it work? Is it scientific? Is it safe?
Some Christians speak about demonic influence. What do you think about this?

Notes to Appendices

[1] Total membership of 103 minus myself and two members living abroad.

[2] Total membershiip of 53 at the time of the telephone survey (November 1997).

[3] Figures from the whole membership of 179, not the sample.

[4] Figures from the whole membership of 103, not the sample.

[5] Figures from the then whole membership of 53, not the sample.

[6] This question was modified for the St James's and questionnaire to include more options.

[7] Inland Revenue figures cited in Rose (1996:373). In July 1999, the average national income was £20,000.

[8] Due to an oversight, there was no category on Omega and Evangelical questionnaires for employed/self-employed.

[9] Including "post-denominational Christian", "very ecumenical", "use Christian form", and similar qualifications.

[10] This question was analysed after the others, so all responses were included. For the Omega Order this was 190, for St James's 56, for CANA 56 also. Figures for this question are not percentages, but responses, and multiple responses were the norm. Only answers with two or more respondents have been included in the tables.

[11] *Gallup* 1993 cited in Heelas 1996a:166.

[12] In 1990, 59% of Europeans claimed to pray or meditate (Barker et al 1992:48).

[13] Although these figures tell a story in themselves – namely, that a high proportion of New Age –oriented people have experienced paranormal phenomena – there is another result from the survey that is not revealed in the figures. My question also asked people to state what kind of experience they had, and New Age Christians typically specified telepathy, visions, clairaudience, coincidences, ESP; whereas the evangelicals, although they have had a lower but still relatively high level of paranormal experiences, spoke differently of feeling the Holy Spirit move within them.

[14] The apparent discrepancy is due to rounding errors.

[15] Figures from Heelas 1996a:109

[16] Multiple answers were allowed. The percentages given in this question disregard blank entries.

[17] This question was analysed after the others, so all responses were included. For the Omega Order this was 190, for St James's 56, for CANA 56 also. Figures for this question are not percentages, but responses, and multiple responses were the norm. Only answers with two or more respondents have been included in the tables.

[18] Exactly 50% of *Omega News* respondents have been to a church service at St James' and/or Alternatives.

[19] According to the *European Values Survey* (Barker et al 1992:42), 23% of the population in Great Britain attend church monthly.

[20] 22% of the population in the United States of America are said to believe in reincarnation, according to George Gallup, 1997, *The Gallup Poll: Public Opinion 1996*, Wilmington DE: Scholarly Research Inc (quoted in Saliba 1999:235).

[21] 22% of the population in the United States of America are said to believe in reincarnation, according to George Gallup, 1997, *The Gallup Poll: Public Opinion 1996*, Wilmington DE: Scholarly Research Inc (quoted in Saliba 1999:235).

REFERENCES

Note: where two publication dates are given, the first date is the edition used and referenced, the second date that of the original publication.

Adler, Margot, 1986, *Drawing Down the Moon: Witches, Druids, Goddess-Worshippers, and Other Pagans in America Today*, Boston: Beacon Press.

Albanese, Catherine L, 1988, "Religion and the American Experience: A Century After", *Church History* 57 337-351.

Albanese, Catherine L, 1990, *Nature Religion in America from the Algonkian Indians to the Ne w Age*, Chicago: University of Chicago Press.

Albanese, Catherine L, 1992, "The Magical Staff: Quantum Healing in the New Age", 68-84 in Lewis, James R & J Gordon Melton eds, 1992, *Perspectives on the New Age,* New York: SUNY.

Albanese, Catherine L, 1993, "Fisher Kings and Public Places: The Old New Age in the 1990s", *Annals of the American Academy of Political and Social Science* 527 131-143.

Amis, Robin, 1995, *A Different Christianity: Early Christian Esotericism and Modern Thought*, Albany NY: SUNY.

Anglarès, Michel, 1992, *Nouvel Age et Foi Chrétienne*, Paris: Centurion.

Anonymous, 1985/1975, *A Course in Miracles*, Harmondsworth: Penguin Arkana.

Bailey, Alice A, 1994/1951, *T'he Unfinished Autobiography*, London: Lucis Press.

Bainbridge, William Sims, 1997, *The Sociology of Religious Movements*, New York: Routledge.

Barker, David et al, 1992, *The European Values Study 1981-1990: Summary Report*, London: The Gordon Cook Foundation.

Barker, Eileen, 1992, *New Religious Movements: A Practical Introduction*, London: HMSO.

Beckford, James A, 1985, *Cult Controversies: The Societal Response to New Religious Movements,* London: Tavistock.

Bednarowski, Mary Farrell, 1989, *New Religions and the Theological Imagination in America,* Bloomington: Indiana University Press.

Bednarowski, Mary Farrell, 1991, "Literature of the New Age: A Review of Representative Sources", *Religious Studies Review* 17.3 209-216.

Berger, Peter L et al, 1981/1973, *The Homeless Mind,* Harmondsworth: Penguin.

Berger, Peter L, 1954, "Sociological study of sectarianism", *Social Research* 21.4 467-85.

Berger, Peter L, 1980/1979, *The Heretical Imperative*, London: Collins.

Best, Steven & Douglas Kellner, 1991, *Postmodern Theory: Critical Interrogations*, Basingstoke: MacMillan.

Beth, Rae, 1990, *Hedge Witch: A Guide to Solitary Witchcraft*, London: Hale.

Bischofberger, Otto, Oswald Eggenberger, Carl-A Keller, Joachim Müller eds, 1987, *New Age – aus christlicher Sicht*, Freiburg: Paulusverlag.

Bloom, William, 1986, *Devas, Fairies and Angels: A Modern Approach,* Glastonbury: Gothic Image.

Bloom, William, 1990, *Sacred Times: A New Approach to Festivals,* Forres:

Findhorn Press.

Bloom, William, 1992/1976, *The Sacred Magician: a ceremonial diary,* 2nd edn Glastonbury: Gothic Image.

Bloom, William, 1992/1989, *Personal Identity, National Identity and International Relations*, Cambridge: Cambridge University Press.

Bloom, William, 1993, *First Steps: An Introduction to Spiritual Practice,* Findhorn: Findhorn Press.

Bloom, William, 1995, *The Christ* Sparks: *The Inner Dynamics of Group Consciousness,* Findhorn: Findhorn Press.

Bloom, William, 1996, *Psychic Protection: Creating positive energies for people and places,* London: Piatkus.

Bloom, William, 1996/1987, *Meditation in a Changing World,* rvsd edn Glastonbury: Gothic Image.

Bloom, William, 1998, *Working with Angels, Fairies and Nature Spirits*, London: Piatkus.

Bloom, William ed, 1991, *The New Age: An Anthology of Essential Writings,* London: Rider.

Bloom, William ed, 2000, *Holistic Revolution*, Harmondsworth: Penguin.

Bochinger, Christoph, 1991, "Theorien des »New Age« und der Geist der Gegenwart", 34-46 in Haneke, Burkhard & Karltheodor Huttner, 1991, *Spirituelle Aufbrüche: New Age und »Neue Religiosität « als Herausforderung an Gesellschaft und Kirche*, Regensburg: Verlag Friedrich Pustet.

Bochinger, Christoph, 1995/1994, *»New Age« und moderne Religion: Religioswissenschaftliche Analysen,* rvsd edn Gutersloh: Chr Kaiser.

Bond, Mark, 1998, "Sacraments for the New Age", *Chrism* 8-10.

Bowman, Marion, 1993, "Reinventing the Celts", *Religion* 23 147-156.

Braden, Charles S, 1966/1963, *Spirits in Rebellion: The Rise and Development of New Thought*, Dallas: Southern Methodist University Press.

Brown-Keister, Katherine, 1982, *Legitimation Strategies of an Alternative Health Occupation: the lay holistic health practitioner in the Bay Area*, Columbia University: PhD thesis.

Bryant, Christopher, 1978, *The River Within: The Search for God in Depth,* London: Darton Longman and Todd.

Bryant, Christopher, 1988/1983, *Jung and the Christian Way,* Darton Longman and Todd.

Burke, T Patrick, 1984, "Must the Description of a Religion be Acceptable to a Believer?", *Religious Studies* 20 631-636.

Burton, Ursula & Janice Dolley, 1984, *Christian Evolution: Moving Towards a Global Spirituality,* Wellingborough: Turnstone Press.

Burton, Ursula, & Janice Dolley, 1990, *Christianity and the New Age,* Edinburgh & London: unpublished manuscript.

Buttiglione, Rocco, 1988, "Zur Frage der Bewegungen", *Zeitschrift für Politik* 35 219-236.

Button, John & William Bloom eds, 1992, *The Seeker's Guide: A New Age Resource Book*, London: Aquarian Press.

Byrne, Peter, 1980, "Does religion have an essence?", *Scottish Journal of Religious Studies* 1.i 62-67.

Campbell, Colin, 1972, "The Cult, the Cultic Milieu and Secularization", 119-136 in Michael Hill ed *A Sociological Yearbook of Religion in Britain* 5 London: SCM.

Campbell, Colin, 1987, "Cultural Sources of Support for Contemporary Occultism", *Social Compass* 34.1 41-60.

CANA, 1999, "Exploring Ways Forward for Christianity into the Twenty-First Century", Oxford: CANA.

Capel, Evelyn Francis, 1989, *An Introduction to Counselling from a Spiritual Perspective,* London: Temple Lodge Press.

Capra, Fritjof, 1992/1976, *The Tao of Physics*, London: Flamingo.

Central Statistical Office, 1996, *Social Trends,* London: HMSO.

Chandler, Russell, 1989/1988, *Understanding the New Age,* Milton Keynes: Word (UK).

Chavchavadze, Marina, 1995, *Dorothy Kerin As I Knew Her,* np: The Executors of the Estate of Marina Chavchavadze.

Christian Research, 2000, *UK Christian Handbook*, London: Christian Research & HarperCollinsReligious.

Church of Scotland Board of Social Responsibility, 1993, *Young People and the Media*, Edinburgh: Church of Scotland.

Clarke, Peter B & Peter Byrne, 1993, *Religion Defined and Explained,* London: Macmillan.

Clarke, Peter B, 1996, "Why NRMs succeed or fail", London: paper delivered at the King's College social sciences and anthropology postgraduate seminar, 12 December.

Clarke, Peter B, 1998, "The Internet and Recruitment to New Religious Movements", London: paper delivered at the King's College social sciences and anthropology postgraduate seminar, 15 October.

Clifford, Ross and Philip Johnson, 2001, *Jesus and the Gods of the NewAge: Communicating Christ in Today's Spiritual Supermarket*, Oxford: Lion.

Coelho, Paulo, 1997/1987, *The Pilgrimage,* trns Alan Clarke, London: Thorsons.

Coelho, Paulo, 1994/1988, *L'Alchimiste,* trns Jean Orecchioni, Paris: Editions J'ai lu.

Coelho, Paulo, 1996/1992, *The Valkyries: An Encounter* with *Angels,* trns Alan R Clarke, London: Thorsons.

Coelho, Paulo, 1997/1994, *By the River Piedra I Sat Down & Wept,* trns Alan Clarke, London: Thorsons.

Cole, Michael et al, 1990, *What is the New Age?,* London: Hodder and Stroughton.

Congregation for the Doctrine of the Faith, 1998, "Notification concerning the writings of Father Anthony de Mello, SJ", 22 August.

Conn, Eileen & James Stewart eds, 1995, *Visions of Creation*, Alresford: Godsfield Press.

Corrywright, Dominic, 2001, *Theoretical and Empirical Investigations into New Age Spiritualities with special reference to the South West of England*, University of Bristol: PhD thesis.

Cumbey, Constance, 1983, *The Hidden Dangers of the Rainbow,* rvsd edn Lafayette LA: Huntington House.

Cuming, Kenneth G, 1975, *God and the New Age,* Tunbridge Wells: Michael Link.

Cupitt, Don, 1998, "Post-Christianity", pp 218-232 in Paul Heelas ed, 1998, *Religion, Modernity and Postmodernity*, Oxford: Blackwell.

D'Andrea, Anthony, 1997/1996, *O Self Perfeito e a Nova Era: Individualism e Reflexividade em Religiosidades Pos-Tradicionais,* 2nd version Rio de Janeiro: Masters thesis.

Dawson, Lorne L, 1997, "Creating 'Cult' Typologies: Some Strategic Considerations", *Journal of Contemporary Religion* 12.3 363-382.

Dawson, Lorne L, 1998, "Anti-Modernism, Modernism, And Postmodernism: Struggling with the Cultural Significance of New Religious Movements", *Sociology of Religion* 59.2 131-156.

Déchanet, JM, 1960, *Christian Yoga*, London.

de Chardin, Pierre Teilhard, 1965/1955, *The Phenomenon of Man*, London: Fontana.

de Chardin, Pierre Teilhard, 1967/1957, *Le Milieu Divin*, London: Fontana.

della Porta, Donatella & Mario Diani, 1999, *Social Movements: An Introduction*, Oxford: Blackwell.

de Mello, Anthony, 1984/1978, *Sadhana: A Way to God. Christian Exercises in Eastern Form,* New York: Image.

de Mello, Anthony, 1997/1990, Awareness, London: Fount.

Dery, Mark, 1996, *Escape Velocity: Cyberculture at the End of the Century*, London: Hodder & Stoughton.

Diani, Mario, 1995, *Green Networks: A Structural Analysis of the Italian Environmental Movement*, Edinburgh: Edinburgh University Press.

Dobroczynski, Bartlomiej, 1991, "Proteeuszowe oblicze Wodnika. Co to jest "New Age"?", *Znak* 71-91.

Dobroczynski, Bartlomiej, 1995, "Protokoly Medrcow Nowej Ery: O „Chrzescijankiej" Krytyce Swiatopogladu „Wodnika"", *Znak* 76-90.

Dole, Arthur A, Michael D Langone & Steve Dubrow-Eichel, 1990, "The New Age Movement: Fad or Menace?", *Cultic Studies Journal 7.1* 69-91.

Dole, Arthur A, Michael D Langone & Steve K Dubrow-Eichel, 1993, "Is the New Age Movement Harmless? Critics Versus Experts", *Cultic Studies Journal* 10.1 53-77.

Donahue, Michael J, 1993, "Prevalence and Correlates of New Age Beliefs In Six Protestant Denominations", *Journal for the Scientific Study of Religion* 32.2 177-184.

Dostoyevsky, Fyodor, 1971/1871-1872, *The Devils*, trns David Magarshack Harmondsworth: Penguin.

Dowling, Levi H, 1987/1907s, *The Aguarian Gospel of Jesus the Christ,* Marina del Rey CA: DeVorss & Co.

Drane, John, 1991, *What is the New Age Saying to the Church?,* London: Marshall Pickering.

Drane, John, Ross Clifford and Philip Johnson, 2001, *Beyond Prediction: The Tarot and Your Spirituality*, Oxford: Lion.

Duncan, Anthony, 1969, *The Christ, Psychotherapy and Magic*, London: George & Allen Unwin.

Duncan, Anthony, 1972, *The Lord of the Dance: An Essay in Mysticism*, London: Helios Book Service.

Eckberg, Douglas Lee & T Jean Blocker, 1989, "Varieties of Religious

Involvement and Environmental Concerns: Testing the Lynn White Thesis",
  Journal for the Scientific Study of Religion 28.4 509-517.

Eddy, Mary Baker, 1934/1875, *Science and Health with Key to the Scriptures*,
  Boston: Trustees of the Will of Mary Baker G Eddy.

Ellwood, Robert S Jr, 1979, *Alternative Altars: Unconventional and Eastern
  Spirituality in America*, Chicago: University of Chicago Press.

English, Barton Dean, 1994, *The Challenge of the New Age to Christian Theology
  and Life*, Edinburgh: PhD thesis.

English, June Anne, 1985, *A Place for Healing: An Ethnography of Holistic
  Health Practitioners in Southern California*, Santa Barbara: PhD thesis.

Enomiya-Lassalle, 1974, *Zen Meditation for Christians*, Illinois.

Epperly, Bruce G, 1996, *Crystal & Cross: Christians and New Age in Creative
  Dialogue*, Connecticut: Twenty-Third Publications.

Faith and Order Committee, 1994, "The New Age Movement : Report to
  Conference 1994", Peterborough: Methodist Publishing House.

Faivre, Antoine, 1994, "Une discipline universitaire nouvelle: l'ésotérisme", pp
  35-44 in Jean-Baptiste Martin & François Laplantine eds, *Le Défi Magique*,
  Lyon: Presses Universitaires de Lyon.

Farr, Ruth, 1986/1970, *Will You Go Back?,* Tunbridge Wells: K&SC.

Ferguson, Marilyn, 1989/1980, *The Aquarian Conspiracy,* London: Paladin.

Festinger, Leon, 1962/1957, *A Theory of Cognitive Dissonance*, London:
  Tavistock Publications.

Festinger, Leon, Henry W Riecken & Stanley Schachter, 1956, *When Prophecy
  Fails*, New York: Harper & Row.

Filoramo, Giovanni, 1992/1990, *A History of Gnosticism*, trsn Anthony Alcock,
  Oxford: Blackwell.

Forman, Robert KC, 1991, *Meister Eckhart: Mystic as Theologian*, Rockport
  Mass: Element Books.

Fortune, Dion, 1941, Letters to Members and Friends of the Fraternity of the
  Inner Light, London: typescripts in the British Library.

Fox, Matthew, 1981/1976, *Whee! We, Wee All the Way Home: A Guide to
  Sensual, Prophetic Spirituality*, Santa Fe NM: Beaar & Co,

Fox, Matthew, 1983, *Original Blessing*, Santa Fe NM: Bear and Co.

Fox, Matthew, 1988, *The Coming of the Cosmic Christ*, New York:
  HarperSanFrancisco.

Fox, Matthew, 1991, *Creation Spirituality: Liberating Gifts for the Peoples of the
  Earth*, New York: HarperSanFrancisco.

Fox, Matthew, 1996, *Confessions: The Making of a Post-Denominational Priest*,
  San Francisco: HarperSanFrancisco.

Freeman, Anthony, 1993, *God in Us: A Case for Christian Humanism*, London:
  SCM.

Frieling, Rudolf, 1977/1974, *Christianity and Reincarnation*, trns Rudolf &
  Margaret Koehler, Edinburgh: Floris.

Gallagher, Eugene V, 1994, "A Religion without Converts? Becoming a Neo-
  Pagan", *Journal of the American Academy of Religion* LXII.3 851p 867.

Gartrell-Mills, Claire F, 1991, *Christian Science: an American Religion in
  Britain,* Oxford: DPhil thesis.

Gerlach, Luther P, 1971, "Movements of revolutionary change", *American*

Behavorial Scientist 14.6 812-836.

Gerlach, Luther P & Virginia H Hine, 1968, "Five factors crucial to the growth and spread of a modern religious movement", *Journal for the Scientific Study of Religion* 7.1 23-40.

Gerson, Lloyd P ed, 1996, *The Cambridge Companion to Plotinus*, Cambridge: Cambridge University Press.

Giddens, Anthony, 1995/1990, *The Consequences of Modernity*, Cambridge: Polity Press.

Gimbutas, Marija, 1982, *The Goddesses and Gods of Old Europe, 7000-3500 BC*, Berkeley: University of California Press.

Gimbutas, Marija, 1991, *The Civilisation of the Goddess*, San Francisco: HarperSanFrancisco.

Glock, Charles Y & Rodney Stark, 1965, *Religion and Society in Tension*, Chicago: Rand McNally.

Godwin, Joscelyn, 1994, *The Theosophical Enlightenment*, Albany: SUNY.

Goffman, Erving, 1974, *Frame Analysis*, Cambridge MA: Harvard University Press.

Goodrick-Clarke, Nicholas, 1992/1985, *The Occult Roots of Nazism*, London: IB Tauris.

Gottschalk, Stephen, 1973, *The Emergence of Christian Science in American Religious Life,* Berkeley: University of California Press.

Graham, Billy, 1975, *Angels – God's Secret Agents*, Doubleday.

Graham, Dom Aelred, 1994/1963, Zen *Catholicism,* Crossroad.

Greeley, Andrew, 1993, "Religion and Attitudes toward the Environment", *Journal for the Scientific Study of Religion* 32.1 19-28.

Greer, Paul, 1994, *The Spiritual Dynamics of the New Age Movement,* Stirling: PhD thesis.

Greer, Paul, 1995, "The Aquarian Confusion: Conflicting Theologies of the New Age", *Journal of Contemporary Religion* 10.2 151-168.

Griffiths, Bede, 1979/1954, *The Golden String: An Autobiography*, Glasgow: Fount.

Griffiths, Bede, 1973, *Vedanta and Christian Faith*, London: Fount.

Griffiths, Bede, 1982, *The Marriage of East and West*, London: Fount.

Griffiths, Bede, 1992/1989, *A New Vision of Reality: Western Science, Eastern Mysticism and Christian Faith*, London: Fount.

Groothuis, Douglas R, 1988 *Confronting the New Age,* Leicester: InterVarsity Press.

Groothuis, Douglas R, 1990, *Revealing the New Age Jesus,* Leicester: InterVarsity Press.

Groothuis, Douglas R, 1991/1986, *Unmasking the New Age,* Leicester: InterVarsity Press.

Grove, Daisy M, 1926, *The Apocalypse and Initiation*, London: Theosophical Publishing House.

Gusfield, Joseph R, 1994, "The Reflexivity of Social Movements: Collective Behavior and Mass Society Theory Revisited", 58-78 in Enrique Laraña, Hank Johnston & Joseph R Gusfield eds, *New Social Movements: From Ideology to Identity*, Philadelphia: Temple University Press.

Hackett, Rosalind IJ, 1992, "New Age Trends in Nigeria: Ancestral and/or Alien

Religion?" 215-231 in James Lewis and J Gordron Melton eds, 1992, *Perspectives on the New Age*, Albany: SUNY.

Hall, John R & Philip Schuyler, 1997, "The Mystical Apocalypse of the Solar Temple", pp 285-312 in Thomas Robbins & Susan J Palmer, 1997, *Millennium, Messiahs, and Mayhem: Contemporary Apocalyptic Movement*, New York: Routledge.

Hanegraaff, Wouter J, 1991, "Channeling-literatuur: een vergelijking tussen de boodschappen van Seth, Armerus, Ramala, en 'A course in miracles'", *Religieuze Bewegingen in Nederland 22* 9-44.

Hanegraaff, Wouter J, 1992a, "A Dynamic Typological Approach to the Problem of 'Post-Gnostic' Gnosticism", *ARIES* (Association pour la Recherche et l'information sur l'Esoterisme) 16 5-43.

Hanegraaff, Wouter J, 1992b, "Esoterie, occultisme en (neo)gnostiek: Historische en inhoudelijke verbanden", *Religieuze Bewegingen in Nederland 25* 1-28.

Hanegraaff, Wouter J, 1994, "Nieuwe Religieuze Bewegingen", *Religieuze Bewegingen in Nederland 29* 1-49.

Hanegraaff, Wouter J, 1995, "Empirical Method in the Study of Esotericism", *Methods and Theory in the Study of Religion 7.2* 99-129.

Hanegraaff, Wouter J, 1996, *New Age Religion and Western Culture*, Leiden: Brill.

Hanegraaff, Wouter J, 1998, "The New Age Movement and the Esoteric Tradition", 359-382 in van den Broek, Roelof & Wouter J Hanegraaff eds, 1998, *Gnosis and Hermeticism from Antiquity to Modern Times*, Albany: SUNY.

Haneke, Burkhard & Karltheodor Huttner, 1991, *Spirituelle Aufbrüche: New Age und »Neue Religiosität« als Herausforderung an Gesellschaft und Kirche*, Regensburg: Verlag Friedrich Pustet.

Hardy, Jean, 1996/1987, A *Psychology with a Soul: Psychotherapy in Evolutionary Contex,* London: Woodgrange Press.

Hardyck, Jane Allyn & Marcia Braden, 1962, "Prophecy Fails Again: A Report of a Failure to Replication", *Journal of Abnormal and Social Psychology* 65 136-141.

Harper, Charles L, 1982, "Cults and Communities: The Community Interfaces of Three Marginal Religious Movements", *Journal for the Scientific Study of Religion* 21.1 26-38.

Heelas, Paul, 1982, "Californian Self Religions and Socializing the Subjective", 69-85 in Barker, Eileen ed, 1982, *New Religious Movements: A Perspective for Understanding Society*, New York: Edwin Mellen.

Heelas, Paul, 1988, "Western Europe: Self Religions", 925-931 in *The World's Religions,* ed Stewart Sutherland et al Boston MA: GK Hall & Co.

Heelas, Paul, 1993, "The New Age in Cultural Context: the Premodem, the Modern and the Postmodern", *Religion* 23 103-116.

Heelas, Paul, 1996a, *The New Age Movement: The Celebration of the Self and the Sacralization of Modernity,* Oxford: Blackwell.

Heelas, Paul, 1996b, "De-traditionalisation of Religion and Self: The New Age and Postmodernity", pp 64-82 in in Kieran Flanagan & Peter C Jupp eds, 1996, *Postmodernity, Sociology and Religion*, London: Macmillan.

Heelas, Paul & Leila Amaral, 1994, "Research Report: Notes on the 'Nova Era':

Rio de Janeiro and Environs", *Religion* 24 173-180.

Heelas, Paul, 1998, "Introduction: On differentiation and Dedifferentiation", 1-18 in Paul Heelas ed, 1998, *Religion, Modernity and Postmodernity*, Oxford: Blackwell.

Heelas, Paul ed, 1998, *Religion, Modernity and Postmodernity*, Oxford: Blackwell.

Heline, Corinne, 1992/1935, *New Age Bible Interpretation*, vol 5, Santa Monica CA: New Age Bible & Philosophy Center.

Hendershott, Carmen, 1989, *Stranger than Paradise: Hosts and Guests in a New Age Community*, Ann Arbor MI: PhD thesis.

Hetherington, Ralph, 1993, "Universalism and Spirituality", Wallingford Pennsylvania: Pendle Hill.

Hick, John, 1983, "Christ in a Universe of Faiths", Leicester: The Quaker Universalist Group.

Hirst, Désirée, 1964, *Hidden Riches: Traditional Symbolism from the Renaissance to Blake*, London: Eyre.

Hobsbawm, Eric & Terence Ranger eds, 1983, *The Invention of Tradition*, Cambridge: CUP.

Houston, Siobhan, 1994, "Turning to Orthodoxy: The Evolution of the Holy Order of MANS", *Gnosis*.

Howard, Roland, 1996, *The* Rise *and Fall of the Nine O'Clock Service: A cult within the church?,* London: Mowbray.

Hunt, Dave & TA McMahon, 1985, *The Seduction of Christianity*, Eugene, Oregon: Harvest House.

Hunt, Dave & TA McMahon, 1988, *The New Spirituality*, Eugene, Oregon: Harvest House.

Hutton, Ronald, 1991, *The Pagan Religions of the Ancient British Isles*, Oxford: Blackwell.

Huxley, Aldous, 1946, *The Perennial Philosophy*, London: Chatto & Windus.

Icke, David, 1992, *Love Changes Everything,* London: The Aquarian Press.

Icke, David, 1993a, *Heal the World,* Bath: Gateway Books.

Icke, David, 1993b, *In the Light of Experience,* London: Warner.

Icke, David, 1994, *The Robot's Rebellion,* Bath: Gateway.

Icke, David, 1995, *...and the truth shall set you free,* Ryde: Bridge of Love.

Inaba, Keishin, 1999, "Accounting for Altruism and Ethical Opinion in the Jesus Army and Friends of the Western Buddhist Order", London: paper delivered at the King's College postgraduate seminar in athropology and sociology of religion, 11 March.

Introvigne, Massimo, 1994, *Storia del New Age 1962-1992*, Piacenza: Cristianita.

Introvigne, Massimo, 1995, "Ordeal by Fire: The Tragedy of the Solar Temple", *Religion 25* 267-283.

Introvigne, Massimo, 1997, "Lectorium Rosicrucianum: A Dutch Movement Becomes International", paper read at CESNUR International Conference, Free University of Amsterdam.

Irish Theological Commission, 1994, *A New Age of the Spirit? A Catholic Response to the New Age Phenomenon*, Dublin: Veritas.

Jameson, Fredric, 1984, "Postmodernism, or the Cultural Logic of Late Capitalism", *New Left Review* 146 53-93.

Johnston, Hank, Enrique Laraña & Joseph R Gusfield, 1994, "Identities, Grievances and New Social Movements", 3-35 in Enrique Laraña, Hank Johnston & Joseph R Gusfield eds, *New Social Movements: From Ideology to Identity*, Philadelphia: Temple University Press.

Johnston, William,1978/1974, *Silent Music*, London: Fount.

Johnston, William, 1989/1988, *Being in Love: The Practice of Christian Prayer*, London: Fount.

Johnston, William, 1979, *Christian Zen*, 2nd end, Dublin: Gill & Macmillan.

Johnston, William, 1991, *Letters to Contemplatives*, London: Fount.

Jones, Chesly, Geoffrey Wainwright & Edward Yarnold eds, 1992/1986, *The Study of Spirituality*, London: SPCK.

Jorgensen, Danny L, 1982, "The Esoteric Community: An Ethnographic Investigation of the Cultic Milieu", *Urban Life* 10.4 383-407.

Jorgensen, Danny L, 1983, "Psychic Fairs: A Basis for Solidarity and Networks Among Occultists", *California Sociologist* 6.1 57-75.

Jorgensen, DL & L Jorgensen, 1982, "Social Meanings of the Occult", *The Sociological Quarterly* 23 373-389.

Kehl, Medard, 1988, *New Age oder Neuer Bund? Christen im Gespräch mit Wendezeit, Esoterik und Okkultismus*, Mainz: Matthias-Grünewald-Verlag.

Kelsey, Morton T, 1973, *Tongue Speaking: An Experiment in Spiritual Experience*, London: Hodder.

Kelsey, Morton T, 1991, *Prophetic Ministry: The Psychology and Sprituality of Pastoral Care*, Longmead: Element Books.

Kemp, Daren, 1992, "Cosmic Capers", *Gair Rhydd* 415 3 February 10-11.

Kemp, Daren, 1994a, "The Gospel according to Saint David ...", *Gair Rhydd* 485, 2 May.

Kemp, Daren, 1994b, "Anglicanism and the New Age", paper presented to an international conference on The Future of Anglicanism at Christ Church College, Canterbury, 4 September available at www.Christaquarian.net.

Kemp, Daren, 2000, "A Platonic Delusion: The Identification of Psychosis and Mysticism", *Mental Health, Religion & Culture* 3.2 157-172.

Kemp, Daren, 2001a, "Christaquarianism: An Implicit Religion of Postmodern Society?", *Implicit Religion* 4.1 27-40.

Kemp, Daren, 2001b, "The Christaquarians? A Sociology of Christians in the New Age", *Studies in World Christianity* 7.1 95-110.

Kemp, Daren, 2003a, "The Christaquarians? A Sociology of Christians in the New Age" in James R Lewis ed, 2003, *The Encyclopedic Sourcebook of New Age Religions*, Buffalo NY: Prometheus Books.

Kemp, Daren, forthcoming a, *New Age: A Guide – Alternative Spiritualities from Aquarian Conspiracy to Next Age*, Edinburgh: Edinburgh University Press.

Kemp, Daren, forthcoming b, *A New Age Christian Theology: The Christaquarian Conspiracy*, New Alresford: John Hunt.

Kerin, Dorothy, 1960/1952, *Fulfilling*, 3rd rvsd edn Tunbridge Wells: Kent.

Kerin, Dorothy, 1987/1914, *The Living Touch*, Groombridge:Dorothy Kerin Trust.

Knight, Gareth, nd, "Dion Fortune and the Three-Fold Way", np.

Knoblauch, Hubert, 1989, "Das unsichtbare neue Zeitalter. 'New Age', privatisierte Religion und kultisches Milieu", *Kölner Zeitschrift für Soziologie*

41.3 504-515.

Kornhauser, William, 1959, *The Politics of Mass Society*, Glencoe Ill: Free Press.

Kranenborg, Reender, 1998, "The Presentation of the Essenes in Western Esotericism", *Journal of Contemporary Religion* 13.2 245-256.

Kriesi, Hanspeter, 1996, "The organizational structure of new social movements in a political context", pp 152-184 in Doug McAdam, John D McCarthy & Mayer N Zald, 1996, *Comparative perspectives on social movements*, Cambridge: CUP.

Kubiak, Anna E, 1999, "Le Nouvel Age, conspiration postmoderne", *Social Compass* 46.2 135-145.

Kuhn, Thomas S, 1970/1962, *The Structure of Sceintific Revolutions,* 2nd edn, Chicago: University of Chicago Press.

Kuykendall, Richard E, 1992, *Liturgies of the Earth*, Phoenix Arizona: Educational Ministries Inc.

Kuykendall, Richard E, 1996, "Where Christian Liturgy and Neo-Pagan Ritual Meet" pp327-337 in James R Lewis ed, 1996, *Magical Religion and Modern Witchcraft,* New York: SUNY.

Lacroix, Michel, 1995, *La Spiritualité Totalitaire: Le New Age et les Sectes*, Paris: Plon.

Legere, Thomas E, 1993, A *Popular Book: Christianity for a New Age,* Union Institute Graduate School: PhD thesis.

Lewis, IM, 1975/1971, Ecstatic Religion: An Anthropological Study of Spirit Possession and Shamanism, Harmondsworth: Penguin.

Lewis, James, 1991, *A Bibliography of Conservative Christian Literature on the New Age Movement.* Santa Barbara, Calif: Santa Barbara Center for Humanistic Studies, occasional paper no.2.

Lewis, James R & J Gordon Melton eds, 1992, *Perspectives on the New Age,* New York: SUNY.

Lewis, James R ed, 2003, *The Encyclopedic Sourcebook of New Age Religions*, Buffalo NY: Prometheus Books.

Livesey, Roy, 1988/1983, *More Understanding Alternative Medicine,* 3rd ed, Chichester: New Wine Press.

Livesey, Roy, 1989, *Understanding the New World Order,* Chichester: New Wine Press.

Livesey, Roy, 1990a/1987, *Understanding Deception: New Age Teaching in the Church,* Chichester: New Wine Press.

Livesey, Roy, 1990b, *More Understanding the New Age,* Chichester: New Wine Press.

Lofland, John, 1977, "'Becoming a World-Saver' Revisited", *American Behavioral Scientist* 20.6 805-818.

Lofland, John & Norman Skonovd, 1981, "Conversion Motifs", *Journal for the Scientific Study of Religion* 20.4 373-385.

Lofland, John & Rodney Stark, 1965, "Becoming a World-Saver: A Theory of Conversion to a Deviant Perspective", *American Sociological Review* 30 862-874.

Lucas, Philip, 1992, "The New Age Movement and the Pentecostal/Charismatic Revival: Distinct Yet Parallel Phases of a Fourth Great Awakening?", 189-212 in Lewis, James R & J Gordon Melton eds, 1992, *Perspectives on the New*

Age, New York: SUNY.

Lucas, Philip, 1995, *The Odyssey of a New Religion; The Holy Order of MANS from New Age to Orthodoxy,* Bloomington: Indiana University Press.

Luhrmann, TM, 1994/1989, *Persuasions of the Witch's Craft,* London: Picador.

Lynch, Frederick R, 1977, "Toward a Theory of Conversion and Commitment to the Occult", *American Behavioral Scientist* 20.6 887-908.

Lynch, Frederick R, 1979, " 'Occult Establishment' or 'Deviant Religion'? The Rise and Fall of a Modern Church of Magic", *Journal for the Scientific Study of Religion* 18.3 281-298.

Lyon, David, 1993, "A Bit of a Circus: Notes on Postmodernity and New Age", *Religion 23* 117-126.

Lyon, David, 1994, *Postmodernity,* Buckingham: Open University.

MacGregor, Don, 2003, *Christian Reincarnation?* Eastleigh: CANA Publications.

MacGregor, Geddes, 1982, *Reincarnation as a Christian Hope,* London: Macmillan.

Maciejko, Pawel, 1994, "Bóg New Age", *Spoleczenstwo Otwarte* 3.

Maddocks, Morris, 1991/1981, *The Christian Healing Ministry,* 2nd edn London: SPCK.

Main, John, 1985, *The Present Christ,* London: DLT.

Main, John, 1987, *The Inner Christ,* London: DLT.

Main, John, 1989, *The Way of Unknwoing,* London: DLT.

Manabu, Haga & Robert J Kisala, 1995, "Editor's Introduction: The New Age in Japan", *Japanese Journal of Religious Studies* 22.3-4 235-247.

Mangalwadi, Vishal, *In Search of Self Beyond the New Age,* Spire 1992.

Martin, Walter, 1989, *The New Age Cult,* Minneapolis: Bethany House.

Marty, Martin, 1970, "The occult establishment", *Social Research* 37.2:212-230.

Marx, Karl & Friedrich Engels, 1990/1848, *The Communist Manifesto* pp 221-247 in David McLellan, 1990/1977, *Karl Marx: Selected Writings,* Oxford: OUP.

Matrisciana, Caryl, 1985, *Gods of the New Age,* London: Marshall Pickering.

Mattausch, J, 1986, A *Commitment to Campaign: A Sociological Study of C.N.D.,* Edinburgh University: PhD thesis.

Mayer, Jean-François, 1993, *Les Nouvelles Voies Spirituelles: Enquête sur la religiosité parallèle en Suisse,* Lausanne: L'Age d'Homme.

Mayer, Jean-François, 1999, " "Our Terrestrial Journey is Coming to an End": The Last Voyage of the Solar Temple", *Nova Religio* 2.2.

McAdam, Doug, 1994, "Culture and Social Movements", 36-57 in Enrique Laraña, Hank Johnston & Joseph R Gusfield eds, *New Social Movements: From Ideology to Identity,* Philadelphia: Temple University Press.

McAdam, Doug, John D McCarthy & Mayer N Zald eds, 1996, *Comparative perspectives on social movements,* Cambridge: CUP.

McCarthy, John D and Mayer N Zald, 1987, *Social Movements in an Organizational Society,* New Brunswick NJ: Transaction.

McCarthy, John D, 1996, "Constraints and opportunities in adopting, adapting, and inventing", 141-151 in McAdam, Doug, John D McCarthy & Mayer N Zald eds, 1996, *Comparative perspectives on social movements,* Cambridge: CUP.

McGuire, Meredith B, 1988, *Ritual Healing in Suburban America,* New

Brunswick: Rutgers University Press.

McGuire, Meredith B, 1993, "Health and Healing in New Religious Movements", 139-155 in David G Bromley & Jeffrey K Hadden eds, 1993, *Religion and the Social Order,* Hampton Hill: JAI Press.

McLynn, Frank, 1997/1996, *Carl Gustav Jung,* London: Black Swan.

Melton, J Gordon, 1992/1986, *Encyclopedic Handbook of Cults in America*, New York: Garland Publishing.

Melton, J Gordon et al, 1991, *New Age Almanac,* Detroit MI: Visible Ink Press.

Melton, J Gordon, 1998/1994, "The Future of the New Age Movement", 133-149 in Eileen Barker & Margit Warburg eds, *New Religions and New Religiosity*, Aarhus: Aarhus University Press.

Merton, Thomas, 1975/1947, *The Seven Storey Mountain*, London: Sheldon Press.

Merton, Thomas, 1976/1951, *The Ascent to Truth*, London: Burns & Oates.

Miller, Elliot, 1990/1989, A *Crash Course on the New Age Movement,* Eastbourne: Monarch Publications.

Millikan, David & Nevill Drury, 1991, *Worlds Apart? Christianity and the New Age*, Crows Nest NSW: Australian Broadcasting Corporation.

Mission Theological Advisory Group, 1996, *The Search for Faith and the* witness *of the church,* London: Church House.

Moore, L David, 1992, *Christianity and the New Age Religion: A Bridge Toward Mutual Understanding*, Atlanta: Pendulum Plus.

Needham, R, 1975, "Polythetic classification: convergence and consequences", *Man* (New Series) 10 349-369.

Needleman, Jacob, 1985/1980, *Lost Christianity: A Journey of Rediscovery*, San Francisco: Harper & Row.

Nelson, Geoffrey K, 1969, "The Spiritualist Movement and the Need for a Redefinition of Cult", *Journal for the Scientific Study of Religion* 8.1 152-160.

Nelson, Geoffrey K, 1987, *Cults, New Religions & Religious Creativity*, London: Routledge & Keegan Paul.

Nettleton, Mollie, nd, "The Technique in Light: An Introduction", Winford: Nettleton.

Niebuhr, HR, 1929, *The Social Sources of Denominationalism*, New York: Henry Holt & Co.

Noll, Richard, 1996/1994, *The Jung Cult: Origins of a Charismatic Movement,* 2nd rvsd edn, London: Fontana.

Noll, Richard, 1997, *The Aryan Christ: The Secret Life of Carl Gustav Jung*, London: Macmillan.

Olson, Mancur, 1965, *The Logic of Collective Action*, Cambridge Mass: Harvard University Press.

Omega Trust, 1994, *The Omega Offices*, 5th edn, Winford: Omega Publications.

Ó'Murchú, Diarmuid, 1989, *The Prophetic Horizon of Religious Life,* London: Excalibur.

Ó'Murchú, Diarmuid, 1995, *Reframing Religious Life,* Middlegreen: St Paul's.

Ó'Murchú, Diarmuid, 1997a, *Quantum Theology,* New York: Crossroad.

Ó'Murchú, Diarmuid, 1997b, *Reclaiming Spirituality,* Dublin: Gill & Macmillan.

Ó'Murchú, Diarmuid, 1997/1992, *Our World* in *Transition: Making Sense of a Changing World,* Lewes: The Book Guild.

Osborn, Lawrence, 1992, *Angels of Light? The Challenge of New Age Spirituality*, London: Daybreak DLT.

Osborn, Lawrence, 1993, *Guardians of Creation: Nature in theology and the Christian life,* London: APOLLOS.

Pagels, Elaine, 1992/1975, *The Gnostic Paul*, Philadelphia: Trinity International Press.

Pagels, Elaine, 1982/1977, *The Gnostic Gospels*, Harmondsworth: Pelican.

Palmer, Martin, 1993a, *Coming of Age: An Exploration of Christianity and the New Age*, London: Aquarian Press.

Palmer, Martin, 1993b, *Living Christianity*, Longmead: Element Books.

Paschkes-Bell, Gillian, 1998, *Christian Belief and the 'New Awareness' a qualitative sociological study and a theological critique*, Oxford University: MTh dissertation.

Peck, M Scott, 1993, *Further Along the Road Less Travelled,* London: Simon & Schuster.

Pepper, David, 1991, *Communes and the Green Vision: Counterculture, Lifestyle and the New Age*, London: Green Print.

Peretti, Frank, 1997/1986, *This Present Darkness*, Eastbourne: Kingsway.

Peretti, Frank, 1997/1989, *Piercing the Darkness*, Eastbourne: Kingsway.

Perry, Michael, 1992, *Gods Within: A Critical Guide to the NewAge,* London: SPCK.

Peters, Ted, 1991, *The Cosmic Self: A Penetrating Look at Today's New Age Movements*, New York: HarperCollins.

Pixley, Olive CB, 1978/1957, *The Armour of Light: A Technique of Healing the Self and Others*, Oxford: Holywell Press.

Pontifical Council for Culture and the Pontifical Council for Interreligious Dialogue, 2003, *Jesus Christ the Bearer of the Water of Life: A Christian reflection on the "New Age"* http://www.vatican.va/roman_curia/pontifical_councils/interelg/documents/rc_pc_interelg_doc_20030203_new-age_en.html.

Porquet, Jean-Luc, 1994, *La France des Mutants: Voyage au cœur du Nouvel Age*, np: Flammarion.

Prince, Ruth, 1992, *An Anthropology of the 'New Age' with special reference to Glastonbury Somerset,* St Andrews: MPhil thesis.

Raine, Kathleen, 1968, *Blake and Tradition*, London.

Redfield, James, 1994, *The Celestine Prophecy*, London: Bantam.

Reeves, Donald, 1988, *For God's Sake,* London: Collins Fount.

Reeves, Donald, 1989, *Making Sense of Religion: A Fresh Look at Christianity,* London: BBC.

Reeves, Donald, 1996, *Down to Earth: A New vision for the Church,* London: Mowbray.

Rhodes, Ron, 1986, *An Examination and Evaluation of the New Age Christology of David Spangler*, Dallas Theological Seminary: ThD thesis.

Rhodes, Ron, 1991/1990, *The Counterfeit Christ of the New Age Movement,* Grand Rapids, MI: Baker Book House.

Roberts, Susan Fries, 1989, *Consciousness Shifts to Psychic Perception: the strange world of New Age services and their providers*, California: PhD thesis.

Robertson, Roland, 1970, *The Sociological Interpretation of Religion*, Oxford:

275

Basil Blackwell.

Robins, Mary, 1990, *Desert Flowers,* Sheffield: Cairns Publications.

Robins, Mary, 1992, *Still We* Rise: *Here and now reflections on the timeless story unfolded through* St *Mark's Gospel,* HatField: Robins.

Robinson, John, 1963, *Honest to God,* London: SCM.

Roof, Wade Clark et al, 1994/1993, A *Generation of Seekers: The Spiritual Journeys of the Baby Boom Generation,* San Francisco: Harper San Francisco.

Rose, Stuart, 1996, *Transforming the World: An examination of the roles played by Spirituality and Healing in the New Age Movement: "The Aquarian Conspirators Revisited",* Lancaster University: PhD thesis.

Roszak, Theodore, 1969, *The Making of a Counter Culture,* Garden City NY: Doubleday.

Roxburgh, Alan J, 1991, *On Being the Church in a New Age,* Northern Seminary Toronto: DMin thesis.

Rudolph, Kurt, 1987/1977, *Gnosis: The Nature and History of Gnosticism,* trns Robert McLachlan Wilson, San Francisco: HarperSanFrancisco.

Russell, Peter, 1991/1982, *The Awakening Earth: The Global Brain,* rvsd edn Harmondsworth: Arkana.

Saliba, John A, 1995, *Perspectives on New Religious Movements,* London: Geoffrey Chapman.

Saliba, John A, 1999, *Christian Responses to the New Age Movement: A Critical Assessment,* London: Geoffrey Chapman.

Sanford, John A, 1987/1970, *The Kingdom Within,* New York: HarperCollings.

Sanford, John A, 1992, *Healing Body and Soul. The Meaning of Illness in the New Testament and in Psychotherapy,* Gracewing: Leominster.

Scholem, Gershom, 1974, *Major Trends in Jewish Mysticism,* New York: Random House.

Schorsch, Christoph, 1988, *Die New Age-Bewegung. Utopie und Mythos der Neuen Ziet. Eine kritische Auseinandersetzung,* Gütersloh: Gütersloher Verlagshaus Gerd Mohn.

Scott, Alan, 1995/1990, *Ideology and the New Social Movements,* London: Routledge.

Scott, Chris, 1996, *Between the Poles: Creative living between atheism and religion,* London: New Millenium.

Scott, Gini Graham, 1980, *Cult and Countercult: A study of a spiritual growth group and a witchcraft order,* Westport Connecticut: Greenwood Press.

Scovel-Shinn, Florence, 1989/1925, *The Game of Life and How to Play it,* Romford: LN Fowler & Co.

Seddon, Philip, 1990, *The New Age – an Assessment,* Nottingham: Grove Books.

Seeger, Dan, 1986, "The Place of Universalism in the Society of Friends", Leicester: The Quaker Universalist Group.

Sheldrake, Rupert and Matthew Fox, 1996, *Natural Grace: Dialogues on Science & Spirituality,* London: Bloomsbury.

Simes, Amy Caroline, 1995, *Contemporary Paganism in the East Midlands,* Nottingham: PhD thesis.

Smith, Adrian B, 1977, *Bridging the Gap,* Eldoret Kenya: Gaba Publications.

Smith, Adrian B, 1978a, *Applying Scripture to Life,* Eldoret Kenya: Gaba Publications.

Smith, Adrian B, 1978b, *God's Word for Today: An Introduction to the Biblical Apostolate*, Lusaka: World Catholic Federation for the Biblical Apostolate.

Smith, Adrian B, 1982, *Interdenominational Religious Education in Africa: The Emergence of a Common Syllabus*, Ledien: Interuniversitair Instituut voor Missilogie en Oecumenica.

Smith, Adrian B, 1986, A *Reason for Hope: The Hurnan Experience of the Kingdom of God,* Great Wakering Essex: McCrimmons.

Smith, Adrian B, 1990, *God and the Aguarian Age,* Great Wakering, Essex: McCrimmons.

Smith, Adrian B, 1993, A *Key to the Kingdom of Heaven,* Lewes: Temple House.

Smith, Adrian B, 1996, *The God Shift: Our* Changing *Percpetion of the UTtirnate Mystery,* London: New Millenium.

Smith, Adrian B, 2002, *A New Framework for Christian Belief*, New Alresford: John Hunt Publishing.

Smith, Adrian B, 2003, *New Age Spirituality: A Christian Perspective*, London: Catholics for a Changing Church.

Smith, Adrian B ed, 1983, *TM. An Aid to Christian Growth,* Great Wakering Essex: Mayhew McCrimmon.

Snow, David A & Robert D Benford, 1988, "Ideology, Frame Resonance, and Participant Movilization", pp197-217 Bert Klandermans, Hanspeter Kriesi & Sidney Tarrow eds, *From Structure to Action: Comparing Social Movement Research across Cultures*, Greenwich, Conn: JAI Press.

Snow, David A, Burke E Rochford, Steven Worden & Robert Benford, 1986, "Frame Alignment Processes, Micromobilization, and Movement Participation", *American Sociological Review* 51 464-481.

Snow, David A, Louis A Zurcher & Sheldon Ekland-Olson, 1980, "Social Networks and Social Movements: A Microstructural Approach to Differential Recruitment", *American Sociological Review* 45 787-801.

Southwold, Martin, 1978, "Buddhism and The Definition of Religion", *Man* (New Series) 13.3 362-379.

Spangler, David, 1978/1971, *Revelation: The Birth of a New Age*, Forres: Findhorn Foundation.

Spangler, David, 1984, *Emergence. The Rebirth of the Sacred,* New York: Dell.

Spangler, David, 1993, "The New Age: The Movement Toward the Divine", 79-105 in Duncan Ferguson, 1993, *New Age Spirituality: An Assessment*, Louisville, Kentucky: Westminster/John Knox Press.

Spangler, David, 1996, A *Pilgrim in Aquarius,* Forres: Findhorn Press.

Spangler, David & William Irwin Thompson, 1991, *Reimagination of the World: A Critique of the New Age, Science, and Popular Culture*, Santa Fe NM: Bear & Co.

Spezzano, Chuck, 1991, *Awaken the Gods: Aphorisms to Remember on the Way Home*, London: Wellspring Publications.

Spink, Peter, 1980, *Spiritual Man in a New Age*, Tunbridge Wells: Michael Link.

Spink, Peter, 1983a, *The Path of the Mystic,* London: DLT.

Spink, Peter, 1983b, *The End of an Age,* Tunbridge Wells: Michael Link.

Spink, Peter, 1984, A *Time for Knowledge,* Tunbridge Wells: Michael Link.

Spink, Peter, 1988, *The Sevenfold Call,* 2nd edn, Winford, Avon: Omega Trust Publications.

Spink, Peter, 1991a, *A Christian in the New Age,* London: Darton, Longman and Todd.

Spink, Peter, 1991b, "Healing in the New Age – from Confusion to Authenticity", Winford: Omega Trust (tape 91/6).

Spink, Peter, 1996, *Beyond Belief. How to develop mystical consciousness and discover the God within,* London: Piatkus.

Spink, Peter, nda, *Religion in the New Age,* Tunbridge Wells: Michael Link.

Spink, Peter, ndb, *Christ in the New Age,* Tunbridge Wells: Michael Link.

Spink, Peter, ndc, *The Third Way, or The Christian in a New Age,* Tunbridge Wells: Michael Link.

Spink, Peter ed, 1990, *The Universal Christ: Daily Readings with Bede Griffiths,* London: Darton, Longman and Todd.

St Romain, Philip, 1995, *Kundalini energy and Christian Spirituality,* New York: Crossroad.

Stanley, Michael ed, 1988, *Emanuel Swedenborg: Essential Readings,* Wellinborough: Crucible.

Stark, Rodney & William Sims Bainbridge, 1979, "Of Churches, Sects, and Cults", *Journal for the Scientific Study of Religion* 18 117-133.

Stark, Rodney & William Sims Bainbridge, 1985, *The Future of Religion: Secularization,* Revival *and Cult Formation,* Berkeley CA: University of California Press.

Stark, Rodney, 1996, "Why Religious Movements Succeed or Fail", *Journal of Contemporary Religion* 11.2 133-146.

Stark, Rodney, 1998, "The Rise and Fall of Christian Science", *Journal of Contemporary Religion* 13.2 189-214.

Stein, Stephen J, 1982, "Retrospection and Introspection: the Gospel According to Mary Baker Eddy*, Harvard Theological Review* 75.

Steyn, Chrissie, 1994, *Worldviews in Transition: An Investigation of the New Age Movement in South Africa*, Pretoria: University of South Africa.

Strachan, Gordon, 1985, *Christ and the Cosmos*, Dunbar: Labarum.

Streiker, Lowell D, 1990, *New Age Comes to Main Street: What worried Christians must know*, Nashville: Abingdon Press.

Sudbrack, Josef, 1987, *Neue Religiosität. Herausforderungen für die Christen*, Mainz: Matthias-Grünewald-Verlag.

Sutcliffe, Steven 1995a, "The Authority of the Self in New Age religiousity: the example of the Findhorn Community", Bath: *Diskus* 3.2 23-42.

Sutcliffe, Steven, 1995b, "Some Notes on a Sociology of New Age and Related Countercultural Religiosity in Scotland", *Journal of Contemporary Religion* 10.2 181-184.

Sutcliffe, Steven, 1997, "Seekers, Networks, and 'New Age'", *Scottish Journal of Religious Studies* 18.2 97-114.

Sutcliffe, Steven, 1998a, *'New Age' in Britain: An Ethnographical and Historical Exploration*, Stirling Open University: PhD thesis.

Sutcliffe, Steven, 1998b, "Between Apocalypse and Self-Realisation: "Nature" as an Index of New Age Religiosity", in J Pearson, R Roberts and G Samuel eds, 1998, *Nature Religion Today: The Pagan Alternative in the Modern World*, Edinburgh: Edinburgh University Press.

Sutcliffe, Steven, 2003, *Children of the New Age: A History of Spiritual*

Practices, London: Routledge.

Swatos, William H, 1976, "Weber or Troeltsch?: Methodology, syndrome and the development of church-sect theory", *Journal for the Scientific Study of Religion* 15.2 129-144.

Talbot, Michael, 1981, *Mysticism and the New Physics*, Harmondsworth: Arkana.

Tarrow, Sidney, 1998/1994, *Power in Movement: Social Movements and Contentious Politics*, 2nd edn, Cambridge: CUP.

Tart, Charles ed, 1975, *Transpersonal Psychologies,* New York: HarperSanFrancisco.

Terrin, Aldo Natale, 1992, *New Age: La Religiosità del Postmoderno*, Bologna: Centro Editoriale Dehoniano.

Thompson, Damian, 1997/1996, *The End of Time: Faith and Fear in the Shadow of the Millennium*, expanded edition London: Minerva.

Thompson, EP, 1993, *Witness against the Beast,* Cambridge: Cambridge University Press.

Tiryakian, Edward A ed, 1974, *On the Margin of the Visible: Sociology, the esoteric and the occult*, Englewood Cliffs NJ: Prentice Hall.

Tlalim, Ronit Yoeli, 1998, *On-Line Zen: A Phenomenological and Epistemic Outlook*, Tel-Aviv: MA thesis.

Tomlinson, Dave, 1995, *The Post-Evangelical,* London: Triangle.

Touraine, Alan, 1981, *The Voice and the Eye: an Analysis of Social Movements*, Cambridge: CUP.

Touraine, Alan et al, 1983/1980, *Anti-nuclear protest: The opposition to nuclear energy in France*, trns Peter Fawcett, Cambridge: Cambridge University Press.

Touraine, Alan et al, 1990/1982, *Solidarity: Poland 1980-81*, trns David Denby, Cambridge: CUP.

Trigg, Joseph W, 1998, *Origen*, London: Routledge.

Troeltsch, Ernst, 1931, *The Social Teaching of the Christian Churches*, trns O Wyon. London: Macmillan.

Tucker, Ruth, 1991/1989, *Strange Gospels,* London: Marshall Pickering.

Tuckwell, Gareth & David Flagg, 1995, A *Question of Healing: The Reflections of a Doctor and a Priest,* London: Fount.

Underhill, Evelyn, 1993/1911, *Mysticism: The Nature and Development of Spiritual Consciousness*, Oxford: One World.

van den Broek, Roelof & Wouter J Hanegraaff eds, 1998, *Gnosis and Hermeticism from Antiquity to Modern Times*, Albany: SUNY.

Vaughan, David, 1967, *A Faith for the New Age*, London: Regency Press.

Vernette, Jean, 1990, *Le Nouvel Age: A l'aube de l'Ere du Irerseau,* Editions Tequi.

Vermes, Geza, 1981, *The Dead Sea Scrolls: Qumran in Perspective*, Revd edn, Philadelphia: Fortress Press.

Verney, Stephen, 1989/1976, *Into the New Age*, np: Fount.

Versluis, Arthur, 1999, *Wisdom's Children: A Christian Esoteric Tradition*, Albany: SUNY.

Vitz, Paul C, 1994/1977, *Psychology as Religion: The Cult of Self-Worship,* 2nd edn, Carlisle: Paternoster Press.

Wallace, Teresa ed, 1998, *This Is My Story: Voyages on the Sea of Faith*, Loughborough: Sea of Faith Network (UK).

Wallis, Roy, 1975, "Scientology: Therapeutic cult to religious sect", *Sociology 9* 89-100.

Wallis, Roy, 1979, *Salvation and Protest,* London: Frances Pinter.

Wallis, Roy, 1984a, *The Elementary Forms of the Religious Life*, London: Routledge.

Wallis, Roy, 1984b, "The Stark-Bainbridge Theory of Religion: A critical analsysis and counter proposals", *Sociological Analysis* 45 11-27.

Walsh, Edward J, 1981, "Resource Mobilization and Citizen Protest in communities around Three Mile Island", *Social Problems* 29 1-21.

Walter, Tony, 1993, "Death in the New Age", *Religion* 23 127-145.

Wapnick, Kenneth, 1990/1989, *Love Does Not Condemn: The Word, the Flesh, and the Devil According to Platonism, Christianity, Gnosticism, and A Course in Miracles*, Roscoe NY: Foundation for Inner Peace.

Wapnick, Kenneth, 1992/1978, *Christian Psychology in A Course in Miracles,* 2nd ed, New York: Foundation for 'A Course in Miracles'.

Wapnick, Kenneth, 1994, *Forgiveness and Jesus: The Meeting Place of A Course in Miracles and Christianity,* 5th ed, New York: Foundation for A Course in Miracles.

Wapnick, Kenneth & W Norris Clarke, 1995, *A Course in Miracles and Christianity: A Dialogue,* Roscoe NY: Foundation for Inner Peace.

Washington, Peter, 1993, *Madame Blavatsky's Baboon: A History of the Mystics, Mediums, and Misfits Who Brought Spiritualism to America,* London: Secker & Warburg.

Weatherhead, Leslie D, 1951, *Psychology, Religion and Healing,* 2nd rvsd edn London: Hodder & Stoughton.

Webb, James, 1976, *The Occult Establishment,* La Salle IL: Open Court.

Weber, Max trns Ephraim Fischoff, 1956/1922, *The Sociology of Religion,* Boston: Beacon Press.

Weddle, David L, 1991, "The Christian Science Textbook: An Analysis of the Religious Authority of *Science and Health* by Mary Baker Eddy", *Harvard Theological* Review 84.3 273-297.

Whaling, Frank, 1996, *Christianity and New Age Thought*, Oxford: Religious Experience Research Centre Occasional Paper 2.1.

Williams, Michael Allen, 1996, *Rethinking "Gnosticism": An Argument for Dismantling a Dubious Category*, Princeton NJ: Princeton University Press.

Williams, Nick, 2000, *The Work We Were Born to Do*, Longmead: Element Books.

Wilson, Bryan R ed, 1984/1970, *Rationality,* Oxford: Basil Blackwell.

Wilson, Bryan R, 1970, *Religious* Sects: *a sociological study,* London: Weidenfeld and Nicolson.

Wilson, Bryan R, 1975/1973, *Magic and the Millenium,* St Albans: Paladin.

Wilson, Bryan R, 1979/1976, *Contemporary Transformations of Religion,* Oxford: OUP.

Wittgenstein, Ludwig trns GEM Anscombe, 1994/1953, *Philosophical Investigations*, Oxford: Blackwell.

Wood, Matthew, 1999a, "Kinship Identity and Nonformative Spiritual Seerkership", Durham: paper delivered at the BSA Sociology of Religion Study Group annual conference, 10 April.

Wood, Matthew, 1999b, *Spirit Possession in a Contemporary British Religious Network A Critique of New Age Movement Studies through the sociology of power*, Nottingham: PhD thesis.

Wuthnow, Robert, 1976, *The Consciousness Reformation*, Berkeley: University of California Press.

Yinger, J Milton, 1970, *The Scientific Study of Religion*, London: Macmillan.

Yinger, J Milton, 1984/1982, *Countercultures: The Promise and Peril of a World Turned Upside Down*, New York: Free Press.

York, Michael, 1995, *The Emerging Network: A Sociology of the New Age and Neo-Pagan Movements,* Lanham, Maryland: Rowman & Littlefield.

Zoccatelli, Pierluigi, 1998, *Il New Age*, Turin: Editrice Elle Di Ci.

Zoutewelle, Rende, 1980, *Attunement to the Vision*, Groningen: MA thesis.